Introduction to Mass Communication and Journalism

Introduction to Mass Communication and Journalism

Javed Shaikh

RANDOM PUBLICATIONS
NEW DELHI (INDIA)

Introduction to Mass Communication and Journalism

ISBN 978-93-5111-213-6

Published in 2014 in India by

RANDOM PUBLICATIONS

4376-A/4B, Gali Murari Lal, Ansari Road
New Delhi-110 002
Phone : +91-11-43580356, +91-11-23289044
e-mail: randomexports@gmail.com, sales@randompublications.com, info@randompublications.com

Reprinted 2024

Type Setting by : Keystoneprintads, Delhi-110051
Digitally Printed at : Replika Press Pvt. Ltd.

Preface

Mass communication is the study of how individuals and entities relay information through mass media to large segments of the population at the same time. It is usually understood to relate to newspaper, magazine, and book publishing, as well as radio, television and film, as these mediums are used for disseminating information, news and advertising. Mass communication differs from the studies of other forms of communication, such as interpersonal communication or organizational communication, in that it focuses on a single source transmitting information to a large group of receivers. The study of mass communication is chiefly concerned with how the content of mass communication persuades or otherwise affects the behavior, attitude, opinion, or emotion of the person or people receiving the information.

Mass communication is "the process by which a person, group of people, or large organization creates a message and transmits it through some type of medium to a large, anonymous, heterogeneous audience." Mass communication is regularly associated with media influence or media effects, and media studies. Mass communication is a branch of social science that falls under the larger umbrella of communication studies or communication. The history of communication moves from prehistoric forms of art and writing through modern communication methods such as the internet. Mass communication fits in when humans began to be able to transmit messages from a single source to multiple receivers.

Mass communication has moved from theories such as the hypodermic needle model through more modern theories such as computer-mediated communication. In the United States, the study of mass communication is often associated with the practical applications of journalism , television and radio broadcasting, film, public relations, or advertising. With the diversification of media options, the study of communication has extended to include social media and new media, which have stronger feedback models than traditional media sources. While the field of mass communication is continually evolving, the following four fields are generally regarded to be the major areas of study within mass communication. They exist in different forms and configurations at different schools or universities, but are practiced at most institutions that study mass communication.

Journalism is the collection and editing of news for presentation through the media, in this sense, refers to the study of the product and production of news. The study of journalism involves looking at how news is produced, and how it is disseminated to the public through mass media outlets such as newspapers, news channel, radio station, television station, and more recently, e-readers and smartphones.

Journalism delves deep into society which constantly undergoes changes; however, it is not immune to this change itself. It is heavily dependent on advancing communications technology-and upon experts in technological fields. At the heart of the enterprise however, are individual journalists including reporters, columnists, editors, correspondents' photographers, cartoonists, etc. The book has been designed for students appearing for UGC-NET/SLET in mass communication and journalism. The book is very comprehensive and covers almost all possible objective type questions on the subject. Many of the questions set in UGC-NET/SLET and various other competitive examinations in the previous years have been used for preparing this book.

I thank all members of my team who have helped in the preparation of the book. My special thanks go to "Random Publications" who have published the book.

– Javed Shaikh

Contents

1

The Importance of Communication

Although the Internet may be portrayed as a communication technology unique to the 1990s, this depiction is somewhat misleading. The Internet's origins are in fact traceable to the 1960s development of the military-funded communication network, ARPANET, with the Internet officially making its debut as a civilian tool for communication in 1983.

However, widespread public awareness of the Internet's existence did not occur within the United States until the early 1990s when it was privatized and online services such as America Online (AOL) were developed to serve the general public. Hence, there is a tendency to think of it as a turn-of-the-twenty-first-century phenomenon.

Prior to the 1990s, early public access to the Internet was limited mostly to government agencies, universities, and computer-related organizations, such as hardware and software developers. Initially, users experienced the Internet in the form of text-based communication applications such as e-mail and navigation systems such as Telnet. In 1992, the World Wide Web (WWW) became publicly available in the United States and began to diffuse widely in 1993 with the release of the iconbased web browser Mosaic, which made web navigation more "user friendly" and visually appealing. Subsequently, use of the Web helped to popularize the Internet in general. As use of the Internet has shifted from a small community of researchers and government employees to a worldwide community, researchers recognize the Internet as an important area in need of study. The widespread diffusion and adoption of the Internet in the United States and abroad provides scholars with numerous research opportunities. Because the Internet functions as a channel for communication, this is especially true for the field of communication. However, as with any innovation, it can be difficult at first to know how to approach the investigation of an innovation's contribution to and effects on the society into which it is introduced.

With regard to the Internet, communication researchers, as well as others, must grapple with numerous decisions, such as determining how applicable existing theories and methods of inquiry are to this newest communication technology.

While the arguments for why and how to study the Internet vary, a common theme to arise within our discipline concerns the unique opportunity that today's communication scholars have to witness and record, first hand, the introduction of a major communication technology.

Scholarly journals are one forum where communication researchers record the results of their research for the benefit of current and future generations of scholars. Published articles inform other researchers of the types of approaches being used to study a wide variety of topics, including the Internet.

A number of disciplines are conducting Internet research as is evident when searching electronic databases. For example, a simple keyword search conducted in December 1999 in the Social Sciences Abstracts database on the term "Internet" yielded a return of 969 articles published across a diversity of disciplines, most notably in the areas of business, demographics, law, and policy studies.

Each discipline, including communication, typically contains a core set of journals considered to be "leaders" among all others in terms of their coverage of subject matter, length of publication, and quality of published articles. The question asked in this study concerns how leading journals in the field represent Internet-based research conducted by communication scholars, because an important goal of scholarly journals is to document a field's evolution over time.

This study examines the content, frequency, and pattern of published Internet-based research articles-studies that focus on some aspect of the Internet-in leading communication journals for the purpose of assessing how these journals are keeping pace with the Internet's influence on the communication process. It also considers how these journals represent our response to these changes to other disciplines in the social sciences.

THE IMPORTANCE OF COMMUNICATION SCHOLARS RESEARCHING THE INTERNET

Within the discipline, a handful of articles has addressed the importance of communication scholars studying the Internet. The reasons for study as well as the ways in which the Internet should be studied are varied. For example, in 1996, the Journal of Communication devoted the majority of its winter issue to "The Net."

Within this issue, in a dialogue between Newhagen & Rafaeli, Rafeali pointed out that the development of the Internet, in part, is rooted in academe and, as such, "this alone behooves our involvement" in its study. Beyond this statement Rafeali suggested that researchers focus on what he called the "five defining qualities of communication" on the Internet which, although somewhat abstract, included "multimedia, hypertextuality, packet switching, synchronicity, and interactivity." Newhagen argued that communication researchers must take a more active role in understanding the Internet by first understanding computer architecture, an area often left to engineers. A bridge must be constructed between the worlds of communication and engineering so that communication researchers no longer find themselves in the position "where the engineers roll out a new technology, and we hold up numbers from 1 to 10, rating it."

Concerning the benefits of studying virtual reality, Biocca stated, "Communication researchers rarely have had the chance to observe the introduction, diffusion, and sociocultural presence of what may become the next dominant communication medium." However, he cautioned against viewing new communication technologies as a revolutionary by stating that many "new" technologies build upon, and borrow from, existing ones.

As such, researchers are likely to start out using existing theories and methods to study a new technology. He suggested focusing on questions such as the shape the medium is taking, and how the medium shapes and is shaped by the user-areas well suited to communication research. In a 1993 article, writing more broadly about humancomputer interface design, Biocca, as Newhagen was to do later in 1996, called for communication scholars to be more proactive in researching computer-mediated communication (CMC) by taking part in the design and development of new communication technologies. Although, both of Biocca's articles were written just prior to the Internet's widespread public diffusion, his ideas, as if in anticipation of its introduction, are very applicable to the Internet and have been echoed in the later writing of Newhagen and Rafaeli.

Other communication scholars assuming the importance of studying the Internet have suggested additional approaches to its study. December argued for the need to define specific units of analysis for Internet research that would act as guideposts for researchers, helping to facilitate cross study comparisons.

These four units were defined as media space, media class, media object, and media instance. He also proposed a definition of Internet-based computer-mediated communication as that which involves information exchange that takes place on the global, cooperative collection of networks using the TCP/IP protocol suite and the client-server model for data communication. Messages may undergo a range of time and distribution manipulations and encode a variety of media types. The resulting information content exchanged can involve a wide range of symbols people use for communication.

As such, he argued that the Internet is not a single medium but is instead made up of several media. Additionally, he cautioned that researchers studying on-line services such as Prodigy or America OnLine (AOL) should be aware that they were not actually conducting Internet-based research because these access providers offer proprietary services not available on the Internet.

While this caveat is technically correct, it is perhaps overly restrictive. In addition to offering proprietary services to its users, on-line vendors such as

AOL also function as Internet Service Providers (ISPs), allowing for communications to be exchanged via the global network. In contrast to December, Morris and Ogan viewed the Internet as a single flexible mass medium capable of the synchronous and asynchronous transmission of text, audio, and video communication.They argued that the Internet provides the opportunity for communication researchers to rethink rather than abandon traditional views on mass media and to adopt a more flexible perspective on communication models.

Additionally, they suggested that researchers study the Internet using a variety of existing frameworks, such as network analysis, and theories, such as social presence. In summary, these scholars essentially argue that communication in relation to other disciplines should be a leader, if not the leader, in researching the Internet because it is a communication phenomenon.

Communication scholars need to be proactive and creative in their research designs in order to reach this goal. To do this, they must possess a thorough understanding of how the technology works by taking an active role in the design and evaluation of future Internet applications.

RATIONALE

Knowledge of the extent to which Internet-related topics have been addressed and what methods of inquiry have been applied can assist communication researchers in placing their work within a broader range of studies. This information also identifies over- and under-emphasized topics and methods.

Lastly, knowledge of the degree to which the Internet is represented within a discipline can provide researchers with a sense of the area's development and relative importance to the field as a whole. It is not uncommon for communication researchers to analyse articles within an individual journal or a range of journals in order to assess the status of the discipline as a whole with respect to a particular issue.

Examples of these studies include analyzing the frequency with which qualitative research is published, investigating the content and quality of published content analyses, and assessing the status of published mass communication articles by women across eight journals. Continuing this type of inquiry, this study examines the publication history of Internet research among five leading journals in the field.

JOURNAL SELECTION CRITERIA

While acknowledging the presence of newer electronic Internet and new technology-specific publications such as Internet Research and Journal of Computer-Mediated Communication, this study purposely focuses on mainstream, established communication journals. The reasons for this emphasis are threefold.

First, and most obvious, the Internet is a channel for communication and as such it falls within the realm for study by communication researchers and, in turn, publication in our leading, established communication journals. Second, established journals-those in existence for a period of decades-have the distinct advantage of having built both a reputation and a following over time. These journals are widely read within the discipline, contributing to scholars' perceptions of and currency with changes in the field. A third reason, closely related to the second, is that established journals can be viewed as historical records that document the field's evolution. Ideally, these journals reflect trends in the development of a discipline and the segments of society with which it deals as accurately as possible for the benefit of current and future scholars.

Selection of the five journals examined in this study employed two criteria: previous research identifying leading journals in the field and the reputation of Social Sciences Abstracts as a valid resource for communication research. In a content analysis of women's published research in mass communication, Dupagne, Potter, and Cooper identified eight leading communication journals, defined according to high circulation counts and low acceptance rates.

The journals identified in their study included: Communication Monographs, Communication Research, Critical Studies in Mass Communication, Human Communication Research, Journal of Broadcasting and Electronic Media, Journal of Communication, Journalism Quarterly, and Quarterly Journal of Speech.

These journals functioned as a starting point for this study; however, application of the second criterion, communication research indexed in Social Sciences Abstracts, resulted in the omission of four titles from the original list. The decision to further limit the journals examined was based on a twofold rationale. First, electronic databases are increasingly used by scholars to conduct literature searches because of their ease of use and convenience in comparison to print indexes. Within the vast realm of electronic indexes available for searching, Social Sciences Abstracts is a widely used leading index published by the highly reputable indexing service, H. W. Wilson Company.

Second, subject-specific indexes, such as Social Sciences Abstracts, are typically more useful to and more likely to be used by scholars than general indexes, such as Expanded Academic Index, because they cover indexed journals in more detail, are more likely to index all articles in a journal rather than a chosen few, and they provide longer, more detailed abstracts.

By restricting the focus to leading communication journals indexed in Social Sciences Abstracts, this study attempts to take into consideration a broader view concerning how scholars in other disciplines might perceive the role of our discipline in the area of Internet research based on the presence of communication journal articles contained in the index. With the application of this second criterion, the final list of journals examined in this study include:

Communication Research, Human Communication Research, Journal of Broadcasting & Electronic Media, Journal of Communication, and Journalism & Mass Communication Quarterly. Measures. This study uses December's definition of Internet-based communication but with a slightly more liberal view on what constituted Internet-based communication.

An article was considered Internetbased if it focused on computer-mediated communication technologies requiring access to an ISP, including services such as AOL or Prodigy, or closely simulated an Internet-based communication environment (e.g., intranets, e-mail exchange between AOL members). This definition broadly included the Internet in general, intranets, World Wide Web (WWW), e-mail, mailing lists, bulletin boards, newsgroups, chat, virtual reality games such as multi-user domains (MUDs), and video/ audio/text computer conferencing. From the interfaces specified above, it can be seen that in most instances Internet access was necessary for communication to occur. As with any area of research, certain information is useful in providing scholars with an overall sense of an area's progress or current status. For the purpose of this study, the concept of current status is operationalized into nine measures-author name, authorship, author rank, affiliation, topic, interface, method, total number of Internet-based articles per issue, and total number of research articles per issue. Identification of an area's primary researchers provides scholars with a sense of which perspectives may be dominant in an area of study. While quantity of publication by an author does not necessarily equate with quality of research, it can provide scholars, especially those new to an area, with a starting point in the literature. The same can be said for the order of authorship on an article.

Distinguishing between primary and secondary authors can indicate, but not necessarily guarantee, which researchers are initiating studies, taking primary responsibility for the studies, and acting as primary contacts or "experts" in an area. Knowledge of which universities or organizations are conducting research in a particular area is beneficial for those interested in matters such as networking, educational, and employment opportunities.

The rank (e.g., faculty, staff, student) of an author provides information on the diversity or homogeneity of the contributors to an area of research. This study attempts to answer two basic questions. First, what is the frequency and pattern, if any, of published Internet-based research articles in five of the leading communication journals? Second, what do the contents of these articles reveal about the status of Internet research within and outside of the communication discipline?

METHOD

UNIT OF ANALYSIS

The unit of analysis for this study was the scholarly communication research article that focused on Internet-based communication. This included "research in brief" articles but excluded editorials, rejoinders, and book reviews. Coders primarily read titles and abstracts to determine if an article fit this study's definition of Internetbased research. In instances where article titles and abstracts did not provide sufficient information, coders skimmed the articles for details.

POPULATION DATA

All research articles were examined in four major communication journals between the years 1994-1999. Because frequency of publication over time was one question asked by this study, population data were used instead of sample data in an effort to obtain a more accurate depiction of publishing trends across time by these journals.

The four journals selected for the main study included Communication Research, Human Communication Research, Journal of Broadcasting & Electronic Media, and Journal of Communication. A fifth journal, Journalism fa Mass Communication Quarterly, was selected for a pilot study to test the codebook. To identify leading communication journals publishing Internet-related articles, a basic keyword search was conducted using the term "Internet" in the Social Sciences Abstracts electronic database; four journals were consistently referenced in the search results and thus selected for closer examination. One limitation of this selection process concerns the exclusion of some communication journal titles from the Social Sciences Abstracts index. However, this limitation was considered acceptable given the broader focus of the study discussed earlier.

Despite this limitation, the five journals selected for this study are examples of the mainstream publication outlets available through most of the field's major associations: the Association for Education in Journalism and Mass Communication, Broadcast Education Association, and International Communication Association. The starting year for the study, 1994, was selected because, based on the Social Sciences Abstracts search results, in general, Internet publications did not begin to increase until that point in time. The first recorded Internet article in the database occurred in 1992; one article was referenced in 1993. However, in each year thereafter, the number of articles increased steadily. This pattern is consistent with the growing popularity of the Internet with the general public in the United States. The communication journals selected for study during this time frame contained a total of 961 research articles (323 from the pilot study and 638 from the main study). Each article was examined to determine if it met the definition of Internet-based research. Those articles that qualified were then coded.

OPERATIONAL DEFINITIONS

To answer the questions proposed in this study, nine measures were recorded for each Internet-based research article: author name, authorship, author rank, affiliation, topic, interface, method, total number of Internet-based articles per issue, and total number of research articles per issue. For each article the last name and initials of all authors were recorded.

Authorship was coded as primary (first author) or secondary (all additional authors). The rank of each author was coded as faculty, student, staff (university affiliated, nonfaculty/non-student employees), government employee, business employee, or other. Author affiliation was recorded as the name of the university or organization with which the author was identified at the time of publication.

Rather than attempt to anticipate the range in subject matter, article topic was recorded as open text by each coder and then later grouped into six broad categories: access, adoption/diffusion, policy, research/theory, social interaction, and other. Interface, the application used to communicate via a computer, was divided into eight categories: World Wide Web, e-mail, mailing lists/newsgroups/bulletin boards, chat rooms, virtual reality game sites (e.g., MUDs, MOOs), video/audio/text-based conferencing, Internet in general (no specific interface identified), and other (coders recorded the specific interface).

Method of inquiry was coded as policy study, critique/essay (non-policy studies), interview/case study, content analysis (qualitative and quantitative), experiment, survey, other (coders recorded the specific method) and combination for multiple methods used within a single study (each method was recorded and then weighted). Lastly, for each journal issue, coders recorded the total number of Internet-based articles and overall total number of research articles.

CODING PROCEDURES

The author and another communication researcher acted as coders. The codebook was created by the author and reviewed for clarity by the second coder. A pilot test to check for intercoder reliability was conducted on all issues of Journalism & Mass Communication Quarterly, 1994-1999, resulting in a 100% overlap of 323 articles. Discrepancies in coding were discussed, and slight modifications for the purpose of clarification were made to the codebook before proceeding to the four journals selected for the main study.

Reliabilities for the number of Internet-based research articles and total number of articles for the pilot test were at the acceptable levels allowing for the inclusion of these articles in the study, under separate reporting. Intercoder reliability for the main study was calculated using a 20% overlap. Issues for the reliability check were selected using a stratified random sample. The total overlap between the coders contained 128 articles.

INTERCODER RELIABILITY

For the main study, the level of agreement concerning which articles qualified as Internet-based research was 98.4%. Percentages of agreement and Scott's pi corrections for chance (where applicable) were as follows for the measures: author name, 97.9%; authorship, 97.9%.96; author rank, 97.9%.97; affiliation, 97.9%; topic, 94.3%; interface, 96.9%.96; method, 97.7%.97; and total number of research articles per issue, 96.9%.

For the pilot study, percentage of agreement for Internet-based research articles was 84.6% and 99.7% for total number of articles per issue. Frequency analyses are reported for each measure. With the exception of overall trends in publishing, all other measures report data collected from the four journals in the main study. This is because intercoder reliability for the pilot study was only reached on the two measures: Internet-based articles per issue and total articles per issue.

TRENDS IN PUBLISHING

Of the 961 research articles analysed, 37 (3.9%) were Internet-based. Among the four journals in the main study, 4.1% (26 of 638 articles) were Internet-based. Trends in the publication of Internet-based articles across the five journals revealed no distinct pattern of increase, decrease, or stabilization during the six-year time period. This finding was also the case within each of the five journals.

Overall, the Journal of Communication (32%) published Internet research articles the most frequently followed by Journalism & Mass Communication Quarterly (30%), Journal of Broadcasting & Electronic Media (24%), Human Communication Research (8%), and Communication Research (6%).

The percentage of published Internet-based research articles varied widely by year; however, a trend line reflecting a moving average suggests that the number of articles has increased over time.

TOPIC, INTERFACE, AND METHOD

Social interaction (31%) was the topic most often researched. This was followed by research/theory (23%); other (15%), which included the topics of competition among local news web sites, digital art on the WWW, TV audience feedback via email, and portrayals of the Internet in magazines; access (12%) and adoption/diffusion (12%); and policy issues (7%).

The interface studied most often was the Internet in general (42%) followed by mailing lists/newsgroups/bulletin boards (19%), WWW (15%), email (12%), and chat rooms (4%), video/audio/text conferencing (4%), and other (4%) which included an Internet-based interactive health programme. The two most frequently used methods of inquiry were content analysis (27%) and critique/essay (27%).

These were followed by experiment (11%) and survey (11%), and, lastly, policy study (8%), interview/case study (8%), and combination (8%), which included groupings such as network analysis and content analysis, and surveys and content analysis. The results of this study present a somewhat vague picture as to where this newest area of study is positioned within the selected journals.

In part, this is due to the low number of Internet articles available for examination and thus discussion. The results also indicate that scholars searching the Social Sciences Abstracts would find a scarcity of Internet-related research in our leading journals. It may be that the infrequent and uneven publication of Internet research in the journals examined is simply a typical reflection of any field's initial attempts to come to terms with a new area of study.

This finding suggests that Internet research is an area within the field that is clearly open for study. Within the four journals analysed, only two authors stood out in total number of publications potentially providing greater opportunity for other scholars to become better known through their research in comparison to more established areas in communication.

Not surprisingly, faculty are the dominant group publishing Internet research articles, but, again, because of the newness of the area student authors may have more opportunities to publish than in more established areas. While certain universities are represented more than others, it remains to be seen which programs will eventually come to the fore regarding Internet-based communication research.

In the areas of topic, interface, and methods, similar opportunities for growth exist. However, as speculated by Biocca and Morris and Ogan, thus far, communication researchers primarily are using traditional methods to study the Internet (e.g., content analysis, essays/critiques) with a few studies employing network analysis, as suggested by Morris and Ogan.

Additionally, research has tended to focus largely on the Internet in general, leaving specific interfaces such as mailing lists and e-mail in need of attention. Topics also seem to follow widely used categories (e.g., adoption/ diffusion, social interaction) in communication research. This trend may be useful for making comparisons across different types of media; however, it also risks overlooking effects that may be unique to the Internet.

The low number of Internet-based research articles (3.9%) and the sporadic publication of the articles within the five communication journals examined may be attributed to several factors. To begin with, the Internet, despite nearly a three-decade history, is still a relatively new area of study. Although the World Wide Web, which helped make the Internet popular, became publicly available in 1992, it was not until 1995 that awareness of the Internet by the media and the general public began to increase.

With this increased awareness among the populace, researchers are realizing the importance of researching the Internet, but this can be a slow process. In 1995, Dennis Davis, the editor of Journal of Broadcasting & Electronic Media, wrote in his annual summary, "One of my editorial priorities is to increase the number of articles dealing with new technologies. To do this, the number of submissions will need to be increased. This past year 10 submissions (4.9%) dealt with new industries or new technologies. Three times as many manuscripts dealt with existing industries (30 papers, 14.8%). I would like to see a more even balance between submissions dealing with old and new industries."

To its credit, the Journal of Communication published a symposium on "The Net" in its 1996 winter issue. Factoring in the timeframe necessary for the review, decision, and printing process, the calls to action contained within this issue may partially explain the noticeable increase in the publication of articles during 1998. The drop off in 1999 may be a reflection of this cycle as well, or possibly a reflection of changes in editors' interests. Still, it seems clear that some of these journals are demonstrating a desire to publish Internet-based research articles; however, as Davis indicates, perhaps few studies are being submitted. Alternatively, it may be that a number of studies are being submitted; however, because of the relative newness of Internet-based research some of these studies may lack the theoretical grounding often desired in published works by our leading journals. A review of the literature reveals that communication researchers are attempting to unveil the parallels and distinctions between new and traditional technology theories and methodologies, but the research waters are still murky in this area.

Additionally, the emergence of new technology journals such as Internet Research and New Media and Society, may serve as alternative outlets for these studies, thus siphoning off submissions to the mainstream, established communication journals. As well, given the crossdisciplinary nature of the Internet (e.g., computing, communication, human factors), depending on the topic, communication researchers may be submitting their works to journals in other fields. If this is the case, then the communication journals examined might more actively solicit Internet research submissions in an attempt to better represent the amount and type of research being conducted in this area. While this author does not advocate the lowering of acceptance standards for research articles, communication journals could potentially foster increased publication of Internet research, following the lead of the Journal of Communication, by dedicating issues to symposia on the topic.

These symposia could be viewed as debuts of Internet research that, while possibly less theoretically rigorous, would be considered valuable contributors to the development of future, more theoretically based studies. The main point to be emphasized is that the communication research community is widely dispersed across numerous universities and organizations worldwide.

Scholarly journals function, in part, as a communication link between researchers. Communication scholars interested in studying the Internet benefit most by knowing who else is researching in the area and what results have been found. Leading journals play an important role in conveying this information, but only if that information is being published. If it is the case, which remains to be seen, that Internet research is not being published because of a lack of strong theoretical foundations, then an important question needs to be addressed. Namely, how are scholars to build theory if they do not have access, which these journals can provide, to studies on which to build a foundation? The answer may lie in the emergence of topic-specific journals such as New Media and Society.

In 1996, Morris and Ogan, commenting on the Internet's growth (25 million at the time), asked, "Why, then, have communication researchers, historically concerned with exploring the effects of mass media, nearly ignored the Internet?" This is a question still in need of an answer, or possibly reformulation. We might also ask why our leading journals appear to be slow on the uptake.

Notably, Wartella and Reeves, in a 1985 study that examined historical trends in publishing about children and the media, observed "that the relationship between research activity and media popularity is not simultaneous." Their findings illustrated that research related to a communication technology (e.g., film, radio, television) often lags behind the diffusion rate of the technology, a pattern confirmed in this study.

Nevertheless, Internet research appears to be an area of study with which communication researchers must become more comfortable and skilled at conducting. Unlike television, radio, or print media, the computer requires certain knowledge and skills to operate-and ultimately to study.

As Biocca and Newhagen and Rafaeli argue, communication scholars are being called upon to take a more active role in the understanding and design of new communication technologies. These challenges, as well as knowledge and skills requirements, may act as barriers for some researchers who are less technically oriented. This particular barrier may be offset over time as communication programs develop tracks of study in new technologies on both the graduate and undergraduate levels that emphasize familiarity with and understanding of computer communication technologies.

Additionally, the Internet can simultaneously function as an interpersonal and mass channel for communication. This hybrid nature tends to blur the traditional lines used to distinguish different types of communication from one another. Is the Internet really a form of mass communication? Questions such as this one make it difficult for communication scholars to identify perspectives from which to study the Internet.

Finally, because Internet research is more or less in its infancy and as such lacks a strong history of research on which to build, communication researchers must be especially thoughtful about and creative in their approach to its study. They must also make the effort to network, outside of journal publications, with other Internet researchers to share research strategies and results.

Certainly, not every communication researcher is interested in studying the Internet nor, given the numerous areas available for study within the field, should it be the focus of every communication scholar or the sole topic of our leading publications. However, in general, to overlook the Internet as an area for study is to be remiss as a discipline.

Before concluding, two limitations must be addressed regarding the narrow focus of the research. First, the conclusions drawn from this study are primarily limited to the five journals examined.

It should be noted, though, that these journals have historically attempted to keep pace with changes in the discipline so that cautious speculations of a more general nature about the discipline's response to the Internet might be made. However, additional research examining a broader range of communication journals is necessary to confirm these speculations.

Second, the definition used to identify Internet-based research excluded articles examining computer-mediated communication more generally. Future studies may wish to examine this broader category of research as well. This study makes two primary contributions to the field. First, it informs communication scholars of the content and amount of published Internet research in leading journals that represent our research efforts both within and outside of the discipline. Second, it generates discussion concerning why the numbers are relatively low in light of earlier calls to action regarding the importance of studying the Internet. Both communication journals and communication scholars play important roles in determining where Internet research will be positioned within the discipline, as well as where the discipline will be placed relative to other fields investigating the technology.

Despite the small number of Internetbased articles published by five of our leading journals during the sixyear time period examined, communication scholars studying the Internet should be encouraged in that, overall, the number of articles published appears to be increasing.

However, to more accurately reflect the Internet's importance as a research topic within the discipline, it is hoped that the findings in this study will encourage communication scholars to submit more of their Internet-based research to our leading journals while current and future editors of these journals will be encouraged to include more of these articles in their publications. As a discipline we possess the potential be a leader in Internet research, and our core journals can, and should, reflect this potential not only to scholars within the field but also to the larger academic community.

2

Communicative Rationality

German critical theorist and philosopher Jürgen Habermas has become a challenging source of ideas for many communication scholars, particularly those concerned with community communication ecology, cultural studies, discourse ethics, participatory communication, and public journalism. Habermas's critical-theoretical project has evoked a great deal of interest among scholars in the social sciences and the humanities. Dryzek asserts that Habermas's critical theory stands out in its ability to engage social science in fruitful dialogue. Capra says that by integrating numerous philosophical strands, Habermas has become a leading intellectual force and a major influence on philosophy and social theory. Scholars have paid particular attention to his analysis of the transformation of the public sphere and the formal pragmatics he used to develop his theory of communicative action.

However, a number of scholars have criticized these two aspects of Habermasian social theory because of their implicit Eurocentric bias and their "universalizing" tendencies that promote domination through globalization. For instance, Giddens asserts that Eurocentrism raises its head when Habermas treats "oral cultures as inferior to civilizations, and particularly to the modernized West".

Kaufman argues that "Habermas's theory of communicative rationality relies strongly on notions of common sense and, more seriously, cannot stand without the notion of Western superiority on which it is founded". Huang argues that the binary opposition between state and society in Habermas's theory of public sphere "is an ideal abstracted from early modern and modern Western experience that is inappropriate for China".

On the other hand, Tong contends that Habermas's theory of modernity associated with his theory of communicative action "provides an ideal basis for a new and rewarding interpretation of the Chinese discourse on modernization and the idea of 'socialist modernization with Chinese characteristics'". The relationship between the theory of the public sphere and the theory of communicative action, which I shall elaborate in greater detail in the next section, needs a brief explanation here. Habermas began his early scholarship by analyzing the emergence and spread of an enlightened, politicized "public sphere" of open rational debate in the 18th century and its gradual emasculation under advanced capitalism.

He described the public sphere as the realm that enabled a "discursive will formation" or free uncoerced debate among equals. The bourgeoisie, which emerged with the rise of capitalism, sought to limit the authority of the state and affirm the principle of public accountability.

Eventually, Habermas developed the notion of communicative rationality based on an in-depth reading of what he originally termed "universal" pragmatics and implanted the public sphere in the lifeworld realm, as opposed to the system realm, of society built into his communicative action theory.

He divided the lifeworld into private and public sectors-the former revolving primarily around the intimacy and solitude of the nuclear family, and the latter concerned with the networks that shape public opinion and social identity through rational social dialogue. The system realm, divided into the economy and the state (public administration), uncoupled itself from the lifeworld with the rise of the welfare state-the economy from the lifeworld's private sphere and the state from the public sphere.

This uncoupling gave rise to the pathologies of modernity, or "colonization of the lifeworld," because the system realm, associated with the media of money and power, used cognitive instrumental rationality to impose purposive-rational action upon the lifeworld. The latter, on the other hand, used communicative rationality for action related to cultural and societal reproduction.

Habermas's critical theory is an attempt to emancipate the lifeworld from system "colonization" through the revival of an uncoerced and unrestricted public sphere operating on the "universal" pragmatics of communicative rationality. Its modus operandi helped participants reach agreement through argumentation based on the validity claims of truth, moral rightness, and sincerity. Max Pensky says that Habermas has been an influential advocate "for an unashamed universalism in political and moral questions" as reflected in Habermas's insistence that "we find a universal, if modest, basis for the great political innovations of popular sovereignty, legally enforceable human rights, democratic procedures, and the inconspicuous but vital solidarity that binds humans together". Pensky goes on to say that globalization "has also globalized the political public spheres of citizens, and has thus globalized the focus of public intellectuals operating within these public spheres as well".

In the light of the attempts to globalize the public sphere in this putative age of globalization, which is more or less a euphemism for Westernization, it is pertinent to re-evaluate the Habermasian metatheory of society, particularly with regard to the aspect of the public sphere, which Habermas developed for his post-doctoral Habilitationschrift, and the aspect of communicative action, which he consummated two decades later. His Legitimation Crisis served as a crucial transitional work separating his public sphere concerns and his work on communicative action. His Gauss lectures and essays of the early 1970s, which provide a good introduction to the theory of communicative action, also formed a bridge between his work of the 1960s and that of the 1980s.

The purpose of this monograph is to examine the thesis that Habermas's theory of the public sphere, as well as the more elaborate theory of communicative action, requires revision in order to remove the "universalizing" tendencies that promote domination through globalization. Universalism at the level of theory-whether it is the theory of the public sphere or the theory of communicative action-has its counterpart at the level of practice through lending support, perhaps uncritical support, to dominant versions of globalization.

The themes of universalism tend to be associated with the negative expressions of globalization (viz., Eurocentric hegemony). Habermasian theory is clearly a product of Eurocentric verticality, for it sees no positives in the historical development of non-Western societies or non-Western epistemology.

"Verticality," therefore, refers to the tendency to interpret world developments through the narrow confines of a particular region or civilization.] Habermas's depth hermeneutics or critical theory, a dialectical synthesis of the empirical-analytic and the historical-hermeneutical disciplines, relies heavily on evolutionary theory to claim the "universalism" of rationality in communicative action. The move to "universalize" the Enlightenment concept of rationality in this manner through a global public sphere, associated with putative globalization, is tantamount to a revival of the "developmentalism" notion of the Parsonsian structural-functionalist modernization paradigm.

Although Pensky credits Habermas as an advocate of an "unashamed universalism," Habermas himself had decided to abandon the term "universal" and related forms as early as the 1970s, when, for example, he selected the term "formal pragmatics" in place of the term "universal pragmatics" for his theory of communicative action, a point he seems consistently bound to repeat against several critics. In a footnote to the 1979 English translation of his 1976 essay on "universal pragmatics," Habermas expresses his dissatisfaction with the label "universal" and his preference for the term "formal pragmatics." The footnote states Hitherto the term "pragmatics" has referred to the analysis of particular contexts of language use and not to the reconstruction of universal features of using language (or of employing sentences in utterances). To mark this contrast, I introduced the distinction between "empirical" and "universal" pragmatics.

I am no longer happy with this terminology; the term "formal pragmatics" - as an extension of "formal semantics" - would serve better. Substituting his preferred terminology, the first sentence of his 1976 essay would read: "The task of formal pragmatics is to identify and reconstruct formal conditions of possible mutual understanding (Verständigung)." This change in terminology led to an important problematization of the critique of Habermasian "universalism," including by Habermas himself in the book Postmetaphysical Thinking, after which "one is hard-pressed to charge Habermas with the development of something like hegemonic universalism, grand in its ambition though Habermas's project may be." Habermas himself has said that his work is of importance only to Western societies because of its Eurocentrically limited view; and that "modernization" is not synonymous with "Westernization".

Therefore, the questions one must ask is: What remains of the Habermasian universalizing impulse today? Can we not circumvent the dangers of globalizing its Eurocentrism-or rather the lingering traces or remaining strains of Eurocentrism-through what subaltern historians call provincializing "Europe" or what Robertson and others call "glocalization"?

PROVINCIALIZING AND GLOCALIZATION

Provincializing "Europe," Chakrabarty explains, is not a project of shunning European thought, but rather a project of "globalizing" such thought by exploring how it may be renewed both for and from the margins-"how we create conjoined and disjunctive genealogies for European categories of political modernity as we contemplate the necessarily fragmentary histories of human belonging that never constitute a one or a whole".

Elaborating further, Chakrabarty says that the project of provincializing Europe "refers to a history that does not yet exist"; and that it does not involve "a simplistic, out-of-hand rejection of modernity, liberal values, universals, science, reason, grand narratives, totalizing explanations, and so on". Thus, "it cannot be a project of cultural relativism," and "it cannot originate from the stance that the reason/science/universals that help define Europe as the modern are simply 'culture-specific' and therefore only belong to European cultures".

Chakrabarty argues that not only Europeans but also Third World nationalisms have been equal partners in equating a certain version of Europe with "modernity." For example, both have been responsible for the universalization of the nation-state as the most desirable form of political community.

Drawing from Marx, Chakrabarty (2000) distinguishes between two types of history: the linear, developmental, and universal type (analytical histories) anchored on rationalism, objectivity, and the driving force of capital (History 1); and the nontotalizing, heterogenizing, and pluralizing type (affective narratives) that examines the lifeworlds of postcolonial people (History 2).

The project of provincializing "Europe" entails the production of History 2 "charged with the function of constantly interrupting the totalizing thrusts of History 1"-the instrument of Western hegemony, repression, and violence on the modern, the contemporary, and the historical.

The subaltern project of provincializing "Europe" is not the same as what Robertson defines as globalization-"a process involving the increasing domination of one societal or regional culture over all others".

Robertson identifies "glocalization" (roughly meaning "global localization") as the heterogenizing aspects of globalization. Robertson maintains that "globalization-in the broadest sense, the compression of the world-has involved and increasingly involves the creation and the incorporation of locality, a process which itself largely shapes, in turn, the compression of the world as a whole".

More recent studies have refined the concept of glocalization. For example, Helvacioglu (2000) used Robertson's notion of glocalization, Castells' notion of polarization, Sassen's notion of global city, and Appadurai's conception of imaginary worlds to elucidate, both in theory and in practice, a series of contradictions, ambiguities, and irregularities that result from particular articulations of global and local developments.

Using Turkey as a case study, Helvacioglu analysed the practical implications of globalization(s) at both the national and local levels and at the level of neighborhoods. Ritzer (2003), on the other hand, sees globalization as the sum of two conflicting sub-processes: glocalization and grobalization [sic], which form a continuum.

Glocalization is "the interpenetration of the global and the local resulting in unique outcomes in different geographic areas" whereas grobalization focuses on "the imperialistic ambitions of nations, corporations, organizations, and the like, and their desire and the need to impose themselves on various geographic areas". Ritzer argues Supporting the glocal as an alternative to the grobal may be a more successful strategy, recognizing the fact that the glocal is an increasingly important source not only of cultural diversity, but also of cultural innovation.

Subaltern scholars may argue that Robertson's "spin" on globalization via glocalization has some serious flaws from the point of view of non-Western contexts, whereas Chakrabarty's poststructuralist position seeks to open up a conceptual space to understand contemporary postcolonial realties.

Because of this monograph uses the framework of the theory of living systems (incorporating the theories of autopoiesis, cognition, and dissipative structures) to detect the scientific fallibility of Habermasian theory, it adheres to the same framework to derive the relevance of the concepts of provincializing "Europe" and globalization/glocalization.

The theory of living systems presumes that the world-system is a far-from-equilibrium dissipative structure wherein nation-states function as autopoietic cells that recursively reproduce themselves. Each nation-state is operationally closed but cognitively and structurally open to its environment-the other nation-states, organizations, and the world-system at large, all of which are structurally coupled through cognition, the process of living.

Autopoiesis is what enables nation-states to preserve their distinctive cultures. Nation-states differ from one another in their receptivity toward globalization/glocalization or toward provincializing "Europe." Thus, the two concepts, irrespective of how they are defined, can relate to different nation-states in different ways. I use the concept of provincializing "Europe" in the sense of translating "modern" universale (associated with Eurocentric historicism and discourse) into the History 2s of non-"Europe" and the concept of glocalization in the sense of adapting "Europe"-imposed globalization trends to suit the socio-cultural contexts of "non-Europe."

It would have been much more appropriate had Chakrabarty avoided the term "globalizing," which implies the deleterious domination of all aspects of Westernization as well, to argue the case for embracing the universals of "modernity." In the subaltern sense, the history of non-Europe has much to do with these universals although they bear the European imprint, and digging that history is part of the project of provincializing "Europe."

Elsewhere, Chakrabarty clarifies that thinking about political modernity is impossible without engaging some universels of "European thought." However, he points out, the problem with these universals is that they come packaged as though they have transcended the particular histories in which they were born.

Chakrabarty says, "When we translate them-practically, theoretically-into our languages and practice, we make them speak to other histories of belonging, and that is how difference and heterogeneity enter these words". Thus, Chakrabarty elucidates that the project of provincializing "Europe" also involves "the translational processes through which concepts and practices are made one's own". Chakrabarty continues that being attentive to the translational processes makes people aware of horizons of human existence that speak of histories other than those encoded into European political thought. Now it is up to us to build an archive or repository of these other horizons so that we can use them creatively to fabricate our lives as we live them. It means further that while one can acknowledge, without seeking revenge, what one owes to Europe, one can at the same time also investigate the histories that provided the grounds on which European thought was situated and translated in our pasts. At present, most of us studying modern Indian history do not do this digging.

This statement makes it quite clear that subaltern scholars are keen to dig the local links to "modern" universals associated with Eurocentric discourse. Thus, differences between provincializing "Europe" and glocalization is a matter of how one perceives the phenomenon of globalization. In what follows, I shall first describe the Habermasian theory in some detail (relegating those criticisms that do not strictly concern the focus of this monograph to two appendices for the benefit of the broad spectrum of readers). Second, I shall examine the relevant concepts of Habermasian theory-civil society/public sphere, communicative rationality, and liberal democracy-in terms of Eastern philosophy and history, as well as modern subaltern historiography. Thereby I hope to uncover the Eurocentric strands of Habermas's project that have received inadequate attention in the ardor for globalizing his theory of modernity based on communicative rationality and formal ("universal") pragmatics.

This attempt also complies with Dhareshwar's call to "interrogate the western theories to construct a metatheory which specifies the intelligibility conditions of the claims and problems of those theories"-a call based on Balagangadhara's theory of religion that unravels Orientalism. Third, I shall examine Habermas's critical theory through the lens of the emerging theory of living systems-incorporating the theories of autopoiesis, cognition, and dissipative structures-to show that operationally closed but structurally and cognitively open subsystems comprising a dissipative structure like the world-system form a formidable barrier against the emergence of a global public sphere. Fourth, I shall briefly present my conclusions.

HABERMASIAN THEORY

Habermas was not the originator of the notion of "civil society" or the idea of the "public" (or the "public sphere") that are central to Habermasian theory. Rather he reconstructed some of the essential philosophical and sociological discussions since the Age of Enlightenment culminating in Hegel and Marx. The concept of civil society as a realm distinct from the state emerged in the 17th-century works of Hobbes and Locke and of the later thinkers of the French and Scottish enlightenments.

The distinction between the private and the public spheres also arose in the 17th century when almost all Enlightenment theorists followed the lead of Locke's famous Letter on Toleration in demanding freedom of religion. They argued for the removal of religion from public life and public authority, so it would fall into the private sphere of individual preference and individual practice. Kant linked the concept of public space with the right to publicity that provided the moral legitimacy of democracy. Negt and Kluge say that Kant ascribed to the public sphere the status of a transcendental principle, that of the mediation between politics and ethics. The public sphere is, according to Kant, a principle of the legal framework of society and simultaneously a method of enlightenment; it is the only medium within which the politics of the revolutionary bourgeoisie can articulate itself.

Some identify Habermas as the last rationalist, for he borrowed the concept from the Enlightenment rationalists via Weber and gave it a new twist. Rationality, science, liberalism, and individualism, all of which emerged as interlinked concepts in the late 17th-century Europe, reached a high point during the Enlightenment. As Wallerstein points out, the presumed rationality of the social world, just like the presumed rationality of the physical world, implied the ability to formulate lawlike propositions that held true across space-time. Because Habermas thought it essential to mix the empirical-analytical approach with the historical-hermeneutical to develop his version of critical theory, he too implicitly subscribed to linear thinking associated with Newtonian mechanics.

One may interpret Western rationality as the pragmatic formulation of the ontological concept of "rationalism," a philosophical view that goes back to Pythagoras, Plato, and Aristotle in ancient Greece, and was later adopted by Descartes, Spinoza, Leibniz, Kant, and Hegel. Rationalism, which has long been the rival of empiricism, has come under severe challenge by the 20th-century logical positivists.

Habermas believed that philosophy in its postmetaphysical, post-Hegelian currents was "converging toward the point of a theory of rationality". He used Weber's theory of rationalization-perhaps a subtle attack on historical materialism, which explains capitalism as a mode of systematizing consciousness rather than of class exploitation-as the groundwork to derive the concept of communicative rationality. Habermas attempted to establish a cooperative relationship between rationality and empiricism by introducing a theory of communicative action that clarifies the normative foundations of a critical theory of society. Thus, Habermas emerges as a different kind of "pragmatist" than Mead, whose pragmatism is highly tilted toward instrumental manipulation of man and nature-not the rules of communicative understanding and democratic will formation.

Habermas conceptualized the bourgeois public sphere as "the sphere of private people come together as a public". They "soon claimed the public sphere regulated from above against the public authorities themselves, to engage them in debate over the general rules governing relations in the basically privatized but publicly relevant sphere of commodity exchange and social labour". The public use of reason was "peculiar and without historical precedent". The apolitical literary precursor of the public sphere, which was not "autochthonously bourgeois", provided them the training ground for critical-rational public debate. Economically, culturally and politically, the "town"-with its coffee houses, the salons, and the table societies (Tischgesellschaften)-served as the life centre of civil society. The line between state and society divided the public sphere from the private realm.

The public sphere in the political realm evolved from the public sphere in the world of letters, and "through the vehicle of public opinion put the state in touch with the needs of society". Thus, Habermas argued for the existence of two kinds of public spheres: the political public sphere concerned with rational discourse leading to agreement on public policy, and the literary public sphere concerned with matters of taste and general social behaviour.

Some version of the public sphere has always existed as an appendage to democratic theory. Benhabib identifies three different versions of public space that correspond to three main currents of Western political thought: the agonistic, the legalistic, and the discursive. The agonistic view, associated with Hannah Arendt, belongs to the "republican virtue" or "civic virtue" tradition.

The legalistic view, exemplified by Bruce Ackerman's conception of "public dialogue," belongs to the liberal tradition of Kant that emphasizes a just and stable political order. The discursive view, associated with Habermas, envisages a democratic socialist accommodation within late capitalist society in hopes of reforming it. Benhabib says that because questions of democratic legitimacy are central to Habermas's public sphere, it has strengths that the other two lack. Villa, who compares the public realm theory of Arendt with that of Habermas, says that both attempted to theorize the minimal conditions necessary for a discursive realm free of structural coercion or manipulation. Both saw the public sphere as a specifically political space-distinct from the state and the economy-for citizen debate, deliberation, agreement, and action.

Antipolitical forces unleashed by modernity, however, overwhelmed the public sphere. Arendt argued that "household" concerns had "devoured" the public sphere while Habermas argued that the universalization of instrumental rationality had enabled technical-administrative imperatives to "colonize" the public sphere. As developed by Habermas, the concept of the bourgeois public sphere should be understood as an analytic category. It emerged along with the development of capitalism as a dynamic nexus that linked "a variety of actors, factors and contexts together in a cohesive theoretic framework". It was this configurational quality, with its emphasis on institutional and discursive contingencies that gave the concept its analytical power.

The ascending bourgeois classes generated this new social space between the private sphere (consisting of the economy and family) and the sphere of the public authorities (formed by the state and the judiciary), especially during the 18th century. Early to mid-19th century saw the highpoint of the bourgeois public sphere, which disintegrated in the modern industrialized welfare states of advanced capitalism.

The bourgeois public sphere was a forum accessible to as many people as possible to express and exchange a large variety of social experiences. Individuals used this forum for rational discussion to confront various arguments and views. Its primary task was to check on government policies systematically and critically. The public sphere functioned on the basis of rational critical argument. The Frankfurt School's attempt to ground a vision of social transformation and human emancipation on the proletariat had foundered. The public sphere, which provided a mode of social integration by ignoring the Marxian concept of class, was an attempt to reground the project of critical theory. Public discourse (or communicative action) enabled the coordination of human life with state power and market economies. Britain, France, and Germany served as the models to trace the development of the public sphere.

A refeudalization of society occurred as private organizations began increasingly to assume public power while the state penetrated the private realm. Thus, the public sphere became more an arena for advertising than a setting for rational-critical debate. The public sphere designates a theater in modern societies in which the medium of talk enacts political participation. Fraser sees it as an institutionalized arena of discursive interaction conceptually distinct from the state, as well as from the official economy.

Ambrozas argues that Habermas salvaged "the emancipatory promise of the bourgeois public sphere," where any and all individuals came together (in principle), around issues of general interest, without concern for social status, to achieve rational consensus by means of critical discussion. Here, Ambrozas presents the consensus theory à la Parsons: All actors more or less possess the same values, which necessarily must cut across all classes and cultural strata. They created public opinion.

The public sphere first emerged in 17th-century England in dialectical opposition to the nuclear family and the modern state. Ambrozas says, "The family was a necessary precondition for the public sphere as the realm where private persons were individuated. Factors promoting individuation in the family were humane interpersonal relations as well as solitary reading, especially of the new domestic novels that depicted bourgeois family life".

COMMUNICATIVE ACTION THEORY

Habermas's theory of communicative action represents the outcome of his efforts to develop a new critical theory of modern society by "synthesizing a tremendous range of approaches and elucidating their implications and interconnectedness". His social theory of rationality appropriated the major currents of 20th-century Western philosophy and social theory-speech-act theory and analytic philosophy, classical social theory, hermeneutics, phenomenology, developmental psychology, and systems theory.

Venturelli says that Habermas's theory of communicative action, which redefines the problem of reason and rationalization, "recentres the principle of communication into the emancipatory project of modernity". Habermas says his theory intertwines three topic complexes: a concept of rationality that is free from the subjectivistic and individualistic premises of contemporary Western philosophy and social theory, a two-level concept of society that connects the lifeworld and system paradigms, and a theory of modernity that explains the social pathologies and paradoxes of modernity.

By exhaustively assessing and recasting the ideas of classical social theorists and critical theorists to meet his own immediate needs, he formulated a new theoretical approach that combined the methods and problematics of both philosophy and empirical social science.

On the first topic complex, Habermas tried to compensate for the weaknesses inherent in the older subject-object paradigm by formulating a paradigm of intersubjectivity. Whereas the former emphasized purposive rational action (based on cognitive-instrumental rationality), the latter emphasized the pragmatics of communicative action (based on communicative rationality).

His aim was to derive a universalistic (and, therefore, nonrelativistic) theory of rationality, which he grounded socially rather than transcendentally. Arens clarifies this point: Because Habermas's discourse ethics stood in the neo-Kantian tradition, it attempted to be not only universalistic, but also deontological, cognitivistic, and formalistic. Habermas used Weber's treatment of world religions to derive a broader theory of cultural rationalization (of worldviews). He did so by drawing upon Mead's communication-theoretic approach ("social behaviorism") and from Durkheim's theory of the origins of religions and ritual. Applying the speech-act theory, Habermas claims that reaching understanding (rather than action oriented to instrumental success) is the essential aspect of language. Thus, he "roots communicative rationality in the very nature of language-mediated communication, and thereby implicitly claims that it has universal significance".

On the second topic complex, Habermas argues that modern society reflects both lifeworld (a concept derived from phenomenology and hermeneutics) and system (as conceptualized by Parsons and carried further by Luhmann) dimensions as differentiated aspects of social life. Forms of action and reason differentiate these two dimensions. Habermas relates each of the two dimensions to a determinate form of action and rationality-communicative versus cognitive-instrumental.

Outlining a theory of social evolution, Habermas grounds the lifeworld in an evolutionary development of societal learning whose superstructural location vitiates the analytic truth claims of Marxist materialism. (This method makes him axiologically neutral on issues of moral judgments and assertions.) System evolution, on the other hand, reflects a linear increase in a society's steering capacity-engendered by the steering media of money and power-that encodes purposive-rational action and instrumental reason.

This dialectical interaction between the two dimensions results in an uncoupling of system integration from social integration entailing the differentiation of state and economy. From a methodological point of view, social integration presents itself as part of the lifeworld's symbolic reproduction while functional integration becomes the standard for system maintenance at the level of organizing the political and economic spheres.

Both paradigms, life-world and system, are important From the life-world perspective, we thematize the normative structures (values and institutions) of a society. We analyse events and states from the point of view of their dependency on functions of social integration (in Parsons's vocabulary, integration and pattern maintenance), while the non-normative components of the system serve as limiting conditions.

From the system perspective, we thematize a society's steering mechanisms and the extension of the scope of contingency. We analyse events and states from the point of view of their dependency on functions of system integration (in Parsons's vocabulary, adaptation and goal-attainment), while the goal values serve as data.

The public and the private spheres served as the environments of the system. Habermas says the imperatives of capitalism and democracy clash in the political public sphere, "where the autonomy of the lifeworld has to prove itself in the face of the administrative system". What emerges as public opinion there takes a different meaning from the action-theoretic lifeworld perspective than it does from the system-theoretic systemic perspective of the state apparatus. From the lifeworld perspective, social consensus is identified "as the first link in the chain of political will formation and as the basis of legitimation," whereas from the systemic perspective, "the same consensus counts as the result of engineering legitimation".

On the third topic complex, Habermas reformulates the notion of the loss of meaning and loss of freedom in terms of his thesis on the colonization of the lifeworld by the system world, which advances his analysis of postliberal capitalism. Habermas says that neither the secularization of worldviews nor the structural differentiation of society is the cause of the pathologies and paradoxes of modernity. He attributes these effects to "the penetration of forms of economic and administrative rationality into areas of action that resist being converted over to the media of money and power because they are specialized in cultural transmission, social integration, and child rearing, and remain dependent on mutual understanding as a mechanism for coordinating action".

Habermas's system perspective, like Parsons's, excludes any meaningful consideration of class, mode of production, and the thermodynamics of nature. Nevertheless, Habermas introduces the dynamic of capitalist market imperatives into his model of interaction between system and lifeworld-an essential characteristic of his critical theory.

Drawing from Weber, Habermas argues that the enduring features of modernity are the three institutionally differentiated cultural value spheres of science and technology, law and morality, and art. As a specification of these three value spheres, Habermas's theory of communicative action takes the following form: The modern differentiation of the lifeworld into three structured components (culture, society, and personality) is the opening up to experience of three 'worlds' (objective, social, and subjective), along with basic attitudes that can be adopted to those worlds (objectivating, norm-conformative, and expressive), their corresponding rationalities (cognitive-instrumental, moral-practical, and aesthetic-practical), and the three validity claims (truth, rightness, and truthfulness) thematized respectively in three uses of language (constative, interactive, and expressive). In this description, each of the three structural components of the lifeworld is assigned its own validity claim, and each is conceived of as having a unique 'inner logic" that expresses itself in a specific type of rationalization. According to this model of three autonomous spheres, the validity claim of truth is lodged in the cultural space of science and institutionalized in the 'scientific enterprise," whereas the rightness validity claim is attached to post-conventional law and morality and the institutions of the liberal democratic state.

As for the cultural and institutional space of the truthfulness validity claim, Habermas refers to an 'artistic enterprise". Billings and Scott (1994) provide a thumbnail sketch of Habermasian theory for contextualizing national religious conflicts over legitimation. They say that for Habermas world mastery meant instrumental rationality, social interaction meant communicative rationality, and rationalization of the lifeworld meant "linguistification of the sacred". Heath (2001) argues that "despite being pitched as a critique of instrumental rationality, Habermas's work is informed by only a somewhat vague grasp of the details of the instrumental views".

Therefore, Heath has brought Habermas's theory into dialogue with Bayesian decision and game theory, "the most sophisticated articulation of the instrumental conception of practical rationality".

LINGERING TRACES OF EUROCENTRISM

I shall now examine the relevant concepts of Habermasian theory in terms of Eastern philosophy and history, as well as modern subaltern historiography, to uncover the Eurocentric strands of Habermas's project that have received inadequate attention in the ardor for globalizing his critical theory of society and modernity. Habermas's metatheory encompasses two aspects of particular interest to communication scholars-the public sphere and communicative action. An exploration of these two aspects will help the project of provincializing or glocalizing the emancipatory potential of Habermas's work for the benefit of non-"Europe" while circumventing the "universalizing" tendencies that promote domination through globalization. I begin with some insights from the project of subaltern studies.

Although postcolonial subaltern studies recognize the value of European thought for modernizing non-"Europe," subaltern historian Chakrabarty (2000) points out the negative impact that "Europe"-centered "universalism" (History 1) has had on the lifeworld of the colonial subjects. He says that "Europe" remains the sovereign, theoretical subject of all other histories because "Europe" is reified and celebrated in the phenomenal world of everyday relationships of power as the scene of the birth of the modern.

Philosophers and thinkers, Chakrabarty says, have produced theories that embraced the entirety of humanity in relative, and sometimes absolute, ignorance of the majority of humankind.

He refers to Husserl's identification of Greek-European science as theoria (universal science) while characterizing oriental philosophies as "practical-universal," and hence "mythical-religious." Also, Marx's categories-such as capital and pre-capital-carry a similar epistemological proposition.

Chakrabarty (2000) then goes on to point out that British rule had put in place the practices, institutions, and discourse of bourgeois individualism in the Indian subcontinent, which became the staging ground of many of the public and private rituals of modern individualism. India became a nation-state, a conceptual entity "whose theoretical subject was Europe," and in Gandhi's words India continued with "English rule without the Englishmen". Indians became constitutionally recognized citizens in the classically liberal sense-a modern individual with a private self.

This modern individual ? is also supposed to have an interiorized "private" self that pours out incessantly in diaries, letters, autobiographies, novels, and, of course, in what we say to our analysts. The bourgeois citizen is not born until one discovers the pleasures of privacy. But this is a very special kind of "private self - it is, in fact, a deferred "public" self, for this bourgeois private self, as Jürgen Habermas has reminded us, is "always already oriented to an audience [Publikum]".

Thus, Chakrabarty says, "Indian public life may mimic on paper the bourgeois legal fiction of citizenship" but the fiction of bourgeois private self fails to come through even in Indians' autobiographies. The ambiguity of the public-private distinction may appear to be another example of the "incompleteness" of bourgeois transformation of India. The metaphor of the sanctified and patriarchal extended family in India and elsewhere clearly does not fit the private-public dichotomy so central to Habermasian social theory.

However, Chakrabarty argues, European imperialism and Third World nationalism have combined to universalize the nation-state as the most desirable form of political community. He rejects the "stance that the reason/science/universals that help define Europe as the modern are simply 'culture-specific' and therefore only belong to the European cultures".

Our task should be to "find a form of social thought that embraces analytical reason in pursuit of social justice but does not allow it to erase the question of heterotemporality from the history of the modern subject". Chakrabarty disagrees with Rorty for crossing cudgels with Habermas and implying that democratic societies had self-contained histories of their own when Habermas stated that modern philosophy had backed the democratic societies' attempts at self-assurance.

Chakrabarty writes, "Rorty ignores the role that the 'colonial theater' (both external and internal)-where the theme of 'freedom' as defined by modern political philosophy was constantly invoked in aid of the ideas of 'civilization,' 'progress,' and latterly 'development'-played in the process of this 'reassurance'". Chakrabarty takes the position that European thought is at once indispensable and inadequate in helping the non-Western nations to think through the experiences of political modernity.

The thesis of this monograph-that Habermas's theory of the public sphere requires provincializing or glocalizing in order to remove its "universalizing" tendencies that promote domination through globalization-does not mean an aversion to Western thought. Chakrabarty asserts that non-"Europe" needs universals derived through European analytical heritage and hermeneutical heritage to produce critical readings of social injustices. Perhaps, one can construe that Chakrabarty's call for History 2s also justifies the glocalization (in the Ritzer sense rather than Robertson's) of such Eurocentric universals (like those built into Habermas's social theory) to reflect the realities of each country's lifeworld.

If such "glocalization" were possible, an exploration of the Eurocentric verticality of the Habermasian project should help determine its adaptability in the non-Western social environment. In the rest of this section, I do this exploration in terms of Habermas's (a) description of the evolution of the public sphere and civil society; (b) use of formal pragmatics in hopes of "universalizing" communicative rationality; (c) treatment of non-Western philosophy and history; and (d) idealization of liberal democracy associated with a discursive public sphere.

My intention is to show the consequences of attempts to push Habermasian theories in the direction of universalism, which promote a Eurocentric discourse of Western universalism that makes non-Western theories relatively invisible in the global academy. Because much of Habermas's work is rooted in modern Europe, I shall examine the usefulness of his concepts in the context of not only classical Eastern philosophy but also of modern subaltern perspective of Chakrabarty.

PUBLIC SPHERE AND CIVIL SOCIETY

The Habermasian blueprint of the public sphere represents an evolutionary phase of European history, although Sparks (2000) rejects the existence of a "bourgeois public sphere" in the 18th century. This blueprint asserts that a political public sphere (preceded by a literary public sphere) evolved between the realm of public authority (viz., state and judiciary) and the private realm (viz., family and civil society, including the economy).

The bourgeoisie used the public sphere for rational debate on matters of public concern that often challenged the realm of public authority. The question arises whether this model conducive to promoting liberal democracy and emancipation can claim "unashamed" universalism. Baynes clarifies that the model of the public sphere that Habermas envisioned comprised a vast array of institutions in which a wide variety of practical discourses overlapped. It ranged "from the more or less informal movements and associations in civil society where solidarities are formed, through the various institutions of the mass media, to the more formal institutions of parliamentary debate and legal argumentation". Under European imperialism, the public spheres that emerged in the colonies from the second half of the 19th century onwards contradicted the Habermasian mold. For instance, in British India, the public constituted the European elite, not the native nationalists. Public opinion was the opinion of the "nonofficial" European community.

The imperial government enacted the Vernacular Press Act of 1878 to suppress native public opinion. In colonial society, as Chatterjee points out, the political domain was under the control of aliens, who excluded the colonized from its decisive zones. In colonial society, the public sphere in the political domain, and its literary precursors in the debating societies and learned bodies, did not emerge out of the discursive construction of a social world peopled by "individuals."

Nor was there an "audience-oriented subjectivity," by which the new conjugal family's intimate domain became publicly transparent and thus consistent with and amenable to the discursive control of the public sphere in the political domain. Clearly, the putative public sphere that arose in colonial India was not associated with civil society of sovereign individuals. It contrasted with the Habermasian public sphere that supposedly functioned in a space outside the supervision of the political authority and thereby marked both the distinction and the unity of state and civil society.

Li points out that the Western division of public sphere and private sphere simply does not exist in Confucianism, the pervasive philosophy in East Asia. De Bary explains that in Chinese philosophy, "private (si) is a familial concept, marked by a cooperative spirit that extends into the community or public sphere (gong) as a single interdependent continuum". This is in general true of Indian philosophy as well.

Therefore, Habermas's public sphere theory, which connects the rise of a market economy with the emergence of civil society in which contractual ties and horizontal integration between economic actors challenge primordial ties to the family and to the state, cannot fit the socio-cultural patterns of much of the non-Western world.

Under alien rule, however, the conflict between the culturally disparate state and its subjects disrupted the cooperative spirit that marked the single interdependent family-community-state continuum-the indigenous "public sphere." Apparently, just like the modernization theorists, Habermas implies that the non-West must eventually go through Europe's "exceptional" historical experience before a bourgeois, rational public sphere can emerge.

This aporetic presumption, in fact, becomes evident in his reliance on the empirically weak evolutionary theories or the "reconstructive sciences" of Piaget and Kohlberg to claim a connection between language and rationality. Calhoun says the notion of civil society is basic to Habermas's account of the public sphere. Habermas asserts that in the 17th and 18th centuries, civil society developed as "the genuine domain of private autonomy [that] stood opposed to the state".

Capitalist market economies formed the basis of this civil society, which "came into existence as the corollary of a depersonalized state authority". Doctrines of laissez-faire and free trade among nations brought the development of "civil society as the private sphere emancipated from the directives of public authority". Civil society served as the precondition for free, rational, informed discourses on the political ends of society.

[However, the links between the public sphere and history are disputatious. Pinter says recent research into the history of the public sphere questioned some interpretation of facts on which Habermas based his early theory.] Contrary to the presumptions of the bourgeois public sphere, Flower and Leonard point out that the notion of a clear boundary between state and society implicit in the discourse of civil society is problematic in the Chinese context, where the vectors of social interaction involve both horizontal and vertical linkages of exchange and expectation.

If the idea of civil society were to have salience in the Chinese countryside, they argue, it must be reworked to embrace the blurry interpenetration of state and society, and understood in terms of cooptation, negotiation, and historicity at the heart of the interaction. Hann too argues the need for a more inclusive usage of civil society such that it is not defined negatively in opposition to the state, but positively in the context of ideas and practices through which cooperation and trust are established in social life.

He says the narrow, Western liberal-individualist idea of civil society has long been in need of such ethnographic investigation because the term civil society is riddled with contradictions, with its current vogue predicated on a fundamental ethnocentricity. Furthermore, he says that the exploration of civil society requires paying careful attention to a range of informal interpersonal practices that scholars have overlooked.

White adds that the term civil society has become entangled in political currents wherein it has become a litmus test for the democratic potential of non-Western regimes. "The meanings attributed to the term have followed the trajectory of Western philosophical thought, beginning in the seventeenth century when the term took on attributes of reason and rationality in opposition to revelation and the state of nature".

The "classical" sense of civil society is of little or no use in describing most of the non-Western world below the level of government and the activities of a segment of educated Westernized elites. Moon, on the other hand, uses the concept of civil society in the "classical" sense when she blames Korea's Chosön dynasty for choosing neo-Confucianism as the state ideology thereby excluding women from the civil society and the public sphere.

However, Moon concedes that the Korean women do not fit the "liberal model of the self as atomized individual isolated from social relations". Koo clarifies that the public sphere that might have existed in Chosön society "was too limited in scope and nature to comprise what can legitimately be called a civil society" because of the lack of an economic base. Rabo asks not to create a dichotomy between state and society in which the state is simply a locus of repression. Instead, one should look at the interdependencies between state and civil society. He adds that Western scholars lean heavily on traditional Orientalism to show that the Orient, the Middle East, and the Islamic world are always lacking some basic ingredient for a happy marriage between the rulers and the ruled.

The Eastern perspective of state as part of the public is also evident in the writings of American philosopher Dewey (1927/1954), who defines the state as "the organization of the public effected through officials for the protection of the interests shared by its members". He points out that for long periods of human history, especially in the Orient, the state ruled but did not regulate. Dewey sees the state as inseparable from the community, which thrives on associated (rather than individualistic) activity thereby bringing into existence a public. The state, Dewey asserts, is "a distinctive and secondary form of association". Implying a Confucian view, Dewey claims that the democratic ideals of fraternity, liberty, and equality are inherent in the "communal experience," and not in individualism. Implicit in Dewey's notion of associational connections is the concept of civil society.

In retrospect, Habermas explains that contemporary discussions of the central question in The Structural Transformation of the Public Sphere nowadays take place under the rubric of the "rediscovery of civil society." He says the current meaning of civil society no longer includes a sphere of an economy regulated via labour, capital, and commodity markets.

The institutional core of civil society is constituted by voluntary unions outside the realm of the state and the economy and ranging from churches, cultural associations, and academies to independent media, sport and leisure clubs, debating societies, groups of concerned citizens, and grassroots petitioning drives all the way to occupational associations, political parties, labour unions, and "alternative institutions". He says that the concept of civil society owes its rise in favour to the criticism leveled against the totalitarian annihilation of the political public sphere. Just as much as Habermas willingly takes "the apologetic role of a Western participant in a cross-cultural discussion of human rights", he appears to say that the non-West must catch up with the modern West by striving to achieve the preconditions necessary for the emergence of a discursive public sphere conducive to the operation of a liberal democracy.

If this interpretation is correct, then the claim for a global public sphere falls apart while strengthening the case for a value-free sphere of the "third realm" (wherein the state and society work in harmony). Such a "third realm," as Huang points out, reflects the reality of the Chinese lifeworld. Elaborating further, Huang says "the value-laden teleology of Habermas's bourgeois public sphere" does not fit either contemporary China or its conditions under the Qing dynasty and the republic. Huang argues that what's relevant to China is a value-free "third realm" that shows the simultaneous influence of the state and society. In late imperial China, the "third realm" played a major role in the justice system, subcounty administration, and local public services.

Since the reform era began in the late 1970s, China has witnessed a tremendous expansion in the realm of private society and economy, but the private realm pales in comparison with the third realm. Thus: Instead of continuing to insist on equating China and Europe, we need to try to explain the difference between the two. Contrary to the vision of the public sphere/ civil society models, actual sociopolitical change in China has really never come from any lasting assertion of societal economy against the state, but rather from the workings out of state-society relations in the third realm.

Chakrabarty's subaltern analysis also points out that even in modern India the private-public dichotomy in the lifeworld remains a fiction, particularly in the context of the extended family system. The rural Bengali institution of adda or majlish-the customary gatherings where people talked informally about all kinds of things affecting their lives-was far from a fledgling public sphere. The ideals of the adda and those of the modern civil society were mutually antithetical. Conversations in an adda were "by definition opposed to the idea of achieving any definite outcome".

However, because of the imperial imposition of British institutional structure, India is perhaps more ready than China to mimic a glocalized version of the public sphere or more likely two versions-one serving the minority of "Europe"-oriented urban elite, a carryover from the British rule; the other serving the "third-realm" sphere associated with the large majority of the non-Westernized "citizens," who have exercised universal franchise since India's independence from Britain in 1947.

Chatterjee distinguishes between a public sphere appropriated within the narrative of capital, and a community public sphere that belongs to the domain of the natural. Chatterjee clarifies that in the contemporary Indian context, "the old idea of civil society as bourgeois society" is limited to "a relatively small section of the population whose social locations can be identified with a fair degree of clarity" whereas the large majority belongs to political society because they have a certain political relationship with the state although "this relationship does not always conform to what is envisaged in the constitutional depiction of the relation between the state and members of civil society".

Chatterjee's political society represents the "third realm" that befits Eastern thinking. These two-civil and political-represent the capital/community opposition, "the great unsurpassed contradiction in Western philosophy". Provincializing the Habermasian public sphere in terms of History 2s has its distinct advantages for non"Europe": Whenever the state attempts to move toward authoritarianism, the "citizens" can cry foul, invoking the emancipatory properties of the fictive "public sphere" and the notion of "communicative rationality" associated with it. Some may argue that the idea of the East implicit in the term Eastern philosophy posits a major problem because the formation of public spheres and differential rationalities in the Third World societies as a product of the encounters with modernity have left the East in a much more complicated situation. The dominance of History 1 in postcolonial society clearly documents this complexity.

However, as Chakrabarty points out, History 1 does not document the achievement of a bourgeois revolution in non-"Europe." Thus, in the absence of bourgeois revolutions in postcolonial societies, bourgeois public spheres or a global public sphere in the Habermasian mold are unlikely to take hold. The more likely are the capital-detached community public spheres in the domain of the natural-the grist for History 2s.

Chatterjee hypothesizes that "an investigation into the idea of the nation, by uncovering a necessary contradiction between capital and community, is likely to lead us to a fundamental critique of modernity from within itself.". He elucidates that the alien rulers introduced the institutions of civil society, in the form in which they had arisen in Europe, into the colonies precisely to create a public domain for the legitimation of colonial rule.

However, this process was fundamentally limited because the colonial state could confer only subjecthood but not citizenship on the colonized, who refused to become members of this civil society. Instead, they chose to build their national identities within the traditional narrative of community, which differed from the domain of the bourgeois civil-social institutions. Chatterjee points out The irony is, of course, that this other narrative is again violently interrupted once the postcolonial national state attempts to resume its journey along the trajectory of world-historical development.

This interpretation clearly shows the problems of provincializing the Habermasian public sphere and civil society, as well as the tension between History 1 and History 2s. Rajeev Bhargava concludes that if one were to conduct an empirical-cum-interpretative inquiry into the presence of civil society, political society, public sphere, and the state in Indian society and polity applying the mainstream (Western) understandings of these terms, one may not find these entities in India.

CONCEPT OF RATIONALITY

For Habermas, rationalization is a two-world process-instrumental (or means-end) rationality, as conceptualized by Weber and the earlier critical theorists, associated with the operation of the system world; and communicative rationality associated with the lifeworld, the corner stone of Habermas's contribution to critical theory.

Communicative rationality supersedes instrumental rationality because the latter is a byproduct of the former, whose communicative action created the system world. As already noted, Habermas developed his theory of communicative action on the foundation of formal pragmatics, which claims to have universal characteristics. Communicative rationality, which refers to "the institutionalization of mechanisms of open criticism and defence", is a distinct feature of Habermas's project. Habermas says that one has to analyse communicative rationality in connection with achieving understanding in language.

This suggests a rationally motivated agreement among participants that one can measure against "criticizable validity claims". Because objectivity in social-theoretical knowledge is essential from both metatheoretical and methodological points of view, the corresponding concepts of communicative action and interpretation, Habermas says, "would have to be shown to be universally valid" and not "interwoven with a particular cultural tradition".

He, therefore, anchors those concepts into an internal structure of processes of reaching understanding in terms of (a) the three-world relations of actors [originally proposed by Popper] and the corresponding concepts of the objective, social, and subjective worlds; (b) the validity claims of propositional truth, normative lightness, and sincerity or authenticity; (c) the concept of rationally motivated agreement, that is, one based on the intersubjective recognition of criticizable validity claims; and (d) the concept of reaching understanding as the cooperative negotiation of common definitions of the situation.

Habermas's main contribution to philosophy has been the development of a theory of rationality. Rationality, in a general sense, means the ability to think logically and analytically. In the Habermasian sense, rationality is a form of communicative action aimed at achieving agreement with others in an "ideal speech situation" where people put forward moral and political claims and defend them based on rationality alone.

However, despite the admirable criteria Habermas applied "to expound the universality of the concept of communicative rationality", his grand theory does not reflect an effort on his part to understand or analyse the non-Western philosophical thinking on action and rationality. This is because he chose to pursue that task by following the path of Occidental sociological approaches to a theory of societal rationalization by using the "conceptual strategies, assumptions, and lines of argument from Weber to Parsons".

Habermas says his concept of rationality is a reconstruction of Weber's theory of rationalization built on "the restricted idea of purposive rationality"- a concept that Marx, Horkheimer, and Adorno also shared. Habermas asserts that Weber "did not regard rationalization process as a phenomenon peculiar to the Occident". Habermas then goes on to work out the logic of the rationalization of worldviews from Weber's studies on the sociology of religion. Weber had differentiated three rationality complexes derived in formal pragmatic terms from basic attitudes and world-concepts: cognitive-instrumental rationality institutionalized in science and social technologies;

aesthetic-practical rationality instituted in eroticism and art; and the moral-practical rationality instituted in law and morality.

In Weber's account, modern life had increasingly become an "iron cage" resulting from the institutionalization of cognitive-instrumental rationality (associated with purposive-rational action) in the economy and the state. Habermas finds conceptual bottlenecks in Weber's theory of action because of Weber's action-theoretic assumption that "processes of societal rationalization could come into view only from the standpoint of purposive rationality". Habermas asserts that from a sociological point of view, it makes more sense to begin with a communication-theoretic line of inquiry. Then he goes on to connect Karl Bühler's theory of language functions-cognitive, expressive, and appellative-with the methods and insights of the analytic theory of meaning to make it "the centerpiece of a theory of communicative action oriented toward reaching understanding".

Habermas takes the view that it is not possible to deal with rationalization adequately within the conceptual framework of the philosophy of consciousness. Therefore, he shifts the paradigm from purposive activity to communicative action by incorporating Mead's communication-theoretic concept of "social behaviorism" and Durkheim's theory of social solidarity connecting social integration to system integration. Habermas says communicative action serves as a reference point for analyzing the contributions of the components of the lifeworld-culture, society, and personality, which, together with organism, make up the four subsystems of every action system in the Parsonsian theory of social evolution. Parsons specified society as an autarchic action system placed in an environment. Habermas delves into general systems theory, as does later Parsons, to give system characteristics to state and economy dimensions of society that intrude into its lifeworld dimension. Predominantly, the lifeworld operates on communicative rationality whereas the two system-dimensions operate on cognitive-instrumental rationality.

The Indian perspective: In contrast, Eastern philosophy in general does not recognize such gradations of rationality. Habermas's treatment of different types of rationality as separate, autonomous validity spheres has come under criticism in the Occident as well because he fails to explain how actors determine the specific standard to apply in a given situation. Fleming has drawn attention to McCarthy's concern that Habermas's schema of three spheres of validity-truth, rightness, and truthfulness-might be Western and idiosyncratic rather than universal features of human interaction. Fleming says that Habermas "seems strangely untroubled by suggestions that his theory might contain Eurocentric prejudices".

Delanty points out that Habermas "fails to grasp that universal morality can be articulated in more than one cultural form and in more than one logic of development". To lessen the residual Eurocentrism still pervading the

Habermasian theory, Delanty suggests a shift of its emphasis from a de-contextualized and transcendental critique of communication rooted in Occidental rationalism to a cosmopolitan model of contemporary cultural transformation.

According to Indian philosophy, as Dissanayake points out, "the realization of truth is facilitated neither by language nor by logic and rationality. It is only intuition that will ensure the achievement of this objective". Thus, Habermas's reliance on speech-act theory on the presumption that linguistically mediated interaction would promote understanding (communicative rationality) appears to clash with this interpretation of Indian thought. However, as White asserts, Habermas relies on the "intuitive knowledge" of participants in imputing the ideal speech situation, a condition necessary for actual discourse when a validity claim is explicitly challenged and justification demanded for it.

Mohanty takes issue with the interpretation that Indian philosophies (darsanas) focus on intuition rather than intellect. He asserts that no Indian philosophy uses a pramäna (or means of true knowledge) that "suffers rendering into the much misused word 'intuition'".

He points out that in the Sanskrit philosophical vocabulary, the words "reason" and "experience," which are so fundamental to Western philosophy, have no exact synonyms. The epistemological question the Indian philosophies asked was whether perception is the only pramäna or whether anumäna (or inference) is also pramäna. Unlike the Western epistemologists, who also worried about the subjective and the objective, as well as the private and the public, Indian philosophers made "unabashed use of 'mentalistic' discourse and never really [worried] about problems such as psychologism or private language". Moreover, unlike the abstract ontologies of Western philosophy, the Indian prameya (ontologies) dealt with more concrete entities.

According to Indian tradition, science and metaphysics are one continuum. This Indian tradition is in accord with the modern philosophy of monistic idealism, which combines quantum physics with transcendent consciousness to explain how sentient beings collapse coherent superpositions or possibility waves into manifest reality.

Habermas was not concerned with the notion of rationality derived from the Indian darsanas even though Matilal points out that India's dharma tradition-as evident in the discourses in the two great epics, folktales, stories, and fables told at different times-exhibits the rudiments of a theory of rationality. Matilal argues that neither Hinduism nor Jainism or Buddhism is incompatible with the search for a rational basis of dharma because none of them cites God as the authority on dharma. He claims that the dharma tradition, which does not have a definitive form, developed through an attempt of rational criticism of itself. Stories in the epics and the puranas mention Cärväka's use of tarka or hetusastra, the science of reasoning, to ask questions and challenge the validity of Vedic rituals. Matilal concedes that probably the karma doctrine "was intended to provide a 'rational' basis for the apparently irrational practice of caste-hierarchy or social inequality".

Sankara, the Indian philosopher who flourished about C.E. 800, expounded thoughts that had the closest parallel to Occidental rationalism. Sankara held that the Absolute is the unattainable goal toward which the finite intellect strives. In the Buddhist sphere, Nägärjuna, the third-century founder of the Mädhyamika school of Mahayana philosophy, used logic to show that nothing in the phenomenal world had full being, and all was ultimately unreal.

Therefore, every rational theory about the world would be a theory about something unreal evolved by an unreal thinker with unreal thoughts. Such ontological nihilism, practiced by the Präsangika sub-school of logic that produced works of great subtlety, reduced all rational argument to absurdity.

However, Siderits asserts that to understand the force of the Mädhyamika claim that the ultimate truth is that there is no ultimate truth, one must begin with the traditional Buddhist distinction between conventional truth (based on warranted assertiblity or community standards) and ultimate truth (based on philosophical rationality). The point of Nägärjuna's dialectic is not that reality transcends conceptualization, but that truth must conform to human practice, that philosophical rationality is doomed precisely insofar as it seeks a truth free of all taint of human needs and interests.

Bitbol (2003), who points out some similarities between the philosophy of Kant and that of the Mädhyamika, asserts that both involve an analysis of the dialectic of reason, and that Kant's distinction between phenomenon and noumenon is similar to the Mädhyamika distinction between conventional (samvrti) and ultimate/absolute (paramärtha) truth. Wallace argues that "many Buddhist theories are obviously expressions of rational public discourse" and that Buddhism presents rational descriptions of how the mind functions. Moreover, considering that scholars have very often called Buddha "a rationalist" for various reasons (e.g., for being non-dogmatic, non-mystical, and non-metaphysical, and for implanting his views on the strong ground of reason with emphasis on empiricism), a theory of rationality would be incomplete without delving into Buddhist scholarship.

An examination of Buddhist rationality methodically vis-à-vis Occidental rationalism, outside of Weber's prejudiced analysis of Eastern philosophies, would help the project of provincializing or glocalizing Habermasian theory. Jayatilleke points out that Buddhist rationality is incongruent with the rationalism (i.e., the anti-empirical theory of philosophy wherein the criterion of truth is not sensory but intellectual and deductive) of Descartes, Leibniz, and Spinoza, whose stand was similar to the rational metaphysics associated with tarka or hetusästra in the time of the Buddha.

As evident in Sandaka Sutta, the Buddha rejected theories based on mere reasoning as unsatisfactory because such reasoning may be valid or invalid;

and even if valid (i.e., internally consistent), it may or may not correspond with fact. Drawing from Sunakkhatta, a monk who left the Buddhist order dissatisfied, Jayatilleke, in almost dialectical contrast to Weber's view of Buddhism, asserts

Buddha's doctrines were a product of pure reasoning and were not based on extrasensory perception or extraordinary insight ? Nothing in the Nikäyas suggests that any doctrines were taught or were considered to follow from premises which were held to be true in an a priori sense. On the contrary, we always find the Buddha recommending doctrines which are claimed to be true in an empirically or an experientially verifiable sense.

Because subaltern studies see the need for provincializing "Europe" in the context of Indo-European hybridization of postcolonial Indian society, Habermas's theory of communicative action has a degree of relevance to the "Europe"-oriented urban elite. An essential task of the project of glocalizing Habermasian theory would be to examine India's dharma tradition, including Carvaka's use of the science of reasoning to ask questions and challenge the validity of Vedic rituals, to distinguish between ontological rationalism and empirical rationality. A provincialized (glocalized) version of the theory of communicative rationality would see the remarkable similarity between the validity claim of prepositional truth (related to the objective world) and the Buddhist focus on empirically verifiable truth, and between the validity claim of moral lightness (related to the social world) and the Mädhyamika concept of conventional truth (based on warranted assertiblity or community standards). The Mädhyamika concept of ultimate truth (based on philosophical rationality) belongs to the realm of rationalism, which Habermas opposed.

A revision of the concept of communicative action on the suggested lines will help diminish the perceived extent of Western universalism that makes non-Western theories relatively invisible in the arena of global academic discourse. It will also help counterbalance Habermas's Eurocentric, evolutionary, or civilizational analysis of what I call non-"Europe" as exemplified by his acceptance of what Levy-Bruhl calls the "savage mind" of the African Azande. In a remarkable rebuff to Habermas's Eurocentrism, Kim has documented that "(a) scientists are not more able to distinguish what is social from what is objective than the Azande, and (b) scientists are not freer to express dissenting views than the Azande, and therefore their discourse not closer to the ideal speech situation than that of the Azande".

The Chinese perspective: The work of the Chinese sage Zhu-xi shows the nearest parallel to thoroughgoing rationalism in Chinese thought. Zhu-xi believed that a single reason, "the Way," was at work in all human minds that enabled the understanding of the world. However, classical Chinese philosophy does not readily agree with Habermas's distinctions of rationality, or his use of formal pragmatics in the theory of communicative action.

At least three basic principles of Chinese philosophy-embodiment of reason in experience, epistemological-pragmatic unity, and infinite interpretation-appear to conflict with the Occidental concept of rationality. The epistemological separation of reason and experience rooted in the ontological separation of form and substance stands in contrast to the Chinese view of unity of all things.

Shalin points out that in Habermas's communicative action theory, reason appears primarily as thinking (consciousness, understanding, cognition) with no obvious relation to the human body and the noncognitive processes (emotion, feeling, sentiment).

Shalin says that Habermas shows little appreciation for "nondiscursive communication." Because Habermas elevates the cognitive form of universality above all others, he "inadvertently devalues human experience as merely private and intellectually mute". Shalin implicitly agrees with Chinese philosophy when he asserts that to "divest reason from living experience is to disembody it" and that "knowledge uninformed by feelings and stripped of emotive elements can be rational without being reasonable".

As Kupperman points out, neither Confucius nor Mencius had anything to say about reason if one thinks of reason along the lines of what is operative in mathematics or in formal logic. Although irrationalism had no place in Chinese thought, philosophical Daoism remained anti-rationalist in contrast to orthodox Confucianism, which was often "rational" but not "rationalistic," and Later Mohism, which was "rationalistic".

Furthermore, as Cheng explains, "Reason is not simply logic as such; it is also the respecting of norms and conventions that have been accepted in the community and that have a practical and aesthetic value". Because the concept of rationality in China differs from Habermas's concept, its relevance to the emergence of a political public sphere, where citizens put forth and defend their claims based on communicative rationality alone, becomes a moot point. Jung says that the Confucian idea of ren (humanity) emphasizes intersubjectivity or sociality. Thus, Habermas comes closer to Chinese philosophy in general when he nearly concedes rationality for communicative action presupposed on the actor's social world and the validity claim of normative rightness.

However, he adds the caveat that "the teleological structure is fundamental to all concepts of action". Responding to his critics, Habermas says, "The critique of reason contends that every tradition, worldview, or culture has inscribed its own-always incommensurable-standards for what is true and false. But this leveling critique fails to notice the peculiar self-referential character of the discourse of modernity". However, this defence is not adequate to buttress Habermas's view that the public sphere must invariably lie between the state and the economy, and his insistence that it is the space where citizens put forth and defend their claims based on communicative rationality alone. Glocalizing Habermas's concept of communicative rationality-the three-world paradigm requiring three types of validity claims-in terms of classical Chinese philosophy presents a dilemma. The principle of infinite interpretation states:

Reality can be understood in an indefinite number of ways, and there is absolutely no fixed procedure for generating understanding because the object of understanding has no absolutely fixed nature, and there are no two things which are the same.

Based on the elaboration of this principle by Daoist philosopher Zhuangzi, Cheng provides two conclusions in terms of modern communication theory: first, participants should explore parallel modes of representation, determine a specific point of view, but use many points of view to illuminate what is communicated; second, communication should not be limited to the application of conventional means, such as language. Thus, in relation to the second conclusion, Habermas's formal pragmatics-communicative action in the form of argumentation or discourse-represents a limiting case.

The project of provincializing "Europe" does not call for "a simplistic, out of-hand rejection of modernity, liberal values, science, reason, grand narratives, totalizing explanations, and so on". In this sense, Tong (2000) appears to play the role of subaltern scholar in China, for he sees parallels between Habermas and the modernity advocate Li Dazhao, who tried to blend communism and liberalism into an organic unity. Li sought to find a middle path between communitarianism and liberalism or universalism. Because China is, at present, trying to combine socialism with a capitalist market economy, Tong asserts that "a modern civil society as conceived by Habermas can help to tame not only the subsystem of state administration, but also the subsystem of market economy" by, inter alia, setting normative standards for the economic system. Tong, as an apologist for Habermas, ignores the fit of the Chinese concept of rationality to that of Habermas, as well as the potentially deleterious effects of "globalization."

DE-EMPHASIS OF NON-WESTERN HISTORY/PHILOSOPHY

As Chakrabarty mentions, philosophers and thinkers have produced theories that embraced the entirety of humanity in relative, and sometimes absolute, ignorance of the majority of humankind. Habermas ignores non-Western history altogether when he traces the emergence of a literary public sphere to Europe alone.

He fails to acknowledge the existence of a literary sphere (undifferentiated as "public" or "private") in China, where widespread block printing produced a literati several centuries prior to Europe. Tsien writes. In both (East and West) printing promoted culture, widened the scope of subjects that interested scholars, helped shift the bias from religious to classical learning, popularized education, spread literacy, and enriched art and literature; though it did so to a different degree in each. [In China, printing] facilitated the continuity and niversality of the written language and thus became an important vehicle for sustaining the cultural tradition [as evident] in the printing of the Confucian classics and similar material for the civil service examinations.

Moreover, Tsien says, China had always produced an optimum number of books without pecuniary motivation because of its extensive literary tradition. This suggests the existence of a literary sphere in China at the time when China was also the centre of global trade. Poetry made up the mainstream of Chinese literature. Tam points out that in the ancient Confucian ideal, poetry served "both functions of expressing personal wishes and admonishing the ruling body as well as the people". Daoist philosophers Laozi and Zhuangzi were renowned poets as well. The poetry of Li Bo, Wang Wei, and Du Fu marked the reign of Tang emperor Xuan-zong.

Poet Bo Zhui appeared thereafter with two of the dominant figures in the Confucian revival: Yan Yu and Liu Zong-yuan. Another notable development was the appearance of fiction writers who produced the so-called "tales of marvels." Drama flourished during the Yuan dynasty. Ming China stood out for its voluminous scholarship in many realms.

The short story and the novel developed, e.g., The Romance of the Three Kingdoms, The Water Margin, The Journey to the West, and The Golden Lotus. Tang Xianzu emerged as a leading playwright. The Ming literati were avid bibliophiles, both collectors and publishers. They established public libraries, such as the Dien-i-ko collection of the Fan family at Ming-po.

Scholars put together huge anthologies of esteemed writings of the entire Chinese heritage. An example was the 11,000-volume Yong-luo-da-dian of 1407. Yan Shen, one of the all-around literati of the Ming period, produced poetry and belles lettres in huge quantities.

Weber too refers to China's literary tradition of more than 2000 years. The literati of the feudal period were officially called bo-shi (living libraries). Weber says the literati were "opponents of feudalism from the very beginning"; and "the originally free mental mobility of the literati came to a halt" with the growth of Chinese prebendalism. The literati exhibited "a highly exclusive and bookish literary education".

However, a bourgeois political public sphere did not materialize in China as it did in Europe probably because such a concept was inconsistent with Confucian philosophy. De Bary and Bloom say that in 1017 the Northern Song set up a board of policy criticism (jianyuan), a sort of political sphere identified in the West with "civil society," by which "public opinion" could be brought to bear on the formulation of state policy.

The board, which "was intended to provide oversight, policy options, and even criticism for the emperor himself lasted only 65 years when autocratic rule resumed. Scholar-poet Su Shi lamented the subversion of the board and the Censorate (yushi tai) in his Ten Thousand Word Memorial of 1069.

During the Ming Dynasty, De Bary says, China had "no infrastructure by which popular sentiment could become informed, articulated, or autonomously structured so as to contribute its authentic voice to the decision-making process".

Habermas, despite his original ardor for universalism, failed to analyse why a bourgeois political sphere failed in China despite its long-standing literary tradition. Nevertheless, Habermas has argued that regardless of different cultural traditions, "autarkic isolation against external influences is no longer an option in today's [globalized] world".

The underlying presumption behind this assertion is that modernization requires the absorption of Europe-centered "universals" by the "non-modern" non-"Europe"-a point of view that receives qualified support from subaltern historians. Despite the absence of printing, a literary sphere of the Brahmans (scholars/priests caste) and the Kshatriyas (warrior caste) emerged in India as well, particularly during the Gupta dynasty (320-550). Epics, lyrics, drama, and fiction flourished under literary giants like Kalidasa and Vishnu Sharman. Other celebrated literary figures followed them in the seventh century: Arnaru, Bana, Bhartrihari, and Dandin, among others.

Of course, India's literary tradition goes far back to the Vedas (dated from about 16th to 10th centuries BCE) and Upanishads (dated from eighth to fifth centuries BCE). India also produced the Buddhist Tripitakas, which it exported to the Far East, and the epics Mahabharata (attributed to Vyasa) and Ramayana (attributed to Valmiki) well before the Gupta period. The Vedas, the Upanishads, and the epics were so much a part of Hinduism that they affected the lifeworld of Vaisyas (merchant caste) and Sudras (laborer caste) as well. It appears that Habermas chose not to compare and contrast these non-Western literary spheres with the "unique" European literary public sphere.

Despite the alleged Eurocentric bias of Weber's Protestant-ethic thesis, Habermas has leaned heavily on Weber's analysis of non-Western religious-metaphysical worldviews to derive the claimed "universalism" for his work. Although Habermas points out the deficiencies of the Weberian analysis, he does not do so with a thorough grounding of non-Western philosophers, philosophy, and history.

However, in the long chapter on Weber's theory of rationalization, he shows a degree of second-hand awareness of non-Western religion and philosophy. He accepts Weber's classification, according to content, of Buddhism and Hinduism as cosmocentric and world rejecting, Confucianism and Daoism as cosmocentric and world affirming, and Judaism and Christianity as theocentric and world rejecting. On attitudes toward the world based on rejection of the world in salvation religions, he again accepts Weber's analysis that Judaism and Christianity exhibit mastery of the world while Hinduism exhibits flight from the world. On the rationalization potential of worldviews, he places the Orient in the low category: Hinduism low on the ethical dimension, and Confucianism low on the cognitive dimension; and he places the Occident in the high category: Judaism and Christianity high on the ethical dimension, and Greek philosophy high on the cognitive dimension. He comments, "It is remarkable that the two worldviews with the structurally greatest potential for rationalization came together within the same European tradition".

Habermas says that rationalized Western culture seems to be developing in the direction of a morally skeptical, purely purposive-rational type of action although early Buddhism provides evidence of the converse case of rationalization of value orientations while impeding purposive-rational action. Weber had identified early Buddhism as a rationalized ethic "in the sense of constant, alert mastery of all natural instinctive drives," but which at the same time leads its followers away from getting hold of the world in a disciplined way. As examples of irrationality of action that are technically rationalized, Weber had mentioned "methods of mortificatory or of magical asceticism or contemplation, in their most consistent forms, for instance in yoga or in the manipulation of the prayer machines of later Buddhism". On the other hand Weber, in his book The Religion of India, hailed the linkage between caste and karma as a pure product of rational ethical thought.

Weber wrote: "Karma doctrine transformed the world into a strictly rational, ethically-determined cosmos; it represents the most consistent theodicy ever produced by history"-a point that Habermas fails to record.

Habermas does not deal with Islam because "Weber was not able to carry out his plan to include Christianity and Islam in his comparative studies" of religious-metaphysical worldviews. It's puzzling why Habermas depended predominantly on Weber's rather controversial interpretations of Asian religious philosophies without a serious attempt to seek other, balanced interpretations of both Western and non-Western authorities.

In passing, Habermas (1984) does refer to Joseph Needham's "pioneering investigations," which show that the Chinese "were evidently more successful than the West in developing theoretical knowledge and in using this knowledge for practical purposes" until the 15th century. Therefore, Habermas suggests that the "rationalization potential of these [East Asian] traditions might have been studied first of all from the standpoint of cognitive and not of ethical rationalization" as Weber had done.

Habermas expresses his suspicion that "the Chinese traditions would appear in another light if one considered them primarily from the standpoint of theory rather than of ethics and compared them with the classical Greek traditions". Tong (2000) latches on to this Habermasian concession to Chinese traditions to argue that Habermas's "theory of modernity and modernization based on his theory of communicative action is most relevant to modernization in China and provides the ideal basis for a new rewarding interpretation of the Chinese discourse of modernization and the idea of 'socialist modernization with Chinese characteristics'" even though Habermas "rarely mentioned China, or developing countries in general, in his discussions".

Tong admits that the Japanese case of modernization "poses difficult problems to Habermas's theory of modernity and modernization". Yet, Tong goes on to assert that the Chinese tradition of dialectical logic-the paired concepts of ti (substance) and yong (function)-that contemporary neo-Confucians like Liang Shuming, Mou Zongsan, and Yu Yingshi frequently used in the discourse of modernization can also be looked at in terms of lifeworld (ti) and system (yong) or value rationality (ti) and instrumental rationality (yong). Tong (2000) sees much merit in Habermasian theory in contrast to Huang. Tong disregards the criticisms of Fleming, who says that "Habermas's theory is not universalistic enough because the basic categories of the theory are gender coded". Tong rejects the criticisms of Habermas's theory of modernity because they relate only to the dynamics of modernization whereas Habermas was mainly concerned with the logic of modernization. Tong goes on to say that the anomalies found in the Japanese case against Habermas's theory "can be seen as anomalies of Japanese society itself according to this theory". Tong skips Huang's point about the "third realm" in China. Rather than "glocalizing" Habermasian theory, Tong glorifies it to support "the official Chinese programme of modernization", namely, a socialist modernization with Chinese characteristics, with high emphasis on science and democracy.

Provincializing Habermasian theory requires the inclusion of the missing literary spheres in China and India, among other histories, and modifying the emphasis on the distinction between the public and the private spheres. We cannot skip the past to enter the future. As Chakrabarty says, "Pasts are there in taste, in practices of embodiment, in the cultural training the senses have received over generations".

IDEALIZATION OF LIBERAL DEMOCRACY

Even though Fleming has pointed out the flaws in Habermas's expansionist strategy in relation to rationality, Habermas presents communicative rationality (associated with the lifeworld) as the ingredient that lends "universalism" to his critical theory. The problem, however, lies in linking this society-contextualized (self-referential) rationality with his idealization of liberal democracy.

Habermas wanted to make "democracy an integral part of philosophy" because he saw the need to avoid a repetition of the traumas of German history. His idealization of liberal democracy-the liberal constitutional state prior to its transformation into the constitutional social-welfare state-implicit in his theory of communicative action and the concept of public sphere becomes explicit in his later political essays, with statements such as

- "Asiatic societies cannot participate in capitalistic modernization without taking advantage of the achievements of an individualistic legal order."

- "These dictatorships [Singapore, Malaysia, Taiwan, and China] consider themselves authorized by the 'right of social development'-apparently understood as a collective right-to postpone the realization of liberal rights and rights of political participation until their countries have attained a level of economic development that allows them to satisfy the basic material needs of the population equally,".

Li has already documented the incompatibility of Confucianism with liberal democracy. However, Perera says that democracy, in its sense as rule by majority decision, has historically appeared in three forms: direct democracy, representative democracy, and liberal or constitutional democracy. Sharma says that his analysis of the Vedic texts reveals the existence of at least four forms of "government by discussion" in the early Vedic period from 1500 BCE to 1000 BCE. Buddhist and Jain texts, as well as the works of Pänini and Kautilya, also attest to the existence of a number of republican states from 600 BCE to 480 BCE.

Domes defines (liberal) democracy in terms of three principles: liberty (guaranteed and institutionalized human rights for everyone and guaranteed and institutionalized civil rights for all adult citizens), equality (securing equal life chances for all citizens), and pluralism (guaranteed existence and operation of competing organizations that articulate and aggregate the different political, economic, social, and cultural interests).

His definition also includes three basic rules: people's sovereignty, division of powers, and competitive elections. Schumpeter provides a minimal definition of democracy: "institutional arrangement for arriving at political decisions in which individuals acquire the power to decide by means of a competitive struggle for the people's vote".

Habermas's concept of the public sphere is primarily related to the democratic value of pluralism, which includes the division of powers. However, his concept of rationality fails to appear as an integral characteristic of democracy in most definitions. Of the three strands of Chinese philosophy-Confucianism, Daoism, and Chan Buddhism-Buddhism comes closest to the values of democracy.

The democratic value of liberty is compatible with both Daoism and Buddhism; equality is both a democratic and Buddhist value; and freedom is a characteristic that Daoism (negative freedom), Buddhism (positive freedom), and democracy (negative or positive freedom) all share. Li has argued that because the Chinese can adjust their minds to accommodate three different philosophies, it would not be too difficult for them to accommodate democratic values as well. Ironically, this shows the greater capacity of the Chinese, as well as others in the so-called Orient, to accommodate pluralistic thinking much more readily than their counterparts in the Occident. Habermas is an advocate of "deliberative democracy," in which a government's laws and institutions would be a reflection of free and open rational discussion in the public sphere. Habermas claims that the "universalism" of his theory of communicative action comes from communicative rationality, which denotes agreement on propositional truth (in the objective domain of culture and science), moral rightness (in the social domain of society), and sincerity (in the subjective domain of personality).

Thus the cultural and social context of the individual determines what is rational. If that were the case, how that process ipso facto leads to an ideal democracy incorporating liberty, equality, and pluralism needs further elucidation. Would communicative rationality based on the cultural and social context of Confucianism promote the ideals of liberal democracy when they are inconsistent with Confucian values? Tu Wei-ming says that the dominant ideology in the Western world today is still that of 18th-century Enlightenment marked by "the arrogance of rationality". Tu claims that Habermas's writing holds that the task of Enlightenment is in fact far from completed, and that this state of being unfinished explains all of the social problems that have surfaced in the course of modernization.

Therefore, our historical task is not to find a new model but to reform the old value system by placing greater emphasis on the ideas of liberty and equality, and to reconfigure the democratic system so as to assure greater freedom and a fairer distribution of power and wealth. Tu's view stands in contrast to that of Tong and the subaltern school. Can liberal democracy dominate the world through globalization? Gunaratne points out that libertarianism cannot exist without its complement authoritarianism. The principles of part-whole interdetermination and the dialectical completion of relative polarities in Chinese philosophy, as well as the revelation of modern physics that every particle has an antiparticle, attest to this. A revision of Habermasian theory requires the dissociation of communicative rationality with libertarian democracy alone, although this should be the most desirable outcome. The public sphere, by Habermas's own admission, has been rendered ineffective by advanced capitalism. Under such circumstances, the prospects for a global public sphere, which would further strengthen Western domination, appear to be unrealistic.

On the other hand, as subaltern scholars would argue, "modernity" demands the propagation of universals enshrined in History 1 (such as democracy, liberalism, rationality, liberty, equality, and pluralism) for which the subjugated colonial people also fought. The continual tension between these universals and the axial-age Eastern philosophies would engender creative solutions reflecting what Chakrabarty calls the "translational processes through which concepts and practices are made one's own"-the grist for narrating History 2s.

HABERMAS AND THEORY OF LIVING SYSTEMS

I shall now examine Habermas's critical theory through the lens of the emerging theory of living systems-incorporating the theories of autopoiesis, cognition, and dissipative structures -to show that operationally closed but structurally and cognitively open subsystems comprising a dissipative structure like the world-system form a formidable barrier against the emergence of a global public sphere.

Although Capra (2002) praises Habermas for "integrating insights from the natural sciences, the social sciences and from cognitive philosophies, while rejecting the limitations of positivism", Capra's assessment is based largely on Baert's review of 20th-century social theory.

Habermas's underestimation of Eastern philosophy stands in stark contrast to Capra's attempt to show the parallels between modern physics and Eastern "mysticism." Moreover, Habermas's quasi-systems theory lacks the three fundamental characteristics that Capra says are essential for a new scientific understanding of living systems: autopoiesis, the pattern of organization of living systems as defined by Maturana and Varela; cognition, the process of life as defined by Maturana and Varela; and dissipative structure, the structure of living systems as defined by Prigogine and Stengers.

Habermas has subjected his critical theory, which he calls deep hermeneutics, to many of the weaknesses inherent in nomothetic social science by merging in it both empirical-analytic and historical-hermeneutic disciplines. Although some may argue that Habermas's theory is "critical-hermeneutical rather than analytical" because his "notion of publicness, particularly in the sense of critical publicity, can only play the role of some kind of comparative standard or of a radical democratic vision on the normative level," Habermas thinks otherwise. For Habermas says unequivocally "any sociology that claims to be a theory of society has to face the problem of rationality simultaneously on the metatheoretical, methodological, and empirical levels". Moreover, Habermas identifies his work as a "theory of society based on the theory of communicative action", and as a "theory of modernity"-a quasi-systems theory sans non-linear dynamics or autopoiesis.

First, Habermas explicitly distances his quasi-systems theory from Luhmann's "boundary maintaining and autopoietic" systems theory, which says that "actions and interactions can be understood as psychological and social systems that form environments for and reciprocally observe one another". Habermas criticizes Luhmann's systems functionalism for cutting "itself off from the intuitive knowledge of the lifeworld and its members".

Elsewhere, Habermas expresses "fundamental doubts about the usefulness of a systems theoretic concept of social crisis" because of the difficulty of systems theory to clearly determine "the boundaries and persistence of social systems". Thus, by excluding autopoiesis as a feature of society, Habermasian theory fails to meet the first of Capra's criteria for a new scientific understanding of living systems. The key characteristic of a living network, including any social system, is that it continually produces itself. This is the pattern of life called autopoiesis. Because all components of an autopoietic network are produced by other components in the network, the entire system is operationally closed even though it is structurally open to its environment (e.g., other social systems) with regard to the flow of energy and matter (e.g., goods, services, and information).

Autopoiesis is the pattern underlying the phenomenon of self-organization. In this sense, autopoiesis of each social system acts as a natural defence against globalization. What is more likely to happen is adaptation, which I call glocalization. Thus, the emergence of a global public sphere is incompatible with the theory of living systems. Habermas adamantly maintains, "I am by no means sure whether a surplus value will accrue to social theory from the most recent developments which systems theory has undergone and which have been labeled autopoiesis".

Second, although Habermas deals extensively with rationality, he does not deal with cognition-the next requirement for a new scientific understanding of living systems-as the process of life. Cognition, the activity involved in the continual embodiment of the system's pattern of organization, is inextricably linked to autopoiesis. Interpreting the Santiago theory, Capra says Human cognition involves language and abstract thinking, and thus symbols and mental representations, but abstract thought is only a small part of human cognition and generally is not the basis for our everyday decisions and actions. Human decisions are never completely rational but are always colored by emotion, and human thought is always embedded in the bodily sensations and processes that contribute to the full spectrum of cognition.

Eastern philosophy, in general, is consistent with this interpretation of cognition as a continual bringing forth of a world through the process of living. Habermas focuses on rationality as if emotion were less significant in human decision making.

The theory of living systems is at odds with the Habermasian preoccupation with rationality, a concept that reached a peak during the Age of Enlightenment when science and rationality fit hand in glove. Nonlinear dynamics, however, has made it abundantly clear that a preoccupation with rationality is rather inconsistent with how things occur in reality in a predominantly nonlinear universe.

The phenomenon of nonlocality (or nonseparability that transcends space-time) and the uncertainty principle in quantum physics make a mockery of rationality. Luhmann's self-referential autopoietic systems theory also rejects the Habermasian system's obsession with consensus-oriented communicative action because communication requires dissent to continue its operation. "If universal consensus could ever be reached, it would terminate the system's autopoiesis".

Third, despite Habermas's "integrating insights," he remains within the fold of classical linear thinking. Habermas does not look at society as a far-from-equilibrium dissipative structure-another essential requirement for a new scientific understanding of living systems. Gunaratne sums up the underlying presumptions of classical (social) science as follows:

- That precisely determinable initial conditions determined every element in natural processes. (Heisenberg's uncertainty principle challenges this presumption.)
- That trajectories of most natural phenomena are linear and that such trajectories always tend to return to equilibrium conditions. (Quantum jumps do not follow predictable trajectories. The second law of thermodynamics says equilibrium is virtual "death.")
- That time is not relevant to the understanding of natural processes because all laws are mathematically "reversible" as the fundamental relations of those processes never evolve. (Time may not be relevant to quantum particles, which cannot have a history because they die quickly. But the arrow of time applies to all "matter.")
- That knowledge is universal and can ultimately be expressed in simple covering laws. (The Aspect experiment's proof of nonlocality-the superluminal interaction of correlated quanta beyond space-time-defies causation.)

Thus, classical (social) science presumed the ability to predict outcomes with the knowledge of the initial conditions and the relevant universal law. Although Habermas calls his theory of communicative action "less a promise than a conjecture", he apparently developed it as an empirically testable "simple covering law," which can both predict and retrodict. It clearly reflects the attributes of determinism, linearity, reversibility, and reductionism.

The concept of the public sphere illustrates this point well. The 16th-century take-off of modern capitalism in Europe resulted in the creation of a potent bourgeois civil society, which initiated a political public sphere (preceded by a literary public sphere) for the rational discussion of issues within a framework of deliberative democracy. When these initial conditions appear elsewhere, they would reproduce similar linear developments conducive to deliberative democracy irrespective of time. The structural-functionalist modernization paradigm, which presumed that nation-states changed in parallel lines from tradition to modernity, belonged to the same genre of Newtonianism. On the other hand, nonlinear dynamics asserts that irreversibility (or the arrow of time, which can only move forward) leads to continuing change and increasing complexity in open systems, where even a small input of change could trigger positive feedback that engenders massive, unpredictable structural changes.

Thus, the theoretical approach of nonlinear dynamics precludes the repeatability of the circumstances that produced Europe's bourgeois public sphere or the so-called Protestant ethic within the world system of interdependent states. Van Ginneken demonstrates the importance of positive feedback, which involves amplification and circular reaction, in understanding communicative action-a phenomenon that Habermas ignores.

Whereas Habermas analyses communication solely in terms of rationality, Van Ginneken asserts There is hardly any rational behaviour that is not colored by accompanying emotions, and there is hardly any emotional behaviour that does not also have an underlying ratio. The theory of communicative action says that social disequilibrium occurs when the imperatives of the system dimensions, engendered by cognitive-purposive rationality, clash with the lifeworld dimension of cultural reproduction, social integration, and socialization. Habermas says that in modernized societies, "stubborn systemic disequilibria"-in the form of crises or pathologies in the lifeworld-appear because of such disturbances.

Prigogine and Stengers have pointed out that far-from-equilibrium conditions are the norm in all dissipative systems, which thrive in open system environments. Had Habermas adopted the dissipative-systems approach of nonlinear dynamics, he could have explained the resulting tension between lifeworld and systemic dimensions as reflecting the usual far-from-equilibrium state associated with all dissipative structures.

Habermas explains that he used the system-environment model of the general systems theory for his two-level concept of society because "it is more suited to application in the social sciences than are the earlier biological equilibrium models". My thesis of the uncoupling of lifeworld and system only implies that the dynamics of demarcation vis-à-vis a more complex environment infiltrates into society itself... The system model.. submits that subsystems mark themselves off from one another in the course of processes of differentiation and define themselves reciprocally as environments.

He adds that the systems model is appropriate for purely analytical use, as does Parsons, but not for essentialist use, as does Luhmann. Habermasian theory, in its current formulation, presumes that social equilibrium is the norm. Thermodynamically, however, equilibrium means the virtual "death" of a system. Habermas (2001b) praises Weber for brilliantly conjoining the rational choice theory on the purposive rationality of individual actors and the systems theory on the functional rationality of large organizations. Parsons used Weber's formulation as a reference system.

Habermas says, "Unlike many systems theorists of a more recent vintage, Parsons was not tempted to forget the constitution of the object domain 'action' or 'society' in the process of applying the systems model to it". This makes it clear that Habermas did not favour the new systems theory or nonlinear dynamics. He points out that systems theory isolates and overgeneralizes the systemic aspect while action theory does the same for the lifeworld aspect; the theory of structural differentiation, on the other hand, does not sufficiently separate either of these two aspects. Because the theories of modernity derived from these three approaches remained insensitive to what Marx called "real abstractions," Habermas says he formulated his theory so as to get at such abstractions "through an analysis that at once traces the rationalization of lifeworlds and the growth in complexity of media-steered subsystems".

In other words, he rejected the "systems theorists of more recent vintage," as well as their reliance on nonlinear dynamics, because of the primacy he attached to the Occidental concept of rationality. For him, the arrow of time was not a matter of concern.

Habermas (2001b) goes on to explain, "For systems theory, modern societies collapse into a multiplicity of independently operating, self-referential closed [my emphasis] systems, which constitute environments for one another and can communicate with one another only indirectly, through mutual observation". However, he omits the distinctive aspects of a living system-the pattern of organization, the process of life, and the structure. It's the pattern that's operationally closed. The dissipative structure itself is always open to its environment. Referring to human rights, Habermas observes, "The autarkic isolation against external influences is no longer an option in today's world". To be sure, it is the fact that a living system is cognitively opens that allows external influences; and it is the fact that it is operationally closed that allows each system to maintain its distinctive culture and choose from among the external influences. Is it not autopoiesis that prevents cultural annihilation through globalization/Westernization?

This monograph has documented that Habermas's emancipatory critical theory of society and modernity is a totalizing Eurocentric product, which contains some significant "universalistic" elements. Habermas carried further the sociological preconditions of universalism that Parsons set through the crucial dimension of rationality.

Piaget allowed Habermas to claim that universalistic critical thought is grounded in the normal development of the human mind. Habermas used formal pragmatics to claim universalism for his theory of communicative action. One may construe the uncritical globalization of such "universalistic" theory as a kind of Eurocentric hegemony as we move from theory to practice. We can circumvent the potential dangers of Eurocentric hegemony through the process of glocalization (revising Eurocentric theory to fit non-"Europe") or, in the jargon of subaltern studies, through provincializing "Europe." The latter means discarding the chaff and retaining the wheat irrespective of Eurocentrism in theory.

From the postcolonial perspective, the emancipatory elements of Habermasian critical theory provide a useful purpose against non-democratic tendencies in non-"Europe," for the colonies too were participants in upholding liberty, equality, and other rights in the fight against European imperialism.

Habermas's theory of communicative action was an attempt to clarify the normative foundations of a critical theory of society, and to provide an alternative to the philosophy of history on which the earlier critical theory of the Frankfurt School relied. Habermas comments that he "attempted to free historical materialism from its philosophical ballast".

He constructed a theory of rationality to establish a cooperative relationship between social science and philosophy. The task he completed was indeed monumental. Yet, as this monograph has documented, his achievement suffers from vast cultural shortcomings. The project of glocalizing the public sphere and communicative rationality should proceed.

In implementing this project, we should incorporate the history of the literary sphere in China and India that preceded the bourgeois literary sphere in Europe. We should also note that democracy had an early start in pre-Buddhist India with republics such as those of Sakiyas and Vajjians. Because Habermas is involved in the implicit political project of promoting democracy, linking his theory to the history of democracy in the East would be a worthy strategy. Global public sphere: Although a global public sphere may appear to be on the horizon because of the ongoing process of globalization, a euphemism for Western domination within the context of the highly lopsided telecommunication infrastructure of the world, the very absence of distinct public and private spheres in many societies in non-"Europe," renders such a concept unviable. The pattern of autopoiesis in living systems would engender local public spheres, if any.

A revision of this concept is imperative because of the prevalence of the "third realm," which is neither public nor private, in many societies. Thus, the call by Habermas (2001b) to bring global economic networks-the postnational constellation-under democratic political control is premature. As Hill (2002) observes, Habermas's model of global political participation is devoid of a global, normative standpoint.

Hill points out that a single public sphere may not befit multicultural societies. Moreover, Hill says, principles of popular sovereignty, commonly embedded in national constitutions, are not necessarily applicable at the global level. In addition, "critics have targeted a perceived ethnocentric bias in the universalistic ambitions of the [public sphere] theory". Sparks (2000) has concluded that there is at present no global public sphere because of regulation and control of satellites, and the small audience for global channels and global newspapers. He has pointed out that the local public sphere is not an aspect of globalization. Furthermore, Sparks has said that the function of the state-oriented public sphere remains crucial, and that, very far from replacing the state, the new localities need the state to represent them.

Communicative rationality: As documented in this monograph, contrary to Weber's Eurocentric analysis, there is much in Eastern philosophy that pertains to communicative rationality. Buddhist philosophy encourages the validity claim of propositional truth through empirical observation. Both Buddhist and Chinese philosophy recognize the validity claim of rightness (conventional truth) derived through social consensus.

The provincializing of the theory of communicative action on these lines would make the theory more appealing to non-"Europe" and help bring nonWestern theories back to visibility in the global academy. The project of provincializing or glocalizing Habermasian theory should also involve looking at the public sphere, communicative rationality, modernity, and related concepts through the lens of the theory of living systems and world-system analysis. These theories are more consistent with the cosmological philosophy of the so-called Orient, which has unabashed faith in the ability of nature to spontaneously derive order out of chaos ad infinitum. Occidental "science," which slighted the Oriental "myths," used empirical measurements to derive universal "laws" without pausing to think about the unseen Supreme Ultimate (in the Daoist sense) behind such (teleological?) "laws." Thus, "myth" is common to all humanity.

Scholars should reconcile the separate worlds of Western and Eastern philosophy and theory. Balagangadhara (1998), on the one hand, attributes the East-West separation to Orientalism: Social sciences generate Orientalism when the West looks at other cultures. Looked at in isolation from Orientalism, social sciences are how the West experiences itself. Social sciences teach us about Western culture. Patomäki (2002), on the other hand, asserts, "Globalization as a coming together of humanity requires an open-ended dialogue about philosophical and religious fundamentals".

3

Advertising

Advertising is a form of communication intended to persuade an audience to take some action. It usually includes the name of a product or service and how that product or service could benefit the consumer, to persuade potential customers to purchase or to consume that particular brand. Modern advertising developed with the rise of mass production in the late 19th and early 20th centuries.

Commercial advertisers often seek to generate increased consumption of their products or services through branding, which involves the repetition of an image or product name in an effort to associate related qualities with the brand in the minds of consumers. Different types of media can be used to deliver these messages, including traditional media such as newspapers, magazines, television, radio, outdoor or direct mail; or new media such as websites and text messages.

Advertising may be placed by an advertising agency on behalf of a company or other organization. Non-commerical advertisers that spend money to advertise items other than a consumer product or service include political parties, interest groups, religious organiz-ations and governmental agencies. Nonprofit organizations may rely on free modes of persuasion, such as a public service announcement.In 2007, spending on advertising was estimated at more than $150 billion in the United States and $385 billion worldwide.

HISTORY

Egyptians used papyrus to make sales messages and wall posters. Commercial messages and political campaign displays have been found in the ruins of Pompeii and ancient Arabia. Lost and found advertising on papyrus was common in Ancient Greece and Ancient Rome.

Wall or rock painting for commercial advertising is another manifestation of an ancient advertising form, which is present to this day in many parts of Asia, Africa, and South America. The tradition of wall painting can be traced back to Indian rock art paintings that date back to 4000 BC. History tells us that Out-of-home advertising and billboards are the oldest forms of advertising. As the towns and cities of the Middle Ages began to grow, and the general populace was unable to read, signs that today would say cobbler, miller, tailor or blacksmith would use an image associated with their trade such as a boot, a suit, a hat, a clock, a diamond, a horse shoe, a candle or even a bag of flour. Fruits and vegetables were sold in the city square from the backs of carts and wagons and their proprietors used street callers (town criers) to announce their whereabouts for the convenience of the customers.

As education became an apparent need and reading, as well as printing, developed advertising expanded to include handbills. In the 17th century advertisements started to appear in weekly newspapers in England. These early print advertisements were used mainly to promote books and newspapers, which became increasingly affordable with advances in the printing press; and medicines, which were increasingly sought after as disease ravaged Europe.

However, false advertising and so-called "quack" advertisements became a problem, which ushered in the regulation of advertising content. As the economy expanded during the 19th century, advertising grew alongside. In the United States, the success of this advertising format eventually led to the growth of mail-order advertising.

In June 1836, French newspaper La Presse was the first to include paid advertising in its pages, allowing it to lower its price, extend its readership and increase its profitability and the formula was soon copied by all titles. Around 1840, Volney Palmer established a predecessor to advertising agencies in Boston. Around the same time, in France, Charles-Louis Havas extended the services of his news agency, Havas to include advertisement brokerage, making it the first French group to organize. At first, agencies were brokers for advertisement space in newspapers. N. W. Ayer & Son was the first full-service agency to assume responsibility for advertising content. N.W. Ayer opened in 1869, and was located in Philadelphia.

At the turn of the century, there were few career choices for women in business; however, advertising was one of the few. Since women were responsible for most of the purchasing done in their household, advertisers and agencies recognized the value of women's insight during the creative process. In fact, the first American advertising to use a sexual sell was created by a woman – for a soap product. Although tame by today's standards, the advertisement featured a couple with the message "The skin you love to touch".

In the early 1920s, the first radio stations were established by radio equipment manufacturers and retailers who offered programs in order to sell more radios to consumers. As time passed, many non-profit organizations followed suit in setting up their own radio stations, and included: schools, clubs and civic groups. When the practice of sponsoring programs was popularised, each individual radio programme was usually sponsored by a single business in exchange for a brief mention of the business' name at the beginning and end of the sponsored shows. However, radio station owners soon realised they could earn more money by selling sponsorship rights in small time allocations to multiple businesses throughout their radio station's broadcasts, rather than selling the sponsorship rights to single businesses per show.

This practice was carried over to television in the late 1940s and early 1950s. A fierce battle was fought between those seeking to commercialise the radio and people who argued that the radio spectrum should be considered a part of the commons – to be used only non-commercially and for the public good. The United Kingdom pursued a public funding model for the BBC, originally a private company, the British Broadcasting Company, but incorporated as a public body by Royal Charter in 1927. In Canada, advocates like Graham Spry were likewise able to persuade the federal government to adopt a public funding model, creating the Canadian Broadcasting Corporation. However, in the United States, the capitalist model prevailed with the passage of the Communications Act of 1934 which created the Federal Communications Commission. To placate the socialists, the U.S. Congress did require commercial broadcasters to operate in the "public interest, convenience, and necessity". Public broadcasting now exists in the United States due to the 1967 Public Broadcasting Act which led to the Public Broadcasting Service and National Public Radio.

In the early 1950s, the DuMont Television Network began the modern practice of selling advertisement time to multiple sponsors. Previously, DuMont had trouble finding sponsors for many of their programs and compensated by selling smaller blocks of advertising time to several businesses. This eventually became the standard for the commercial television industry in the United States. However, it was still a common practice to have single sponsor shows, such as The United States Steel Hour. In some instances the sponsors exercised great control over the content of the show—up to and including having one's advertising agency actually writing the show. The single sponsor model is much less prevalent now, a notable exception being the Hallmark Hall of Fame.

The 1960s saw advertising transform into a modern approach in which creativity was allowed to shine, producing unexpected messages that made advertisements more tempting to consumers' eyes. The Volkswagen ad campaign—featuring such headlines as "Think Small" and "Lemon" (which were used to describe the appearance of the car)—ushered in the era of modern advertising by promoting a "position" or "unique selling proposition" designed to associate each brand with a specific idea in the reader or viewer's mind. This period of American advertising is called the Creative Revolution and its archetype was William Bernbach who helped create the revolutionary Volkswagen ads among others. Some of the most creative and long-standing

American advertising dates to this period. The late 1980s and early 1990s saw the introduction of cable television and particularly MTV. Pioneering the concept of the music video, MTV ushered in a new type of advertising: the consumer tunes in for the advertising message, rather than it being a by-product or afterthought. As cable and satellite television became increasingly prevalent, specialty channels emerged, including channels entirely devoted to advertising, such as QVC, Home Shopping Network, and ShopTV Canada.

Marketing through the Internet opened new frontiers for advertisers and contributed to the "dot-com" boom of the 1990s. Entire corporations operated solely on advertising revenue, offering everything from coupons to free Internet access. At the turn of the 21st century, a number of websites including the search engine Google, started a change in online advertising by emphasizing contextually relevant, unobtrusive ads intended to help, rather than inundate, users. This has led to a plethora of similar efforts and an increasing trend of interactive advertising.

The share of advertising spending relative to GDP has changed little across large changes in media. For example, in the US in 1925, the main advertising media were newspapers, magazines, signs on streetcars, and outdoor posters. Advertising spending as a share of GDP was about 2.9 per cent. By 1998, television and radio had become major advertising media. Nonetheless, advertising spending as a share of GDP was slightly lower—about 2.4 per cent.

A recent advertising innovation is "guerrilla marketing", which involve unusual approaches such as staged encounters in public places, giveaways of products such as cars that are covered with brand messages, and interactive advertising where the viewer can respond to become part of the advertising message.

Guerrilla advertising is becoming increasing more popular with a lot of companies. This type of advertising is unpredictable and innovative, which causes consumers to buy the product or idea. This reflects an increasing trend of interactive and "embedded" ads, such as via product placement, having consumers vote through text messages, and various innovations utilizing social network services such as MySpace.

Public Service Advertising

The same advertising techniques used to promote commercial goods and services can be used to inform, educate and motivate the public about non-commercial issues, such as HIV/AIDS, political ideology, energy conservation and deforestation.

Advertising, in its non-commercial guise, is a powerful educational tool capable of reaching and motivating large audiences. "Advertising justifies its existence when used in the public interest—it is much too powerful a tool to use solely for commercial purposes." Attributed to Howard Gossage by David

Ogilvy. Public service advertising, non-commercial advertising, public interest advertising, cause marketing, and social marketing are different terms for (or aspects of) the use of sophisticated advertising and marketing communications techniques (generally associated with commercial enterprise) on behalf of non-commercial, public interest issues and initiatives.

In the United States, the granting of television and radio licenses by the FCC is contingent upon the station broadcasting a certain amount of public service advertising. To meet these requirements, many broadcast stations in America air the bulk of their required public service announcements during the late night or early morning when the smallest percentage of viewers are watching, leaving more day and prime time commercial slots available for high-paying advertisers. Public service advertising reached its height during World Wars I and II under the direction of several governments.

TYPES OF ADVERTISING

Virtually any medium can be used for advertising. Commercial advertising media can include wall paintings, billboards, street furniture components, printed flyers and rack cards, radio, cinema and television adverts, web banners, mobile telephone screens, shopping carts, web popups, skywriting, bus stop benches, human billboards, magazines, newspapers, town criers, sides of buses, banners attached to or sides of airplanes ("logojets"), in-flight advertisements on seatback tray tables or overhead storage bins, taxicab doors, roof mounts and passenger screens, musical stage shows, subway platforms and trains, elastic bands on disposable diapers, doors of bathroom stalls, stickers on apples in supermarkets, shopping cart handles (grabertising), the opening section of streaming audio and video, posters, and the backs of event tickets and supermarket receipts. Any place an "identified" sponsor pays to deliver their message through a medium is advertising.

Television

The TV commercial is generally considered the most effective mass-market advertising format, as is reflected by the high prices TV networks charge for commercial airtime during popular TV events. The annual Super Bowl football game in the United States is known as the most prominent advertising event on television. The average cost of a single thirty-second TV spot during this game has reached US$3 million. The majority of television commercials feature a song or jingle that listeners soon relate to the product.

Virtual advertisements may be inserted into regular television programming through computer graphics. It is typically inserted into otherwise blank backdrops or used to replace local billboards that are not relevant to the remote broadcast audience. More controversially, virtual billboards may be inserted into the background where none exist in real-life. Virtual product placement is also possible.

Infomercials

An infomercial is a long-format television commercial, typically five minutes or longer. The word "infomercial" is a portmanteau of the words "information" & "commercial". The main objective in an infomercial is to create an impulse purchase, so that the consumer sees the presentation and then immediately buys the product through the advertised toll-free telephone number or website. Infomercials describe, display, and often demonstrate products and their features, and commonly have testimonials from consumers and industry professionals.

Radio Advertising

Radio advertising is a form of advertising via the medium of radio. Radio advertisements are broadcasted as radio waves to the air from a transmitter to an antenna and a thus to a receiving device.

Airtime is purchased from a station or network in exchange for airing the commercials. While radio has the obvious limitation of being restricted to sound, proponents of radio advertising often cite this as an advantage.

Press Advertising

Press advertising describes advertising in a printed medium such as a newspaper, magazine, or trade journal. This encompasses everything from media with a very broad readership base, such as a major national newspaper or magazine, to more narrowly targeted media such as local newspapers and trade journals on very specialized topics.

A form of press advertising is classified advertising, which allows private individuals or companies to purchase a small, narrowly targeted ad for a low fee advertising a product or service.

Online Advertising

Online advertising is a form of promotion that uses the Internet and World Wide Web for the expressed purpose of delivering marketing messages to attract customers. Examples of online advertising include contextual ads that appear on search engine results pages, banner ads, in text ads, Rich Media Ads, Social network advertising, online classified advertising, advertising networks and e-mail marketing, including e-mail spam.

Billboard Advertising

Billboards are large structures located in public places which display advertisements to passing pedestrians and motorists. Most often, they are located on main roads with a large amount of passing motor and pedestrian traffic; however, they can be placed in any location with large amounts of viewers, such as on mass transit vehicles and in stations, in shopping malls or office buildings, and in stadiums.

MOBILE BILLBOARD ADVERTISING

Mobile billboards are generally vehicle mounted billboards or digital screens. These can be on dedicated vehicles built solely for carrying advertisements along routes preselected by clients, they can also be specially-equipped cargo trucks or, in some cases, large banners strewn from planes. The billboards are often lighted; some being backlit, and others employing spotlights. Some billboard displays are static, while others change; for example, continuously or periodically rotating among a set of advertisements.

Mobile displays are used for various situations in metropolitan areas throughout the world, including:

- Target advertising
- One-day, and long-term campaigns
- Conventions
- Sporting events
- Store openings and similar promotional events
- Big advertisements from smaller companies
- Others

In-store Advertising

In-store advertising is any advertisement placed in a retail store. It includes placement of a product in visible locations in a store, such as at eye level, at the ends of aisles and near checkout counters, eye-catching displays promoting a specific product, and advertisements in such places as shopping carts and in-store video displays.

Covert Advertising

Covert advertising, also known as guerrilla advertising, is when a product or brand is embedded in entertainment and media. For example, in a film, the main character can use an item or other of a definite brand, as in the movie *Minority Report*, where Tom Cruise's character John Anderton owns a phone with the *Nokia* logo clearly written in the top corner, or his watch engraved with the *Bulgari* logo. Another example of advertising in film is in *I, Robot*, where main character played by Will Smith mentions his *Converse* shoes several times, calling them "classics," because the film is set far in the future. *I, Robot* and *Spaceballs* also showcase futuristic cars with the *Audi* and *Mercedes-Benz* logos clearly displayed on the front of the vehicles.

Cadillac chose to advertise in the movie *The Matrix Reloaded*, which as a result contained many scenes in which Cadillac cars were used. Similarly, product placement for Omega Watches, Ford, VAIO, BMW and Aston Martin cars are featured in recent James Bond films, most notably *Casino Royale*. In "Fantastic Four: Rise of the Silver Surfer", the main transport vehicle shows a large Dodge logo on the front. *Blade Runner* includes some of the most obvious product placement; the whole film stops to show a Coca-Cola billboard.

Celebrities

This type of advertising focuses upon using celebrity power, fame, money, popularity to gain recognition for their products and promote specific stores or products. Advertisers often advertise their products, for example, when celebrities share their favourite products or wear clothes by specific brands or designers. Celebrities are often involved in advertising campaigns such as television or print adverts to advertise specific or general products.

The use of celebrities to endorse a brand can have its downsides, however. One mistake by a celebrity can be detrimental to the public relations of a brand. For example, following his performance of eight gold medals at the 2008 Olympic Games in Beijing, China, swimmer Michael Phelps' contract with Kellogg's was terminated, as Kellogg's did not want to associate with him after he was photographed smoking marijuana.

MEDIA AND ADVERTISING APPROACHES

Increasingly, other media are overtaking many of the "traditional" media such as television, radio and newspaper because of a shift toward consumer's usage of the Internet for news and music as well as devices like digital video recorders (DVRs) such as TiVo.

Advertising on the World Wide Web is a recent phenomenon. Prices of Web-based advertising space are dependent on the "relevance" of the surrounding web content and the traffic that the website receives.

Digital signage is poised to become a major mass media because of its ability to reach larger audiences for less money. Digital signage also offer the unique ability to see the target audience where they are reached by the medium. Technology advances has also made it possible to control the message on digital signage with much precision, enabling the messages to be relevant to the target audience at any given time and location which in turn, gets more response from the advertising. Digital signage is being successfully employed in supermarkets. Another successful use of digital signage is in hospitality locations such as restaurants. and malls.

E-mail advertising is another recent phenomenon. Unsolicited bulk E-mail advertising is known as "e-mail spam". Spam has been a problem for email users for many years. Some companies have proposed placing messages or corporate logos on the side of booster rockets and the International Space Station. Controversy exists on the effectiveness of subliminal advertising, and the pervasiveness of mass messages. Unpaid advertising (also called "publicity advertising"), can provide good exposure at minimal cost. Personal recommendations ("bring a friend", "sell it"), spreading buzz, or achieving the feat of equating a brand with a common noun (in the United States, "Xerox" = "photocopier", "Kleenex" = tissue, "Vaseline" = petroleum jelly, "Hoover" = vacuum cleaner, "Nintendo" (often used by those exposed to many video games) = video games, and "Band-Aid" = adhesive bandage) — these can be seen as the pinnacle of any advertising campaign. However, some companies oppose the use of their brand name to label an object. Equating a brand with a common noun also risks turning that brand into a genericized trademark - turning it into a generic term which means that its legal protection as a trademark is lost.

As the mobile phone became a new mass media in 1998 when the first paid downloadable content appeared on mobile phones in Finland, it was only a matter of time until mobile advertising followed, also first launched in Finland in 2000. By 2007 the value of mobile advertising had reached $2.2 billion and providers such as Admob delivered billions of mobile ads.

More advanced mobile ads include banner ads, coupons, Multimedia Messaging Service picture and video messages, advergames and various engagement marketing campaigns. A particular feature driving mobile ads is the 2D Barcode, which replaces the need to do any typing of web addresses, and uses the camera feature of modern phones to gain immediate access to web content. 83 per cent of Japanese mobile phone users already are active users of 2D barcodes. A new form of advertising that is growing rapidly is social network advertising. It is online advertising with a focus on social networking sites. This is a relatively immature market, but it has shown a lot of promise as advertisers are able to take advantage of the demographic information the user has provided to the social networking site.

Friendertising is a more precise advertising term in which people are able to direct advertisements toward others directly using social network service. From time to time, The CW Television Network airs short programming breaks called "Content Wraps," to advertise one company's product during an entire commercial break. The CW pioneered "content wraps" and some products featured were Herbal Essences, Crest, Guitar Hero II, CoverGirl, and recently Toyota. Recently, there appeared a new promotion concept, "ARvertising", advertising on Augmented Reality technology.

CRITICISM OF ADVERTISING

While advertising can be seen as necessary for economic growth, it is not without social costs. Unsolicited Commercial Email and other forms of spam have become so prevalent as to have become a major nuisance to users of these services, as well as being a financial burden on internet service providers. Advertising is increasingly invading public spaces, such as schools, which some critics argue is a form of child exploitation. In addition, advertising frequently uses psychological pressure (for example, appealing to feelings of inadequacy) on the intended consumer, which may be harmful.

Hyper-commercialism and the Commercial Tidal Wave

Criticism of advertising is closely linked with criticism of media and often interchangeable. They can refer to its audio-visual aspects (e. g. cluttering of public spaces and airwaves), environmental aspects (e. g. pollution, oversize packaging, increasing consumption), political aspects (e. g. media dependency, free speech, censorship), financial aspects (costs), ethical/moral/social aspects (e. g. sub-conscious influencing, invasion of privacy, increasing consumption and waste, target groups, certain products, honesty) and, of course, a mix thereof. Some aspects can be subdivided further and some can cover more than one category.

As advertising has become increasingly prevalent in modern Western societies, it is also increasingly being criticized. A person can hardly move in the public sphere or use a medium without being subject to advertising. Advertising occupies public space and more and more invades the private sphere of people, many of which consider it a nuisance. "It is becoming harder to escape from advertising and the media. ... Public space is increasingly turning into a gigantic billboard for products of all kind. The aesthetical and political consequences cannot yet be foreseen." Hanno Rauterberg in the German newspaper 'Die Zeit' calls advertising a new kind of dictatorship that cannot be escaped.

Ad creep: "There are ads in schools, airport lounges, doctors offices, movie theaters, hospitals, gas stations, elevators, convenience stores, on the Internet, on fruit, on ATMs, on garbage cans and countless other places. There are ads on beach sand and restroom walls." "One of the ironies of advertising in our times is that as commercialism increases, it makes it that much more difficult for any particular advertiser to succeed, hence pushing the advertiser to even greater efforts." Within a decade advertising in radios climbed to nearly 18 or 19 minutes per hour; on prime-time television the standard until 1982 was no more than 9.5 minutes of advertising per hour, today it's between 14 and 17 minutes. With the introduction of the shorter 15-second-spot the total amount of ads increased even more dramatically. Ads are not only placed in breaks but e. g. also into baseball telecasts during the game itself. They flood the internet, a market growing in leaps and bounds.

Other growing markets are "product placements" in entertainment programming and in movies where it has become standard practice and "virtual advertising" where products get placed retroactively into rerun shows. Product billboards are virtually inserted into Major League Baseball broadcasts and in the same manner, virtual street banners or logos are projected on an entry canopy or sidewalks, for example during the arrival of celebrities at the 2001 Grammy Awards. Advertising precedes the showing of films at cinemas including lavish 'film shorts' produced by companies such as Microsoft or DaimlerChrysler. "The largest advertising agencies have begun working aggressively to co-produce programming in conjunction with the largest media firms" creating Infomercials resembling entertainment programming.

Opponents equate the growing amount of advertising with a "tidal wave" and restrictions with "damming" the flood. Kalle Lasn, one of the most outspoken critics of advertising on the international stage, considers advertising "the most prevalent and toxic of the mental pollutants. From the moment your radio alarm sounds in the morning to the wee hours of late-night TV microjolts of commercial pollution flood into your brain at the rate of around 3,000 marketing messages per day. Every day an estimated twelve billion display ads, 3 million radio commercials and more than 200,000 television commercials are dumped into North America's collective unconscious". In the course of his life the average American watches three years of advertising on television.

More recent developments are video games incorporating products into their content, special commercial patient channels in hospitals and public figures sporting temporary tattoos. A method unrecognisable as advertising is so-called ''guerrilla marketing'' which is spreading 'buzz' about a new product in target audiences. Cash-strapped U.S. cities do not shrink back from offering police cars for advertising. A trend, especially in Germany, is companies buying the names of sports stadiums. The Hamburg soccer Volkspark stadium first became the AOL Arena and then the HSH Nordbank Arena. The Stuttgart Neckarstadion became the Mercedes-Benz Arena, the Dortmund Westfalenstadion now is the Signal Iduna Park. The former SkyDome in Toronto was renamed Rogers Centre. Other recent developments are, for example, that whole subway stations in Berlin are redesigned into product halls and exclusively leased to a company. Düsseldorf even has 'multi-sensorial' adventure transit stops equipped with loudspeakers and systems that spread the smell of a detergent. Swatch used beamers to project messages on the Berlin TV-tower and Victory column, which was fined because it was done without a permit. The illegality was part of the scheme and added promotion.

It's standard business management knowledge that advertising is a pillar, if not "the" pillar of the growth-orientated free capitalist economy. "Advertising is part of the bone marrow of corporate capitalism." "Contemporary capitalism could not function and global production networks could not exist as they do without advertising."

For communication scientist and media economist Manfred Knoche at the University of Salzburg, Austria, advertising isn't just simply a 'necessary evil' but a 'necessary elixir of life' for the media business, the economy and capitalism as a whole. Advertising and mass media economic interests create ideology. Knoche describes advertising for products and brands as 'the producer's weapons in the competition for customers' and trade advertising, e. g. by the automotive industry, as a means to collectively represent their interests against other groups, such as the train companies. In his view editorial articles and programmes in the media, promoting consumption in general, provide a 'cost free' service to producers and sponsoring for a 'much used means of payment' in advertising. Christopher Lasch argues that advertising leads to an overall increase in consumption in society; "Advertising serves not so much to advertise products as to promote consumption as a way of life."

Advertising and Constitutional Rights

Advertising is equated with constitutionally guaranteed freedom of opinion and speech. Therefore criticizing advertising or any attempt to restrict or ban advertising is almost always considered to be an attack on fundamental rights (First Amendment in the US) and meets the combined and concentrated resistance of the business and especially the advertising community.

"Currently or in the near future, any number of cases are and will be working their way through the court system that would seek to prohibit any government regulation of... commercial speech (e.g. advertising or food labelling) on the grounds that such regulation would violate citizens' and corporations' First Amendment rights to free speech or free press." An example for this debate is advertising for tobacco or alcohol but also advertising by mail or fliers (clogged mail boxes), advertising on the phone, in the internet and advertising for children. Various legal restrictions concerning spamming, advertising on mobile phones, addressing children, tobacco, alcohol have been introduced by the US, the EU and various other countries. Not only the business community resists restrictions of advertising.

Advertising as a means of free expression has firmly established itself in western society. McChesney argues, that the government deserves constant vigilance when it comes to such regulations, but that it is certainly not "the only antidemocratic force in our society....corporations and the wealthy enjoy a power every bit as immense as that enjoyed by the lords and royalty of feudal times" and "markets are not value-free or neutral; they not only tend to work to the advantage of those with the most money, but they also by their very nature emphasize profit over all else....Hence, today the debate is over whether advertising or food labelling, or campaign contributions are speech...if the rights to be protected by the First Amendment can only be effectively employed by a fraction of the citizenry, and their exercise of these rights gives them undue political power and undermines the ability of the balance of the citizenry to exercise the same rights and/or constitutional rights, then it is not necessarily legitimately protected by the First Amendment."

In addition, "those with the capacity to engage in free press are in a position to determine who can speak to the great mass of citizens and who cannot". Critics in turn argue, that advertising invades privacy which is a constitutional right. For, on the one hand, advertising physically invades privacy, on the other, it increasingly uses relevant, information-based communication with private data assembled without the knowledge or consent of consumers or target groups. For Georg Franck at Vienna University of Technology advertising is part of what he calls "mental capitalism", taking up a term (mental) which has been used by groups concerned with the mental environment, such as Adbusters. Franck blends the "Economy of Attention" with Christopher Lasch's culture of narcissm into the mental capitalism: In his essay "Advertising at the Edge of the Apocalypse", Sut Jhally writes: "20. century advertising is the most powerful and sustained system of propaganda in human history and its cumulative cultural effects, unless quickly checked, will be responsible for destroying the world as we know it.

The price of Attention and Hidden Costs

Advertising has developed into a billion-dollar business on which many depend. In 2006 391 billion US dollars were spent worldwide for advertising. In Germany, for example, the advertising industry contributes 1.5% of the gross national income; the figures for other developed countries are similar. Thus, advertising and growth are directly and causally linked. As far as a growth based economy can be blamed for the harmful human lifestyle (affluent society) advertising has to be considered in this aspect concerning its negative impact, because its main purpose is to raise consumption. "The industry is accused of being one of the engines powering a convoluted economic mass production system which promotes consumption."

Attention and attentiveness have become a new commodity for which a market developed. "The amount of attention that is absorbed by the media and redistributed in the competition for quotas and reach is not identical with the amount of attention, that is available in society. The total amount circulating in society is made up of the attention exchanged among the people themselves and the attention given to media information.

Only the latter is homogenised by quantitative measuring and only the latter takes on the character of an anonymous currency." According to Franck, any surface of presentation that can guarantee a certain degree of attentiveness works as magnet for attention, e. g. media which are actually meant for information and entertainment, culture and the arts, public space etc.

It is this attraction which is sold to the advertising business. The German Advertising Association stated that in 2007 30.78 billion Euros were spent on advertising in Germany, 26% in newspapers, 21% on television, 15% by mail and 15% in magazines. In 2002 there were 360.000 people employed in the advertising business. The internet revenues for advertising doubled to almost 1 billion Euros from 2006 to 2007, giving it the highest growth rates.

Spiegel-Online reported that in the US in 2008 for the first time more money was spent for advertising on internet (105.3 billion US dollars) than on television (98.5 billion US dollars). The largest amount in 2008 was still spent in the print media (147 billion US dollars). For that same year, Welt-Online reported that the US pharmaceutical industry spent almost double the amount on advertising (57.7 billion dollars) than it did on research (31.5 billion dollars). But Marc-André Gagnon und Joel Lexchin of York University, Toronto, estimate that the actual expenses for advertising are higher yet, because not all entries are recorded by the research institutions. Not included are indirect advertising campaigns such as sales, rebates and price reductions. Few consumers are aware of the fact that they are the ones paying for every cent spent for public relations, advertisements, rebates, packaging etc. since they ordinarily get included in the price calculation.

Influencing and Conditioning

The most important element of advertising is not information but suggestion more or less making use of associations, emotions (appeal to emotion) and drives dormant in the sub-conscience of people, such as sex drive, herd instinct, of desires, such as happiness, health, fitness, appearance, self-esteem, reputation, belonging, social status, identity, adventure, distraction, reward, of fears (appeal to fear), such as illness, weaknesses, loneliness, need, uncertainty, security or of prejudices, learned opinions and comforts. "All human needs, relationships, and fears – the deepest recesses of the human psyche – become mere means for the expansion of the commodity universe under the force of modern marketing. With the rise to prominence of modern marketing, commercialism – the translation of human relations into commodity relations – although a phenomenon intrinsic to capitalism, has expanded exponentially." 'Cause-related marketing' in which advertisers link their product to some worthy social cause has boomed over the past decade. Advertising exploits the model role of celebrities or popular figures and makes deliberate use of humour as well as of associations with colour, tunes, certain names and terms. Altogether, these are factors of how one perceives himself and one's self-worth.

In his description of 'mental capitalism' Franck says, "the promise of consumption making someone irresistible is the ideal way of objects and symbols into a person's subjective experience. Evidently, in a society in which revenue of attention moves to the fore, consumption is drawn by one's self-esteem. As a result, consumption becomes 'work' on a person's attraction.

From the subjective point of view, this 'work' opens fields of unexpected dimensions for advertising. Advertising takes on the role of a life councillor in matters of attraction. The cult around one's own attraction is what Christopher Lasch described as 'Culture of Narcissism'."

For advertising critics another serious problem is that "the long standing notion of separation between advertising and editorial/creative sides of media is rapidly crumbling" and advertising is increasingly hard to tell apart from news, information or entertainment. The boundaries between advertising and programming are becoming blurred. According to the media firms all this commercial involvement has no influence over actual media content, but, as

McChesney puts it, "this claim fails to pass even the most basic giggle test, it is so preposterous." Advertising draws "heavily on psychological theories about how to create subjects, enabling advertising and marketing to take on a 'more clearly psychological tinge'. Increasingly, the emphasis in advertising has switched from providing 'factual' information to the symbolic connotations of commodities, since the crucial cultural premise of advertising is that the material object being sold is never in itself enough.

Even those commodities providing for the most mundane necessities of daily life must be imbued with symbolic qualities and culturally endowed meanings via the 'magic system of advertising. In this way and by altering the context in which advertisements appear, things 'can be made to mean "just about anything"' and the 'same' things can be endowed with different intended meanings for different individuals and groups of people, thereby offering mass produced visions of individualism."

Before advertising is done, market research institutions need to know and describe the target group to exactly plan and implement the advertising campaign and to achieve the best possible results. A whole array of sciences directly deal with advertising and marketing or is used to improve its effects.

Focus groups, psychologists and cultural anthropologists are '"de rigueur"' in marketing research". Vast amounts of data on persons and their shopping habits are collected, accumulated, aggregated and analysed with the aid of credit cards, bonus cards, raffles and internet surveying. With increasing accuracy this supplies a picture of behaviour, wishes and weaknesses of certain sections of a population with which advertisement can be employed more selectively and effectively.

The efficiency of advertising is improved through advertising research. Universities, of course supported by business and in co-operation with other disciplines, mainly Psychiatry, Anthropology, Neurology and behavioural sciences, are constantly in search for ever more refined, sophisticated, subtle and crafty methods to make advertising more effective.

"Neuromarketing is a controversial new field of marketing which uses medical technologies such as functional Magnetic Resonance Imaging (fMRI) — not to heal, but to sell products. Advertising and marketing firms have long used the insights and research methods of psychology in order to sell products, of course.

But today these practices are reaching epidemic levels, and with a complicity on the part of the psychological profession that exceeds that of the past. The result is an enormous advertising and marketing onslaught that comprises, arguably, the largest single psychological project ever undertaken. Yet, this great undertaking remains largely ignored by the American Psychological Association." Robert McChesney calls it "the greatest concerted attempt at psychological manipulation in all of human history."

Dependency of the Media and Corporate Censorship

Almost all mass media are advertising media and many of them are exclusively advertising media and, with the exception of public service broadcasting are privately owned. Their income is predominantly generated through advertising; in the case of newspapers and magazines from 50 to 80%. Public service broadcasting in some countries can also heavily depend on advertising as a source of income (up to 40%). In the view of critics no media that spreads advertisements can be independent and the higher the proportion of advertising, the higher the dependency. This dependency has "distinct implications for the nature of media content.... In the business press, the media are often referred to in exactly the way they present themselves in their candid moments: as a branch of the advertising industry."

In addition, the private media are increasingly subject to mergers and concentration with property situations often becoming entangled and opaque. This development, which Henry A. Giroux calls an "ongoing threat to democratic culture", by itself should suffice to sound all alarms in a democracy. Five or six advertising agencies dominate this 400 billion U.S. dollar global industry.

"Journalists have long faced pressure to shape stories to suit advertisers and owners .... the vast majority of TV station executives found their news departments 'cooperative' in shaping the news to assist in 'non-traditional revenue development." Negative and undesired reporting can be prevented or influenced when advertisers threaten to cancel orders or simply when there is a danger of such a cancellation. Media dependency and such a threat becomes very real when there is only one dominant or very few large advertisers. The influence of advertisers is not only in regard to news or information on their own products or services but expands to articles or shows not directly linked to them. In order to secure their advertising revenues the media has to create the best possible 'advertising environment'. Another problem considered censorship by critics is the refusal of media to accept advertisements that are not in their interest. A striking example of this is the refusal of TV stations to broadcast ads by Adbusters. Groups try to place advertisements and are refused by networks.

It is principally the viewing rates which decide upon the programme in the private radio and television business. "Their business is to absorb as much attention as possible. The viewing rate measures the attention the media trades for the information offered. The service of this attraction is sold to the advertising business" and the viewing rates determine the price that can be demanded for advertising.

"Advertising companies determining the contents of shows has been part of daily life in the USA since 1933. Procter & Gamble (P&G) .... offered a radio station a history-making trade (today know as "bartering"): the company would produce an own show for "free" and save the radio station the high expenses for producing contents. Therefore the company would want its commercials spread and, of course, its products placed in the show. Thus, the series 'Ma Perkins' was created, which P&G skilfully used to promote Oxydol, the leading detergent brand in those years and the Soap opera was born ..."

While critics basically worry about the subtle influence of the economy on the media, there are also examples of blunt exertion of influence. The US company Chrysler, before it merged with Daimler Benz had its agency, PentaCom, send out a letter to numerous magazines, demanding them to send, an overview of all the topics before the next issue is published to "avoid potential conflict". Chrysler most of all wanted to know, if there would be articles with "sexual, political or social" content or which could be seen as "provocative or offensive". PentaCom executive David Martin said: "Our reasoning is, that anyone looking at a 22.000 $ product would want it surrounded by positive things.

There is nothing positive about an article on child pornography." In another example, the USA Network held top-level, off-the-record meetings with advertisers in 2000 to let them tell the network what type of programming content they wanted in order for USA to get their advertising." Television shows are created to accommodate the needs for advertising, e.g. splitting them up in suitable sections. Their dramaturgy is typically designed to end in suspense or leave an unanswered question in order to keep the viewer attached. The movie system, at one time outside the direct influence of the broader marketing system, is now fully integrated into it through the strategies of licensing, tie-ins and product placements.

The prime function of many Hollywood films today is to aid in the selling of the immense collection of commodities. The press called the 2002 Bond film 'Die Another Day' featuring 24 major promotional partners an 'ad-venture' and noted that James Bond "now has been 'licensed to sell'" As it has become standard practise to place products in motion pictures, it "has self-evident implications for what types of films will attract product placements and what types of films will therefore be more likely to get made".

Advertising and information are increasingly hard to distinguish from each other. "The borders between advertising and media .... become more and more blurred.... What August Fischer, chairman of the board of Axel Springer publishing company considers to be a 'proven partnership between the media and advertising business' critics regard as nothing but the infiltration of journalistic duties and freedoms".

According to RTL-executive Helmut Thoma "private stations shall not and cannot serve any mission but only the goal of the company which is the 'acceptance by the advertising business and the viewer'. The setting of priorities in this order actually says everything about the 'design of the programmes' by private television." Patrick Le Lay, former managing director of TF1, a private French television channel with a market share of 25 to 35%, said: "There are many ways to talk about television. But from the business point of view, let's be realistic: basically, the job of TF1 is, e. g. to help Coca Cola sell its product. (…) For an advertising message to be perceived the brain of the viewer must be at our disposal.

The job of our programmes is to make it available, that is to say, to distract it, to relax it and get it ready between two messages. It is disposable human brain time that we sell to Coca Cola." Because of these dependencies a widespread and fundamental public debate about advertising and its influence on information and freedom of speech is difficult to obtain, at least through the usual media channels; otherwise these would saw off the branch they are sitting on. "The notion that the commercial basis of media, journalism, and communication could have troubling implications for democracy is excluded from the range of legitimate debate" just as "capitalism is off-limits as a topic of legitimate debate in US political culture".

An early critic of the structural basis of US journalism was Upton Sinclair with his novel The Brass Check in which he stresses the influence of owners, advertisers, public relations, and economic interests on the media. In his book "Our Master's Voice – Advertising" the social ecologist James Rorty wrote: "The gargoyle's mouth is a loudspeaker, powered by the vested interest of a two-billion dollar industry, and back of that the vested interests of business as a whole, of industry, of finance.

It is never silent, it drowns out all other voices, and it suffers no rebuke, for it is not the voice of America? That is its claim and to some extent it is a just claim..." It has taught us how to live, what to be afraid of, what to be proud of, how to be beautiful, how to be loved, how to be envied, how to be successful.. Is it any wonder that the American population tends increasingly to speak, think, feel in terms of this jabberwocky? That the stimuli of art, science, religion are progressively expelled to the periphery of American life to become marginal values, cultivated by marginal people on marginal time?"

THE COMMERCIALISATION OF CULTURE AND SPORTS

Performances, exhibitions, shows, concerts, conventions and most other events can hardly take place without sponsoring. The increasing lack arts and culture they buy the service of attraction. Artists are graded and paid according to their art's value for commercial purposes. Corporations promote renown artists, therefore getting exclusive rights in global advertising campaigns. Broadway shows, like 'La Bohème' featured commercial props in its set.

Advertising itself is extensively considered to be a contribution to culture. Advertising is integrated into fashion. On many pieces of clothing the company logo is the only design or is an important part of it. There is only little room left outside the consumption economy, in which culture and art can develop independently and where alternative values can be expressed. A last important sphere, the universities, is under strong pressure to open up for business and its interests.

Competitive sports have become unthinkable without sponsoring and there is a mutual dependency. High income with advertising is only possible with a comparable number of spectators or viewers. On the other hand, the poor performance of a team or a sportsman results in less advertising revenues. Jürgen Hüther and Hans-Jörg Stiehler talk about a 'Sports/Media Complex which is a complicated mix of media, agencies, managers, sports promoters, advertising etc. with partially common and partially diverging interests but in any case with common commercial interests. The media presumably is at centre stage because it can supply the other parties involved with a rare commodity, namely (potential) public attention. In sports "the media are able to generate enormous sales in both circulation and advertising."

"Sports sponsorship is acknowledged by the tobacco industry to be valuable advertising. A Tobacco Industry journal in 1994 described the Formula One car as 'The most powerful advertising space in the world'. .... In a cohort study carried out in 22 secondary schools in England in 1994 and 1995 boys whose favourite television sport was motor racing had a 12.8% risk of becoming regular smokers compared to 7.0% of boys who did not follow motor racing."

Not the sale of tickets but transmission rights, sponsoring and merchandising in the meantime make up the largest part of sports association's and sports club's revenues with the IOC (International Olympic Committee) taking the lead. The influence of the media brought many changes in sports including the admittance of new 'trend sports' into the Olympic Games, the alteration of competition distances, changes of rules, animation of spectators, changes of sports facilities, the cult of sports heroes who quickly establish themselves in the advertising and entertaining business because of their media value and last but not least, the naming and renaming of sport stadiums after big companies.

"In sports adjustment into the logic of the media can contribute to the erosion of values such as equal chances or fairness, to excessive demands on athletes through public pressure and multiple exploitation or to deceit (doping, manipulation of results ...). It is in the very interest of the media and sports to counter this danger because media sports can only work as long as sport exists.

Occupation and Commercialisation of Public Space

Every visually perceptible place has potential for advertising. Especially urban areas with their structures but also landscapes in sight of through fares are more and more turning into media for advertisements. Signs, posters, billboards, flags have become decisive factors in the urban appearance and their numbers are still on the increase. "Outdoor advertising has become unavoidable.

Traditional billboards and transit shelters have cleared the way for more pervasive methods such as wrapped vehicles, sides of buildings, electronic signs, kiosks, taxis, posters, sides of buses, and more. Digital technologies are used on buildings to sport 'urban wall displays'. In urban areas commercial content is placed in our sight and into our consciousness every moment we are in public space. The German Newspaper 'Zeit' called it a new kind of 'dictatorship that one cannot escape'. Over time, this domination of the surroundings has become the "natural" state. Through long-term commercial saturation, it has become implicitly understood by the public that advertising has the right to own, occupy and control every inch of available space. The steady normalization of invasive advertising dulls the public's perception of their surroundings, re-enforcing a general attitude of powerlessness toward creativity and change, thus a cycle develops enabling advertisers to slowly and consistently increase the saturation of advertising with little or no public outcry."

The massive optical orientation toward advertising changes the function of public spaces which are utilised by brands. Urban landmarks are turned into trademarks. The highest pressure is exerted on renown and highly frequented public spaces which are also important for the identity of a city (e.g. Piccadilly Circus, Times Square, Alexanderplatz). Urban spaces are public commodities and in this capacity they are subject to "aesthetical environment protection", mainly through building regulations, heritage protection and landscape protection. "It is in this capacity that these spaces are now being privatised. They are peppered with billboards and signs, they are remodelled into media for advertising."

Socio-cultural Aspects: Sexism, Discrimination and Stereotyping

"Advertising has an "agenda setting function" which is the ability, with huge sums of money, to put consumption as the only item on the agenda. In the battle for a share of the public conscience this amounts to non-treatment (ignorance) of whatever is not commercial and whatever is not advertised for. Advertising should be reflection of society norms and give clear picture of target market. Spheres without commerce and advertising serving the muses and relaxation remain without respect. With increasing force advertising makes itself comfortable in the private sphere so that the voice of commerce becomes the dominant way of expression in society." Advertising critics see advertising as the leading light in our culture. Sut Jhally and James Twitchell go beyond considering advertising as kind of religion and that advertising even replaces religion as a key institution.

"Corporate advertising (or commercial media) is the largest single psychological project ever undertaken by the human race. Yet for all of that, its impact on us remains unknown and largely ignored.

When I think of the media's influence over years, over decades, I think of those brainwashing experiments conducted by Dr. Ewen Cameron in a Montreal psychiatric hospital in the 1950s. The idea of the CIA-sponsored "depatterning" experiments was to outfit conscious, unconscious or semiconscious subjects with headphones, and flood their brains with thousands of repetitive "driving" messages that would alter their behaviour over time....Advertising aims to do the same thing."

Advertising is especially aimed at young people and children and it increasingly reduces young people to consumers. For Sut Jhally it is not "surprising that something this central and with so much being expended on it should become an important presence in social life. Indeed, commercial interests intent on maximizing the consumption of the immense collection of commodities have colonized more and more of the spaces of our culture.

For instance, almost the entire media system (television and print) has been developed as a delivery system for marketers its prime function is to produce audiences for sale to advertisers. Both the advertisements it carries, as well as the editorial matter that acts as a support for it, celebrate the consumer society. The movie system, at one time outside the direct influence of the broader marketing system, is now fully integrated into it through the strategies of licensing, tie-ins and product placements. The prime function of many Hollywood films today is to aid in the selling of the immense collection of commodities. As public funds are drained from the non-commercial cultural sector, art galleries, museums and symphonies bid for corporate sponsorship."

In the same way effected is the education system and advertising is increasingly penetrating schools and universities. Cities, such as New York, accept sponsors for public playgrounds. "Even the pope has been commercialized ... The pope's 4-day visit to Mexico in ...1999 was sponsored by Frito-Lay and PepsiCo. The industry is accused of being one of the engines powering a convoluted economic mass production system which promotes consumption.

As far as social effects are concerned it does not matter whether advertising fuels consumption but which values, patterns of behaviour and assignments of meaning it propagates. Advertising is accused of hijacking the language and means of pop culture, of protest movements and even of subversive criticism and does not shy away from scandalizing and breaking taboos (e.g. Benneton). This in turn incites counter action, what Kalle Lasn in 2001 called ''Jamming the Jam of the Jammers''. Anything goes. "It is a central social-scientific question what people can be made to do by suitable design of conditions and of great practical importance. For example, from a great number of experimental psychological experiments it can be assumed, that people can be made to do anything they are capable of, when the according social condition can be created." Advertising often uses stereotype gender specific roles of men and women reinforcing existing clichés and it has been criticized as "inadvertently or even intentionally promoting sexism, racism, and ageism... At very least, advertising often reinforces stereotypes by drawing on recognizable "types" in order to tell stories in a single image or 30 second time frame."

Activities are depicted as typical male or female (stereotyping). In addition people are reduced to their sexuality or equated with commodities and gender specific qualities are exaggerated. Sexualized female bodies, but increasingly also males, serve as eye-catchers.

In advertising it is usually a woman being depicted as:

- Servants of men and children that react to the demands and complaints of their loved ones with a bad conscience and the promise for immediate improvement (wash, food)
- A sexual or emotional play toy for the self-affirmation of men
- A technically totally clueless being (almost always male) that can only manage a childproof operation
- Female expert, but stereotype from the fields of fashion, cosmetics, food or at the most, medicine
- As ultra thin, slim, and very skinny.
- Doing ground-work for others, e.g. serving coffee while a journalist interviews a politician

A large portion of advertising deals with promotion of products that pertain to the "ideal body image." This is mainly targeted toward women, and, in the past, this type of advertising was aimed nearly exclusively at women. Women in advertisements are generally portrayed as good-looking women who are in good health. This, however, is not the case of the average woman. Consequently, they give a negative message of body image to the average woman. Because of the media, girls and women who are overweight, and otherwise "normal" feel almost obligated to take care of themselves and stay fit. They feel under high pressure to maintain an acceptable bodyweight and take care of their health. Consequences of this are low self-esteem,eating disorders, self mutilations, and beauty operations for those women that just cannot bring themselves eat right or get the motivation to go to the gym.

The EU parliament passed a resolution in 2008 that advertising may not be discriminating and degrading. This shows that politicians are increasingly concerned about the negative impacts of advertising. However, the benefits of promoting overall health and fitness are often overlooked. Men are also negatively portrayed as incompetent and the butt of every joke in advertising.

CHILDREN AND ADOLESCENTS AS TARGET GROUPS

The children's market, where resistance to advertising is weakest, is the "pioneer for ad creep". "Kids are among the most sophisticated observers of ads. They can sing the jingles and identify the logos, and they often have strong feelings about products.

What they generally don't understand, however, are the issues that underlie how advertising works. Mass media are used not only to sell goods but also ideas: how we should behave, what rules are important, who we should respect and what we should value." Youth is increasingly reduced to the role of a consumer. Not only the makers of toys, sweets, ice cream, breakfast food and sport articles prefer to aim their promotion at children and adolescents. For example, an ad for a breakfast cereal on a channel aimed at adults will have music that is a soft ballad, whereas on a channel aimed at children, the same ad will use a catchy rock jingle of the same song to aim at kids.

Advertising for other products preferably uses media with which they can also reach the next generation of consumers. "Key advertising messages exploit the emerging independence of young people". Cigarettes, for example, "are used as a fashion accessory and appeal to young women.

Other influences on young people include the linking of sporting heroes and smoking through sports sponsorship, the use of cigarettes by popular characters in television programmes and cigarette promotions. Research suggests that young people are aware of the most heavily advertised cigarette brands." "Product placements show up everywhere, and children aren't exempt. Far from it. The animated film, Foodfight, had 'thousands of products and character icons from the familiar (items) in a grocery store.' Children's books also feature branded items and characters, and millions of them have snack foods as lead characters." Business is interested in children and adolescents because of their buying power and because of their influence on the shopping habits of their parents.

As they are easier to influence they are especially targeted by the advertising business. "The marketing industry is facing increased pressure over claimed links between exposure to food advertising and a range of social problems, especially growing obesity levels."

In 2001, children's programming accounted for over 20% of all US television watching. The global market for children's licensed products was some 132 billion US dollars in 2002.

Advertisers target children because, e.g. in Canada, they "represent three distinct markets:

1. Primary Purchasers ($2.9 billion annually)
2. Future Consumers (Brand-loyal adults)
3. Purchase Influencers ($20 billion annually)

Kids will carry forward brand expectations, whether positive, negative, or indifferent. Kids are already accustomed to being catered to as consumers. The long term prize: Loyalty of the kid translates into a brand loyal adult customer" The average Canadian child sees 350,000 TV commercials before graduating from high school, spends nearly as much time watching TV as attending classes. In 1980 the Canadian province of Québec banned advertising for children under age 13.

"In upholding the consititutional validity of the Quebec Consumer Protection Act restrictions on advertising to children under age 13 (in the case of a challenge by a toy company) the Court held: '...advertising directed at young children is per se manipulative.Such advertising aims to promote products by convincing those who will always believe.'"

Norway (ads directed at children under age 12), and Sweden (television ads aimed at children under age 12) also have legislated broad bans on advertising to children, during child programmes any kind of advertising is forbidden in Sweden, Denmark, Austria and Flemish Belgium. In Greece there is no advertising for kids products from 7 to 22 h. An attempt to restrict advertising directed at children in the US failed with reference to the First Amendment. In Spain bans are also considered undemocratic.

Opposition and Campaigns Against Advertising

According to critics, the total commercialization of all fields of society, the privatization of public space, the acceleration of consumption and waste of resources including the negative influence on lifestyles and on the environment has not been noticed to the necessary extent. The "hyper-commercialization of the culture is recognized and roundly detested by the citizenry, although the topic scarcely receives a whiff of attention in the media or political culture".

"The greatest damage done by advertising is precisely that it incessantly demonstrates the prostitution of men and women who lend their intellects, their voices, their artistic skills to purposes in which they themselves do not believe, and .... that it helps to shatter and ultimately destroy our most precious non-material possessions: the confidence in the existence of meaningful purposes of human activity and respect for the integrity of man."

"The struggle against advertising is therefore essential if we are to overcome the pervasive alienation from all genuine human needs that currently plays such a corrosive role in our society. But in resisting this type of hyper-commercialism we should not be under any illusions.

Advertising may seem at times to be an almost trivial of omnipresent aspect of our economic system. Yet, as economist A. C. Pigou pointed out, it could only be 'removed altogether' if 'conditions of monopolistic competition' inherent to corporate capitalism were removed. To resist it is to resist the inner logic of capitalism itself, of which it is the pure expression."

"Visual pollution, much of it in the form of advertising, is an issue in all the world's large cities. But what is pollution to some is a vibrant part of a city's fabric to others. New York City without Times Square's huge digital billboards or Tokyo without the Ginza's commercial panorama is unthinkable. Piccadilly Circus would be just a London roundabout without its signage.

Still, other cities, like Moscow, have reached their limit and have begun to crack down on over-the-top outdoor advertising." "Many communities have chosen to regulate billboards to protect and enhance their scenic character.

The following is by no means a complete list of such communities, but it does give a good idea of the geographic diversity of cities, counties and states that prohibit new construction of billboards. Scenic America estimates the nationwide total of cities and communities prohibiting the construction of new billboards to be at least 1500.

A number of States in the US prohibit all billboards:

- *Vermont*: Removed all billboards in 1970s
- *Hawaii*: Removed all billboards in 1920s
- *Maine*: Removed all billboards in 1970s and early 80s
- *Alaska*: State referendum passed in 1998 prohibits billboards
- Almost two years ago the city of Sao Paulo, Brazil, ordered the downsizing or removal of all billboards and most other forms of commercial advertising in the city."

Technical appliances, such as Spam filters, TV-Zappers, Ad-Blockers for TVs and stickers on mail boxes: "No Advertising" and an increasing number of court cases indicate a growing interest of people to restrict or rid themselves of unwelcome advertising.

Consumer protection associations, environment protection groups, globalization opponents, consumption critics, sociologists, media critics, scientists and many others deal with the negative aspects of advertising. "Antipub" in France, "subvertising", culture jamming and adbusting have become established terms in the anti-advertising community.

On the international level globalization critics such as Naomi Klein and Noam Chomsky are also renown media and advertising critics. These groups criticize the complete occupation of public spaces, surfaces, the airwaves, the media, schools etc. and the constant exposure of almost all senses to advertising messages, the invasion of privacy, and that only few consumers are aware that they themselves are bearing the costs for this to the very last penny. Some of these groups, such as the 'The Billboard Liberation Front Creative Group' in San Francisco or Adbusters in Vancouver, Canada, have manifestos. Grassroots organizations campaign against advertising or certain aspects of it in various forms and strategies and quite often have different roots.

Adbusters, for example contests and challenges the intended meanings of advertising by subverting them and creating unintended meanings instead. Other groups, like 'Illegal Signs Canada' try to stem the flood of billboards by detecting and reporting ones that have been put up without permit. Examples for various groups and organizations in different countries are

'L'association Résistance à l'Agression Publicitaire' in France, where also media critic Jean Baudrillard is a renown author. The 'Anti Advertising Agency' works with parody and humour to raise awareness about advertising. and 'Commercial Alert' campaigns for the protection of children, family values, community, environmental integrity and democracy. Media literacy organisations aim at training people, especially children in the workings of the media and advertising in their programmes.

In the US, for example, the 'Media Education Foundation' produces and distributes documentary films and other educational resources. 'MediaWatch', a Canadian non-profit women's organization works to educate consumers about how they can register their concerns with advertisers and regulators.

The Canadian 'Media Awareness Network' offers one of the world's most comprehensive collections of media education and Internet literacy resources. Its member organizations represent the public, non-profit but also private sectors. Although it stresses its independence it accepts financial support from Bell Canada, CTVGlobeMedia, CanWest, TELUS and S-VOX.

To counter the increasing criticism of advertising aiming at children media literacy organizations are also initiated and funded by corporations and the advertising business themselves. In the US 'The Advertising Educational Foundation' was created in 1983 supported by ad agencies, advertisers and media companies. It is the "advertising industry's provider and distributor of educational content to enrich the understanding of advertising and its role in culture, society and the economy" sponsored for example by American Airlines, Anheuser-Busch, Campbell Soup, Coca-Cola, Colgate-Palmolive, Walt Disney, Ford, General Foods, General Mills, Gillette, Heinz, Johnson & Johnson, Kellogg, Kraft, Nestle, Philip Morris, Quaker Oats, Nabisco, Schering, Sterling, Unilever, Warner Lambert, advertising agencies like Saatchi & Saatchi Compton and media companies like American Broadcasting Companies, CBS, Capital Cities Communications, Cox Enterprises, Forbes, Hearst, Meredith, The New York Times, RCA/NBC, Reader's Digest, Time, Washington Post, just to mention a few.

Canadian businesses established 'Concerned Children's Advertisers' in 1990 "to instill confidence in all relevant publics by actively demonstrating our commitment, concern, responsibility and respect for children". Members are CanWest, Corus, CTV, General Mills, Hasbro, Hershey's, Kellogg's, Loblaw, Kraft, Mattel, McDonald's, Nestle, Pepsi, Walt Disney, Weston as well as almost 50 private broadcast partners and others.

Concerned Children's Advertisers was example for similar organizations in other countries like 'Media smart' in the United Kingdom with offspring in Germany, France, the Netherlands and Sweden. New Zealand has a similar business-funded programme called 'Willie Munchright'.

"While such interventions are claimed to be designed to encourage children to be critical of commercial messages in general, critics of the marketing industry suggest that the motivation is simply to be seen to address a problem created by the industry itself, that is, the negative social impacts to which marketing activity has contributed.

By contributing media literacy education resources, the marketing industry is positioning itself as being part of the solution to these problems, thereby seeking to avoid wide restrictions or outright bans on marketing communication, particularly for food products deemed to have little nutritional value directed at children. The need to be seen to be taking positive action primarily to avert potential restrictions on advertising is openly acknowledged by some sectors of the industry itself.... Furthermore, Hobbs suggests that such programs are also in the interest of media organizations that support the interventions to reduce criticism of the potential negative effects of the media themselves."

Taxation as Revenue and Control

Public interest groups suggest that "access to the mental space targeted by advertisers should be taxed, in that at the present moment that space is being freely taken advantage of by advertisers with no compensation paid to the members of the public who are thus being intruded upon.

This kind of tax would be a Pigovian tax in that it would act to reduce what is now increasingly seen as a public nuisance. Efforts to that end are gathering more momentum, with Arkansas and Maine considering bills to implement such a taxation. Florida enacted such a tax in 1987 but was forced to repeal it after six months, as a result of a concerted effort by national commercial interests, which withdrew planned conventions, causing major losses to the tourism industry, and cancelled advertising, causing a loss of 12 million dollars to the broadcast industry alone".

In the US, for example, advertising is tax deductible and suggestions for possible limits to the advertising tax deduction are met with fierce opposition from the business sector, not to mention suggestions for a special taxation. In other countries, advertising at least is taxed in the same manner services are taxed and in some advertising is subject to special taxation although on a very low level. In many cases the taxation refers especially to media with advertising (e.g. Austria, Italy, Greece, Netherlands, Turkey, Estonia).

Tax on advertising in European countries:

- *Belgium*: Advertising or billboard tax (taxe d'affichage or aanplakkingstaks) on public posters depending on size and kind of paper as well as on neon signs
- *France*: Tax on television commercials (taxe sur la publicité télévisée) based on the cost of the advertising unit
- *Italy*: Municipal tax on acoustic and visual kinds of advertisements within the municipality (imposta communale sulla publicità) and municipal tax on signs, posters and other kinds of advertisements

(diritti sulle pubbliche offisioni), the tariffs of which are under the jurisdiction of the municipalities

- *Netherlands*: Advertising tax (reclamebelastingen) with varying tariffs on certain advertising measures (excluding ads in newspapers and magazines) which can be levied by municipalities depending on the kind of advertising (billboards, neon signs etc.)
- *Austria*: Municipal announcement levies on advertising through writing, pictures or lights in public areas or publicly accessible areas with varying tariffs depending on the fee, the surface or the duration of the advertising measure as well as advertising tariffs on paid ads in printed media of usually 10% of the fee.
- *Sweden*: Advertising tax (reklamskatt) on ads and other kinds of advertising (billboards, film, television, advertising at fairs and exhibitions, flyers) in the range of 4% for ads in newspapers and 11% in all other cases. In the case of flyers the tariffs are based on the production costs, else on the fee
- *Spain*: Municipalities can tax advertising measures in their territory with a rather unimportant taxes and fees of various kinds.

In his book "When Corporations Rule the World" US author and globalization critic David Korten even advocates a 50% tax on advertising to counterattack what he calls "an active propaganda machinery controlled by the world's largest corporations" which "constantly reassures us that consumerism is the path to happiness, governmental restraint of market excess is the cause of our distress, and economic globalization is both a historical inevitability and a boon to the human species."

REGULATION

In the US many communities believe that many forms of outdoor advertising blight the public realm. As long ago as the 1960s in the US there were attempts to ban billboard advertising in the open countryside. Cities such as Sao Paulo have introduced an outright ban with London also having specific legislation to control unlawful displays.

There have been increasing efforts to protect the public interest by regulating the content and the influence of advertising. Some examples are: the ban on television tobacco advertising imposed in many countries, and the total ban of advertising to children under 12 imposed by the Swedish government in 1991. Though that regulation continues in effect for broadcasts originating within the country, it has been weakened by the European Court of Justice, which had found that Sweden was obliged to accept foreign programming, including those from neighboring countries or via satellite.

In Europe and elsewhere, there is a vigorous debate on whether (or how much) advertising to children should be regulated. This debate was exacerbated by a report released by the Kaiser Family Foundation in February

2004 which suggested fast food advertising that targets children was an important factor in the epidemic of childhood obesity in the United States. In New Zealand, South Africa, Canada, and many European countries, the advertising industry operates a system of self-regulation. Advertisers, advertising agencies and the media agree on a code of advertising standards that they attempt to uphold.

The general aim of such codes is to ensure that any advertising is 'legal, decent, honest and truthful'. Some self-regulatory organizations are funded by the industry, but remain independent, with the intent of upholding the standards or codes like the Advertising Standards Authority in the UK.

In the UK most forms of outdoor advertising such as the display of billboards is regulated by the UK Town and County Planning system. Currently the display of an advertisement without consent from the Planning Authority is a criminal offense liable to a fine of £2,500 per offence. All of the major outdoor billboard companies in the UK have convictions of this nature. Naturally, many advertisers view governmental regulation or even self-regulation as intrusion of their freedom of speech or a necessary evil.

Therefore, they employ a wide-variety of linguistic devices to bypass regulatory laws (e.g. printing English words in bold and French translations in fine print to deal with the Article 120 of the 1994 Toubon Law limiting the use of English in French advertising).

The advertisement of controversial products such as cigarettes and condoms are subject to government regulation in many countries. For instance, the tobacco industry is required by law in most countries to display warnings cautioning consumers about the health hazards of their products. Linguistic variation is often used by advertisers as a creative device to reduce the impact of such requirements.

FUTURE

Global Advertising

Advertising has gone through five major stages of development: domestic, export, international, multi-national, and global. For global advertisers, there are four, potentially competing, business objectives that must be balanced when developing worldwide advertising: building a brand while speaking with one voice, developing economies of scale in the creative process, maximising local effectiveness of ads, and increasing the company's speed of implementation.

Born from the evolutionary stages of global marketing are the three primary and fundamentally different approaches to the development of global advertising executions: exporting executions, producing local executions, and importing ideas that travel. Advertising research is key to determining the success of an ad in any country or region. The ability to identify which elements and/or moments of an ad that contributes to its success is how economies of scale are maximised. Once one knows what works in an ad, that idea or ideas can be imported by any other market. Market research measures, such as Flow of Attention, Flow of Emotion and branding moments provide insight into what is working in an ad in any country or region because the measures are based on the visual, not verbal, elements of the ad.

Trends

With the dawn of the Internet came many new advertising opportunities. Popup, Flash, banner, Popunder, advergaming, and email advertisements (the last often being a form of spam) are now commonplace.

In the last three quarters of 2009 mobile and internet advertising grew by 18.1% and 9.2% respectively. Older media advertising saw declines: -10.1% (TV), -11.7% (radio), -14.8% (magazines) and -18.7% (newspapers). The ability to record shows on digital video recorders (such as TiVo) allow users to record the programs for later viewing, enabling them to fast forward through commercials. Additionally, as more seasons of pre-recorded box sets are offered for sale of television programs; fewer people watch the shows on TV. However, the fact that these sets are sold, means the company will receive additional profits from the sales of these sets. To counter this effect, many advertisers have opted for product placement on TV shows like Survivor. Particularly since the rise of "entertaining" advertising, some people may like an advertisement enough to wish to watch it later or show a friend. In general, the advertising community has not yet made this easy, although some have used the Internet to widely distribute their ads to anyone willing to see or hear them.

Another significant trend regarding future of advertising is the growing importance of the niche market using niche or targeted ads. Also brought about by the Internet and the theory of The Long Tail, advertisers will have an increasing ability to reach specific audiences. In the past, the most efficient way to deliver a message was to blanket the largest mass market audience possible. However, usage tracking, customer profiles and the growing popularity of niche content brought about by everything from blogs to social networking sites, provide advertisers with audiences that are smaller but much better defined, leading to ads that are more relevant to viewers and more effective for companies' marketing products.

Among others, Comcast Spotlight is one such advertiser employing this method in their video on demand menus. These advertisements are targeted to a specific group and can be viewed by anyone wishing to find out more about a particular business or practice at any time, right from their home. This causes the viewer to become proactive and actually choose what advertisements they want to view. In the realm of advertising agencies, continued industry diversification has seen observers note that "big global clients don't need big global agencies any more". This trend is reflected by the growth of non-traditional agencies in various global markets, such as Canadian business TAXI and SMART in Australia and has been referred to as "a revolution in the ad world".

In freelance advertising, companies hold public competitions to create ads for their product, the best one of which is chosen for widespread distribution with a prize given to the winners. During the 2007 Super Bowl, PepsiCo held such a contest for the creation of a 30-second television ad for the Doritos brand of chips, offering a cash prize to the winner. Chevrolet held a similar competition for their Tahoe line of SUVs. This type of advertising, however, is still in its infancy. It may ultimately decrease the importance of advertising agencies by creating a niche for independent freelancers. Advertising education has become widely popular with bachelor, master and doctorate degrees becoming available in the emphasis.

A surge in advertising interest is typically attributed to the strong relationship advertising plays in cultural and technological changes, such as the advance of online social networking. A unique model for teaching advertising is the student-run advertising agency, where advertising students create campaigns for real companies. Organizations such as American Advertising Federation and AdU Network partner established companies with students to create these campaigns.

ADVERTISING RESEARCH

Advertising research is a specialized form of research that works to improve the effectiveness and efficiency of advertising. It entails numerous forms of research which employ different methodologies.

Advertising research includes pre-testing (also known as copy testing) and post-testing of ads and/or campaigns—pre-testing is done before an ad airs to gauge how well it will perform and post-testing is done after an ad airs to determine the in-market impact of the ad or campaign on the consumer. Continuous ad tracking and the Communicus System are competing examples of post-testing advertising research types.

4

Television Advertisement

A television advertisement or television commercial – often just commercial or TV ad (US), or advert or ad (UK/US), or ad-film (India) – is a span of television programming produced and paid for by an organization that conveys a message. Advertisement revenue provides a significant portion of the funding for most privately owned television networks.

The vast majority of television advertisements today consist of brief advertising spots, ranging in length from a few seconds to several minutes (as well as programme-length infomercials). Advertisements of this sort have been used to sell every product imaginable over the years, from goods and services to political campaigns. The effect of television advertisements upon the viewing public has been so successful and so pervasive that in some countries, the United States in particular, it is considered impossible for a politician to wage a successful election campaign without the purchase of television advertising.

In other countries, such as France, political advertising in television is strictly restricted, and some, like Norway, even completely ban it.The USA's first television advertisement was broadcast July 1, 1941.

The watchmaker Bulova paid $4 for a placement on New York station WNBT before a baseball game between the Brooklyn Dodgers and Philadelphia Phillies. The 10-second spot displayed a picture of a clock superimposed on a map of the United States, accompanied by the voice-over "America runs on Bulova time." The first TV ad broadcast in the UK was on ITV on 21 September 1955, advertising Gibbs S.R Toothpaste

CHARACTERISTICS

Many television advertisements feature catchy jingles (songs or melodies) or catch-phrases (slogan) that generate sustained appeal, which may remain in the minds of television viewers long after the span of the advertising campaign. Some of these ad jingles or catch-phrases may take on lives of their own, spawning gags or "riffs" that may appear in other forms of media, such as comedy movies or television variety shows, or in written media, such as magazine comics or literature. These long-lasting advertising elements may therefore be said to have taken a place in the pop culture history of the demographic to which they have appeared. One such example is the enduring phrase, "Winston tastes good like a cigarette should," from the eighteen-year advertising campaign for Winston cigarettes from the 1950s to the 1970s. Variations of this catchy dialogue and direct references to it appeared even as long as two decades after the ad campaign expired.

Another is, "Where's the Beef?", which grew so popular that it was used in the 1984 presidential election by Walter Mondale. And yet another popular catch-phrase is "I've fallen and I can't get up", which still appears occasionally, decades after its first use. Advertising agencies often use humor as a tool in their creative marketing campaigns. In fact, many psychological studies have attempted to demonstrate the effects of humour and their relationship to empowering advertising persuasion. Animation is often used in advertisements. The pictures can vary from hand-drawn traditional animation to computer animation. By using animated characters, an advertisement may have a certain appeal that is difficult to achieve with actors or mere product displays.

For this reason, an animated advertisement (or a series of such advertisements) can be very long-running, several decades in many instances. A notable example is the series of advertisements for Kellogg's cereals, starring Snap, Crackle and Pop. The animation is often combined with real actors.

Other long-running ad campaigns catch people by surprise, or even tricking the viewer, such as the Energizer Bunny advertisement series. It started in the late 1980s as a simple comparison advertisement, where a room full of battery-operated bunnies was seen pounding their drums, all slowing down...except one, with the Energizer battery. Years later, a revised version of this seminal advertisement had the Energizer bunny escaping the stage and moving on (according to the announcer, he "keeps going and going and going..."). This was followed by what appeared to be another advertisement: viewers were oblivious to the fact that the following "advertisement" was actually a parody of other well-known advertisements until the Energizer bunny suddenly intrudes on the situation, with the announcer saying "Still going..." (the Energizer Battery Company's way of emphasizing that their battery lasts longer than other leading batteries). This ad campaign lasted for nearly fifteen years. The Energizer Bunny series has itself been imitated by others, via a Coors Light Beer advertisement, in motion pictures, and even by current advertisements by Geico Insurance.

TV ADVERTISEMENTS AROUND THE WORLD

UNITED STATES OF AMERICA

Frequency

Television advertisements appear between shows, but also interrupt them at intervals. This method of screening advertisements is intended to capture or grab the attention of the audience, keeping the viewers focused on the television show so that they will not want to change the channel; instead, they will (hopefully) watch the advertisements while waiting for the next segment of the show. However, remote controls have now made it easier for audiences to "tune out" advertisements simply by allowing them to turn down the volume or even switch channels when the advertisement comes on.

Also people tend to do other things while the advertisements are on, while waiting for the programme to resume. Additionally, television recording mechanisms such as DVR and TiVo have also allowed viewers to skip advertising completely during television programming. Entire industries exist that focus solely on the task of keeping the viewing audience interested enough to sit through advertisements. The Nielsen ratings system exists as a way for stations to determine how successful their television shows are, so that they can decide what rates to charge advertisers for their advertisements. Advertisements take airtime away from programs. In the 1960s a typical hour-long American show would run for 51 minutes excluding advertisements.

Today, a similar programme would only be 42 minutes long; a typical 30-minute block of time now includes 22 minutes of programming with 6 minutes of national advertising and 2 minutes of local. In other words, over the courses of 10 hours, American viewers will see approximately 3 hours of advertisements, twice what they would have seen in the sixties.

Furthermore, if that sixties show is rerun today it may be cut by 9 minutes to make room for the extra advertisements (some modern showings of Star Trek exhibit this). In more recent years, that number has grown by an average of 2 minutes. This is due in large part to the economic recession that has hit broadcast television programming especially. In the 1950s and 1960s, the average advertisement's length was one minute. As the years passed, the average length shrank to 30 seconds (and often 10 seconds, depending on the television station's purchase of ad time), but more of them are now shown during the break, while in the '60's, only one or two advertisements would be shown at each break. However, today a majority of advertisements run in 15-second incre-ments (often known as "hooks"). TV advertisements are identified by an ISCI code.

POPULARITY

In the United States, the TV advertisement is generally considered the most effective mass-market advertising format, and this is reflected by the high prices TV networks charge for commercial airtime during popular TV events. The annual Super Bowl American football game is known as much for its commercial advertisements as for the game itself, and the average cost of a single 30-second TV spot during this game (seen by 90 million viewers) has reached US$2.7 million (as of February 2008).

In general, advertisers covet the 18-49 age demographic; older viewers are of almost no interest to most advertisers. The number of viewers within the target demographic is more important to ad revenues than total viewers. According to *Advertising Age*, during the 2007-08 season, *Grey's Anatomy* was able to charge $419,000 per advertisement, compared to only $248,000 for an advertisement during *CSI*, despite CSI having almost five million more viewers on average.

Due to its demo strength, *Friends* was able to charge almost three times for an advertisement as *Murder, She Wrote*, even though the two series had similar total viewer numbers during the seasons they were on the air together. Broadcast networks are concerned by the increasing use of DVRs by young viewers, resulting in aging of the live viewing audience and consequently, lower ad rates. Also TV advertisers may also target certain audiences of the population such as certain races, income level, and gender. In recent years, shows that tend to target young women tend to be more profitable for advertisements than shows targeted to younger men, this is due to the fact that younger men are watching TV less than their female counterparts.

Because a single television advertisement can be broadcast repeatedly over the course of weeks, months, and even years (the Tootsie Roll company has been broadcasting a famous advertisement that asks "How many licks does it take to get to the tootsie centre of a Tootsie Pop?" for over three decades), television advertisement production studios often spend enormous sums of money in the production of one single thirty-second television spot.

This vast expenditure has resulted in a number of high-quality advertisements, ones which boast of the best production values, the latest in special effects technology, the most popular personalities, and the best music. A number of television advertisements are so elaborately produced that they can be considered miniature thirty-second movies; indeed, many film directors have directed television advertisements both as a way to gain exposure and to earn a paycheck. One of film director Ridley Scott's most famous cinematic moments was a television advertisement he directed for the Apple Macintosh computer, that was broadcast in 1984. Even though this advertisement was broadcast only once (aside from occasional appearances in television advertisement compilation specials and one 1 a.m. airing a month before the Super Bowl so that the advertisement could be submitted to award ceremonies for that year), it has become famous and well-known, to the point where it is considered a classic television moment.

Despite the popularity of some advertisements, many consider them to be an annoyance for a number of reasons. The main reason may be that the sound volume of advertisements tends to be higher (and in some cases much higher) than that of regular programming.

The increasing number of advertisements, as well as overplaying of the same advertisement, are secondary annoyance factors. A third might be that television is currently the main medium to advertise, prompting ad campaigns by everyone from cell-phone companies, political campaigns, fast food restaurants, to local businesses, and small businesses, prompting longer commercial breaks. Finally, another reason is that advertisements often cut into certain parts in the regular programming that are either climaxes of the plot or a major turning point in the show, which many people find exciting or entertaining to watch. From a cognitive standpoint, the core reason people find advertisements annoying is that the advertisement's offer is not of interest at that moment, or the presentation is unclear. A typical viewer has seen enough advertisements to anticipate that most advertisements will be bothersome, prompting the viewer to be mercilessly selective in their viewing.

Conversely, if an advertisement strikes a chord with the viewer (such as an ad for debt relief shown to a viewer who has received a late notice in the mail), or has entertainment value beyond the basic message (such as the classic humorous spots for Wendy's "Where's the beef?" campaign), then viewers tend to stay with the advertisement, perhaps even looking forward to viewing it again.

Restrictions

Beginning on January 2, 1971, advertisements featuring cigarettes have been banned from American TV. Advertisements for alcohol products are allowed, but the consumption of any alcohol product is not allowed in a television advertisement. Since the late 1990s TV advertisements have become far more diverse, and in addition household products and foods that are not new are no longer generally advertised as they were in the mid to late 20th century. Also subliminal messaging has been banned.

Advertisements also as Programming

Since the 1960s, media critics have claimed that the boundaries between "programming" and "advertisements" have been eroded to the point where the line is blurred nearly as much as it was during the beginnings of the medium, when television shows were sponsored by corporations.

For much of the 1970s, '80s, and '90s, the FCC imposed a rule requiring networks that broadcast programming on Saturday morning and Sunday nights at 7 PM/6 PM Central air bumpers ("We'll return after these messages...", "...now back to our programming" and variations thereof) to help younger audiences distinguish programs from advertisements. The only programs that were exempt from this rule were news shows and information shows relating to news (such as *60 Minutes*). Conditions on children's programming have eased a bit since the period of the 1970s and 1980s.

Europe

In many European countries television advertisements appear in longer, but less frequent advertising breaks. For example, instead of 3 minutes every 8 minutes, there might be around 6 minutes every half hour. European Union legislation limits the time taken by commercial breaks to 12 minutes per hour (20%), with a minimum segment length of 20 or 30 minutes, depending on the programme content. However, these are maximum limits and so specific regulations differ widely from both within and outside the EU, and indeed from network to network. Unlike in the United States, in Europe the advertising agency name may appear at the beginning or at the end of the advert.

United Kingdom

In the UK, the British Broadcasting Corporation (BBC) is funded by a licence fee and does not screen adverts. On the commercial channels, the amount of airtime allowed by the UK broadcasting regulator Ofcom for advertising is an overall average of 7 minutes per hour, with limits of 12 minutes for any particular clock hour (8 minutes per hour between 6pm and 11pm). With 42-minute American exports to Britain, such as *Lost*, being given a one hour slot, nearly one third of the slot is taken up by adverts or trailers for other programmes. Live imported tv programmes such as WWE Raw show promotional material that is shown in place of US advert breaks. Infomercials (known as "admags") were originally a feature of the main commercial channel ITV when it was launched in 1955 but were banned in 1963.

The first advert to be shown in the UK was an advert for S.R. Toothpaste in 1955. Freeview has provided a cheap entry level alternative to satellite and cable subscription services and has taken the penetration of digital television to well over 80%. The growth of multi-channel television has changed the face of TV advertising making the medium effective for companies with niche products and a targeted audience. 30-second advertisements on digital channels such as Sky News, MTV or E4 can be bought for less than £50000 and adverts on more targeted channels like the Business Channel, Motors TV or Real Estate TV for less than £500 per 30 seconds. New TV channels are launching every week in the UK and advertising opportunities are plentiful.

In 2008, Ofcom announced a Review of television advertising and teleshopping regulation, with a view to possibly changing their code, *Rules on the Amount and Distribution of Advertising* (RADA), which regulates the duration, frequency and restriction of adverts on television.

Germany

As in Britain, in Germany, public television stations own a major share of the market. Their programming is funded by a licence fee as well as advertisements on specific hours of the day (5 p.m. to 8 p.m.), except on Sundays and holidays. Private stations are allowed to show up to 12 minutes of ads per hour with a minimum of 20 minutes of programming in between interruptions.

Ireland

In the Republic of Ireland, the Broadcasting Commission of Ireland allows up to a maximum of 10 minutes of advertising minutage per hour for all broadcasters. Regarding overall advertising minutes there is a difference between the public funded TV broadcasters and commercial TV broadcasters. Broadcasters funded by a television licence fee, RTÉ and TG4, are permitted to allocate 10% of their broadcast minutage to advertising.

Commercial broadcasters, TV3 and 3e (formerly Channel 6) and Setanta Ireland are permitted a maximum of 15% advertising time vs. overall broadcast time. This effectively gives an average of either 6 minutes or 9 minutes an hour depending on the type of broadcaster.

Finland

In Finland, there are two mainstream non-commercial channels run by the state owned broadcasting company YLE, that run advertisements only on very infrequent occasions, such as important sport events. The three main commercial channels MTV3, SubTV (a subsidiary of MTV3), and Nelonen ("Number Four" in Finnish), all run their advertisements during breaks approximately every 15 minutes.

Since digital TV has been introduced, the number of TV channels has grown, with YLE and the main broadcasters all adding new channels (including some subscription channels). Analogue broadcasts ceased in August 2007 and the nation's TV services are now exclusively digital. A typical break lasts about 4 minutes. The length of *individual* advertisements can vary from a few seconds (7, 10 and 15 are common), but nowadays they are rarely over one minute in length. Many advertisements of supranational companies are dubbed from English language advertisements. Although Swedish is the other official language of Finland, the advertisements do not feature Swedish subtitles nor are any Swedish language advertisements shown with the infrequent exception of some political advertisements at the time of elections. English language advertisements are also uncommon.

Russia

The Russian advertising break consists of 2 parts: federal adverts and regional adverts. The duration for each is 4 minutes and 15 minutes per hour respectively. The Russian government intends to decrease TV advertisements because of a drop in TV channels' ratings.

Denmark

The Danish DR-channels are funded by a television licence, so they do not show any commercials at all. The other Danish television network, TV2 shows commercials only in blocks between the programs. These can take from 2 minutes to 10 minutes depending on the time to the next show. In Denmark, commercial breaks are strictly prohibited. Channels like Kanal 5 and TV3 broadcast via satellite from the United Kingdom to be able to interrupt programs.

ASIA-PACIFIC

Malaysia

All television stations and channels, whether government-owned or private, broadcast advertisements. In Malaysia, a typical break lasts about 5 minutes, while RTM, the nation's state broadcaster, usually has shorter commercial break. There are usually two commercial breaks in a half-hour programme and three commercial breaks in an hour-long programme, with the exception of news programmes.

All television stations (except TV3, which is only used for selected sponsored programmes), broadcast commercial bumper before commercial break, but on selected programmes only. Advertisements are not allowed to be broadcast in-between programmes except in some foreign channels broadcast by Astro and before announcing the breaking of fast in the month of Ramadan.

Malaysian television advertisements were at first identified by KP/YYYY/XXXX which was first introduced in circa 1995. The KP is the abbreviation of the Ministry of Information while the YYYY is the year the advertisement produced and the XXXX is the number of the advert permit, and it was earlier was shown at the beginning or end of the advert.

Other advertising permits includes the KKLIU (Ministry of Health, the Medicine Advertising Authority) for medicinal advertisements, which was has been used before 1995 and the JIRP (Pesticide Advertising Department) for pesticide advertisements. It was also used in advertisements on newspapers and magazines. Since mid-late 2009, advertise-ments are shown with the KPKK/XXXX/YYYY, in which the KPKK is the abbreviation of the Ministry of Information, Communications and Culture and it was shown in the beginning of the advertisement. However, advertisements that use KP/YYYY/XXXX (which was broadcast prior to mid-late) is still broadcasting on television. It is common for advertisements shown on RTM and also common for some advertisements shown on Astro satellite television service and Media Prima-owned television stations, such as TV3, ntv7, 8TV and TV9.

Astro is also known to delay incoming satellite feeds for its purpose of commercial replacement, as government laws forbid advertisements produced from overseas, except those recognizing Malaysia's brands, such as Sony, Panasonic, Nokia and LG, as well as produced from within the country itself. Liquor advertisements which were shown after 10:00 pm during non-Malay programmes has been banned in the country since 1995, while cigarette advertisements have been banned from showing cigarette packaging since

1995, and complete ban since 2003. Fast-food advertisements during children's programmes are also banned in 2007. There are also restrictions on Malaysian television advertisements such as certain feminine care products and unhealthy foods which is prohibited from broadcasting during children's programmes and lottery advertising which is prohibited from broadcasting during Malay programmes. Lingerie advertisements is prohibited from broadcasting in Malaysian television, but allowed in non-Malay magazines published in Malaysia.

Malaysian television advertisements were broadcast in Malay, English and Chinese. On Astro, Tamil-language advertisements are also shown. Malay or Chinese language advertisements can also be broadcast during an English programme if the advertisement is not made in English. Non-Malay, English and Chinese programming, such as Hindi, Finnish and Korean programmes for example, during commercial break, shown commercial in Malay, English and Chinese language, respectively. TV3 has sparked some controversies to Malaysian entertainment in the recent years, with the excessive advertisement space which lead to the anger of the audience. Some of the advertisements were banned from RTM due to some problems, but the broadcast of these advertisements were allowed on Astro and Media Prima-owned television advertisement breaks.

The Philippines

In the Philippines, advertising is self-regulated by individual broadcasters. The Association of Broadcasters of the Philippines, a self-regulatory organization representing most television and radio broadcasters in the country, limit advertising to 18 minutes per hour, a move taken to help "promote public interest."

Australia

Similar to the European Union, advertising on Australian commercial television is restricted to a certain amount in a 24-hour period, but there are no restrictions on how much advertising may appear in any particular hour. Australian television generally has high advertising content. Like Canada, it is one of the few countries in the world where advertisements may appear prior to the closing credits of a programme. There are other restrictions on television advertising in Australia, such as the complete ban on advertising during programmes intended for young children. The ABC, the nation's public broadcaster, broadcasts no external advertisements, but between programmes will broadcast promotions for its own programmes and merchandise, but is restricted to approximately five minutes per hour.

New Zealand

All major New Zealand television channels, whether state-owned or private, screen advertisements, with adverts on average taking up 15 minutes of each hour. There are usually two advert breaks in a half-hour programme, and four advert breaks in an hour-long programme. Television adverts are banned on Christmas Day, Good Friday, Easter Sunday, and also on Sunday mornings before midday (although TV3 did broadcast adverts on Sunday mornings during the 2007 Rugby World Cup). Also, advertising of certain products is restricted (e.g. alcohol, unhealthy foods) or banned (e.g. tobacco).

The Advertising Standards Authority is responsible for advertisement compliance, and deals with advertisement complaints (except for election advertising, in which the Broadcasting Standards Authority is responsible.)

Korea, South

Under the current rules, terrestrial channels cannot take in-programme commercial breaks. So the commercials are usually put between the intro and the start of a programme, and between the end credits and the endcaps. Terrestrial channels often divide some longer-length films like The Ten Commandments into parts and consider each part as an individual programme. Terrestrial channels can take commercial breaks during breaks in action during sporting events.

Pay-television channels can take in-programme commercial breaks, although some pay channels schedule advertisement in the same way that terrestrial channels do. Regulations for commercials on terrestrial channels are more strict than those for pay channels. Non-South Korean channels are not subject to these regulations. Tobacco advertisements are prohibited.

USE OF POPULAR MUSIC

Prior to the 1980s music in television advertisements was generally limited to jingles and incidental music; on some occasions lyrics to a popular song would be changed to create a theme song or a jingle for a particular product. In 1971 the converse occurred when a song written for a Coca-Cola advertisement was re-recorded as the pop single "I'd Like to Teach the World to Sing" by the New Seekers, and became a hit. Some pop and rock songs were re-recorded by cover bands for use in advertisements, but the cost of licensing original recordings for this purpose remained prohibitive until the late 1980s. The use of previously-recorded popular songs in television advertisements began in earnest in 1985 when Burger King used the original recording of Aretha Franklin's song "Freeway of Love" in a television advertisement for the restaurant.

This also occurred in 1987 when Nike used the original recording of The Beatles' song "Revolution" in an advertisement for athletic shoes. Since then, many classic popular songs have been used in similar fashion. Songs can be used to concretely illustrate a point about the product being sold (such as Bob Seger's "Like a Rock" used for Chevy trucks), but more often are simply used to associate the good feelings listeners had for the song to the product on display. In some cases the original meaning of the song can be totally irrelevant or even completely opposite to the implication of the use in advertising; for example Iggy Pop's "Lust for Life", a song about heroin use addiction, has been used to advertise Royal Caribbean International, a cruise ship line. Music-licensing agreements with major artists, especially those which had not previously allowed their recordings to be used for this purpose, such as Microsoft's use of "Start Me Up" by the Rolling Stones and Apple Inc.'s use of U2's "Vertigo" became a source of publicity in themselves.

In early instances, songs were often used over the objections of the original artists, who had lost control of their music publishing the music of Beatles being perhaps the most well-known case; more recently artists have actively solicited use of their music in advertisements and songs have gained popularity and sales after being used in advertisements. Famous case is Levi's company which has used several one hit wonders in their advertisements (songs such as "Inside", "Spaceman" and "Flat Beat").

Sometimes a controversial reaction has followed the use of some particular song on an advertisement. Often the trouble has been that people do not like the idea of using songs that promote values important for them in advertisements. For example Sly and the Family Stone's anti-racism song, "Everyday People", was used in a car advertisement which caused anger among people. Generic scores for advertisements often feature clarinets, saxophones, or various strings (such as the acoustic/electric guitars and violins) as the primary instruments. In the late 1990s and early 2000s, electronica music was increasingly used as background scores for television advertisements, initially for automobiles, and later for other technological and business products such as computers and financial services.

Future of TV Advertisements

The introduction of digital video recorders (also known as digital television recorders or DTRs), such as TiVo, and services like Sky+, Dish Network and Astro MAX, which allow the recording of television programs onto a hard drive, also enable viewers to fast-forward or automatically skip through advertisements of recorded programs.

There is speculation that television advertisements are threatened by digital video recorders as viewers choose not to watch them. However evidence from the UK shows that this is so far not the case. At the end of 2008 22 per cent of UK households had a DTR. The majority of these households had Sky+ and data from these homes (collected via the SkyView panel of more than 33,000) shows that, once a household gets a DTR, they watch 17 per cent more television. 82 per cent of their viewing is to normal, linear, broadcast TV without fast-forwarding the ads. In the 18 per cent of TV viewing that is time-shifted (i.e. not watched as live broadcast), viewers still watch 30 per cent of the ads at normal speed. Overall, the extra viewing encouraged by owning a DTR results in viewers watching 2 per cent more ads at normal speed than they did before the DTR was installed.

The SkyView evidence is reinforced by studies on actual DTR behaviour by the Broadcasters' Audience Research Board (BARB) and the London Business School. Other forms of TV advertising include Product placement advertising in the TV shows themselves. For example, *Extreme Makeover: Home Edition* advertises Sears, Kenmore, and Home Depot by specifically using products from these companies, and some sports events like the Sprint Cup of NASCAR are named after sponsors, and of course, race cars are frequently covered in advertisements. Incidentally, many major sporting venues, in North America at least, are named for commercial companies, dating back as far as Wrigley Field. Television programs delivered through new mediums such as streaming online video also bring different possibilities to the traditional methods of generating revenue from television advertising.

Another type of advertisement shown more and more, mostly for advertising TV shows on the same channel, is an ad overlay at the bottom of the TV screen, which blocks out some of the picture. "Banners", or "Logo Bugs", as they are called, are referred to by media companies as Secondary Events (2E). This is done in much the same way as a severe weather warning is done, only these happen more frequently. they may sometimes take up only 5 to 10 per cent of the screen, but in the extreme, they can take up as much as 25 per cent of the viewing area.

Subtitles that are part of the programme content can be completely obscured by banners. Some even make noise or move across the screen. One example is the 2E ads for Three Moons Over Milford, which was broadcast in the months before the TV show's premiere. A video taking up approximately 25 per cent of the bottom-left portion of the screen would show a comet impacting into the moon with an accompanying explosion, during another television programme.

Google's Eric Schmidt has announced plans to enter the television ad delivery and optimization business. This is despite the fact that Google lacks an immediate video production and network placement foothold. There are few details in place about how this may occur, but some have speculated that they will use a similar model to that of their business strategy directed at radio broadcast, which included the acquisition of operations system support provider.

Online video directories are an emerging form of interactive advertising, which help in recalling and responding to advertising produced primarily for television. These directories also have the potential to offer other value-added services, such as response sheets and click-to-call, which greatly enhance the scope of the interaction with the brand. During the 2008-09 TV season, Fox experimented with a new strategy, which the network dubbed

"Remote-Free TV". Episodes of Fringe and Dollhouse contained approximately ten minutes of advertisements, four to six minutes fewer than other hour-long programs. Fox stated that shorter commercial breaks keep viewers more engaged and improve brand recall for advertisers, as well as reducing channel surfing and fast-forwarding past the ads. However, the strategy was not as successful as the network had hoped and it is unclear whether it will be continued into the next season.

5

Corporate Media

"Corporate media" is a term which refers to a system of mass media production, distribution, ownership, and funding which is dominated by corporations and their CEOs. It is owned by the capitalist imperatives of maximizing profits for investors, stockholders, and advertisers. It is sometimes used as a term of derision to indicate a media system which does not serve the public interest in place of the "mainstream media" or "MSM," which tends to be used by both the political left and the right as a derisive term.

Media critics such as Robert McChesney, Ben Bagdikian, Ralph Nader, Jim Hightower, Noam Chomsky and Amy Goodman suggest that such a media system, especially when allowed to dominate the mainstream media, inevitably will be manipulated by these same corporations to suit their own interests. These critics point out that the main national networks, NBC, CBS, and ABC, as well as most if not all of the smaller cable channels, are owned, funded, and controlled by an interconnected network of large corporate conglomerates and international banking interests, which they say manipulate and filter out news that does not fit their corporate agenda.

They also argue that the programming on these outlets clearly reflects the conservative views of its owners, most notably Fox News Channel, headed by Rupert Murdoch through his parent company News Corp., as well as Roger Ailes, the CEO of FOX News itself.

PROPAGANDA MODEL

Noam Chomsky and Edward S. Herman have established a propaganda model which purports to explain this bias. The common misinterpretation of this model is that all bias is conscious and centralized. The process however is hypothesized to be decentralized and operates as a confluence of factors that includes the overt pressure from owners and advertisers, but also by the gradual internalization of the biases and values of the corporate owners, leading to self-censorship.

Other factors include the tendency of journalists to avoid doing original research, instead obtaining news from the same few wire services, such as Reuters and Associated Press, which themselves tend to cover the same news under the same perspective. Due to the desire to reduce operation costs, the mainstream media favour news pieces that are pre-made by these news agencies instead of conducting their own reporting.

Impact of Public Relations on News and Public Affairs Programming

This same economic pressure makes media susceptible to manipulation by government and other corporate sources through the widespread use of press releases, often created by industry-funded public relations firms.

Impact of the Corporate Media Propaganda Model on World Events and Societies

The point of view and statements made by governments, officials, military, police, national security organizations (such as the FBI and CIA), as well as various other political offices are regularly reported as facts and are published without any (or very little) fact checking by the corporate media. Perhaps the most infamous current example of the impact of the propaganda model on world events and societies was during the two year period following September 11, 2001.

During this time, according to a five year in depth research project conducted by The Centre for Public Integrity; the President of the United States (George W. Bush) and seven high ranking officials in his administration made at least 935 or more false statements about the threat posed to the world and to American national security by Suddam Hussein. These false statements were virtually uncontested by the corporate media and presented as a sound rationale for both the invasion of (and war against) Iraq and "The War on Terror/ism".

The result was the "manufacturing of consent" for the invasion of Iraq and "The Global War on Terror/ism" in which hundreds of thousands of people have lost their lives to date. As an example Jessica Yellin on Anderson Cooper 360 admitted being pressured by corporate executives to present positive stories during the run up to the Iraq war.

Anderson Cooper 360 Transcript of Jessica Yellin

COOPER: Jessica, McClellan took press to task for not upholding their reputation. He writes: "The National Press Corps was probably too deferential to the White House and to the administration in regard to the most important decision facing the nation during my years in Washington, the choice over whether to go to war in Iraq.

The 'liberal media' — in quotes — didn't live up to its reputation. If it had, the country would have been better served." Dan Bartlett, former Bush adviser, called the allegation "total crap." What is your take? Did the press corps drop the ball?

Jessica yellin, cnn congressional correspondent: I wouldn't go that far. I think the press corps dropped the ball at the beginning. When the lead-up to the war began, the press corps was under enormous pressure from corporate executives, frankly, to make sure that this was a war that was presented in a way that was consistent with the patriotic fever in the nation and the president's high approval ratings.

And my own experience at the White House was that, the higher the president's approval ratings, the more pressure I had from news executives — and I was not at this network at the time — but the more pressure I had from news executives to put on positive stories about the president. I think, over time. *Cooper:* You had pressure from news executives to put on positive stories about the president?

Yellin: Not in that exact — they wouldn't say it in that way, but they would edit my pieces. They would push me in different directions. They would turn down stories that were more critical and try to put on pieces that were more positive, yes. That was my experience. Factcheck.org, created by the Annenberg school of Public Policy at the University of Pennsylvania, found hundreds of misrepresentations in political ads that were never corrected by the mainstream media. Studies also show that those who rely on the media for their information have a poor understanding of the issues and are unable to discern misrepresentations in political advertising.

As documented by authors Sheldon Rampton and John Stauber, it is becoming increasingly common for video news releases (VNR) to be created by government and corporations, mimicking TV news story-format to be used straight into broadcasting in a newscast. Other factors include the cost of litigation. Large corporations tend to sue over any news that are against their interests, causing great expense for the news editors. Even if the litigation is lost, the cost of time and pressure will certainly bias a reporter towards avoiding such possibility.

WATCHDOG JOURNALISM

Watchdog journalism is a type of investigative journalism. It refers to forms of activist journalism aimed at holding accountable public personalities and institutions whose functions impact social and political life. The term lapdog journalism is sometimes used as a conceptual opposite to watchdog journalism. Watchdog journalism is most commonly found in think tanks, alternative media, and citizen journalism such as blogs. It is occasionally found in mainstream media as well. Since independent media and think tanks are not profit-oriented, they have more latitude in which to adopt strong positions and cover a wide range of topics. However, it is also more difficult to determine the backing of non-mainstream outlets so those are sometime subject to covert exploitation by well-funded interests. In recent history, a notable example of watchdog journalism was the exposure of Dan Rather's investigative segment which cast George W. Bush's military record in an unfavorable light. The segment was based on the Killian documents, which blogger journalists exposed as being insufficiently verifiable as authentic.

ALTERNATIVE MEDIA

Alternative media are media (newspapers, radio, television, movies, Internet, etc.) which are alternatives to the business or government-owned mass media. Proponents of alternative media argue that the mainstream media are biased. While sources of alternative media can also be biased (sometimes proudly so), proponents claim that the bias is significantly different than that of the mainstream media, hence these media provide an "alternative" viewpoint. As such, advocacy journalism tends to be a component of many alternative outlets. Because the term "alternative" has connotations of self-marginalization, some media outlets now prefer the term "independent" over "alternative".

PROPAGANDA MODEL

The propaganda model is a theory advanced by Edward S. Herman and Noam Chomsky that alleges systemic biases in the mass media and seeks to explain them in terms of structural economic causes.

First presented in their 1988 book Manufacturing Consent: The Political Economy of the Mass Media, the "Propaganda model" views the private media as businesses interested in the sale of a product — readers and audiences — to other businesses (advertisers) rather than that of quality news to the public. Describing the media's "societal purpose", Chomsky writes, "... the study of institutions and how they function must be scrupulously ignored, apart from fringe elements or a relatively obscure scholarly literature". The theory postulates five general classes of "filters" that determine the type of news that is presented in news media.

These five classes are:

1. Ownership of the medium
2. Medium's funding sources
3. Sourcing
4. Flak
5. Anti-communist ideology

The first three are generally regarded by the authors as being the most important. Although the model was based mainly on the characterization of United States media, Chomsky and Herman believe the theory is equally applicable to any country that shares the basic economic structure and organizing principles which the model postulates as the cause of media biases.

THE FILTERS

Ownership

The sheer size, concentrated ownership, immense owner wealth, and profit-seeking imperative of the dominant media corporations could hardly yield any other result. It was not always thus. In the early nineteenth century, a radical British press had emerged which addressed the concerns of workers. But excessive stamp duties, designed to restrict newspaper ownership to the 'respectable' wealthy, began to change the face of the press. Nevertheless there remained a degree of diversity. In postwar Britain, radical or worker-friendly newspapers such as the Daily Herald, News Chronicle, Sunday Citizen (all since failed or absorbed into other publications) and the Daily Mirror (at least until the late 1970s) regularly published articles questioning the capitalist system.

Herman and Chomsky argue that since mainstream media outlets are either large corporations or part of conglomerates (*e.g.* Westinghouse or General Electric), the information presented to the public will be biased with respect to these interests. Such conglomerates frequently extend beyond traditional media fields, and thus have extensive financial interests that may be endangered when certain information is widely publicized. According to this reasoning, news items that most endanger the corporate financial interests of those who own the media will face the greatest bias and censorship. It then follows that if to maximize profit means sacrificing news objectivity, then the news sources that ultimately survive must be fundamentally biased, with regard to news in which they have a conflict of interest.

Funding

The second filter of the propaganda model is advertising. Most newspapers have to attract and maintain a high proportion of advertising in order to cover the costs of production; without it, they would have to increase the price of their newspaper. There is fierce competition throughout the media to attract advertisers; a newspaper which gets less advertising than its competitors is put at a serious disadvantage. Lack of success in raising advertising revenue was another factor in the demise of the 'people's newspapers' of the nineteenth and twentieth centuries.

The product is composed of the affluent readers who buy the newspaper — who also comprise the educated decision-making sector of the population — while the audience includes the businesses that pay to advertise their goods. According to this filter, the news itself is nothing more than "filler" to get privileged readers to see the advertisements which makes up the real content, and will thus take whatever form is most conducive to attracting educated decision-makers. Stories that conflict with their "buying mood", it is argued, will tend to be marginalized or excluded, along with information that presents a picture of the world that collides with advertisers' interests. The theory argues that the people buying the newspaper are themselves the product which is sold to the businesses that buy advertising space; the news itself has only a marginal role as the product.

Sourcing

The third of Herman and Chomsky's five filters relates to the sourcing of mass media news: "The mass media are drawn into a symbiotic relationship with powerful sources of information by economic necessity and reciprocity of interest." Even large media corporations such as the BBC cannot afford to place reporters everywhere. They therefore concentrate their resources where major news stories are likely to happen: the White House, the Pentagon, 10 Downing Street, and other centralised news "terminals".

Although British newspapers may occasionally complain about the "spin-doctoring" of New Labour, for example, they are in fact highly dependent upon the pronouncements of "the Prime Minister's personal spokesperson" for government-related news. Business corporations and trade organisations are also trusted sources of stories considered newsworthy. Editors and journalists who offend these powerful news sources, perhaps by questioning the veracity or bias of the furnished material, can be threatened with the denial of access to their media life-blood - fresh news. Thus, the media become reluctant to run articles that will harm corporate interests that provide them with the resources that the media depend upon.

This relationship also gives rise to a "moral division of labour", in which "officials have and give the facts," and "reporters merely get them". Journalists are then supposed to adopt an uncritical attitude that makes it possible for them to accept corporate values without experiencing cognitive dissonance.

Flak

The fourth filter is 'flak', described by Herman and Chomsky as 'negative responses to a media statement or [TV or radio] programme. It may take the form of letters, telegrams, phone calls, petitions, law-suits, speeches and Bills before Congress, and other modes of complaint, threat and punitive action'. Business organisations regularly come together to form flak machines.

Perhaps one of the most well-known of these is the US-based Global Climate Coalition (GCC) - comprising fossil fuel and automobile companies such as Exxon, Texaco and Ford. The GCC was started up by Burson-Marsteller, one of the world's largest public relations companies, to rubbish the credibility of climate scientists and 'scare stories' about global warming. For Chomsky and Herman "flak" refers to negative responses to a media statement or programme.

The term "flak" has been used to describe what Chomsky and Herman see as targeted efforts to discredit organizations or individuals who disagree with or cast doubt on the prevailing assumptions which Chomsky and Herman view as favorable to established power (*e.g.*, "The Establishment"). Unlike the first three "filtering" mechanisms — which are derived from analysis of market mechanisms — flak is characterized by concerted and intentional efforts to manage public information.

Anti-ideologies; Substitutes for Anti-communism

The fifth and final news filter that Herman and Chomsky identified was 'anti-communism'. *Manufacturing Consent* was written during the Cold War. A more apt version of this filter is the customary western identification of 'the enemy' or an 'evil dictator' - Colonel Gaddafi, Saddam Hussein, or Slobodan Milosevic (recall the British tabloid headlines of 'Smash Saddam!' and 'Clobba Slobba!'.

The same extends to mainstream reporting of environmentalists as 'eco-terrorists'. *The Sunday Times* ran a series of articles in 1999 accusing activists from the non-violent direct action group Reclaim The Streets of stocking up on CS gas and stun guns.

Anti-ideologies exploit public fear and hatred of groups that pose a potential threat, either real, exaggerated, or imagined. Communism once posed the primary threat according to the model. Communism and socialism were portrayed by their detractors as endangering freedoms of speech, movement, the press, *etc.* They argue that such a portrayal was often used as a means to silence voices critical of elite interests.

Empirical Support

Following the theoretical exposition of the propaganda model, Manufacturing Consent contains a large section where the authors seek to test their hypotheses. If the propaganda model is right and the filters do influence media content, a particular form of bias would be expected — one that systematically favors corporate interests.

They also looked at what they perceived as naturally-occurring "historical control groups" where two events, similar in their relevant properties but differing in the expected media attitude towards them, are contrasted using objective measures such as coverage of key events (measured in column inches) or editorials favoring a particular issue (measured in number).

Finally, the authors examine what points of view they believe are expressed in the media. In one case, the authors examined over fifty of Stephen Kinzer's articles about Nicaragua in the New York Times. They criticize Kinzer for failing to quote a single person in Nicaragua who is pro-Sandinista and contrast this with independent polls reporting only 9% support for all the opposition parties taken together. Chomsky states

"The polls show that all of the opposition parties in Nicaragua combined had the support of only 9 per cent of the population, but they have 100 per cent of Stephen Kinzer. Based on this example and select others, the authors argue that such a persistent bias can only be explained by a model like the one they advocate.

APPLICATIONS

Since the publication of Manufacturing Consent, both Herman and

Chomsky have adopted the theory and have given it a prominent role in their writings, lectures, and theoretical frameworks. Chomsky, in particular, has made extensive use of its explanative power to lend support to his own interpretations of mainstream media attitudes towards a wide array of events, including the following:

- Panama invasion (1989)
- Gulf War (1990)
- Iraq invasion (2003)
- *Ethanol as fuel*: energy balance, impact on world food prices and allegations of amazon rainforest depletion (2008)

Herman, seeking to build upon a more institutionalized framework to analyse mainstream media functioning, joined the media watchdog group Fairness and Accuracy in Reporting (FAIR), which has since 1986 attempted to expose media bias through critique, documentation, and statistical analysis. With the emergence of the World Wide Web as a cheap and potentially wide-ranging means of communication, a number of independent websites have surfaced which adopt the propaganda model to subject media to close scrutiny. Several examples of these are, Free Press, FAIR and Media Lens, a British-based site authored by David Edwards and David Cromwell.

In May, 2007, both Chomsky and Herman spoke at the University of Windsor in Canada summarizing developments and responding to criticisms related to the model. Both authors stated they felt the propaganda model is still applicable today (Herman said even more so than when it was originally introduced), although they did suggest a few areas where they believe it falls short and needs to be extended in light of recent developments.

Chomsky has commented in the "ChomskyChat Forum" on the applicability of the Propaganda Model to the media environment of other countries: "That's only rarely been done in any systematic way. There is work on the British media, by a good University of Glasgow media group. And interesting work on British Central America coverage by Mark Curtis in his book Ambiguities of Power. There is work on France, done in Belgium mostly, also a recent book by Serge Halimi (editor of Le Monde diplomatique). There is one very careful study by a Dutch graduate student, applying the methods Ed Herman used in studying US media reaction to elections (El Salvador, Nicaragua) to 14 major European newspapers.

CRITICISM

Inroads: A Journal of Opinion

Gareth Morley argues in an article in *Inroads: A Journal of Opinion* that widespread coverage of Israeli mistreatment of protesters as compared with little coverage of similar (or much worse) events in sub-Saharan Africa is poorly explained. Chomsky responded that when testing a model, examples should be carefully paired to avoid reasons for discrepancies not related to political bias. For instance, general coverage of the two areas compared should be similar. In this case, according to Chomsky, they are not: news from Israel (in any form) is far more common than news from sub-Saharan Africa.

New York Times Review

Historian Walter LaFeber criticized the book *Manufacturing Consent* for overstating its case, in particular with regards to reporting on Nicaragua, and not adequately explaining how a powerful propaganda system would let military aid to the Contra rebels be blocked. Herman responded in a letter by stating that the system was not "all powerful" and that LaFaber did not address their main point regarding Nicaragua. LaFaber replied that:

Mr. Herman wants to have it both ways: to claim that leading American journals "mobilize bias," but object when I cite crucial examples that weaken the book's thesis. If the news media are so unqualifiedly bad, the book should at least explain why so many publications (including my own) can cite their stories to attack President Reagan's Central American policy.

MEDIA LENS

Media Lens is a media analysis website based in the United Kingdom. It was established in 2001 to highlight what its founders consider to be "serious examples of bias, omission or deception in British mainstream media", with a primary emphasis on media intended to be impartial (BBC, Channel 4 News) or generally thought of as liberal (*The Guardian, The Independent*), and to encourage members of the public to challenge the relevant journalist, editor, newspaper or broadcaster. It is run by editors David Cromwell and David Edwards. The editors encourage polite and constructive engagement with journalists and discourage abusive emails. The website is maintained by webmaster Oliver Maw, and is financed through voluntary subscription and donations from grant-funding bodies.

The Media Lens editors have collaborated on two books, Guardians of Power: The Myth of the Liberal Media and Newspeak in the 21st Century. In 2007, Media Lens was awarded the Gandhi International Peace Award. The award was presented by Denis Halliday, former United Nations Humanitarian Co-ordinator in Iraq, and himself a recipient of the award in 2003.

Criticism of Media Lens

Media Lens has been criticised by Peter Beaumont, foreign affairs editor of The Observer, as "controlling Politburo lefties who insist that the only acceptable version of the truth is theirs alone and that everybody else should march to the same step and sing the same (old party) song". Beaumont states the Media Lens does not engage in dialogue with the targets of their criticism, but rather exploits the media to create a virtual soap box for their views.

Beaumont accused the group of a campaign intended to silence John Sloboda and his Iraq Body Count project, because it produced a victim count lower than the academic surveys on the casualties during the Iraq War published in the The Lancet by academics from Johns Hopkins Bloomberg School of Public Health.

Media Lens and its methods have been regularly criticised by The Times commentator Oliver Kamm, who described the organisation as "a shrill group of malcontents who exploit the patience of practising journalists", and its practices as "pernicious and anti-journalistic". Kamm took issue with their criticism of a review of the film Flags of Our Fathers, published by The Independent. Kamm challenged Media Lens' editors' knowledge of source material relevant to the US atomic bombings of Hiroshima and Nagasaki and claimed this was "a subject wholly outwith Cromwell's competence." David Cromwell wrote further on the debate in January 2008.

Praise of Media Lens

- Peter Barron former Editor of the BBC's *Newsnight* and currently Head of PR in Europe for Google: "Another organisation that tries to influence our [*Newsnight's*] running orders is Medialens... In fact I rather like them. David Cromwell and David Edwards, who run the site, are unfailingly polite, their points are well-argued and sometimes they're plain right."
- Noam Chomsky, Professor Emeritus of Linguistics at the Massachusetts Institute of Technology: "Regular critical analysis of the media, filling crucial gaps and correcting the distortions of ideological prisms, has never been more important. Media Lens has performed a major public service by carrying out this task with energy, insight, and care."
- Edward S. Herman, Professor Emeritus of Finance at the Wharton School of the University of Pennsylvania: "Media Lens is doing an outstanding job of pressing the mainstream media to at least follow their own stated principles and meet their public service obligations."
- John Pilger, journalist and film-maker: "The creators of Media Lens, David Edwards and David Cromwell, assisted by their webmaster, Olly Maw, have had such an extraordinary influence since they set up the site in 2001 that, without their meticulous and humane analysis, the full gravity of the debacles of Iraq and Afghanistan might have been consigned to bad journalism's first draft of bad history."

INDEPENDENT MEDIA CENTRE

The Independent Media Centre (aka Indymedia or IMC) is a global participatory network of journalists that report on political and social issues.

It originated during the anti-WTO protests worldwide in 1999 and remains closely associated with the global justice movement, which criticizes neo-liberalism and its associated institutions. Indymedia uses an open publishing and democratic media process that allows anybody to contribute. According to its homepage, "Indymedia is a collective of independent media organizations and hundreds of journalists offering grassroots, non-corporate coverage.

Indymedia is a democratic media outlet for the creation of radical, accurate, and passionate tellings of truth." Indymedia was founded as an alternative to government and corporate media, and seeks to facilitate people being able to publish their media as directly as possible.

The first Indymedia project was started in late November 1999 to report on protests against the WTO meeting that took place in Seattle, Washington, and to act as an alternative media source. This followed a successful experiment in June that year, reporting the events of the Carnival Against Capitalism in London, UK. The Media team there used software and unmediated reports from protest participants. The open publishing script was first developed by video activists in Sydney, Australia.

After Seattle the idea and network spread rapidly. By 2002, there were 89 Indymedia websites covering 31 countries (and the Palestinian territories), growing to over 150 by January 2006. Indymedia websites publish in a number of languages, including English, Spanish, German, Italian, Portuguese, French, Russian, Arabic and Hebrew.

IMC collectives distribute print, audio, photo, and video media, but are most well known for their open publishing newswires, sites where anyone with internet access can publish news from their own perspective. The content of an IMC is determined by its participants, both the users who post content, and members of the local Indymedia collective who administer the site.

While Indymedias worldwide are run autonomously and differ according to the concerns of their users, they share a commitment to provide copyleft content. The general rule is that content on Indymedia sites can be freely reproduced for non-commercial purposes. Indymedia sites run on a number of free software platforms, many developed especially for the purpose; these include DadaIMC, Mir, Oscait, Active, SF-Active, Activismo, Drupal and Plone.

CONTENT AND FOCUS

The origins of IMCs themselves came out of protests against the concentrated ownership and perceived biases in corporate media reporting. The first IMC node, attached as it was to the Seattle anti-corporate globalization protests, was seen by activists as an alternative news source to that of the corporate media, which they accused of only showing violence and confrontation, and portraying all protesters negatively.

As a result, between 1999 and 2001, IMC newswires tended to be focused on up-to-the-minute coverage of protests, from local demonstrations to summits where anti-globalization movement protests were occurring. In 2007, this was still the case, but some IMCs are attempting to broaden their coverage to include more of what "traditional" journalism ignores.

Print Projects

There have been a number of print-based projects under the Indymedia banner, including short-run papers and longer-running newspapers. New York City IMC has produced The Indypendent, a bi-weekly "free paper for free people" for over five years. Winner of numerous awards from the Independent Press Association for original writing, photography, design and art, the Indypendent is currently the most widely circulated underground paper in North America.

During the 2004 Republican National Convention in New York City, the Indypendent printed hundreds of thousands of copies and briefly attained a mass circulation. Contentious issues have included consistent editorial practices, commercial advertising and a diversity of perspectives rare among radical publications. Short-run papers for protests have included the Unconvention during the Philadelphia "R2K" protests during the Republican National Convention in 2000. Other newspapers include the Bay Area's Fault Lines, and papers in Connecticut, Maine, Baltimore and St. Louis in the United States, as well as in Wellington, New Zealand.

Radio projects: They have a global radio project, which aggregates audio RSS feeds from around the world.

Video project: They produce a regular DVD magazine, called newsreal. As well as the American one there is a European one and an Australian one. Some of their footage has been used in evidence in several court cases, eg Genoa.

ORGANIZATIONAL STRUCTURE

Local

Local IMC collectives are expected to be open and inclusive of individuals from a variety of different local anti-capitalist points of view, whether or not these have any definite political philosophy, so that even those without internet access can participate in both content creation and in content consumption.

Editorial policies, locally chosen by any Indymedia collective, generally involve removing articles which the Indymedia editors believe promote racism, sexism, hate speech, and homophobia. All Indymedia collectives are expected to have a locally chosen, thoroughly discussed and clearly stated editorial policy for posts to their website.

Global

The overall Indymedia network is decentralized to the extent that the local IMCs operate independently once they are authenticated into the IMC network. The process of admission into the IMC network is somewhat centralized but is relatively relaxed and transparent compared to the occasionally contentious disputes within local IMCs and has not generated a great deal of criticism.

Local IMC collectives vary widely in their openness, editorial policies and tolerance of different viewpoints. Along with the locally-organised collectives are IMC websites dealing with particular topics (such as biotechnology) or for different media (such as video). Along with contributing their own media, core organizers maintain IMC's open publishing infrastructure, enabling different people throughout the internet to publish their news. IMC editing is done by a system of layered admin which contributors apply to join for each site, by participating on open email lists and attending open meetings.

As an example of different models for collective internal organizing, the DC IMC (one of the older IMCs in the network) became a Coop with dues with a workshop/office, now closed. In contrast, other IMC local collectives are without any formally-defined membership and have minimal organizational structure. Some IMC memberships require its members to sign a mission statement – not every IMC has a formalized policy. Some collectives do ban members for repeated rules violations. Some feel that membership includes only those actively doing organizing or other IMC work, while some feel that it actually extends to every IMC contributor.

Funding

IMCs tend to be funded solely by donations of money and equipment from individuals. In maintaining its independence and anti-corporate stance, Indymedia has had struggles with funding issues.

For example, in September 2002, the Ford Foundation proposed funding for an Indymedia regional meeting. This was ultimately refused because many volunteers, especially some from IMC Argentina, were uncomfortable with accepting money from the Foundation, which some believe to be linked to the CIA.

REPUTATION

Indymedia has a variable reputation, both among its users and outside critics. While some criticize Indymedia for adopting a position hostile to the interests of capital, others believe that this is the purpose of the media.

Still others believe that its editorial policy on feature selection and hiding or deletion of articles is overly biased in certain topic areas, such as the Israeli-Palestinian conflict. Some critics argue that since anyone can publish with little to no editorial process, unsubstantiated allegations and conspiracy theories are often published as fact, along with inaccurate articles and content that can offend.In its favour, others argue Indymedia is a viable or preferable alternative to corporate media.

Its operations are conducted by activists around the world, who, though they may be lacking in journalistic training and corporate funding, tend to make up for this with enthusiasm for reporting issues of social justice and unique related events, which in their view, the corporate media under-reports or censors. For example, the Bolivian Gas War in 2003 was virtually unheard of in the US media, while it received extensive worldwide and multilingual reporting through Indymedia. Another example is the February 15, 2003 anti-war protest in many US and European cities, which received detailed coverage written by its participants. While Indymedia has global aspirations, the vast majority of IMCs are in North America, Latin America and Europe. Although the Middle East is an area of considerable interest to Indymedia, there are only three IMCs in the region, located in Beirut, Lebanon; Cyprus and Israel, although there was a Palestine IMC in Jerusalem between 2001 and 2003. The Lebanon centre is one of three IMCs in Muslim nations; the other two are in Jakarta, Indonesia and Istanbul, Turkey.

Temporary Removal from Google News searches

In early May 2003, after receiving numerous complaints about newswire stories that referred to the Israeli military (IDF) as "Zionazi forces" or to Israelis as "Zionazis", Google temporarily stopped including some IMCs in Google News searches (many non-English IMCs remained in the search).

Google News described the term "Zionazi" as a "degrading, hateful slur" and refused to index the Bay Area IMC because it had appeared there; SF Bay Area Indymedia agreed that it "could be considered hate speech". This spawned a petition which sought to promise that content the Indymedia community finds offensive will be moderated from the front page as a matter of editorial policy. IMCs were still included in normal Google web searches.

CONTROVERSY AND CRITICISM

Hate Speech

Open publishing has left some IMCs in Europe vulnerable to legal action or threats of legal action related to questions of libel or hate speech. In some such cases, local IMC collectives took autonomous decisions to temporarily suspend the site while the different activist groups reorganized to find a consensual, constructive method of dealing with these problems and to increase openness and non-authoritarian organizing methods.

FBI Investigation

In March 2006, the Los Angeles Times alleged that Indymedia had appeared with Food Not Bombs and the Communist Party of Texas on an FBI terrorist watchlist, revealed at a presentation at the University of Texas School of Law. A reference to the 2005 IndyConference was made at the same presentation.

Editorial Policy

Although attempts have been made to formalize global editorial standards, the autonomous and independent nature of Indymedia has meant that many IMCs prefer their own local policies. As a result, many deal with similar issues and complaints, particularly around matters of distinguishing between criticism and hateful comments ("hate speech"); and the criteria for selecting issues and authors for the websites' "featured articles". While freedom of speech is valued by Indymedia collectives, it is rarely the overriding principle guiding editorial policy.

Many IMCs now routinely remove from the front page "newswire" articles copied from corporate-run or state-run press sources. This policy (where implemented) is intended by those IMCs to keep Indymedia as an independent news source, rather than a blog of articles from existing news sources. There is generally an editorial electronic mailing list, to which questions and complaints may be directed.

SERVERS SEIZURES

Seizure of Servers by the FBI

On October 7, 2004, the FBI took possession of several server hard drives used by a number of IMCs and hosted by US-based Rackspace Managed Hosting. The servers in question were located in the United Kingdom and managed by the British arm of Rackspace, but some 20 mainly European IMC websites were affected, and several unrelated websites were affected (including the website of a Linux distribution). No reasons were given at first by the FBI and Rackspace for the seizure, in particular IMC was not informed.

Rackspace claimed that it was banned from giving further information about the incident. Some (but not all) of the legal documents relating to the confiscation of the servers were unsealed by a Texas district court in August 2005, following legal action by the Electronic Frontier Foundation.

The documents revealed that the government never officially demanded the computer servers—the subpoena to Rackspace only requested server log files. This contradicted previous statements by the web host that it took the servers offline because the government had demanded the hardware. Thus, it is unclear whether it is correct to say the servers were seized by the FBI.

The documents also contradicted Rackspace's claim that it had been ordered by the court not to discuss publicly the government's demand. The seized servers were returned on October 13, 2004.

A statement by Rackspace stated that the company had been forced to comply with a court order under the procedures laid out by the Mutual Legal Assistance Treaty, which governs international police co-operation on "international terrorism, kidnapping and money laundering". The investigation that led to the court order was said to have arisen outside of the U.S. Rackspace stated that they were prohibited on giving further detail. Agence France-Presse reported FBI spokesman Joe Parris, who said the incident was not an FBI operation, but that the subpoena had been issued at the request of the Italian and the Swiss governments. Again, no further details on specific allegations were given. UK involvement was denied in an answer given to a parliamentary question posed by Richard Allan, Liberal Democrat MP.

Indymedia pointed out that they were not contacted by the FBI and that no specific information was released on the reasons of seizing the servers. Indymedia also sees the incident in the context of "numerous attacks on independent media by the US Federal Government", including a subpoena to obtain IP logs from Indymedia at the occasion of the Republican National Conference, the shut-down of several community radio stations in the US by the FCC, and a request by the FBI to remove a post on Nantes IMC containing a photograph of alleged undercover Swiss police.

The move was condemned by the International Federation of Journalists, who stated that "The way this has been done smacks more of intimidation of legitimate journalistic inquiry than crime-busting" and called for an investigation. Criticism was also voiced by European civil liberties organisation Statewatch and the World Association of Community Radio Broadcasters (AMARC).

In Italy, the federal prosecutor of Bologna Marina Plazzi confirmed that an investigation against Indymedia had been opened because of suspected "support of terrorism", in the context of Italian troops in the Iraqi city of Nasiriyah. The Italian minister of justice, Roberto Castelli, has refused further details. In November 2003, 17 members of parliament belonging to the right-wing Alleanza Nazionale, including Alessandra Mussolini demanded that Indymedia be shut down. A senior AN member and government official had announced the co-operation with US authorities (AN was a member of the Italian coalition government), and AN spokesman Mario Landolfi welcomed the FBI's seizure of the Indymedia servers. Left-wing Italian politicians denounced the move and called for an investigation.

Bristol Server Seizure

Not long after the Rackspace affair another server in the UK was seized by police in June 2005. An anonymous post on the Bristol Indymedia server, came to police attention for suggesting an "action" against a freight train carrying new cars as part of a protest against cars and climate change in the run up to that year's Gleneagles G8 summit. The police claimed that the poster broke the law by "incitement to criminal damage", and sought access logs from the server operators. Despite being warned by lawyers that the servers were "journalistic equipment" and subject to special laws, the police proceeded with the seizure and a member of the Bristol Indymedia group was arrested. Indymedia was supported in this matter by the National Union of Journalists, Liberty and Privacy International, along with others. This incident ended several months later with no charges being brought by the police and the equipment returned.

Other legal actions - IMC UK

In 2005, Indymedia UK was threatened with a libel action by the US arms company EDO Corporation, for publishing articles accusing their UK branch EDO (UK) of EDO MBM Technology Ltd (who supply the US, UK, and Israel armed forces) of being 'warmongers'. Their lawyers ultimately withdrew the writ. EDO MBM then launched a further High Court lawsuit against the protest group Smash EDO in April 2005, under anti-stalker laws, presenting as evidence articles that had been posted anonymously on Indymedia UK. Although a controversial interim injunction was imposed on this evidence, the suit collapsed without reaching a trial in early 2006.

Other Legal Actions - IMC US

On January 30, 2009, one of the system administrators of the server that hosts indymedia.us received a grand jury subpoena from the Southern District of Indiana federal court. The subpoena asked the administrator to provide all "IP addresses, times, and any other identifying information" for every visitor to the site on June 25, 2008. The subpoena also included a gag order that stated that the recipient is "not to disclose the existence of this request unless authorized by the Assistant U.S. Attorney." The administrator of indymedia.us could not have provided the information because Indymedia sites generally do not keep IP address logs. The Electronic Frontier Foundation determined that there was no legal basis for the gag order, and that the subpoena request "violated the SCA's restrictions on what types of data the government could obtain using a subpoena." Under Justice Department guidelines, subpoenas to news media must have the authorization of the attorney general. According to a CBS News blog, the subpoena of indymedia.us was never submitted for review by the attorney general. On February 25, 2009, a United States Attorney sent a letter to an attorney with the Electronic Frontier Foundation stating that the subpoena had been withdrawn.

ASSAULTS ON JOURNALISTS

On August 15, 2000, The Los Angeles Police Department temporarily shut down the satellite uplink and production studio of the Los Angeles Independent Media Centre on its first night of Democratic National

Convention coverage, claiming explosives were in a van in the adjacent parking lot. No explosives were ever found. In July, 2001 at the 27th G8 summit in Genoa, Indymedia journalists claim to have been seriously assaulted at the Diaz school where Indymedia had set up a temporary journalism centre and radio station. In an ongoing trial, twenty-nine Italian police officers were indicted for grievous bodily harm, planting evidence and wrongful arrest during a night-time raid on the Diaz School, of which thirteen were convicted. A further 45 state officials, including police officers, prison guards and doctors, were charged with physically and mentally abusing demonstrators and journalists held in a detention centre in the nearby town of Bolzaneto. Video evidence from Indymedia and from the video activist group Undercurrents, is being used as key evidence for the prosecution.

On June 1, 2003, Indymedia journalist Guy Smallman was seriously injured by a police grenade in Geneva. He was covering protests against the G8 summit in nearby Evian for Indymedia and Image Sans Frontière.

On June 9, 2003, Alejandro Goldín, a photographer for Indymedia Argentina claims to have been assaulted by Federal Police officers while covering an incident between police and factory workers at the Brukman textile factory in Buenos Aires.Goldín claims that although he identified himself as press and showed his credentials, police tried to smash his equipment. Goldín claims that he was beaten on the head with a shotgun, shoved to the ground and kicked repeatedly by officers. On May 19, 2005, two videographers were roughed up by the Houston Police Department's Mounted Patrol during the Halliburton Shareholders Meeting - both videographers were contributors to Houston Indymedia. Both videographers were charged with assault on a police officer, but the charges were dropped after mainstream media from KTRK-TV (ABC13), KPRC-TV (Local 2 Houston), and KHOU-TV (Channel 11 Houston) provided the Harris County District Attorney's office with video footage that exonerated the journalists.

6

Paying for the Video Revolution

In 1978, the new video technologies of cable TV and home video were relatively uncommon, with fewer than 20 percent of U.S. households receiving cable and just over 1 percent owning videocassette recorders. Just ten years later, both technologies were represented in a majority of households, with 51 percent receiving cable and 58 percent owning videocassette recorders. The social implications and policy consequences of this "video revolution" are the subject of continuing research.

This chapter focuses on the changes in spending patterns that made possible the swift diffusion of new video technologies. Using methods originated by McCombs and extended by Wood, we examine consumer spending on the mass media during the decade when cable television and video recording and playback became majority technologies.

Consumer spending has been thought to be a constant fraction of consumer income. This "constancy principle" would imply that new mass media technologies could be supported only by spending taken away from the income share of established media technologies. As a result, new technologies could threaten the survival of existing technologies.

However, if the constancy principle failed to hold, even for a few years, consumers might devote an increased share of their mass media expenditures to adopting new technologies. Later, when long-term constancy reasserted itself, the new technologies would have become established without having displaced the older mass media.

McCombs originally identified mass media spending as a broad aggregate of six categories of consumer spending kept by the U.S. Department of Commerce. Those categories are newspapers, magazines, and sheet music; books and maps; radio and television receivers, records, and musical instruments; radio and television repairs; motion picture admissions; and other paid admissions. The "mass media" aggregate was expanded by Wood to include the then-emerging videodisc and cassette technologies as well as expenditures on cable television services. The previous studies examined yearly national data on mass media spending and income from 1929 through 1981, before the new video technologies had become firmly established.

The constancy principle can be formally described as the invariance of the proportion of consumer income spent on the mass media aggregate, regardless of changes in levels of income, changes in mass media technologies, or the passage of time. Function A goes through the origin of the graph and remains in place over time. Along that function, consumers adjust their media spending with the passage of time and changes in income, but they always spend the same fraction on media.

In this hypothesis, new technologies can gain a share of income only at the expense of existing technologies. For example, first-run movie theaters might lose income share to home video, or book publishers might lose out to cable television. In the absence of sufficient growth of income, the actual number of dollars spent on the older media would decline, possibly endangering those media's survival.

Constancy could fail to hold in a variety of ways. For example, a function like A could rotate upward or shift upward in parallel fashion. In either case, the fraction of income spent on mass media would change. Because of the multiple ways in which constancy might fail, no one test can indicate decisively whether constancy is present.

Although other interpretations of constancy are possible, we focus here on the more conventional income-share and time-trend tests, which use correlation studies or the statistically equivalent regression approach. The regression approach has the advantage of facilitating corrections for serially correlated error terms, which commonly occur in annual time-series data.

If the fitted function intercepts the vertical axis below zero (function B), then mass media spending as a fraction of income increases if income goes up. The test for constancy is therefore a test of whether the intercept of the fitted function is statistically different from zero. The time-trend constancy test uses multiple regression to estimate the relationship between mass media spending, disposable income, and a time-trend variable.

Including a time-trend variable means that the interpretation of the intercept term is no longer a straightforward indication of the constancy of spending on the mass media. If the regression coefficient of the time-trend variable is not significantly different from zero, the relationship between income and mass media spending is considered constant over time. A coefficient statistically different from zero would cast doubt on the constancy hypothesis. To test for the presence of constancy, we must examine both the incomeshare and time-trend interpretations. It is possible that time-trend constancy would hold while income-share constancy is violated. This would indicate that over long periods of time people spend a constant fraction of their income on the mass media but spend greater proportions of income for shorter intervals. These short-term violations of constancy could be sufficient for new technologies to become established, before mass media spending returned to long-term constancy.

To test the constancy hypothesis during the time of rapid change in video technologies, we extended the data series of earlier studies through 1988. In addition, we amended some of the pre-1981 data because of revisions made by the U.S. Department of Commerce.

For this study, new video technologies were videodisc, videocassette recorders, and cable television services. Videodisc spending first showed up in the government figures for 1981. Videocassette recorders were significant enough to report for the first time in 1975. Cable television had been reported as early as 1955, but it remained a minority technology, with less than 20 percent penetration of households as recently as 1980.

Tests confirmed that serial correlation was present in the time-series sample, with t-statistics for 1929-1988 significant at p d".01. Our regression tests corrected for this serial correlation of error terms and incorporated corrections for taxation of personal income and length of sample period.

Period, when new video technologies became majority technologies, was characterized by an increased share of income being spent on the mass media. The fitted function has an intercept statistically different from zero. Consumers also had spent an increasing share of income on the mass media in 1959-1968 and a decreasing share in 1949-1958 and 1969-1978. The overall constancy for 1929-1988 thus masked significant decade-long departures from constancy.

Departures from constancy could imply dramatic financial gains for new technologies, in times of increasing income share for the mass media, or large losses of revenue for all technologies, in times of decreasing income share for the mass media. The income share spent on mass media is plotted against time and broken down into print, audiovisual, and new video components. The figure reflects increasing income shares for the mass media in 1959-1968 and in 1979-1988, the period of special interest here.

This confirms the long-term constancy of the relationship between mass media spending and consumer income. The time-trend variable is not statistically different from zero; consumer income retains a high degree of explanatory power. The result confirms the absence of persistent increases or decreases in mass media spending over time. The data show that consumers' willingness to spend an increased share of income on the mass media in 1979-1988 prevented major losses by print and conventional audiovisual media. In 1979, mass media spending commanded a 2.57 percent share of income. If that share had remained constant over the decade, consumers would have spent only $89.4 billion on the mass media in 1988 instead of the $113.8 billion that they actually spent. Had consumer spending obeyed the constancy principle for 1979-1988 while new video technologies were adopted, there would have been a dramatic loss of revenue by older technologies.

Although the income share of print media appears to be declining, higher overall levels of income allowed for actual increases in spending on print media. As the totals indicate, real consumer expenditure was higher at the end of the decade than the beginning, despite some year-to-year reductions. Consumer expenditure is, of course, only one variable influencing the survival of specific media; rising costs of production could doom an older media technology if consumers did not increase their spending to keep pace.

The data for 1979-1988 show that new technologies entered the mass media market, attracted significant consumer spending, and did not displace or endanger older technologies. It is possible that the dramatic upturn in consumer spending on the mass media that began in 1979 marks the beginning of a longterm departure from constancy. The introduction of new video technologies may have structurally changed consumer spending, making consumers willing to spend a greater proportion of income on the mass media at the expense of nonmedia goods and services. Such a structural change could leave room in household budgets for older and newer technologies alike. Since the video revolution is a relatively recent occurrence, however, statistical confirmation of this change may be years in coming.

7

News Media Coverage of Popular-culture Culpability

Throughout the twentieth century, certain segments of society have blamed the products of popular culture for lowering moral standards and inciting "had" behaviour. After World War I, for example, many blamed movies for bringing the "loose morals" of Europe to America, resulting in women taking up smoking and wearing dresses that exposed their calves.

In the 1950s, parents worried that doo-wop and rock and roll would provoke sexual promiscuity in their teenage sons and daughters. And in the 1980s, a group of concerned parents known as the PMRC labeled the music of Madonna, Michael Jackson, Motley Crue, and others as a "contributing factor" in teen pregnancy and suicide.

In the 1990s, popular media products (including movies, recorded music, television talk shows, the Internet, tabloid newspapers, and video games) were blamed, at least in part, for a number of high-profile tragedies. Among these were the car crash that killed Princess Diana, the murder associated with the "Jenny Jones" show, and the shootings at several high schools in the United States, including the massacre at Columbine High School in Littleton, Colorado.

In news coverage of these tragedies, the mainstream news media seemed to lead the charge against their popular brethren by unabashedly reporting on, if not initiating, the finger-pointing. This study explores how and why the news media came to assign blame to products of popular culture in coverage of the three recent high-profile tragedies mentioned above. We chose these three events because we see them as variations on a theme: well-publicized, wide-reaching events in which a tragedy occurred that involved popular media in some way and in which a large component of the news discourse that followed involved the blaming of popular media for the tragedies.

We argue that the ways in which the "elite" news media covered these events were not isolated or unique but rather exemplified widely held assumptions, common practices, and consistent perspectives regarding news, popular media, and audiences. We see the analysis of three cases, rather than only one, as compelling evidence of the universality of the themes we raise.

Through case studies based on qualitative content analysis of English-language newspaper coverage of these three events, we will answer the following questions:

- *RQ1:* How did the reporting of each story-Princess Diana's death, the "Jenny Jones" talk show murder, and the Columbine High School shootings-evolve over time?
- *RQ2:* At what point in news coverage of each story did popular-culture culpability arise, and from what source(s) did the blame originate?
- *RQ3:* In news coverage of each story, how were products of popular culture such as video games, the Internet, the paparazzi, and talk shows blamed for each tragedy?
- *RQ4:* How might we explain the news media placing the blame on popular culture?

After presenting the case studies, we employ several theoretical frameworks to discuss why popular-culture products, and occasionally their producers, were blamed for these tragic events.

Our goal is not to exonerate popular-culture products or their producers but to understand how and why they were implicated in news coverage of the tragedies. This research topic has the potential to reveal a great deal about the practices-and perhaps even the motivations-of those involved in the creation and control of the news. Yet little research has been done on the relationship between the "elite" news media and the various forms of "popular" media, those which serve to entertain more than to inform.

Analyses of news media blaming popular media products for causing or contributing to high-profile tragedies are rare. Thus, we briefly review the few studies that look specifically at the coverage of these three tragedies by the news media to provide context for the rather novel study at hand. We also provide a brief overview of the history of blame being assigned to popular media by entities other than the news media.

Finally, we turn toward more broad theoretical foundations that can be applied to the particular occurrence of assignment of blame by news media to popular media. News coverage of the three tragedies studied here implicated many typos of entertainment media and popular culture, all of which have been the subject of similar criticism as well as of more formalized research scrutiny in the past. One popular media form that was blamed, in part, for the Columbine tragedy was recorded music.

In social scientific research, exposure to violence in recorded music has been associated with antisocial and destructive behaviour, as well as sex-role stereotyping and negative attitudes toward women. Yet a direct causal relationship has been elusive because of both the difficulty in extracting the influence of song lyrics in complex decision-making processes and the finding that up to 30% of those adolescents listening do not know the lyrics. The evidence on the topic is sufficient, however, for the American Academy of Pediatrics to make recommendations to parents about "reducing the potential negative effects of music lyrics and videos". There also exists an extensive history of blaming violent films for encouraging antisocial behaviour, as was also the case in news coverage of the shootings at Columbine.

Among the more recent contributions to this literature are analyses finding increases in aggression levels after exposure to violent films, often greater for those aggressively inclined prior to exposure. Similarly, a growing body of research links video-game use-raised as a causal factor for the Columbine shootings-with increased aggressive behaviour and desensitization toward violence.

Other research has found elevations in aggressive play rather than aggressive behaviour directed toward others following violent video-game use. Two other aspects of popular culture widely blamed in the three cases examined here, particularly in the Columbine case, include television violence and extensive news coverage of violent events (because such coverage may lead to copycat behaviour). Both have received attention in studios too numerous to identify here, yet Berkowitz, Surette, Comstock and Scharrer, and Potter provide informative overviews of each.

Analyses of the amount or treatment of violence in newspaper content are surprisingly scant. One exception is Clark and Blankenberg's study of violence across different types of media that found about 18% of newspaper front pages featured violence. There is also a growing amount of research on the topic of news coverage of violent events involving youths, an issue relevant to the Columbine tragedy. For example, an analysis of local television news in California found that over half of the nearly 1,800 stories analysed that contained violence featured youths, similar to the 48% of violent stories that involved children found in an earlier study. A similar study in California the following year found 68% of all violent stories involved youths.

To our knowledge, no scholarly research has linked daytime television talk shows or tabloid publications-the two remaining objects of blame in these cases, particularly in the "Jenny Jones"-related murder and the death of Princess Diana-to adverse media effects, though they have certainly been criticized in the news media. One exception is a study by Tavener, who argues that daytime talk shows elicit moral panics among middle-class cultural critics and mainstream journalists but that, in fact, shows such as "Jerry Springer" and "Jenny Jones" serve to reinforce middle-class values and mores.

However, a few studies conducted over the last decade have examined the often controversial content of talk shows. Brinson and Winn report one reason for the format's popularity has been an increased emphasis on interpersonal conflict. Critics of the "Jerry Springer Show" suggest the show's premise is to spark controversy and conflict in the hopes of elevating the conflict to a physically violent level. As the trend of revealing "secrets" or disclosing private information in front of a national audience became more popular, a few researchers began to explore the role of these programs in society and the nature of talk-show guests themselves. Anderson and Oliver suggest that talk shows are "modern, mass mediated freak shows", and critics, ranging from journalists to political figures to a talk-show host have charged talk shows with emphasizing sexual themes, sexual practices, and sexual deviance.

Abt and Seesholtz found in their analysis of talk-show content that talk shows are dominated by sexuality, themes of deviance and psychopathology, and self-disclosure of private facts. Greenberg and colleagues found in their analysis of 110 talk-show episodes that sexual activity was a major issue of discussion in 36% of the shows and discussion of criminal acts was a major-issue in 24% of the shows. Brinson and Winn analysed representations of interpersonal conflict in 40 randomly selected talk shows and found aggressive behaviour in approximately 25% of the shows.

In another area of talk-show research, Priest and Dominick examined the relationship between talk-show participants, their exposure to television, and their reasons for choosing to disclose sensitive and private information in a public forum. They found that participants on the "Donahue" show reported a "pragmatic attitude toward talk shows as a forum to reach a number of audiences".

Though some talk-show guests were aware that they might face ridicule or embarrassment on the program, they were willing to do so in order to "evangelize" their issue or position. In another investigation of self-disclosure on talk shows, Peck found that talk-show participants viewed the talk-show stage as an extension of therapy, thereby enabling talk-show participants to perceive their participation on the show as a step in the healing process.

A few studies have looked specifically at news-media coverage of one of the three tragedies analysed in this chapter, Princess Diana's death. Real (2000) used print and broadcast news coverage of Diana's death and funeral to explicate a theory that the media serve a religious function in modern society. Real did not focus on the "elite" media blaming popular culture for the tragedy, but he suggested that "the intense controversy over the possible role of media paparazzi in her death functioned largely as a displacement attempting to find blame to explain away the unexplainable finality of death".

Eichholz studied the extent to which German and American newspapers (both "elite" and tabloid) criticized tabloid photographers and the tabloid press for their purported role in Diana's death. He found that "on average, elite newspapers devoted 25% of their coverage to the role the media played, compared with only 5% that the tabloids devoted to the media's role". Eichholz also found "the elite media were more willing to voice media criticism because they aimed most of their critique at the tabloids and the paparazzi, while at the same time differentiating themselves from these groups". Bishop, whose study is most similar to the study at hand, focused primarily on how the news media (both print and broadcast) actively differentiated themselves from tabloid publications in their coverage of Diana's death. Through textual analysis, Bishop identified a pattern of coverage that served to distinguish "elite" journalists and "elite" media from tabloid-press photographers and tabloid publications.

Bishop found that journalists for the "elite" media "struggled to keep their readers and viewers aware that the paparazzi, and British and American tabloids, did not practice journalism with the same level of professionalism".

MEDIA DISCOURSE AND "SERIOUS" vs. TABLOID JOURNALISM

In addition to the particular studies cited above, the works of Bird, Jensen, Pauly, and Eason contribute to our theoretical framework for interpreting the mainstream news media's handling of the three high-profile events studied here. This framework views communication as a symbolic social practice and media content as the negotiated outcome of the social practices of its producers and the public.

Bird writes about supermarket tabloids as cultural phenomena, existing "alongside and because of other cultural phenomena" rather than merely as disconnected parts. She stresses the importance of considering intertextuality, or the relationship of one media product to other media and oral traditions, when studying the role of a media product (in her case, tabloids) in people's lives.

Bird argues that the writer, the reader, and the content itself contribute to "the cultural phenomenon of the tabloid", and she counters criticism of tabloid journalism by "serious" journalists with evidence of the close connection between "serious" and tabloid journalism, both past and present. The connections to be made with our study are several. First, we must consider the cultural phenomenon we are examining, the assignment of blame in newspaper journalism to elements of popular media, in context with other cultural phenomena.

If popular media are being portrayed in a negative light in print news media and the reader is a fan of popular media, a complex intertextual scenario may transpire. How audience members read news coverage that places responsibility for social ills on popular media may certainly be mitigated by audience members' own relationships with popular media.

Also relevant to our study is the relationship between "serious" journalism and tabloid journalism. In our study, we expect tabloid journalism will be directly implicated in both the "Jenny Jones" and the Princess Diana cases. In the Columbine case, we expect that the popular, entertainment-based media (video/computer games, movies, television shows, recorded music) will be implicated in press coverage. Central to our discussion of the treatment of these entities by journalists employed at major newspapers is the apparent division between the popular and the "elite" being drawn by the "serious" journalists in non-tabloid publications. We argue that in order to point the finger of blame at media in general but deflect blame from one's own media outlet, this delineation is drawn. Yet, as Bird suggests, the distinction between "serious" and popular media is not one of opposite sides of a polemic but rather of blurry points on a continuum.

Jensen analyses decades of discourse about ill effects associated with media, although she examines scholarly arguments made by media critics whereas we examine news articles appearing in major newspapers. Jensen argues that when critics rail against the powers and persuasions of media, the underlying assumptions and beliefs they are advancing are fundamentally complaints about modernity or what modern times have wrought.

She does not attempt to determine whether there are unfavorable influences of the media on society or on individuals but rather she analyses the discussion or discourse surrounding that topic. We adopt the same stance in our study in that we do not attempt to determine whether the popular media discussed in newspaper coverage of these three events are to blame for the three tragedies. Rather, we examine the process by which they were blamed, in discourse located in newspaper coverage of the events.

Jensen's argument about modernity can be applied to our study. It is possible that though media criticism is easier to articulate as a cause for these tragic events, perhaps truer culprits are modern issues and circumstances. Among these are an emphasis on commercial interests (e.g., ratings for Jenny Jones, money for the photos of Princess Diana, sales or ratings for the movies, music and video games mentioned in coverage of the Columbine shootings) or the alienation and disconnection experienced by many in contemporary life (e.g., the ostracism of the Columbine perpetrators, the claims of humiliation for the Jenny Jones assailant, the identification with and adoration of Princess Diana).

Jensen presents the key media criticism arguments advanced by Macdonald, that media and mass culture jeopardize the presence of high art; Boorstin, that "pseudo events" created by the media and presented to audiences as fact obscure the truth; Ewen, that consumer culture promotes an ideology of consumption that functions as an agent of social control; and Postman, that television has led to the transformation of serious and important aspects of public affairs into entertainment, thereby robbing audiences of information they need to conduct themselves as citizens.

Jensen identifies a common element in these criticisms: each suggests media change us, as audience members, by offering something more appealing or easier to make sense of compared to those things that would be better for us. Implicit in this criticism are the beliefs that there is consensus regarding what is good for society and that ordinary citizens themselves cannot be trusted to know what that may be. However, in media criticism the blame is often not directly placed on the audience for choosing lazy or flashy options; instead blame is placed on the media for duping the audience into doing so by presenting no better options.

These notions about audience preference and this sense of protectionism are central to our study. The angles chosen, words used, and sources employed in reporting about these events (as part of the social process of news gathering) may reveal a similar "elite" protectionism and unflattering belief about the nature of audience preferences and desires. The news coverage may imply that members of the news media know what is best in order to protect the masses and to sustain social order.

By assigning responsibility to popular media for these three tragedies, "serious" journalists can adopt a prescriptive stance toward improving social conditions by leading audiences away from the ostensibly harmful and salacious content in the popular media to which they are presumably drawn. Jensen discusses the moral element in the comparison of tabloid journalism with "serious" journalism, with the distinction drawn between the two indicating "a moral tension between self-indulgence and self-denial".

The loyalty of tabloid journalists to audience interests and therefore profit making is contrasted in media criticism to the loyalty of "serious" journalists to "higher" processes of rationality and the virtues of high culture.

The distinction is made more obvious in the aspect of media-influence discourse that refers to the "lowest common denominator" presumably appealed to by certain types of media content such as tabloid journalism or popular media. A particular view of audiences as being ill equipped for reason and inevitably drawn to more "shallow symbolic forms" underlies this commonly used phrase. This is central to our discussion in that implicit in the criticism of popular media by elite news media is a sense of shamefulness associated with "pandering" to "base" human instincts toward violence (Columbine, Jenny Jones), intrusivcness (Jenny Jones, Princess Diana), and sex (Jenny Jones).

An essay by Pauly about media mogul Rupert Murdoch in Carey's Media, Myths, and Narratives also informs this discussion of "elite" and "non-elite" media. Murdoch was criticized for his use of "promotional journalism" and accused of devaluing journalistic ideals by not "honoring the stylistic conventions that journalists used to defend the social importance of their occupation". Pauly discusses the defensive strategy of distinguishing between information and entertainment as a primary means of defining "elite" and "non-elite" media. Yet, he argues that this is an artificial construction since news content is increasingly presented in a manner and in a context that seeks to entertain:

Because mass-circulation dailies comprise vast and varied symbolic materials, different groups can argue that the 'essential' part is the one that they most enjoy or that sustains their sense of identification. Thus the professional journalist emphasizes the investigative role of the newspaper out of proportion to the actual number of stories undertaken.

In other words, the investigative, purely informational, "factual" content in a daily newspaper is a small portion of the whole, but is magnified in importance by those with a vested interest in arguing the difference between "serious" and tabloid journalism. This argument is at the centre of our study, which suggests that in order to blame some aspects of media and popular culture, newspaper journalists must imply that this content is fundamentally different (and comparatively "worse") than what they transmit to audiences.

The alleged dichotomy between "what audience members want" and "what audience members need" is also raised in Eason's essay in Carey's Media, Myths, and Narratives, in which Eason discusses the controversy surrounding the fabricated elements in Janet Cooke's award-winning news story, "Jimmy's World." Eason argues that journalism has experienced an evolution away from the repertorial function of transmitting facts and more toward the creation of "reality " with the words and elements of a story chosen by journalists.

We argue similarly that the journalists in the news stories we reviewed about these three high-profile tragedies create a reality in which popular media and popular-culture products bear responsibility for the tragedies. Although the journalists whose stories we review presumably did not fabricate any information they conveyed, they did choose to highlight certain "facts" that appear to have made their stories more marketable to a large audience while downplaying other "facts" that may have been deemed of less interest to readers.

FACTORS AFFECTING MEDIA COVERAGE

A somewhat different though complementary view of the phenomenon of popular-culture culpability is seen from the perspective of Shoemaker and Reese. Their approach examines how media content is influenced by factors in the context in which it is created.

Though one could view their theoretical perspective as examining media content as shaped by external social processes in a unidirectional (external forces lead to media content) manner, we argue that their theory can be expanded to examine the interrelated, multidirectional, dynamic relations between all elements-content, producers, public. In Mediating the Message, Shoemaker and Reese identify five major spheres of influence on media content, from the most microscopic to the most macroscopic.

We use these labels to identify sources of influence on the producers of news content as well as on the content itself. Though the labels are presented individually, we argue for their overlapping, multidirectional relationship with content as journalists go about the social practice of determining how to cover "the news." We introduce the levels of influence here briefly and will then apply them to each of the three events examined in this chapter.

The most microscopic level of influence on media content is the individual level, that is, the influence exerted by the individual reporter or columnist, the copy editor, and the editor-each person who has a hand in creating the news content. This can include deciding what constitutes news, selecting the angle of the story, writing the story, and editing it. Some of the factors that influence content decisions at the individual level are personal feelings, tastes and preferences, values, opinions, and the professional backgrounds and training of those directly involved in content decisions.

The media routines level focuses on the routines, or standard procedures, for gathering and disseminating news. Among the influences found at this level are news values-those characteristics that make an event newsworthy, such as deviance from the norm, sensationalism, prominence, proximity, timeliness, conflict or controversy, human interest, and impact on audience members or society as a whole.

Other media routines include objectivity, the five "Ws" (answering who, what, when, where, and why in every report), pack journalism, competition, reliance on other media for information or for whole stories, localism (getting the local angle on a story that takes place far away), simplicity (offering pat "answers" because complex situations are hard to explain and hard for readers to understand quickly), and over-reliance on a handful of sources.

The next level of influence, moving toward a more macroscopic perspective, is the organizational level. Analysis at the organizational level focuses on the impact of policies, managers, and owners of the organization in which the media content is produced. It is difficult to discuss influences at this level, as we do not know what went on in each newsroom during coverage of these three events. However, the opinions of upper management or concerns of those in the circulation or advertising-sales departments can influence coverage, as can organizational policies such as the degree of autonomy allowed to each reporter.

The extramedia level has to do with elements and factors outside of the media organizations themselves, such as news sources, advertisers, government, interest groups, and the audience. This level includes actual, direct influences as well as the influence that news media personnel's perceptions of what these entities might do or how they might feel that also shape content. While influence of advertisers might weigh against extensive blaming of popular culture in news coverage, for example, pressure from some interest groups and activists, as well as governmental concern, could weigh toward the pursuit of this angle. In terms of perceptions of audience preferences, some journalists may believe that audiences want to see and read about violence, sensationalism, scandal, and the lives of celebrities. This perception could have a profound impact, because giving the audiences "what they want" will presumably sell newspapers and space to advertisers. Thus, angles that have popular appeal may be advanced while more esoteric or abstract angles, such as the notion that society in general is responsible or that a complex nexus of forces are at fault, may take a back seat.

The notion of audience preference is also a cultural one. de Mooij argues the one such preference that is culturally bound is America's adherence to a cause-and-effect paradigm. She argues that it is a cultural norm in the United States to expect to have a logical explanation for any given event and that any event has concrete and measurable answers to the question of what caused it. Journalists, if following this cultural norm or if presuming audiences follow it, may provide a concrete explanation rather than leave the tragedies unexplained. Subscribing to this cause-and-effect paradigm can be viewed as an individual influence on the part of reporters and editors, an extramedia influence that takes the shape of conceptions about audience preferences, or an ideological influence that entails broad-based cultural and societal beliefs.

The ideological level includes the influences that broad systems of beliefs and values have on the news-gathering process. Among the factors at play here are notions of "elite" and "popular" media, representations that define "mainstream" and "deviant" content, and the concept of hegemony. The latter suggests that entities enjoying political and economic power in existing societal structure will act in the interest of thwarting social change in order to protect their dominant status.

We predict that these three case studies will show the use of defensive strategies when other media are, indeed, blamed. Through the use of labels such as "tabloid," "paparazzi," and "trash TV" to draw theoretically distinct lines, journalists may construct readings of their own stories as the dominant discourse and those of "tabloid" media and "trash TV" as deviant.

A subtext exists in this type of criticism that suggests a need to save people from their own tastes in media and popular culture. This is similar to the points raised by Bird and Jensen above, and is the central theoretical element of the study at hand. de Mooij's suggestion that as part of American culture, we-as members of society-need someone or something to blame whenever there is a tragedy, also has implications for hegemony and social order.

In order for members of society to feel secure about the world around them, there has to be a rational cause, with a clearly identifiable source of blame, for each event. Thus, it is much more satisfying to place blame on a specific, tangible targetin this case, the non-elite media-rather than advancing the more unsettling notion that something is amiss in society at large.

PRINCESS DIANA

The first case study involves the death of Princess Diana of Wales and the automobile accident that took her life and the lives of Dodi al Fayed and Henri Paul on August 31, 1997. The accident occurred shortly after midnight in Paris when the Mercedes Benz in which the princess and her friend were travelling crashed in a tunnel near the Seine River. Dodi al Fayed and Henri Paul, the driver, were found dead at the scene. The princess died a few hours later of injuries she sustained in the crash.

The event was reported in newspapers around the world. The larger U.S. and U.K. newspapers gave extensive coverage to the event in the days following the crash. For example, on the first day of coverage The London Observer ran 28 articles, The New York Daily News ran 10 articles, and The Atlanta Journal and Constitution ran four articles.

This case study is based on analysis of those articles and others that were published in English-language newspapers from the day of the crash, August 31, 1997, through the day of Diana's funeral, September 6, 1997, when the focus of coverage shifted from the accident to the funeral. The articles were retrieved from the General News archive of LEXIS-NEXIS Academic Universe. In all, 507 stories were reviewed for relevant content, and those with relevant content were studied more closely.

Often, the first news reports of a tragic and unexpected event will present only the basic facts of the story, answering the fundamental journalistic questions of who was involved, what happened, when it happened, and where it happened, without speculation as to the causes of the event. It usually takes another day or more for the "how" and "why" questions to be answered.

However, this was not the case in the early reporting on Princess Diana's death. Answers to the "how" and "why" questions were included in the initial reports of the event because tabloid-press photographers were said to have been chasing the princess's car at the time of the accident. Approximately 11 photographers, sources said, some on motorcycles and others in a car, set out after Diana and Dodi's Mercedes when it left the Ritz hotel in Paris.

The photographers were apparently trying to get pictures that would confirm rumors of a romance between Diana and Dodi. Several sources in the earliest stories claimed that the photographers caused the accident. Among them were Paris police, unspecified police, French journalists (their sources unnamed), a photographer for a London paper, Agence-France Presse (the French news agency), and British reporters.

No eyewitnesses to the crash were quoted in the early coverage-in other words, no source knew for certain that the photographers had actually caused the accident (and some sources even claimed that the car had lost the photographers). In spite of this, the idea that the photographers caused the accident became a part of every story reporting the facts of the event.

The Boston Heraldbegan an article by Joseph Mallia with "Princess Diana and her companion Dodi Fayed were killed in a high-speed car crash early today in a tunnel near the Seine River in Paris, as their Mercedes was being pursued by photographers." The Hindu of India began a story with "Britain's Princess Diana and her millionaire companion, Dodi El-Fayed, were killed in a car crash early on Sunday while being chased by photographers on motorcycles in a road tunnel in the French capital Paris." The third paragraph of an Associated Press story that ran in The Buffalo News on August 31 read "The crash happened shortly after midnight in a tunnel along the Seine River at the Pont de l'Aima bridge. It came as paparazzi-the commercial photographers who constantly tailed Diana followed her car, police said."

POPULAR-CULTURE CULPABILITY

During the week after the fatal crash, when coverage of the event was at its most intense, nearly every article contained at least one source who blamed the producers of popular culture for Diana's death. Among these were family members and family representatives, dignitaries, ordinary citizens, and journalists themselves. Other sources who blamed "the paparazzi," "the press," "the media," or "the tabloids" (sometimes including tabloid-style television shows) were an Arizona talk-radio host and many of his callers, Britons living in the United States (usually interviewed in pubs), un-named TV commentators, and David Perel, executive editor of the American tabloid The National Enquirer.

Perel was quoted in several newspapers as saying that reckless action by the paparazzi probably caused the accident. Some family members of the crash victims extended the blame to all photographers who pursue celebrities for photos to be printed in tabloid newspapers. Ellen Tumposky and Mike Claffey of The New York Daily News (Aug. 31) reported "The dead Egyptian playboy's father, Mohammed Al-Fayed, blamed the tragedy on the paparazzi, who were being held for questioning by Paris police.

There is no doubt in Mr. Al-Fayed's mind that this tragedy would not have occurred but for the press photographers who have dogged and pursued Mr. Fayed and the princess for weeks,' a spokesman for the Egyptian billionaire said." The Houston Chronicle reported "(Michael Gibbons), a spokesman for Buckingham Palace, noting that the incident occurred while the couple were being chased by photographers, said it was 'an accident waiting to happen.' he repeated the palace's anger at the actions of photographers who pursue the royal family around the world."

Other family members blamed not only tabloid-press photographers but also the editors and publishers of gossipy tabloid publications. The London Observer was one of the first to report a scathing statement from Diana's brother. "This is not a time for recriminations," said Earl Spencer, "but I would say that I always believed the press would kill her in the end. But not even I could imagine that they would take such a direct hand in her death as seems to be the case. It would appear that every proprietor and editor of every publication that has paid for intrusive and exploitative photographs of her, encouraging greedy and ruthless individuals to risk everything in pursuit of Diana's image, have blood on their hands today."

None of the first-day stories reporting the reactions of world leaders and diplomats (such as President Clinton, the Singapore government, and the Pope) contained quotes that blamed popular culture. However, on the second day of coverage, several French government officials made statements blaming the paparazzi, as reported in The Hindu.

The president of the French Parliament, the former prime minister, Mr. Laurent Fabius said that death precipitated by paparazzi proves that "photos, words and attitudes can also, in a certain sense, kill. These people must now face their responsibility." The government's spokeswoman, Ms. Catherine Trautmann, who is also France's Culture Minister, was more vehement in her denunciation of the paparazzi. Princess Diana was the victim of the stubbornness of the press, she declared. "The singlemindedness of the press had increased dramatically these past weeks The circumstances of her death have thrown up questions about the functioning of this profession and above all of our society," Ms. Trautmann added.

Among the stories that reported the reactions of ordinary citizens, most contained at least one source who blamed either the paparazzi who pursued the Mercedes or the press in general. Most of these "average-citizen" sources did not distinguish between the popular press and the elite press or their producers, nor did the reporters attempt to make any distinction for the sources. The blame laid by these sources was among the most vitriolic. The New York Daily News reported:

Britons in New York mixed their grief at Princess Diana's death with criticism of the press for its relentless pursuit of her Beverly Dorking, 25, of Leeds in northern England, said, "she's been dogged and hounded by the media. They've been in her face since she was 19, and now they've taken away the world's most popular woman." Nicola Shigley, 24, of northern England, predicted a backlash against the media. She accused the media of spending "the last 10 years trying to put the woman to an end."

The San Diego Union-Tribune reported '"The press has a lot to answer for,' said Mary Simpson, also of Liverpool. 'They hounded her to death. Literally, now.'" The Seattle Times reported "Mitch Lease, 23, reflected bitterly on the circumstances of her death, a chase by photographers. I think the media should have given her a break a long time ago, and now they've killed her.'"

The London Observer reported "In one bitter outburst on BBC TV, a woman demanded that a reporter and his cameraman slop filmmg. 'You've done this Io her,' she screamed. 'You're to blame. The media, the papers, all of you.'" Some articles blamed popular culture by quoting other publications and thereby demonstrating what seemed to be a world-wide consensus as to who was to blame for the tragedy. A London Observer article read: The French newspaper Liberation gave over its whole front page to a picture of (Diana) with the headline, "One photo too many. " Italy's La Stampa took up the same theme, stating tersely: "Dead for a photo" Hong Kong newspapers agonised over their own home-grown paparazzi, with the Oriental Daily News recalling that a local pop singer, Leslie Cheung, had crashed his Porsche while being pursued by photographers.

It branded paparazzi as "criminals of a thousand years." The Daily Star, a Bangladesh newspaper, said that "Western press and society will need to embark on a long search of their souls to come to terms with the sense of guilt Diana's death must generate."

Alongside the just-the-facts stories and reaction stories were articles focused primarily on the causes of the accident. Many of these stories found some aspect of popular culture (either the photographers who chased Diana's car that night, tabloid-press photographers in general, tabloid newspapers, the editors and publishers of tabloid newspapers, or any member of the press who had purchased paparazzi photos) to be at fault. The tone of these articles was often angry and disgusted. Earl Spencer's statement was used in several of these stories as a starting point for further discussion of the role of the paparazzi in Diana's death. Dave Walker, writing for TAe Arizona Republic (Sept. 1), began such a story by asking "Do the media have blood on their hands for the death of Princess Diana? That's what her brother, Earl Spencer, suggested in the aftermath of the car wreck"

Walker went on to cite several sources who agreed with Spencer, including Dodi's father, Mohamed al Fayed, unnamed network television commentators, and Phoenix-area talk-radio host Charles Goyette, whom Walker quoted: '"The media are clearly to blame,' said Goyette, summing up the majority opinion among his callers. 'The consumers of this trash don't have the culpability, the media do.'" An article in The Glasgow Herald quoted a source who followed Spencer's lead and blamed all the producers of tabloid newspapers: "the Prince of Wales's biographer Jonathan Dimbleby said: 'It isn't only the reporters and photographers, it's those who hired them.' He added: 'It's the editors and proprietors who too often, offer glossy excuses about the public interest who need now to examine their consciences.'"

Some of the stories that discussed causes were actually editorials expressing the views of the writer or writers. For example, The London Observer (no by-line, Aug. 31) expressed the following opinion: "Anyone in the British Press who has bought and used the pictures snatched by paparazzi on so many previous utterly private occasions helped ensure that the ravening pack would be on the trail on Saturday night." Some of these articles were written in a narrative stylo, retelling the facts of the story dramatically while characterizing the photographers as degenerates.

For example, Michael DaIy of The New York Daily News (Aug. 31) wrote: No matter how fast her car sped through the Paris night, the paparazzi on the motorbikes were sure to stay right behind her, for she was with the man said to be her lover (T)he following Sunday, she was swarmed by those only interested in violating her private life. They were still after the couple when she arrived in France. The hounds kept baying, right up to early this morning, when motorcycles sped after Diana's car along the Seine. Her pursuers were right out of the 1961 movie "La Dolce Vita," in which a photographer named Paparazzo chases his prey on a motorscooter (T)hey chased the biggest score ever right to her death.

The frenzy that began with "The Kiss" ended in two children being left without their mother. Similarly, Luke Harding, Owen Bowcott, John Hooper, Paul Webster, Alex Bellos, Stephen Bates, and Chris Mihill of The London Observer (Aug. 31) wrote: Even before Princess Diana and Dodi Fayed had strolled through the baroque central corridor of the Ritz hotel in Paris.

The paparazzi were lurking in wait (Diana and Dodi's) presence was common knowledge among the small, ruthless, multilingual band of photographers who pursue her, very lucratively, for a living Around 7 p.m. on Saturday Diana left the Ritz in a chauffeur-driven car to do some shopping in the Champs Elysee. The press pack were, reportedly, in close pursuit Quite a few stories blamed "the press" in general or "the media" in general, not distinguishing the mainstream press from the tabloid press. Among these were stories reporting that Diana herself had condemned the practices of the British press in an interview published in a French newspaper the week before the accident.

J. Frank Lynch of The Atlanta Journal and Constitution (Aug. 31) reported "In Great Britain, 'the press is ferocious," Diana said in the article in the French daily Le Monde. 'It forgives nothing and is only hunting down mistakes. Each act is twisted; each gesture is criticized."'

SHAHING THE BLAME

A number of stories about the causes of Diana's death divided the blame among several culprits. One of these culprits was Henri Paul, the driver of the Mercedes. On the first day of coverage, many articles noted that Paul had been driving at a speed well above the limit and that he lost control of the car, thus implying that the accident was at least partly his fault.

When the news of Paul's very high blood-alcohol level (which was more than three times the French legal limit) was released on day two, he became the target of finger-pointing in many more articles. However, none of the stories that blamed Paul let the producers of popular culture off the hook completely. An editorial in The Arizona Republic (no byline, Sept. 3) argued:

The swift and reckless rush to judgment, the desire to fix certain blame for the death of Diana, is also destructive and promises to leave victims. Misplaced blame might mask sorrow's pain, but it does not heal. Diana Spencer, queen of celebrity, died from the impaired judgment of millions. We'll name a few.

The paparazzi, a subset of photojournalists identified first and perhaps forever as the villains who ended the strange, fairy-tale existence of a lovely young woman, continue to receive disproportionate blame. Seven photographers face some type of charges related to the fatal crash. So what of the judgment of those editors and publishers who buy sleaze and resell it under some loose definition of news? Impaired? Morally warped? Yes. And, so whal of the judgment of millions of readers who purchase the product now blamed for the death of a princess? Impaired? Warped? Yes. However, in this tragedy, the person whose impaired judgment seems most responsible for the death of Princess Diana, is the man behind the wheel of the car carrying her and her boyfriend

One of the few articles to seriously consider the culpability of Henri Paul was published by The Boston Globe (Sept. 1). (This story also contained several sources who blamed the paparazzi at the scene and the press in general.) Author Peter S. Canellos wrote: Ralph Whitehead, a journalism professor at the University of Massachusetts, said all the hand-wringing over the misdeeds of media is "a momentary hysteria."

Unless proof emerges that paparazzi on motorcycles actually interfered with the progress of Diana's car, responsibility for the accident should rest with the driver, he said. The Mercedes limousine was traveling faster than 60 miles per hour-perhaps much faster-in a tunnel where the speed limit is 30, police said. The princess and her companion, Dodi Fayed, did not appear to be wearing seatbelts. "What would Diana and the rest of the people in the car have lost if they'd been overtaken by photographers?" Whitehead said. "If you're a celebrity, you have a right to regard the paparazzi as a pain in the neck. But it's not the right response to put your life in jeopardy by speeding away."

For a few days, there was a bit of a tug of war between those sources representing the photographers (primarily their lawyers) and those representing the driver (the Fayed family and Paul's co-workers). Some of the stories printed on days two through seven offered opinions as to which party deserved more blame, while others blamed Western society as a whole for its fascination with celebrities. In an article called "Time Has Come to Point Finger in Right Direction," Steve Wilson of The Arizona Republic (Sept. 3) wrote "I would like to interrupt all the finger-pointing in Princess Diana's death-do the paparazzi or the drunken driver deserve the most blame?-for this important message: It's the culture, stupid. Or more precisely, it's the stupid, celebrity-obsessed culture."

Mickey H. Osterreicher of The Buffalo News (Sept. 4) wrote: As a photojournalism I am ashamed and embarrassed by the accusations that "paparazzi, " photographically pursuing the princess, were the cause of the accident. Given that factor, along with alcohol and excessive speed, the comparative negligence in this case would appear to be endless. In a larger sense, we are all somewhat responsible. This tragedy sadly illustrates the life and times in which we live.

POPULAR-CULTURE EXONERATION

In the other cases we examined, some journalists and sources came to the defence of the popular-culture products that were widely blamed for the tragedies. In the case of Diana's death, the paparazzi, the tabloids, and their producers were never fully exonerated. However, quite a few stories published in the days following the crash placed primary responsibility on the readers of tabloid newspapers-for encouraging the practices of the paparazzi.

An editorial in The Atlanta Journal and Constitution (Sept. 1) blamed the consumers of popular culture: "Princess Diana, perhaps the most recognizable woman in the world, was so beautiful and compassionate that people everywhere fell in love with her. And then they loved her to death. The insatiable demand for gossip and pictures involving Diana sot the stage for her tragic end.

" The editorial went on to blame the tabloid audience more explicitly: "The way to stop the stalking is to quit buying the trashy publications that pay for paparazzi pictures. This week, many of Diana's loyal fans will be weeping for their tragic heroine, but if they had not purchased the papers that exploited her in the first place, she might not be dead."

Others concurred. The Arizona Republic's Dave Walker (Sept. 1) wrote "Some observers blame tabloid readers for creating the high-dollar market that would send photographers on a high-speed chase through Paris. " Walker cited "Mary-Lou Galician, an associate professor at the Walter Cronkite School of Journalism and Telecommunications at Arizona State University" as saying "that paparazzi command huge fees for celebrity photos because there's a market demanding them. 'The mathematics suggest that millions of people want these things,' she said. The public has to assume ultimate responsibility and not blame the messengers.'" Interestingly, several other factors could have served to exonerate the photographers and tabloids, at least partially, but these factors were largely ignored by the writers who sought to answer the "why" question.

Among these factors are the 15 minutes it took for an ambulance to reach the Mercedes, where Diana was rapidly losing blood; the fact that neither Diana nor Dodi was wearing a seat belt; the claim made by a few sources that the Mercedes had escaped the photographers before the crash; and, finally, the fact that no one really knew if the photographers actually caused the accident.

Instead of emphasizing or even just exploring these factors, the newspapers chose to focus most of their coverage (and most of the blame) on the paparazzi, the tabloids, their editors and publishers, and the readers of these popular publications.

CONNECTIONS WITH THEORY

Many of the theoretical arguments made by Pauly, Eason, and Bird were apparent in this case study of press coverage of Princess Diana's death. The fact that the photographers who were following Diana were employed at tabloid newspapers invited the discourse of "serious" versus "tabloid" journalism seen throughout the coverage.

The tone of condemnation and blame in coverage of Diana's death was typically directed squarely at the tabloids rather than at press coverage in general, just as in the pointed criticism of fabricated news stories and the reproach of the practices of Rupert Murdoch.

As Bird found in her analysis of tabloid newspapers in general, the tabloid photographers, in this particular situation (as well as editors, reporters, and owners) were implicated for their "base" profit-seeking and sensationalism which was implicitly contrasted with the elevating of the public service function of the "elite" press.

The theoretical contributions of Jensen also apply. In fact, the Princess Diana coverage stands out because the audience was also drawn into tho blame for its apparent attraction to sensationalism and intrusive fascination with the private lives of famous people. This element of the coverage reveals a view of the general public as drawn to "what is bad for them" that Jensen discusses as an underlying element in major strains of media criticism.

By implicitly making a distinction between the "popular" and "elite" news media, the newspapers we reviewed were able to deflect criticism from themselves and take an allegedly prosocial stance as watchdogs standing guard against the practices and content of other media institutions, thereby protecting the public. Finally, we may also examine the press coverage of Diana's death via the levels of influences of news media content as advanced by Shoemaker and Roese. At the individual level, for instance, reporters may have empathized with Diana's plight of being followed and photographed all the time and thus been more inclined to blame the accident on those who hounded her. Individual reporters (and their higher ups) may also have been motivated to try to make sense of and elevate the status of the death of Diana because her life was so extraordinary. In other words, death caused by a car crash-even one in which the driver was under the influence of alcohol-seems too mundane for a princess and a woman of such stature.

Thus, the pursuit ofthat car by paparazzi adds a glamorously tragic element befitting a princess as well as a moralistic element that may help channel the widespread anger and sadness caused by her death. This is exacerbated by the immediate removal of Henri Paul from ongoing blame due to his own demise. The tabloids provide an enduring, monolithic institution to blame rather than one unknown and unknowable individual.

Finally, the professional background of newspaper journalists might have made them prone to view the paparazzi as reckless or unruly because freelance photographers are not required to have journalism training or to adhere to a professional code of ethics, whereas most newspaper journalists are. Media routines were also apparent in the coverage. The selection of sources certainly shaped the stories that were written.

Many newspapers reported either the prepared statements of the victims' family members or the comments of celebrities, all of which sharply criticized the paparazzi. Localism produced some of the most vehement sources. The Britons interviewed in American pubs were quick to blame not only the photographers who chased Diana's car but all tabloid media. This would also serve to separate the "elite" news media from the presumed culprits (though, in the case of Diana's death, a few writers did admit to guilt on the part of the "elite" media, especially after the wall-to-wall coverage of Diana's death in the "elite" media). Extramedia influences on coverage were also apparent. Some sources called for government intervention in the practices of tabloid photographers after Diana's death. Notions of audience preference may well have facilitated the pursuit of the paparazzi angle through the view that many readers of the "elite" press would welcome the criticism of the tabloids and find this element of the event emotionally charged and fascinating.

Influences presumably occurred at the ideological level as well. The potential dissonance involved in newspapers reprimanding other types of print media was alleviated by the strategy of distinguishing between "them" and "us. " This is apparent in the many markers labeling tabloids as a separate entity in "elite" press coverage. We can also see evidence of the cultural belief in the cause-and-effect paradigm in press coverage that is, in fact, magnified here clue to the fact that Diana was the subject of admiration and adulation in many parts of the world. Her revered status may well have heightened the typical North American tendency to try to find a cause for every event, a solution for every "problem."

The criticism of the paparazzi, as well as the alcohol level of the driver, surfaced as an attempt to explain what essentially a senseless death was and thereby to diminish readers' fears, discomfort, and, in some cases, grief. Finally, ideological beliefs about the nature of the masses were also apparent in the Diana case, as some newsppers placed part of the blame squarely at the feet of the public, whose taste for sensationalism, the papers claimed, is merely answered by tabloid publications.

THE "JENNY JONES" MURDER

In 1995, television talk-show host Jenny Jones arranged for Jonathan Schmitz, 34, to appear on her show as a part of her signature "secret admirer" segment. Schmitz was told in front of a national audience that his secret admirer was Scott Amedure, 32, a gay friend. Three days after the show was taped, Schmitz shot Amedure to death. News coverage of the event quickly focused on the way Schmitz was brought in front of a national audience and "humiliated" as the subject of a gay fantasy. Subsequent news coverage was dominated by finger-point-ing-who should be blamed for the death of a talk-show guest? Schmitz was convicted of murder in November 1996, and in May 1999, the Amedure family won $25 million in a negligence suit brought against the "Jenny Jones Show" and Warner Brothers, Jones' employer. Over the five years in which the story has been reported, the object of blame has fluctuated. News stories about the Jenny Jones talk-show murder centreed around four points in time: the initial shooting, a rash of follow-up stories blaming "trash TV" for the murder, Schmitz's first trial, and Schmitz's second trial.

The analysis below reflects quotes taken from newspapers across the country from the day after the murder through August 1999 when Jonathan Schmitz was convicted for a second time in the shooting death of Amedure. Articles were retrieved using the news category in ProQuest. In all, 326 articles with relevant content were reviewed. This case study attempts to illustrate how the print news media covered the Jenny Jones case, with an emphasis on analyzing the sources of blame. News stories on the first day after Scott Amedure's death reported the event as just another murder. Furthermore, news stories published that day implicated Jonathan Schmitz alone for Amedure's murder. While the firstday stories mentioned the "Jenny Jones Show" because both men were guests on the show, neither the show and its producers were directly implicated for the murder until a few days later. Shauna Snow, writing for The Los Angeles Times, dealt with the facts alone in her story on March 10, 1995.

A gay man who took his penchant for talk shows to heart and appeared on the "Jenny Jones Show" to reveal his secret crush on a heterosexual man has been shot dead, and police said the object of his affection admitted the killing. All other stories examined that were published on the first day after the event contained a similar, just-the-facts approach.

POPULAR-CUTURE CULPABILITY

After initial news accounts reported who, what, where, when, and how, analysis and interpretation began to appear in stories about the murder. The "Jenny Jones Show" and the show's producers came under fire the day Jonathan Schmitz was arraigned on first-degree murder charges. In a Washington Post article (no byline) on the second day after the murder, March 11, 1995, the finger pointing at the "Jenny Jones Show" began.

Producers of the "Jenny Jones Show" have come under attack by Michigan prosecutors who allege the nationally syndicated talk show is partly responsible for the murder this week of a guest who professed to have a crush on another man Oakland County Prosecutor Richard Thompson said the talk show's "ambush" tactics-in which guests learn of shocking personal details on camera-may be partly to blame for the death. A Tacoma News article published March 11, 1995, was one of many newspapers to describe the segment as "ambush television." Call it ambush television. It's the latest weapon in daytime talk-show wars, and now it's had deadly consequences. The formula is simple: Bring guests on the air, set off conflict and embarrass them before a national TV audience. Maybe even embarrass them to death.

The "Jenny Jones Show"' brought on John Schmitz, a 24-year-old man from Orion Township, Mich., and told him that a 32-year-old acquaintance, Scott Amedure, was his secret admirer. Today, Amedure is dead and Schmitz has been charged with murder. The "Jenny Jones Show" was further implicated for Amedure's death later in that first week of news coverage after Prosecutor Thompson alleged the talk show was not only partially responsible for the murder of Amedure but also for the "poisoning of society." An article in The Detroit News quoted Thompson as saying Schmitz was "ambushed on national TV, the suggestion being that all Schmitz did was ambush back" at Amedure.

While the other two cases studied here were front-page stories from day one, the "Jenny Jones" talk-show murder only began to make the front page after the talk show's culpability became a part of the story. Most stories, such as this story from The State Journal Registerpublished on day two, contained harsh criticism directed toward the show and its producers and cited ratings as the rationale behind the segment.

A talk show focusing on "Secret Admirers" led to the killing of one guest, allegedly by another. Is 'The "Jenny Jones Show'" to blame? And was this a tragedy just waiting to happen? Yes to both questions, according to talk-show critics, who argue that anything goes to boost ratings. As the story became more prominent, analysis of the event became the "new" news. The event was frequently the subject of newspaper editorials and columns, and these columns went beyond implicating the show and its producers for Amedure's murder-the authors accused the talk show of "trashing society."

By the time this Phoenix Gazette story ran on March 14, many of the "elite" newspapers had spent the previous three days analyzing the culpability of the talk show and its producers. "Our concern now is for the family and friends of the deceased and (for) maintaining the sanctity of the police investigation and the case," Jim Paratore, president of Telepictures Productions, which produces the "Jenny Jones Show," said.

His concern comes a couple of shotgun blasts too late. And his rejection of blame is cynical and without merit. Do Jones or the show's producers ever investigate the temperaments or personality traits of those they seek to embarrass? Did they know anything about Schmitz, or about submerged feelings he may have about homosexuality?

Obviously not. Nor did they care. Someone else pulled the trigger, but they were the ones who blindly spun the chamber. For that reason, they are all accessories. Howard Rosenberg of The Los Angeles Times on March 17, 1995, blamed the daytime talk shows for what he called rampant misbehaviour on the part of daytime television talk shows that play loosely with the lives of some of their guests by seeking to embarrass them with the cameras rolling. Schmitz is surely a man driven by inner demons that "Jenny Jones" didn't know or care about when its staff plotted this high-risk farce, which, in the case of these two men, was based on the premise that a homosexual coming on to someone who is apparently straight equals titillation.

Elsewhere in the column, Rosenberg blamed the "Jenny Jones Show" for driving a mentally unstable Schmitz over the edge in the cause of ratings. "If Schmitz is guilty, he's the one who pulled the trigger. But if so, it was 'Jenny Jones' along with the laws allowing him to purchase a shotgun with apparent ease that provided the trigger." It was at about this point (one week after the murder) that the theories of "who is at fault" seemed to coalesce among the different sources. Schmitz's attorney wholeheartedly defended his client's actions, suggesting the talk show "goaded a lunatic" to take desperate action.

Many of the news stories published at the same time took a similar tone. It was in these articles, published from two days to two weeks after the murder, that the popular-culture culpability angle became so evident. Newspaper headlines alone clearly directed responsibility to the talk show.

- "Critics Link Slaying to Contentious Talk Shows" (News Tribune, March 11, 1995)
- "Ambush-Style Talk Shows Are Playing with Fire" (Detroit News, March 11, 1995)
- "Critics Say Talk Show Partly to Blame in Talk-Show Slaying" (Sun-Sentinel, March 11, 1995)
- "TV's Gutter Talk-Sleaze Takes a Terrible Price" (New York Newsday, March 13, 1995)

Nationally known newspapers such as The Detroit News, The Washington Post, The Los Angeles Times and The Chicago Tribune covered the murder and arraignment from a seemingly objective standpoint; however, the sources used in each of the stories-Schmitz's attorney and Schmitz's family members-primarily represented just one side. The tone in the newspaper stories was not overtly critical, but the inclusion of some points of view and not others suggested the "elite" media were condemning the actions of the daytime talk shows. Not surprisingly, the Detroit newspapers dedicated a great deal of space to the story, and Ron French of The Detroit News wrote several articles and columns dealing with the issue of culpability.

His parents can't understand how a son who cried when he ran over a toad with the lawn mower could shoot a man. "It's darker on this side of the gun," Allyn Schmitz said. "This terror we had lived with came in a worse form. He didn't kill himself, but he killed himself in another way. His life is taken away by prison and by Jenny Jones." Neal Gabler of The Houston Chronicle also faulted the show for putting the gun in Schmitz's hand. How the producers of the "Jenny Jones Show" must have grieved.

During a segment entitled "Secret Admirers," they had surprised a male guest expecting to meet a female admirer by springing a male acquaintance insteadNaturally, the producers made professions of regret, but one suspects what they really regretted was the killer's indecency of not having pulled out his rifle and committed the crime before their cameras. Now, there would have been a ratings coup.

The "Jenny Jones" talk-show murder all but disappeared from newspaper headlines within the first month after the murder. However, as the case moved closer to the trial stage, news stories blaming products of popular culture started to reappear. It was at this time in late 1995 when many politicians jumped on the bandwagon of condemning the daytime talk show for broadcasting "daytime TV smut. "It was also during this time that parents and politicians alike decided daytime television needed regulation. Harry Levins' story in The St. Louis Post Dispatch, October 28, 1995, reported on a "band of influential Washingtonians" who led a campaign of taking the talk show to task, calling it "a matter of citizenship." The main critic of the daytime talk shows was former Education Secretary William Bennett, quoted in The Detroit News. "There was a time," Bennett said Thursday, "when personal failure or marital failure, subliminal desire, and perverse tastes were accompanied by a sense of guilt or embarrassment. Today, these are a ticket to appear on the Sally Jesse Raphael show to be broadcast for children to watch," Bennett said. "This cultural rot is polluting America."

Many news organizations relied regularly on sources such as Prosecutors Thompson or Burdick or politicians such as Bennett, Joseph Lieberman, or Sam Nunn, who were very outspoken about the liability of the talk show. Thompson readily blamed the "Jenny Jones Show," Jenny Jones herself, and the talk show's producers for the murder. Friends and family members of Amedure rarely appeared as sources in news stories.

Yet family members and friends of Schmitz were frequently quoted, as were psychologists and analysts hired by the defence team. Furthermore, newspapers used Thompson and Burdick as sources more than anyone else. Therefore, the voices most critical to the talk show were the ones most frequently cited. In addition to presenting relatively one-sided stories, news organiztions can be considered to have pandered to the audiences of the popular-culture products they were criticizing by giving the story so much news coverage. Joanne Jacobs of The Tulsa World, November 14, 1995, reported on what it was she thought the public wanted.

It's estimated that a million teen-agers and 650,000 pre-teens turn on daytime sleaze, and absorb its perverted values Trash-talk hosts claim their shows serve as morality plays, with the studio audience cast as judges. This lets viewers revel in the lurid confessions and confrontations. Then they get to condemn it. Small-town morality lives, only with hotter gossip and a better choice of sins.

EXONERATING POPULAR CULTURE /SHAKING THE BLAME

As the implication of a popular-culture product in the murder case became old news, new theories of blame started to circulate. During this time, a few weeks after the murder, two key suspects shared the blame for Amedure's murder with the "Jenny Jones Show"-Jonathan Schmitz himself and what was called the "homosexual panic defence." Paul E. Gainor, reporting for The Detroit News, March 26, 1995, was one of many who explored this theory.

Richard S. Sinacola, a Royal Oak therapist for 12 yearssays the case of Scott Amedure and John Schmitzmay have involved homosexual panic as a trigger point Sinacola theorizes that Schmitz "couldn't handle the fact that it involved homosexuality." For him, it touched on some deep-seated homophobia What he was killing was not so much the victim, but his own sense of homosexuality in the victim.

The "homosexual panic defence" theory quickly took centre stage in news articles after stories about Jenny Jones' irresponsible behaviour began to subside. The homosexual panic defence made headlines a few weeks after the murder and reappeared as a secondary object of blame when the media began covering Schmitz's first trial. From The Seattle Times, reporter not listed, on October 6, 1996:

Focusing on the "Jenny Jones Show" shifts blame away from the defendant to homophobia Society's problem is not that these TV shows are on. Society's problem is that we've created a world where a guy feels he can go out and kill a guy because he is gay.

As the "hate, not humiliation" theory became the new focus of news stories, a small contingent began to blame Schmitz again for the murder. Robert Strauss of The Los Angeles Times said that Schmitz would have to be pretty gullible to have no idea what he was in for on the "Jenny Jones Show." Strauss argued that even if the show's producers encouraged Amedure to be "flamboyant" toward Schmitz, Schmitz still purchased the gun, sought out Amodure, and killed him.

UNIQUE ELEMENTS

While Scott Amedure's death is undoubtedly a tragedy, his death did not reach the magnitude, in terms of press coverage or public outrage, of the Columbine High School shootings or Princess Diana's death.

The "Jenny Jones" talk-show case also differed from the other two cases in that it involved two trials and a negligence suit brought against the show. In the late fall of 1995, hearings on the "Jenny Jones" murder case began, and throughout late 1995 and 1996, the "Jenny Jones" talk-show murder began making news again. While more than six months had passed between the murder and the first round of hearings, Jenny Jones, the show, and its producers still remained the objects of blame for Amedure's murder. As the trial neared, Schmitz's new defence attorney again tried to focus on the talk show's tactics. While on the stand, Jenny Jones herself maintained that Schmitz knew his secret admirer could be a man or a woman. Ron French, for The Detroit News on February 21, 1996, wrote several stories about the trial stages of the case. Defence attorney James Burdick will try to deflect responsibility for the slaying from his client to the "Jenny Jones Show" and its ambush interview tactics. Schmitz claims he was misled by producers who persuaded him to fly to Chicago to appear on a show about secret admirers. On November 12, 1996, Jonathan Schmitz was convicted of second-degree murder, yet jurors for the trial said the show deserved at least some of the blame. Ron French of The Detroit News, November 13, 1996, covered the case's outcome from the jury's point of view.

"We saw the show as a catalyst for this," said juror Joyce O'Brien. "They destroyed one person's life and his family, and another young man is dead and his family ruined. It is a terrible injustice all because of the show." As the trial came to a close, reporters from the "elite" media again began bashing the "Jenny Jones Show," the show's producers, and daytime TV for the "corruption of society". An Associated Press story, written by Frazier Moore, discussed the details of the verdict in a November 29, 1996, column. Obviously Jonathan Schmitz wasn't prepared for what he got by Jones or any of the Jenny Jones staff. Quite the opposite. Evidence indicates that for the sake of lively talk TV, Schmitz was set up to believe he would be meeting the girl of his dreams. Instead, he met Jenny Jones.

After the much-publicized trial and verdict, the two years following the trial, 1997 and 1998, were fairly quiet. News of the murder and trial popped up sporadically, mostly in the form of editorials. Schmitz was convicted in 1996, but in 1998, his conviction was overturned on a technicality in an appeals court. In May of 1999, a jury awarded the Amedure family $25 million in a negligence suit against the "Jenny Jones Show." From a Los Angeles Times story (byline merely indicating it was from wire reports) on May 15, 1999:

A jury finds the "Jenny Jones Show" liable for the 1995 shooting death of Scott Amedure, a gay man who admitted during a never-aired show that he had a crush on Jonathan Schmitz. The jury awarded $25 million in damages to Amedure's family, saying the show tricked Schmitz and humiliated him into committing the murder. In September 1999, Jonathan Schmitz was convicted for the second time in the death of Scott Amedure. Circuit Judge Wendy Potts handed Schmitz a 25 to 50-year sentence-the same sentence he received in his first trial. The $25 million civil-suit award for the Amedure family represents a new turn in state and federal courts holding entertainment media liable for a tragedy.

Culpability in the "Jenny Jones" talk-show murder case was easier to prove than the culpability of the violent video games, music, and films linked to the Columbine High School shooting and of the paparazzi linked to the death of Princess Diana. The title of the segment, "Secret Admirers," the "ambush-style" tactics, and the notion that a talk-show guest was allegedly "goaded" to "act flamboyantly" have all been cited as evidence that the show and its producers incited the murder.

CONTEXT OF POPULAR-CULTURE BLAME

At the same time the entertainment industry was being held accountable for Scott Amedure's death, news of other tragedies, including the Columbine High School shootings, hit the airwaves and newsstands, and some producers of popular culture were again the target of blame.

From the time of the murder to the time of Jonathan Schmitz's first trial, the "Jenny Jones Show," the producers of the show, daytime talk shows in general, homophobia, and Schmitz had all been blamed for the death of Amedure. The news stories acknowledged Schmitz was responsible for pulling the trigger; however, many reporters seemed intent on finding an additional source of blame. Through the selection of sources used in news stories to the focus of the news stories themselves, the "elite" media seemed to assign blame to the "less-than-legitimate" talk shows. Within a month after the murder, many of the "elite" media jumped on the bandwagon of accusing the popular media of polluting America. From The Washington Post, on October 31, 1995:

Still, there's no question many talk shows exploit and often humiliate people for entertainment-especially the ambush-style programs like the infamous Jenny Jones episode that was accused of sparking a murder. Some of the news stories even tried to draw distinctions between audiences of the "trashy" daytime talk shows and the audiences for other news-oriented programs. Sharon Waxman in The Washington Post described viewers of the daytime talk shows as "gullibleoften unemployedleeches" who had nothing better to do than to live vicariously through the lives of other "trailer park trash." This cycle of blame became all the more evident as Jonathan Schmitz headed into his first trial and then his second trial. "Elite" newspapers such as The Washington Post, The Los Angeles Times, The Dallas Morning News, The Detroit News, and The Chicago Tribune appeared to draw a clear distinction between themselves and the popular media.

Furthermore, these news outlets criticized the talk shows for uncovering secrets, exposing wrongdoings, and "harping on the perversion in society." Yet many of these publications were doing the same thing by giving the story so much coverage. The difference is that the talk shows were reaching one audience, and the "elite" media used the same "trash" to reach another audience. During the four-and-a-half-year-long evolution of the story, several theories of blame circulated. While the blame was shared, the daytime talk shows took the biggest hit for allegedly causing a larger social problem, "cultural pollution." Jonathan Schmitz's lawyer, James Burdick, said when Jenny Jones asked her television audience, "Is your life better than television?," culpability rested in her hands and in the hands of the show's producers. Burdick's contention is that in Jones' quest to focus on the drama of interpersonal conflict in a public forum, she theoretically put the gun in Schmitz's hands.

CONNECTIONS WITH THEORY

Pauly's (1992) discussion of the "elite" media's criticism of Rupert Murdoch parallels the "elite" media's criticism of the talk shows in the "Jenny Jones" case. Rupert Murdoch was accused by many in the "elite" press of devaluing journalistic ideals, and in a similar sense, journalists covering the "Jenny Jones" case accused the talk shows of not maintaining a high standard of practice. This can be seen quite clearly as many newspaper reporters covering the story implicitly or explicitly distinguished themselves as "serious" journalists. Media mogul Rupert Murdoch was criticized for his style of promotional journalism, and the news organizations covering the "Jenny Jones" story capitalized on the promotional qualities of the pop-culture products they were criticizing by giving the story so much news coverage.

The news media would have a difficult time rationalizing the prominent play the story received, especially the length of time the story was in the news, because over the course of time, new details were not uncovered. More simply, the story was essentially old news with a high level of sensationalism and a presumed high level of public interest. It seems fairly clear that as news editors made decisions regarding the newsworthiness of the story, promotional journalism was a driving factor in continued coverage. The examples from the "Jenny Jones" case parallel Bird's (1992) discussion of the way "serious" journalists speak out about "low taste."

The "elite" journalists and the sources they chose made overt references to the media producers they felt were responsible for Amedure's death. Adjectives such as "trashy" and "tabloid" clearly placed the talk shows in a very different category from the "elite" journalists; thus, by distinguishing the talk shows as a media product very different from what the journalists were producing, the journalists were able to keep the blame away from themselves. The "elite" media's classification of the talk shows as "smut" entertainment is what Jensen would classify as an assumption of the masses as the "lowest common denominator." As the "elite" newspapers critiqued their popular media counterparts by using words such as "trash," "smut," or "tabloid," they elevated their own status by drawing a clear distinction between themselves and those ostensibly not like them.

One application of Jensen's theoretical framework to this study is an understanding of how the popular media were blamed for each of the tragedies. In the "Jenny Jones" case, the "elite" journalists accused the talk shows of pandering to the "sick" predilections of viewers-in a sense, doing anything for ratings. The talk shows were blamed for giving audiences what they wanted rather than news and information they needed. In many news stories, the "elite" journalists directly condemned the talk shows, the talk show producers, the talk show guests and the talk show viewers of lowering the cultural standard of art in America.

This analysis can also be tied to McDonald's discussion of journalists speaking out against "low taste." In the "Jenny Jones" case, some newspaper quotes actually addressed this issue explicitly, arguing that part of the blame lies squarely at the feet of the public whose taste for sensationalism is merely answered by television talk shows. Shoemaker and Reese's discussion of the five levels of influence on media content is central to explaining much of the coverage of the "Jenny Jones" case. At the individual level, reporters and columnists frequently took the show to task in the form of editorials, thereby providing an outlet for their own unfavorable views of the show and others like it. The newspaper journalists covering the "Jenny Jones" case often seemed to have taken a "holier-than-thou" tone in their stories of Scott Amedure's death. It is possible the professional background of these reporters and columnists enabled them to view the talk-show host and producers as professionally careless in their attempts to achieve higher ratings via exploitative means.

At the routines and/or the individual level of influence, newspaper reporters often presented a relatively one-sided story via the sources they used in their stories. Some stories, while seemingly objective, contained a position simply by the use of some sources and not others. It seems as if the "elite" newspapers relied on Thompson, the prosecutor, heavily because he provided a voice for the point of view that was presumed to sell more newspapers. Thompson readily blamed the "Jenny Jones Show, " Jenny Jones herself, and the talk-show producers for the murder. Numerous news stories quoted family members and friends of Schmitz in addition to psychologists and analysts hired by the defence team.

Furthermore, "elite" journalists were able to work many expert and official sources into their stories by relying on murder experts and psychologists who provided a rationale for Schmitz's actions and in some cases even took the blame away from Schmitz and placed more blame on the talk show. Following Amedure's murder, several members of Congress also spoke publicly about the negative and violent content of television talk shows, and some even advocated removing the shows from television altogether.

The inclusion of these sources in the news stories was certainly justifiable, yet few stories provided the depth and analysis that would represent alternative views. Initially, the "Jenny Jones" case did not receive the prominent news coverage of the other cases reviewed here. The murder was not considered newsworthy until the entertainment media were accused of helping to commit the crime. The story seemed to illustrate the routines of "status conferral" and of pack journalism.

As the story and its subjects became more prominent, it began to appear in more and more newspapers. Some newspapers devoted one story and several sidebars to the case for weeks and even months. Other newspapers ran stories for several days in a row, even though new information had not been uncovered or released.

While this behaviour may be standard practice in many newsrooms, it also illustrates the way news editors are often "forced" to allow more space for a story simply because the competition or national newspapers are running the story. From an ideological or hegemonic standpoint, blaming the "Jenny Jones Show" and its producers meant the "cause" for the tragedy was easily pinpointed. American society could point its finger at the media, and then, in a figurative sense, rest comfortably with the thought that the villain was identified. As de Mooij suggests, American culture strives for a source of blame, an identifiable cause, and views tragic events as a consequence of blame-worthy factors.

Blaming the media, in this case, helps maintain order because members of society do not necessarily have question the social forces that pit members of a dominant group (heterosexuals) against those from a non-dominant group (homosexuals) with potentially fatal consequences once the media have been isolated as the villain. The underlying theme of the press coverage is that ordinary citizens do not have to fear for their safety unless they appear on a talk show themselves, rather than suggesting homophobia and hate are all too common in society. Initially, this well-publicized case may have temporarily heightened fear and feelings of uncertainty in members of society. With the elevated fear, they searched for a culprit, and once the talk shows were identified as the "cause," the fear subsided, and members of society, as well as those in the "elite" media, were able to feel more secure about their status quo social world.

It seemed much easier to blame the products of popular culture when the finger-pointers could step back and draw a clear distinction between themselves and those they were blaming for the tragedy. By making daytime television seem sleazy, trashy, and outlandish, the "elite" media improved their own image by comparison. However, the oversight seems to be that these same "elite" media were using similar stunts to draw in larger audiences themselves. Case: Columbine High School Shootings.On April 20,1999, just before lunchtime, 18-year-old Eric Harris and 17-year-old Dylan Klebold, armed with guns and homemade bombs, opened fire on their classmates at Columbine High School in Littleton, Colorado. The siege lasted over four hours and ended with 15 dead, including the two gunmen, and several others wounded.

It was the bloodiest school shooting in the history of the United States and was carried out with well-orchestrated and disturbingly cold and calculated precision-as well as visible glee on the part of the gunmen. The series of events and its aftermath left many to grapple with the difficult question of what had gone so terribly wrong that two young men would wreak such awful havoc on their peers.

This case study attempts to illustrate how the print news media covered this tragedy, with an emphasis on how journalists dealt with the task of addressing the issue of why the shooting occurred. In the course of investigating and discussing possible entities at fault, the news media quickly came to focus on popular-culture and entertainment-media products as causal contributors to the massacre at Columbine High. Extensive quotes drawn from major newspapers around the world (searched via LEXIS-NEXIS) illustrate and also place into context the tendency of the news media to point the finger of blame at popular culture following this tragic event.

JUST THE FACTS

The very first accounts in the news media of the school shooting in Littleton, Colorado, followed traditional journalistic ideals of reporting on who, what, where, when, and how. The first day of coverage was a veritable news media frenzy, with blow-by-blow accounts broadcast live across the United States on the major radio and broadcast television networks and extensive coverage of gory details on cable news networks.

News that day featured terrified testimonials from students. Expressions of immense relief were broadcast as parents were united with their children. But above all, the view of a bloodied student escaping from a second-story window was perhaps the most memorable image, because of both its profundity and the number of times it was shown.

Quotes from print news media on April 20, 1999, document the tragic and frightening sequence of events and reflect the journalistic tradition of conveying the particulars (who, what, when, where, and how) of the event. The first newspaper articles on the topic came out before all the facts were known and thus included attempts to find out what exactly was happening inside the school, reporting the harrowing estimations of how many were killed, how many wounded.

From The Denver Rocky Mountain News, reporters Mike Anton, Manny Gonzalez, Kevin Vaughan, Charley Able, and Lou Kilzer, on April 20, 1999: At least 21 people were injured today when two or three gunmen dressed in black overcoats and masks opened fire inside Columbine High School in Littleton. Witnesses said the gunmen, reportedly students, appeared to fire randomly and set off explosives, possibly pipe bombs, laughing as they went.

From The Denver Rocky Mountain News, reporter Mike Anton, on April 20, 1999: Authorities said some victims were still inside the school as of 2:15 p.m. About 30 students were reported hiding in the choir room Seconds after the shooting began, hundreds of students and teachers poured out of the school while others sought refuge inside, hiding under desks and locking themselves in bathrooms Said another student "We were all under the table and the girl across the table from me was shot in the head right there." A finger pointing of sorts occurred on this day, but served to merely answer the most pressing question at hand: who was responsible for this tragedy? Early blame was narrowly focused on those quickly identified as the gunmen, Eric Harris and Dylan Klebold. News stories traced the steps of the siege, its consequences, and its perpetrators.

POPULAR-CULTURE CULPABILITY

The next day, however, on April 21, 1999, the basic facts had largely already been gathered and disseminated. News coverage would now be dominated by placing blame and assigning responsibility to various people, institutions, and entities. Exceptions to the blame-laying patterns that prevailed in the aftermath of the shooting were stories about vigils and grieving processes, connections made in communities around the country with those involved, and decisions to cancel sporting and other events in light of the tragedy. Most other stories appearing for more than a month later attempted not to repeat the who, what, where, when, and how issues, but rather tackled the far more complex issue of why.

Instances of popular culture being blamed came quickly, on the day of the tragedy to help fill the broad expanse of time that cable news networks devoted to coverage, and in the days immediately following in print. The tradition of many news sources picking up the same angle or the same threads of the story was also readily apparent. Wire reports appeared in newspapers across the nation, and the same shocking footage became less and less troubling as American television news viewers were exposed to it again and again. Once popular-culture products were introduced as culprits in early coverage, journalists across the world made a similar connection.

Those who pointed the finger of blame at media and popular-culture products in newspaper coverage largely fell into three categories: students at Columbine and other area schools, experts-typically professors, counselors, attorneys, and police officers-and reporters and newspaper editorial staff writers themselves. Many popular-culture products were implicated as causal contributors to Harris and Klebold's violence. Movies (especially The Matrix), television, video games, the Internet, and recorded music were all scrutinized as antisocial influences on the gunmen.

In fact, though there is plenty of precedent for a single film or book, for instance, inspiring real-life antisocial behaviour, the Columbine shooting stands out as the one historical incident in which so many different popular-culture products were seen as responsible in so many different ways.

From The Atlanta Journal Constitution, reporter Mike Williams, on April 22, 1999: According to their friends, Harris, 18, and Klebold, 17, were part of a loose-knit group called the 'Trenchcoat Mafia' and often dressed in black, favoring leather and the long coats that have been featured in many violence-filled Hollywood movies. The boys played violent computer games for hours, friends said Harris set up an Internet home page that spouted Nazi ideology and condoned violence. The shootings came on the 110th anniversary of Hitler's birthday. From The Daily Telegraph (London), reporter John Hiscock, on April 22, 1999: The two laughing teenagers who shot and bombed their way though the halls of Columbine High School were members of a Gothic-style group known as the Trenchcoat Mafia.

Students at Littleton, Colorado, yesterday described Dylan Klebold, 17, and Eric Harris, 18, as "satanic individuals" who talked about Nazis and were fans of the "shock rock" star Marilyn Manson. From The New York Daily News, reporter Helen Kennedy, on April 21, 1999: A Web page attributed to one of the members contained crude sketches of demons along with juvenile nihilism like "Anything I don't like sucks." There were song lyrics, from a German underground band called KMFDM an acronym for Kein Mehrfeit Fur Die Mitleid (No pity for the majority) including "What I don't like I waste," "I am your apocalypse," and "Chaos panic/no resistance/detonations in the distance."

From The Daily Telegraph (London), reporter John Hiscock, on April 22, 1999: The Trenchcoat Mafia was born about three years ago when about a dozen students at Columbine started wearing black and listening to German techno music. They often wore German slogans and swastikas on their clothes. Both were obsessed with the Internet-widely used by neo-Nazi groups-and computer games. Their favourites were Doom and Quake-violent fantasies where the aim is to kill everything you meet.

From The Denver Post, reporters Susan Greene and Bill Briggs, on April 21, 1999: "It appears you have a bunch of kids who've been into black metal music-Marilyn Manson-who basically have apocalyptic fantasies and (who operate under) a heavy code of neo-Nazism," said (Dr. Carl) Raschke (author of Painted Black, which explores violent youth culture).

From The Denver Rocky Mountain News, reporter Robert Denerstein, on April 22, 1999: In the enormously popular new movie The Matrix, Keanu Reeves wears a black duster and battles the forces of evil with two-fisted bursts of gunfire. He stages an attack on the conspiracy that has turned his life into a living hell. The movie already is being mentioned as a possible source of influence on the Trench Coat Mafia, two of whose members entered Columbine High School Tuesday carrying weapons and wearing long black coats. It's not the first time movies have been connected with real-life violence

The above quotes demonstrate the wide variation in types of popular-culture products blamed, as well as the unique combinations of those entities that were viewed as responsible. They also demonstrate other aspects of youth culture, including hairstyles, body art, and means of dress, that were indirectly implicated in the news coverage of the Columbine shootings.

The entire nation was introduced to "gothic" culture in a manner that was at times valiant in its pursuit of value-neutral reportage. At other times "gothic" culture was implicated as a menacing desensitization to and even morbid fascination with death and dying that purportedly helped explain why Harris and Klebold acted with such utter disregard for human life.

The short amount of time it took to blame popular media and popular culture was partially explained by the relationship of the events that occurred in Littleton that day to other school shootings with young perpetrators in other areas of the country. It was an eerily familiar formula, and attempts at explanation linked Columbine to these other school shootings as sources and reporters struggled to make sense of the lot. In fact, one newspaper account used the media and popular culture to link the tragedy at Columbine to another recent high-profile student shooting. From The Ottawa Citizen, reporters Bob Harvey and Christopher Guly, on April 22, 1999:

Just last week, parents of three girls killed in 1997 in Paducah, Kentucky, sued the makers of another film, The Basketball Diaries, starring Leonardo DiCaprio. The Paducah killer, Michael Carneal, said his decision to open fire on a school prayer group was influenced by that film.

EXONERATING POPULAR CULTURE/ SHARING THE BLAME

Certainly the media and popular-culture products were not the only entities blamed for the Columbine tragedy, though they were among the most frequent targets. Other sources of blame included poor parenting, unsafe schools, uninformed school and police officials, teen cliques, feelings of ostracism, and, perhaps the most frequent additional target of criticism-the prevalence and accessibility of guns. Some of those who assigned blame in the Columbine shootings chose to focus on only one of these culprits, while others argued that these factors acted in concert to explain the tragedy that had occurred.

Some took the position that other societal factors outweighed the role of popular culture in contributing to the tragedy. Others seemed to feel that those entities should share the responsibility. From The Los Angeles Times, reporter Josh Getlin, on April 22, 1999:

The shooting also brings up an old question. How much responsibility does the culture bear for images of violence and retribution, which fill movies, TV, video games, the Internet, recorded music and even the most elementary cartoons today? "We've seen a steady escalation of violence as entertainment, and it reaches people in disturbing ways," (Joyce) Appleby (American history professor) said. "Billions of people watch these pictures around the globe, but somewhere a handful of boys weren't horrified, they were fascinated."

From The Ottawa Citizen, reporters Bob Harvey and Christopher Guly, on April 22, 1999: Those especially vulnerable to violent media messages are individuals-like the two gunmen in the Denver suburb Tuesday-who are "separated away from the mainstream," said Mr. (Andrew) Osier (media professor at the University of Western Ontario), who researches media and violence at the university's Faculty of Information and Media Studies.

A few reporters and experts alike voiced concern that media and popular-culture products were serving as scapegoats in the wake of Columbine, possibly masking other, ostensibly more important causal factors. Articles defending these entities, however, were in the minority and tended to occur in response to the preceding typos of popular-culture accusations. From The Chicago Sun Times, reporter Richard Roeper, on April 22, 1999:

It's impossible-and unfair-to point to a band or a movie or a TV show and say "That was the cause," and then to turn to a slaughter and say, "This is the effect." If that's the way it worked, how can it be that hundreds of thousands of fans the world over have been exposed to the spine-thumping music of KMFDM without turning violent?

From The Los Angeles Times, reporter Josh Getlin, on April 22, 1999: "The media influences people, but you don't march into a school armed with guns and grenades and kill 13 people overnight. It doesn't come from nowhere," he (Todd Boyd, an author and professor at the USC School of Cinema and Television) added. From The Denver Rocky Mountain News editorial, on April 21, 1999: What, many Americans wonder, is going on? We don't profess to know, yet surely part of the answer is a relatively simple phenomenon: unbalanced, resentful kids imitating the highly publicized actions of other unbalanced kids. Most other explanations-the influence of violent entertainment, for example, or too-easy access to guns-suffer from the weakness of having long predated the recent trend of gun-toting students invading their schools with guns.

Do news accounts merely blame the content of popular entertainment media without assessing the media companies and the production and distribution processes that create that content? The answer in this case appears to be yes. Noticeably absent in coverage of the Columbine school shootings was a larger, more macroscopic context for popular-culture blame.

Newspaper articles that mentioned either the corporations involved in the production of the content that many found objectionable or the commercial structure of American media that de-emphasizes social responsibility in the creation of content were noticeably rare. Indeed, though many an allegation was made against popular-culture products for their role in this shooting, most blamers did not accuse the producers of these products but rather just the products themselves. This seems to suggest media and popular-culture content were "naturalized," perceived as a given in this case.

Most accounts did not tend to acknowledge that there were people making decisions that dictate what types of content we see in entertainment media and popular culture. Though very rare, we will share the few exceptions in which producers of the objectionable content were blamed. From The Boston Globe, reporter John Ellis, on April 22, 1999: The television networks, the major movie studios, record companies, video game software producers, print and other media are spending hundreds of millions of dollars every year to adapt children to this diet of violence and carnage. Once addicted, they'll want more of it, which can and will be provided at a slightly higher price.

From The London Independent, reporter David Aaronovitch, on April 22, 1999: Film-makers who allow violence to seem cool and attractive should examine their consciences. And we should criticise them more. Organisations like CNN, who offered "uninterrupted live coverage" of events at Columbine High School, should consider whether that isn't exactly what the avenging dweebs want. Some news accounts were acutely aware of the blaming tendency and viewed it as a defence mechanism for coping with the tragedy, also noting that at the most fundamental level, there truly was no sufficient explanation for a tragedy of such magnitude. These atypical news articles drew the most macroscopic picture possible, speculating on broad problems at issue in society or simply conceding that an accurate and fair assessment of blame was impossible. From The Arizona Republic editorial, on April 21, 1999:

Whatever that elusive answer may be, it is no longer enough to simply wag our fingers at the usual suspects. This time, we can't allow ourselves to simply scowl at the National Rifle Association. Or at disintegrating families and bleak, cynical television that trivializes life. We can't simply rage at bloody video games. From The Boston Globe, reporter John Ellis, on April 22, 1999: We have surrounded ourselves with violence. It is everywhere we turn. It is in our music. It is on our televisions. It is in our movies. It is on our video games. It is prominently featured in print media and on popular Web sites. If it bleeds it leads and it leads because it sells. Tuesday's massacre at Columbine High School in Littleton, Colo., was not an aberration. It was and is a fact of modern American life. From The Denver Rocky Mountain News editorial, on April 21, 1999: But as we said, we don't know what the explanation is and don't care to speculate right now. The moment is too solemn, the bloodletting too extensive for the mind to even grasp. For the time being, our thoughts remain focused solely on those who lives now will never be the same.

UNIQUE ELEMENTS

The role of popular culture in the Columbine school shooting is a rather complex phenomenon. In addition to the basic and pervasive tendency to blame popular-culture products (films, television, video games, recorded music), there were three additional sources of media-related blame in newspaper coverage. First, many questioned the role of the local news media-universally picked up by the national news media-during the tragedy, in that their actions may have inadvertently jeopardized the safety of the students in the school. Others blamed the news media for being unnecessarily sensationalistic, insensitive to the trauma experienced by those involved, and inordinately intrusive into the lives of members of the community. (It is important to note that still others applauded the local news media for accurate and compassionate reporting, though those accounts are not reported here as they do not involve blame.) These quotes also demonstrate the way in which some news organizations differentiated themselves from others in order to elude blame by association. From The Atlanta Journal Constitution, reporters Don Aucoin and Drew Jubera, on April 21, 1999:

In the heat of the moment, missteps occurred. At one point, the information was broadcast that one youth was trapped inside the schools' "choir room," a potentially risky step if the gunmen were watching TV inside the school. From The Chicago Sun Times, reporter Phil Rosenthal, on April 21, 1999: From ground zero of the melee at Columbine High School in Littleton, Colo., a student hiding under a table with his cell phone called to alert others of his predicament. His call went not to his parents or police, as some did. It went to Denver's KUSA-TV, which broadcast his report live in Denver (and nationally via CNN, MSNBC and CNBC), oblivious to the fact the school had TVs in every classroom and that the inside information might be aiding the gun-toting assailants behind the siege.

From The Boston Herald, reporter Monica Collins, on April 22, 1999: On television yesterday, it was a mop-up operation after Tuesday's horrendous live coverage of the massacre at Columbine High School in Littleton, Colo. Bigfoot network reporters arrived, interviewing shell-shocked student survivors. Sobbing parents who awaited their children's corpses at a nearby elementary school were not spared from the intrusive lenses. Viewers still shudder at the memory of those macabre, unfiltered visions captured at the height of the evil event Second, many critics of the news media also speculated on the possibility of copycat instances following the very extensive coverage the news media gave the event.

Critics mentioned the unwitting tendency of the news media to elevate the perpetrators to cult celebrity status, which may, in turn, encourage similar behaviours from young people elsewhere. One might expect newspaper reporters to omit such instances in which news media were implicated, albeit indirectly, out of self-interest. However, sources consulted for the stories often thrust this angle into the news discourse about the event. Furthermore, newspapers were able to protect their own interests by emphasizing local strategies to avoid hypercoverage that may lead to copycat phenomena.

From The Atlanta Journal Constitution, reporter Phil Kloer, on April 21, 1999: As the sheriff spoke to reporters, news helicopters circled overhead. He was immersed in a sea of reporters, their microphones all lined up in concentric circles, pointing inward. "We've had a lot of media attention of these kinds of situations," the sheriff said, "and you don't know how much that gives other people the idea to do it."

From The Boston Herald, reporter Monica Collins, on April 22, 1999: Detective Sgt. Margot Hill, the Boston police media relations director who helped hammer out the pact (setting standards for the airing of live tragedies) with Boston broadcasters, says "There's no value in airing live. If you air live, you're ghouls and you'll probably create a copycat within a week. We've become a nation of voyeurs."

From The Columbus Dispatch, reporter not listed, on April 22, 1999: "Media attention has given a star quality to such incidents," (Richard) Hazier (a professor in Counselor Education at Ohio University) said. "Kids now have the thought in their minds that it is possible to bring guns into school and get revenge that way," he said"That's why copycat issues are such a concern today." Third, another subtopic of media-related blame involved Harris and Klebold reportedly learning how to make pipe bombs on the Internet. From The New York Daily News, reporter Kevin McCoy, on April 22, 1999:

A Colorado prosecutor confirmed the cybersearch yesterday as new details emerged about violent imagery and pipe bomb assembly instructions on a Web site linked to gunman Eric Harris. "The Internet is very involved in this case," Jefferson County District Attorney David Thomas said when asked whether Harris and Dylan Klebold used computer expertise to plot the rampage. From The London Independent, reporter David Aaronovitch, on April 22, 1999: Ah yes, but Eric and Dylan also had home-made pipe bombs. Where did those come from?

Almost certainly from the pages of the Internet, where Randy from Idaho, or the Urban Terrorist's homepage, will give any teenager all the information he needs to know to blow up his enemiesPerhaps they were rendered immune to the reality of what they were planning to do as a consequence of long, crepuscular hours spent at the keyboard, blasting punks and decapitating jerks to earn record scores. After a while, real flesh may become confused with pixellated gore and guts in the adolescent mind.

CONNECTIONS WITH THEORY

The quotes from the newspaper coverage of the Columbine tragedy demonstrate many of the theoretical foundations outlined earlier in this chapter. Just as Pauly and Eason discuss in essays about Rupert Murdoch and the news story "Jimmy's World," respectively, analysis of the press coverage of the Columbine school shootings reveals rather ingrained, idealized notions about the nature of journalism.

Journalists reporting on Columbine seem to deem themselves above the fray, even when discussing the apparent mistakes made by fellow journalists in covering the story, such as being too intrusive or insensitive or having coverage that is so extensive it could inspire a copycat shooting.

In fact, some of the stories-either through the comments of sources or the words of journalists themselves-suggest disdain on the part of "serious" journalists for their more sensationalistic or entertainment-oriented counterparts. Rarely was a distinction between "serious" journalism and more "frivolous" and presumably "harmful" entertainment media content made explicitly by a reporter in the story.

Rather, the distinction was made implicitly in the tone of the stories, in the words and phrases chosen, and in the angles pursued in the telling of the story. The distinction that we argue is made here is similar to the one discussed by Bird in her analysis of tabloid newspapers and their relationship to "serious" journalism. In the case of Columbine, the distinction may, in fact, be easier for newspaper reporters to argue because the medium is often different, with newspapers or print journalism seen as "serious," informative, and helpful, and video games, recorded music, television, and movies seen as more "frivolous" and "harmful."

The same types of assumptions that Jensen argues underlie major strains of media criticism are apparent here. There is a sense of protectionism that borders on elitism on the part of those who criticized popular media in major newspaper coverage of the Columbine shootings, with the notion that the newspapers provide what is good for the public, and entertainment media provide what is bad. The newspaper's role is one of savior. By pointing out the evils of the popular media that Dylan Klebold and Eric Harris enjoyed, newspaper coverage can help save other impressionable youth or raise a warning flag for their parents. The newspaper coverage of the Columbine school shootings can also be examined in terms of Shoemaker and Reese's levels of influence on media content.

On the individual level, for instance, the tone of the coverage suggests that the journalists may have shared the sadness and outrage of the American public and were thus inclined to point the finger of blame as a way of coping with and trying to make sense of the tragedy. In fact, the immediate deaths of Klebold and Harris served to remove them as a target for continuing feelings of grief and anger. Assigning responsibility to an ongoing social institution such as the popular media provides both reporters and their readers with an enduring target at which they can vent their anger.

The individual reporters and their editors may also have chosen this angle because it corresponds with their own personal values or opinions regarding popular culture and media influence. The quotes that imply disapproval or the ones that adopt a moralistic tone would support this as one factor shaping coverage. Also on the individual level, reporters and editors at the newspapers whose coverage was examined may have felt a "holier than thou" attitude toward entertainment-oriented popular media. This influence bridges the theoretical structure of Shoemaker and Reese with that of Jensen, Bird, Eason, and Pauly. On the media routines level, the routines regarding the selection and use of sources as well as the traditional emphasis on localism were apparent in coverage. For example, schoolmates and area residents were often called upon for first-hand accounts of possible popular-culture blame, and experts such as police officers or college professors were often utilized for verification. The coverage also evolved from reporting "who, what, where, when, and how" to also including "why," the latter leading to the popular-culture blame explored here. Finally, the routine of providing simplified, uncomplicated explanations for events was followed in some of the coverage of the Columbine shootings that advanced one particular or more compelling explanation for the tragedy (often popular culture) rather than discussing multiple and complex factors.

In either the organizational or the extramedia level as defined by Shoemaker and Reese, ownership issues and the chain of command may have influenced coverage of the Columbine shootings. With such a broad range of media and popular-culture products implicated, a conflict of interest was possible because of growing cross-media ownership.

A newspaper owned by the same company that owns a record label whose recording artists or types of music were criticized for their role in the shootings may have been disinclined to emphasize the possible effect ofthat music on the shooters because of pressure from the top.

On the other hand, a newspaper relatively free of those direct connections with the popular media being implicated (or with holdings in competing media that would benefit from a possible boycott of the particular popular media criticized) may be more likely to point the finger of blame.

In the case of Columbine, it is possible that manufacturers and distributors of popular-culture products that advertise in newspapers would be displeased with coverage that implicates those video games, the Internet, television, or movies in such a high-profile tragedy. For instance, the newspapers from which we have quoted may carry lucrative advertising inserts for retail outlets offering or even specializing in media-driven products (TV sets, DVD players, video game consoles). Perhaps popular-culture culpability would havo been even more extensive or scathing if it were not for this influence that may have trickled down from the owners and managers in the newspaper's organizational structure. Also on the extramedia level, the sources used to cover the Columbine tragedy helped shape the content.

The students of Columbine High School were quick to report the violent and nihilistic media and popular culture content that attracted Klebold and Harris, as is apparent in the quotes from coverage above. This early angle may well have helped define the story from that point on.

Similarly, the efforts of other media organizations to establish the popular-media culpability angle, including the hometown Denver newspapers who had the earliest and most extensive coverage, may have set the tone that other media organizations followed. Finally, influences found at the ideological level may have shaped coverage of the Columbine shootings, as well. For instance, in many of the quotes from newspaper coverage outlined above, occasional resistance to assign blame to producers of content is evident, as writers relied instead on accusations against media content itself as divorced from those who created it. This may have been, consciously or not, a defensive strategy on the part of the newspapers to deflect criticism from their possible role in creating "a culture of violence" by helping to obscure the connection between the decisions and approaches of creators of content from content itself.

Also evident in the language used to implicate popular media are the lines of distinction implicitly drawn in coverage of the Columbine tragedy between the news media who covered the event and the entertainment media who were blamed. The emphasis was often on the blood, gore, and generally antisocial content of particular music lyrics, video games, and movies, and the apparently disturbing notion that this is what is used to entertain young people in our society. Thus, responsibility was placed firmly at the feet of media who are merely entertaining the masses rather than the news media who are providing a public service by informing them.

In the case of Columbine, there exists an underlying assumption that something is dreadfully wrong with the people who tune in to violent media fare and that the news media are trying to save them by pointing this out. Also at the ideological level, blaming the media for the Columbine tragedy could help maintain comforting notions of social order and reassure the public of social stability. The discomfort that comes with leaving such a tragedy unexplained is evident in the very few editorials that expressed that they were mystified by the tragedy and admitted this created a disquieting sense of chaos. It is also evident in the majority of newspaper stories that did, indeed, offer the popular-culture culpability argument as an explanation.

As de Mooij suggests, Americans are comforted by a sense of rationality and order, of things occurring for a reason. Advancing the popular-culture culpability attempts to bring rationality to the otherwise senseless nature of the tragedy, compounded because of the young age of the assailants and victims, the seemingly safe setting, and the apparent glee with which Klebold and Harris perpetrated their crimes. This study uses three high-profile cases to investigate conceptions regarding the moral consequences of popular media in contemporary soci-ety. In analyzing the discourse generated in news coverage of the three events, the theme of popular media's moral culpability was quite apparent. Whether it was for the car crash that claimed the life of Princess Diana, for the shooting that followed an apparently incendiary taping of the "Jenny Jones Show," or for the multiple-weapon assault enacted on Columbine High School, newspaper coverage included the assignment of blame to popular media and popular-culture products for these tragedies.

Analysis of the news discourse surrounding these events points to a number of themes regarding cultural and social practices. First, we can examine views and perceptions of "the media" as having potentially different readings and carrying quite disparate critical connotations depending on one's perspective. Some conceptualize "the media" as a relatively homogeneous and powerful force in the contemporary social structure with only slight, if any, important differences based on news versus entertainment content. This view holds that each media outlet exists for the purpose of profit and seeks that profit by appealing to audiences of specific sizes or characteristics.

Differences between news and entertainment are seen as minimal and shrinking, in a time in which "infotainment" abounds and the "news hole" in newspapers and on television is diminished by the amount of space or time allotted to weather, sports, and "light" features. Yet, the discourse examined in newspaper coverage of these three events shows a very different view of "the media." Rather than assuming similarities between news and entertainment and rather than newspapers sharing a sense of responsibility for a "culture of violence" or sensationalism such as is criticized in these cases, "the media" is seen as a heterogeneous collection of very different types of organizations with very different functions.

Implicit distinctions are drawn between those "serious" journalists whose function is to inform the public of important information related to their health and well being and those producers of popular media who allegedly instead jeopardize public health by irresponsible practices and the transmis sion of potentially harmful content.

The notion of irresponsible practices can be seen in the condemning tone in newspaper coverage that discusses the paparazzi in the case of Princess Diana's death and talk show producers and creators in the case of the "Jenny Jones Show" murder. The notion of harmful content is also an explicit element of the news discourse surrounding sensationalism, sex, and violence in talk shows as related to the "Jenny Jones" murder and antisocial and violent themes in popular media as related to the Columbine shootings.

Thus, there are some parallels to the theoretical argument made by Jensen. Jensen would argue that the view of the media described first above, as a homogeneous force, is an example of modern media criticism that may better be viewed as a criticism of modernity. Yet, she would presumably also object to the defensive strategies embarked upon by the newspapers whose coverage we examined because of their underlying assumptions regarding popular preferences and morality. These lines of distinction between "serious" and "popular" media comprise the second major theme revealed in this analysis.

As mentioned in the case studies, the distinction between "us" and "them" was not always made explicitly in the news coverage of the events. However, in the pursuit of the popular-culture culpability angle, in the disapproving tone of sources turned to or in reporters' own words, and in the lack of connection established between the newspaper itself and the other forms of media criticized, the distinction appears as an underlying assumption.

The assumption of a stark distinction between the "elite" press and other media forms is tenuous at best. As Bird andPauly suggest, those who position themselves as "serious" journalists and those who are viewed as "tabloid" journalists (and even those who create and disseminate entertainment media content) have more similarities than differences in terms of practices and goals. Yet, even when the connection between the accuser (the newspaper) and the accused seems most obvious, as in the discussion of excessive news coverage paving the way for a copycat following the Columbine tragedy, no elements of the discourse suggest similarity or recognize potential involvement on the part of the accuser.

Rather, the newspapers reported from a presumed position above the fray, akin to an omniscient and impartial observer, who then adopts an interpretive role to further the public good by helping to cure social ills. This not only reveals a privileged position for "elite" journalists but also suggests an artificial, unrealistic isolation of the newspaper from surrounding society.

At the centre of the issue of what makes a media professional "serious" or not is an assumption about the nature of the audience. The analysis of news discourse provided here shows further evidence of a protectionist, somewhat elitist view of audiences as being drawn, like moths to a flame, to content that is bad for them. Whether one blames the producers of such content or the audience members themselves for this assumed preference, the premise is the same: audience members must be encouraged to see the error of their ways in their enjoyment of or tolerance for violent, sexual, sensationalistic, and intrusive media content.

Some of the quotes we have cited from newspaper coverage of these three events appear to adopt the position that deaths such as these are the price we pay for the moral decline evident in the popularity of certain types of media content. Others reveal a tone of warning for local communities to prevent similar tragedies from occurring or recurring.

Still others call directly for greater governmental regulation, stricter parental control, and more responsibility on the part of the media industry. All such angles suggest a need for those wiser and more moral-led, in this case, by the "serious" journalists - to help save audience members from themselves. Underlying the blame of popular media and culture in the media discourse examined in our study is the "serious" journalists' notion of audience members preferring what is "easier to digest" or more appealing (popular media and culture) rather than what is good for them. What is good for them, in the case of our study, is presumably more "elite" media and culture, including the reading of newspapers such as those that are blaming their more populist counterparts. By focusing on the aspect of each story that involves the purportedly appealing qualities of the popular media criticized, "elite" newspapers can capitalize on those qualities (e.g., violence in the case of Columbine, sex in the case of "Jenny Jones") at the same time that they implicitly draw a distinction that separates them as more "tasteful." Shoemaker and Reese's theory of influences on media content also provides insights about situated, particular practices of news professionals, constraints and traditions in news gathering, and the interplay of producers, content, and public. Of the five spheres of influence identified by Shoemaker and Reese, we would argue that media routines were among the most likely to have a direct and measurable impact on how these three events were covered in the news. Routines including news values, ideas of what makes a "good" story, and traditional practices and constraints of news reportage are also presumably the influences that would most likely be listed by journalists themselves if asked what factors affect how events are covered, because of their practicality and concrete nature.

The other, more microscopic spheres of influence are slightly less compelling in this context. For example, though many journalists would welcome a work environment in which their own preferences, opinions, and values could dictate coverage, few achieve this degree of autonomy and write articles that run unchanged by higher-ups in the organizational structure.

We believe the more macroscopic factors of extramedia influences and ideology also play a crucial role, but one which is less apparent and more insidious. It is this element of the Shoemaker and Reese theory that can be linked to the theoretical contributions of Jensen, Bird, Pauly, and Eason. Though these forces are not always obvious, we argue that the factors comprising them are among the most potent in shaping news content in general, and coverage of these events specifically.

The influence of ideology encompasses cultural elements such as the cause-and-effect paradigm that de Mooij suggests is expected in American culture. This cultural norm is readily apparent in news-media discourse surrounding each of these three events, evident in the attempts to answer "why" the tragedies occurred in a simple and straightforward manner.

The ideological level also encompasses the issues of journalists (and others) holding rather unflattering perceptions of audience members and espousing a somewhat idealized role of the "serious" journalist as watchdog in contemporary society. In this scenario, there is a protectionism that borders on elitism. A key element interwoven throughout these theoretical foundations is hegemony. A revered and respected role reserved for "serious" journalists assures their position in society. Economics also play a crucial part. Newspapers tell stories in a certain way to sell copies in order to sell space to advertisers.

Popular-culture culpability, by its very populist nature, is a virtual guarantee of public interest. Yet, the public may be surprised to find the news discourse generated is one of shame, guilt, and danger associated with popular media. We would like to caution our readers, however, about assumptions that underlie this research endeavor. Our aim here was not to blame the "serious" news media for, in turn, blaming more populist news and entertainment media because we feel that blame is not deserved.

On the contrary (and perhaps contrary to the position Jensen would adopt), we do believe there are irresponsible practices and potentially harmful content in tabloid news and entertainment media that may have contributed-though certainly not as the sole culprit-to these three tragedies, and to other events as well. Our purpose here was to examine how this blame took shape, to illuminate forces and factors that led to the pursuit of this blaming as a common angle, and to elucidate the implicit strategies to keep "serious" journalists above blame.

It is this distinction that is made between accuser and culprit in the news coverage we examined, when the distance between the two is arguably quite small, that we suggest is the most interesting finding from our study.

8

Usage of Various Electronic Media

On the one hand, there have been huge investments by the educational sector on the establishment and maintenance of educational media for students. On the other hand, there has been very little and sporadic knowledge about the usage of such media in education. There is a need to understand the opinions of the target group on the functioning of the educational media and to elicit their suggestions towards the improvement of educational media in terms of content, duration, timings and methods available through them. Media had to be viewed on a comparative note in order to identify the more effective ones among them.

While the growth of the electronic media of radio and TV in terms of reach, popularity and variety has been phenomenal, there has not been a corresponding growth in their education-related usage. Lack of publicity about the contents and timings of the programs, inability of one's electronic equipments to receive the signals and lack of interactive nature of their programs have contributed to the under-utilization of these educational media.

In the case of internet, the problem has been one of access and affordability. Rural students are said to have less familiarity on the availability and contents of various media inputs. Similarly, the students of distance education and regional language medium classes also have been facing limitations in their utilization of educational media resources compared to regular streams and English medium classes.

The objective of the study included identifying the variations among the students of different demographic characteristics in terms of their media usage. As part of the study on various media usage patterns among the students of the state, the researcher carried out an extensive review of literature to identify the various issues and perspectives with regard to the area of focus. Radio is playing a significant role in reaching, informing and educating people.

Radio is still a dominant medium with wide access. Computers and internet have started influencing the way we learn. All these media are very powerful to reach, teach and enrich. But learning from them is quite different from reading a book according to Singhal and Rogers (2001). Reports confirm that educational Radio programs have been tried out in a wide range of subject areas in different countries. In Thailand, the radio is used to teach mathematics to school children Galda and for teacher training and other curricula Faulder; In Mexico, radio was used for literacy training and other programs Ginsburg and Arias-Goding; In Nigeria, radio was used for management courses for the agriculture sector Shears; The Philippines used the radio for nutrition education Cooke and Romweder; The Dominion Republic used radio in support of primary education White; Paraguay used radio to offer primary school instruction according to the Academy for Educational Development.

Radio in education can provide useful answers with diverse learners to solve easily, according to McLeish. Mason has stated that radio can be valuable in distance learning milieus ranging from schools, colleges and universities, from commerce and industry to public sector organizations. Moreover, radio programs can provide flexibility and openness, and easy accessibility to knowledge as well as better higher-order thinking and skill improvements with high-tech learning environments.

Radio can create new distance milieus in which learners are able to take greater responsibility for their own learning and constructing their own knowledge according to Resta. Moore and Tait, focusing on the use of new communication technologies in distance education systems such as e-learning, stated that educators and trainers give up working with radio as a low-tech educational tool. Radio has a unique power to create better interactive distance education environments itself than do emerging communication technologies, which can empower the capacities of radio when being used together in distance education systems.

Radio, moreover, provides life-long learning, professional updating, in-service training and community education from a cradle-to-grave position, which is independent of not only place but time as well.

Mason Learners, for that reason, can gain knowledge about themselves without feeling any digital diversity to share and exchange their experiences with others to promote their understanding with other learners from different culture. Learners can share and exchange their ideas, beliefs, opinions, knowledge, and information with others in interactive distance educational radio programs synchronously and/or asynchronously according to Crisell.

Also, learners and instructors can collaborate with any experts and learners from any places in the world. Synchronous education allows all distance learners taking their educational session at the same time, and interactivity occurs at same time. Synchronous communication in interactive distance radio programs allows live interactions among learners, instructors, experts, resources, etc., as per the views of Bonk and Cunningham.

With the technology growing in leaps and bounds, education does not stop at the borders of the campus and Television (TV) offers another way to reach out into homes and serve people where they live Reddi. Where TV is supposed to be the most effective one. Mohanty and Rath made an appraisal of Country Wide Class Room (CWCR) TV Programs. Among other things they found that the knowledge objective has been realized to a great extent in all the programs whereas understanding and application objectives have been realized to a great extent in 60% and 52% of the programs respectively. Jaiswal and Goel (1991), referring to the CWCR programs suggested that different pedagogical fields such as methods, media, techniques, devices, aids and formats have to be well selected.

There are several pointers to suggest that television, if used appropriately would be one of the powerful educational media. "Tests showed that students did significantly better when they viewed the lessons that demonstrated planned visual continuity, contained visual reinforcement, and had been the result of a team approach to make effective use of the TV medium." Chu and Schramm.

Without the ITV technology students would have limited access to courses" said Garland and Loranger (1996). According to Ranganathan (2002) watching TV is popular among students and not all of them watching TV for entertainment alone. Considerable numbers among them are on the look out for useful and usable information. They seek information that will enhance their general awareness and help them in their educational pursuits. Among the TV viewers there are some who watch CWCR occasionally. Ways to hold on to the existing viewer ship by enhancing viewer interest in our programs and attract others by extending the scope of programs should be found out. It is imperative that the programs are different and contain something special to get noticed among the plethora of programs offered by various channels.

The focus ought to be not on undergraduates but all the information and knowledge seekers. It is necessary to produce need based programs such as preparatory courses for those who take the competitive examinations at various levels. Promotion of CWCR through cross channel publicity is absolutely essential. TV expansion in years has been phenomenal. TV covers over 85% of the country's population. Cable TV is largely used for entertainment but it has great potential of being used for education as well according to Yadava (2000). Saiprasad (1991) carried out a study to elicit opinions and expectations of students and teachers on CWCR programs.

The results implied that there is a need to be conscious of the entry skills of the target group, to produce programs which require student participation and to integrate the CWCR programs into the collegiate education. According to a study Saiprasad (2001), higher education students seek information on education, career guidance, career advancement and a host of other areas through the internet. Research has indicated that computerized learning motivates students to invest more time in a subject-area (time-on-task), in particular when the student can work according to his own pace and time schedule, as described by Worthen, Van Dusen and Sailor. This also happens when the system creates extra possibilities for the student to communicate with other students (through e-mail, bulletin boards and computer conferencing). The enthusiasm of students working with the WWW is a clear illustration of these research findings. Research has shown that using computerized learning can reduce the necessary learning time of students to two-third of the time needed in a conventional course, as per the observations of Kulik and Kulik.

Internet enables citizens to have access to anything and everything of their choice - books, news, bank accounts, shopping, databanks, friends, peer groups and interest groups - and at a time of their choice without stirring out of the comfort of their homes with a flick of buttons on their remote control and computer keyboard.

Voice-activated signals may even do away with all this trouble of pushing buttons. But one may have to pay tolls for using internet. 'Unparalleled and unlimited human connectivity and interactivity without stirring out of homes, is set to transform intellectual, cultural, economic and political life' says Yadava (2000). Internet-based emerging communication tools, such as e-mails, bulletin boards, etc., provide more reflective and useful interactions among learners, instructors and resources according to Picciano (2002). The researcher found that, in the field of education, TV has assumed immense importance not only in terms of its reach but also in improving the quality of education at all levels and promises to play a major role in educational endeavors, towards upgrading as well as enrichment.

Web-based course delivery offers a complex learning and teaching environment. A vibrant learning community can be created using different teaching strategies, activities, and technologies. Thus, review of literature suggests that the number of educational courses that depend on modern educational media, more so in case of distance education. Education has become media technology enabled worldwide.

Methods play a major role in research. This study has adopted the survey method and descriptive research design. The universe or population of the study consisted of the entire set of student population in the graduate level in the state of Tamilnadu. According to the statistical handbook 2005, a total of 7.02 lakhs students are studying of under-graduation (UG) in various colleges in Tamilnadu. A total of 14,000 respondents (2%) of the universe have been covered as the sample. The sample for this study was selected from among the UG students of regular - distance mode and urban - rural students. Samples were drawn from different type of colleges like Arts, Science, Commerce, Engineering and Technology, Medicine and Agriculture.

Totally 14 places were selected for this study including seven major cities and seven small towns. Data were gathered using a self-administered questionnaire prepared specially for these purpose. Over 1,000 questionnaires were collected from each place. Based on the average of incomplete responses, the researcher has taken up 840 respondents from each place for the final analysis. The data was collected during the period from January 2005 to March 2006. Total numbers of respondents whose responses were taken up for analysis were 11,760. The chi-square test, simple percentage, Friedman's two-way anova and cross-tabulation were used for the analysis of this study.

DATA EXPERIENCES

The researcher observed that many of the students had come to know for the first time, about some of the media opportunities available, only at the time of research, by going through the questionnaire. The students expressed regret about the fact that no one had briefed them about the need to use various educational media.

The researcher also found that management bodies of many colleges were quite averse to the idea of researching media usage among their students. A notable facet that was exposed during the data collection was that many Principals and faculty members were ignorant about the latest educational media and programs available.

USAGE OF VARIOUS ELECTRONIC MEDIA

The ensuing part of the article presents the demographic details of the respondents in terms of their place of living, gender, age and academic details like the courses pursued by the candidates and their modes of study.

SAMPLE COMPOSITION

Students of regular mode of study and distance-education mode are likely to differ on several characteristics such as time of direct interaction with faculty members, employment status, time available for education and opportunities to keep oneself up to date in their field of study.

Considering these differences, the researcher thought it necessary to consider viewing the two modes of study as separate groups for further analysis of their responses. There have been exactly equal numbers of respondents from regular as well as distance education streams. Exactly 50% were students in regular mode of study while the remaining 50% were in distance mode. Thus, it may be seen that the mode of study has been taken as the prime parameter for the stratification of respondents.

There have been more male respondents than female. (56.90% were male while the remaining 43.10% were female). This percentage, though unequal in numbers, could be stated to reflect the same proportion of men and women enrolling themselves for studies in the universe of the study.

Needs and wants of people tend to differ with their age in general. Further, age factor could heighten the level of exposure a person is likely to have. Since all the respondents were students, a vast majority of them would belong to a narrow range of age group, namely 17 to 30. Hence their age groups were grouped at narrow intervals. 6146 (52.26%) belonged the age group 17 -

20, while 4438 (37.74%) belonged to the age group 21 - 25 and the remaining 1176 (10%) were above 25 yrs. Thus it may be seen that the study has covered more of undergraduate students, reflecting their relative proportion in the actual student population.

The researcher felt the need for diversity of respondents in terms of the courses they pursue, so as to bring in the pluralist perspective on the usage of media. Out of the total, 28% have their course of study as B.A. while 33.33% have their course of study as B.Sc., and the rest of them pursued B.E, B.Com and other courses. More than nine of ten respondents 93.33% have had English as the medium of instruction while 6.67% have Tamil as the medium of instruction. Of the respondents, 50% belonged to Institutions located in rural area. While the remaining 50% belong to Institutions located in urban area.

POSSESSION OF VARIOUS ELECTRONIC MEDIA

Educational Media could take multiple forms. They could be either mass-based or personalized, containing materials in audio or visual formats. Using them regularly would require the personal possession of the instruments appropriate for each. A comparison of possession patterns with respect to different instruments shows that the costs involved in owning an instrument is inversely proportional to the number of people owning them, the only notable exception being TV, which occupies the second position among the instruments owned closely following the radio sets, despite involving a higher initial investment compared to tape recorder or telephone, which are owned by fewer respondents. The appeal of TV as a media could be understood from the emerging analysis. It is noteworthy to find that 90.24% possess radio, 86.43% possess tape recorder and 96.31% possess TV while 71.90% possess telephone. Merely, a 35.24% possess Personal Computer as compared to 61.31% who possess Satellite/Cable connection, 20.95% who have access to Internet and similarly, 49.64% who possess CD player.

USAGE PATTERN OF RADIO

Distribution of Students by Listening To Radio From the radio listening group 35.71% of the respondents listen to radio everyday a week, while 5.12% listen to radio 4 to 5 days a week, 8.93% listen to radio once a week and 12.86% rarely listen to radio. It is found that 18.10% never listen to radio.

Combining the segment listening to radio every day and at least 4 to 5 times a week, it may be stated that the majority of respondents tend to be frequent radio listeners. However, there remains to be a sizeable segment of nearly one third of the total respondents whose radio usage is almost non-existent to produce any impact.

APPROXIMATE TIME SPENT ON LISTENING TO RADIO

While 30.36% listen to radio less than 30 min., 27.74% listen to radio 30 -

60 min., 18.10% do not listen to radio, 13.57% listen to radio 60-120 min. and 10.24% listen to radio above than 120 min. With regard to the time spent on listening to radio, the emergent data shows a divergence among respondents, with respondents' time ranging from nothing to two hours a week, which could be interpreted to be offering a considerable scope for increase.

PLACE OF LISTENING TO RADIO

Summing up the responses, it is found that 87.35% listen to radio at home, 23.11% listen to radio at friends place. Others listen to radio at their office; place of study or at cyber cafes. Data indicate that home is the place where most of the respondents have been listening to radio, thereby suggesting that timing of the educational programs through radio should match with the time when people are at home.

LISTENING TO RADIO PROGRAMS

With a view to ascertain the purpose of listening to radio, respondents' listening patterns were further enquired. It was found that 37.06% listen to radio for education, 84.30% listen to radio for entertainment and 29.07% listen to radio for Science. 5.23% listen to radio for purpose other than those mentioned above. Analyzing the data on the purpose of listening to radio, there seems to be scope for improvement as the majority of respondents have reported that they do not listen to radio for education or for Science programs.

INTERPRETATIVE ANALYSIS ON RADIO

LISTENING TO RADIO AND MODE OF STUDY

Hence it can be concluded that there is a significant relationship between listening to radio and mode of study. This means that the two streams would differ in their usage of radio, as they have similar syllabus but dissimilar teaching-interaction process.

LISTENING TO RADIO AND AREA OF INSTITUTION

Urban and rural milieu of students tend to differ in the available levels of exposure to co-curricular events, access to educational services like counseling and library services. In the absence of multiple forms of educational assistance, there is a greater likelihood of students becoming dependent on the mass media as a one-stop source for the fulfillment of their educational needs. It was with this assumption that the researcher endeavored to examine the association between place of study and the patterns of listening to radio. It was concluded that there is significant association between area of institution and listening to radio.

The result of this analysis could mean that media planners would have to focus on the target audience according to their place of study. Programs might have to be tailor made to suit the specific needs of the two categories of students.

LISTENING TO RADIO AND MEDIUM OF INSTRUCTION

The medium of instruction in higher education in most of the cases remains to be English, while the mass media offer contents both in regional languages and in English. In order to identify the possibility that mass media like radio caters to students with concerns about the medium of instructions, chi-square analysis was done to find out if there is any association between the two variables. It can be concluded that there is significant association between medium of instruction and listening to radio, which could indicate that language plays a vital role in out-of-classroom learning. Media planners need to carefully address the issue of medium of instruction used in radio as well. With the help of primary data, it was also concluded that there is significant relationship between course of study and listening to radio.

The relationship could be interpreted as arising out of the differing requirements between various types of courses. Whether these differences are also affecting the time spent on listening to radio, is to be analysed further.

APPROXIMATE TIME TO LISTEN TO RADIO

Having established the fact that radio usage is unmatched with the supply, the researcher has undertaken to analyse the various factors that could further influence the increase or decrease in the usage patterns. This analysis is carried out in order to find clues that could be valuable in making students listen more actively to the medium.

There is significant association between mode of study and approximate time spent on listening to the radio. The implication of this finding might be that different strategies would be necessary to address the distance and on-campus learners, as far as improving the time spent on listening to radio. Also there is significant association between the area of institution and the approximate time of listening to the radio.

Rural and urban students spend different amounts of time listening to radio, and within the attention spans of each of the categories, programs should be able to convey the important messages. In the same manner it was concluded with the help of chi square analysis that there is significant association between medium of instruction and approximate time to listen to radio.

Hence it is felt necessary to look into the familiar lingua franca of the local population if the average duration of listening has to be increased. The study also proved that there is significant association between course of study and approximate time to listen to radio. This implies that the media planners should conduct audience research and find out the subjects for which the demand for radio programs are higher and broadcast them accordingly.

USAGE PATTERN OF TV BY HIGHER EDUCATION STUDENTS

DISTRIBUTION OF STUDENTS BY WATCHING PATTERN ON TV

TV tends to occupy a coveted position among the media because of its audio visual presentations. The analysis portrays the respondents' viewing patterns.

FREQUENCY OF WATCHING TV

Data on viewing time suggest that 65.36% watch TV every day in a week, 12.74% watch TV 4 - 5 days in a week, 5.83% watch TV once a week and 5.48% watch TV rarely and 4.64% do not watch TV. From the data on TV viewership, it may be observed that majority of the respondents watch TV every day in a week and that it is a very small segment which abstains from watching TV totally. This response pattern reiterates the general perception about the popularity of TV among people.

TIME SPENT ON WATCHING TV

In order to verify the dependence on TV, respondents were requested to provide data on the time spent on watching TV. The analysis brings out the data on this question. Since media planners and analysts have divided TV slots into durations closer to 30 minutes, this duration was taken as the minimum period. 20.60% watch TV < = 30 min., 29.17% watch TV from 30 min - 1hour, 21.07% watch TV for a duration between 1 to 2 hours, 16.90% watch TV from 3 to 5 hours and 7.62% watch TV for more than 5 hours.

A closer look at the data presented shows that the majority of the viewers' spend not less than an hour on an average and this would imply that educational TV programs should also time their programs accordingly.

PLACE OF WATCHING TV

With regard to the place of watching TV, the response pattern has shown a striking similarity with that of radio. A vast majority of 86.64% of the students watching TV at home, 25.22 % watching TV at friends place and the rest of the people watching TV at other places like study place, office or at cyber cafes.

PROGRAMS WATCHED ON TV

Analyzing the purpose of watching TV, it is seen that 69.91% watching TV for news, 35.08% watching TV for education, while 78.40% watching TV for entertainment, 3.50% watching TV for other than those mentioned above. The pattern of data shows that viewing TV for education purposes should be enhanced among the majority of the students.

TYPES OF MATERIAL/CONTENT WATCHED BY STUDENTS ON TV

Respondents expressing opinions on the contents watched on TV were sought with options for multiple responses. Results showed that, out of the total respondents, 68.12% watched subject-based programs on TV, 38.12% watched scientific programs and expert lectures, 46.77% watched interactive programs, while 58% watched career guidance, higher education information on TV. Interactive video can improve student attitudes and results in increased participation.

Distribution of Students Watching University Grants Commission - Country Wide Class Room (UGC - CWCR) Among the educational programs, a pioneering initiative under the aegis of the UGC was its CWCR. Respondents were enquired on their usage of these unique programs. Of TV watching respondents, 14.61% watch UGC CWCR while 85.39% do not watch UGC CWCR. The results show that a vast majority of the respondents do not watch the programs, even though there are specific programs to suit every student group's needs.

Frequency of Watching CWCR

17.95% stated that they watch UGC on DD1 every day in a week, while 11.11% stated that they watch UGC on DD1 4-5 days in a week, 14.53% stated that they watch UGC on DD1 2-3 days in a week, 13.68% stated that they watch UGC on DD1 once a week and 42.74% stated that they watch UGC on DD1 rarely. It is seen that even among those who watch the programs, majority of them do not watch even twice a week. Only a very small segment is deriving benefits out of the programs, about which there should be some form of interventions from the telecasters.

Reasons for not Watching CWCR

A segment of respondents who stated that the reason for not watching CWCR; opine that they were not interesting. 1063 stated that reason for not watching CWCR as inadequate interaction. 48.15% stated that reason for not watching CWCR was that they received no signal. As high as 74.90% stated that reason for not watching CWCR was lack of periodic information about it.

Knowledge About Gyandarshan (GD) and Receiving

Among the students covered by the study, as large a segment as 82.38% stated that they do not receive GD programs on TV. When compared with other educational programs offered by the Government, very similar results are found with regard to the GD programs. It is evident that there is little awareness about the telecast of GD.

Since the percentage of population using the various educational telecasts is small, the focus of the analysis is shifted towards understanding the opinions of the small segment of users, about the effectiveness of these programs. As the programs have rich and varied contents, all the users might not need all the inputs. Hence the respondents were asked to estimate the percentage of programs which they found GD to be helpful.

Reason for Not Accessing GD

A total of 1112 stated that they do not access GD due to non-availability of signal while 10684 stated other reasons for not accessing GD.

Format of Presentation Followed Mostly in GD

Expressing opinions on the content of programs, a sizeable segment (44.59%) stated that format of presentation followed in GD is mostly lecture based only. A perceptible section of 33.11% stated that format of presentation followed in GD is mostly lecture with demonstrations only. 4.73% stated that format of presentation followed in GD to be other than those mentioned above.

From the data, it is obvious that the major form of presenting lessons has been lecture, which has been vouched as a dependable method for disseminating large quantity of information in a short period of time. However the programs watched by the respondents were apparently confined to lectures not complemented with value enhancing presentations.

Not accessing GD is an area of concern as it could render the investments made in producing educational programs and the costs of telecasting them as unproductive. The reasons for not accessing as stated by the respondents were analysed, to know if it is due to any faults in the contents of the program. The analysis and results discussed so far have shown that mass media's reach is yet to expand in a significant way among students.

INTERPRETATIVE ANALYSIS ON TV

WATCHING TV

While both TV and radio are mass media, their audiences tend to differ in terms of their reach and extent of usage. Therefore, respondents' views on television were sought with regard to the same indicators of usage such as frequency, duration and perceived usefulness of the media, as used in the context of radio.

It can be concluded that there is significant association between the modes of study and watching TV. This association is found to be very much similar to that of radio usage.

Watching TV and Area of Institution

Association between area of institution and watching TV is significant. In respect of this variable too, there is similarity between radio and TV. Consequent to further analysis, it was concluded that there is significant association between medium of instruction and watching TV. Analyzing the result in the light of earlier findings, it is seen that there is inter-media consistency among radio and TV and hence a common approach could be adopted in planning and striving for greater effective usage of the two media. The study also resulted in the conclusion that there is significant association between mode of study and approximate time spent on TV watching. The difference could possibly be the result of unstructured or inadequate time availability to students belonging to any one of the two modes of study.

Analysis of data showed that there was significant association between the area of institution and the approximate time spent on watching TV. Comparing the results with that of earlier findings, it is seen that differences do exist between the areas of institution on almost every parameter taken up for measuring usage patterns of both radio and TV.

There is significant relationship between medium of instruction and approximate time spent on watching TV. This result adds to the general belief that there must be separately designed programs meant for students belonging to different medium of instruction, rather than merely translated versions.

Watching UGC CWCR

The present study took up the task of examining the viewing practices in Tamilnadu between regular and distance mode, rural and urban areas. There is significant association between mode of study and watching UGC CWCR. Similarly there is significant association between area of institution and watching UGC CWCR.

Further, among the respondents viewing the program very frequently, there are more urban students than their rural counterparts. Hence efforts are to be directed towards popularizing the program among rural audience too. Also there is significant association between medium of instruction and watching UGC, CWCR. From the figures, it is seen that there are disproportionately higher levels of students studying in English medium than the regional language. However the frequency of Tamil medium students watching UGC CWCR is more than their expected frequency. Hence there is a great need to fill the gap by supplying programs in the local language.

Watching UGC CWCR was also significantly associated to the course of study pursued by the students. In terms of the frequency, no clear picture can be said to have emerged among the courses as their relationship has not been linear. Initial negative attitude towards educational TV is likely to lessen over time and become more positive or neutral.

RECEIVING GD PROGRAMS

Mode of study can largely be differentiated in terms of the average age groups benefited, the level of expenditure on education and a host of other grounds. However, to eliminate bias, the researcher assumed that there is no significant association between mode of study and receiving GD program on TV. That there is significant association between mode of study and receiving GD program on TV. This reinforces the initial surmise that the two modes would differ on maximum variables used in the study. Receiving GD program could largely depend on the area in which the place where the respondents mostly watch TV.

Earlier the analysis on place of watching TV showed that home is the place most of them used for TV watching. However, in order to verify the data, the relationship between the area of institution and receipt of GD programs was examined.

Hence it can be concluded that there is significant relationship between area of institution and receiving GD program on TV.

There is also significant association between medium of instruction and receiving GD program on TV. In this regard too, the emerging data is similar to that of CWCR and TV in general. It also can be concluded that there is significant relationship between course of study and receiving GD program on TV. The programs are not labeled to be meant as exclusively for students belonging to any particular mode of study. Hence it was assumed that the two are not seen as closely related. On a comparative analysis of the various results discussed in relation to watching educational programs CWCR or GD, it is seen that there have been significant relationships established between this dependent variable and all other independent variables taken up for the study such as the place of the institution, the mode of study and the medium of instruction. The results seem to stress the importance that is to be accorded to these variables while planning and implementing educational programs in various media.

USAGE PATTERN OF INTERNET BY HIGHER EDUCATION STUDENTS

DISTRIBUTION OF STUDENTS BY INTERNET USAGE

Internet being a media of recent origin has evoked the interests of educational researchers and media professionals alike. The various parameters of assessing the reach of this medium, such as favorable opinions on the medium, number of people using it, the frequency at which they use it and the time spent on Internet are analysed.

EVER USED INTERNET

As large as 92.86% have used Internet while 7.14% have not ever used it. Since a vast majority of the respondents have effectively utilized Internet at least once, one could be optimistic about the potential for its growth in the future educational efforts. Internet could be accessed at ones' convenient times.

FREQUENCY OF USING INTERNET

It is seen that the usage frequency is widely dispersed, with majority of the users browsing not less than twice a week. Internet usage is unlike that of others. A user is not an owner and is merely allowed access on payment of charges. The frequency of usage could have been influenced most by the interest levels of the respondents followed by the costs involved in using them.

19.36% use Internet everyday in a week, 14.87% use it 4 - 5 days in a week, 21.28% use it 2-3 days in a week, 28.85% use it once in a week and 15.64% use Internet rarely.

APPROXIMATE TIME SPENT TO USE INTERNET

In using the internet, searching takes a sizeable time. 1hour, 18.33% use it approximately for about 1-2 hours, 5.51% use it approximately for about 2 - 3 hours, and 4.63% use it approximately for more than Shours. The emerging data shows that majority of the respondents have used the net for the optimal time. As the browsing pattern shows that just a small segment comprising of 24% are using it less than 30 minutes, the statistical mode of browsing time is the duration of 31 to 60 minutes. A summary of the analysis on indicators of browsing standards would be that the quantum of browsing within the initial decades of browsing in India could be described as in the right direction. However, the adequacy and quality of browsing would depend on the individual and the connectivity available.

PLACE OF ACCESSING INTERNET

Institutional provision of browsing facilities is still in a rudimentary stage. An ideal situation for education related browsing would be before or after the class room sessions, in which case the place of browsing is a significant influence in the benefits of browsing. 22.56% stated that they browse at home. 62.56% stated that they browse at cyber cafes, 29.36% stated they browse at friends places, 41.28% stated that they browse at institutions and 3.21% stated that they browse at other than those places mentioned above.

PURPOSE OF USING INTERNET

Browsing could be done for different purposes and education is one of them. Majority (59.74%) of browsers answered that they use Internet sometimes to send mail and 24.74% use Internet always to send mail. With 16.41% having stated that they don't use internet for the purpose of seeking information about education, 41.92% use it always to seek information about education. While 20.26% stated that they don't use for the purpose of gathering information about study, 40% use it always to gather information about study. Whereas 25% stated that they don't use for the purpose of fun and entertainment, 27.44% use always for fun and entertainment, 27.86% stated that they don't use the internet for the purpose of chatting with friends, while 22.34% use rarely for chatting with friends and 21.95% use it always for chatting with friends.

INTERPRETATIVE ANALYSIS ON INTERNET

FREQUENCY OF USING INTERNET

Through the chi-square test there is significant association between mode of study and frequency of using Internet. It is also similar to the association between area of institution and frequency of using internet. This could be understood in the context of unequal spread of internet in India.

Frequency of using internet and medium of instruction were also found to be significantly associated. The predominant language medium of the vast majority of web sites would be English. Further, it was concluded that there is significant association between gender and frequency of using internet. There is significant relationship between course of study and frequency of using internet. It can be concluded that there is significant association between year of study and frequency of using Internet. As years go by, a student tends to be more independent and moves towards a wide range of experiences according to personality theorists like Chris Argyris.

Approximate Time Spent on Internet

There is significant association between mode of study and approximate time spent to use internet. Also there is significant association between area of institution and approximate time spent to use internet.

This result could be viewed in relation to the findings of another study described below in which educational media have been found to benefit the rural students than the urban students. Rural students, tested against rural control groups, benefited more than urban students tested against urban control groups as per the writings of Galda & Searle.

The project evaluators hypothesized that radio lessons were particularly effective in raising the level of knowledge of those who knew least, which in this case were the rural students. The findings of the present study could be understood in the light of the earlier finding. Similarly there is significant association between medium of instruction and approximate time spent on Internet. Approximate time spent to use Internet and course of study were also significantly associated. The analysis resulted in the conclusion that there is significant association between course of study and approximate time spent to use Internet.

A comparative analysis of all the suggestions provided by respondents through their answers to the open ended questions reveals noticeable commonality among the suggestions to the various media, they are the need felt for greater subject-orientation, enhanced exposure to scientific advancements, examination-centreed contents, need for user-interface and contribution and the like. As suggestions, the users have provided opinions that more visual, movable content should be available with the facility of interaction. Educational media, when used in classrooms are likely to produce maximum learning then using them elsewhere. This has been the theme of the variables analysed. While data on viewing time suggested that 65.36% watch TV every day a week, 35.71% of those who listen to radio do it everyday a week, only 19.36% of those using internet, do it everyday a week. Majority of the respondents tend to be frequent listeners of radio and TV, while TV has more regular audience than radio. A vast majority of respondents possess radio sets as well as TV sets. It was found that 37.06% listen to radio for education, 35.08% watch TV for education, while 40% use internet always to gather information about study. Data indicate that home is the place where most of the respondents have been listening to radio, while vast majorities of 86.64% of the students watch TV at home; only 22.56% stated that they browse at home. 41.28% stated that they browse the internet at institutions, whereas only a negligible segment of students use radio and TV at their institutions. Among the less interactive media, 61.62% answered that they need interactive programs in radio, while only 21.86% have answered that interactive programs are needed for educational purpose on TV programs. Majority 66.90% use Internet, which, in comparison to the fact that very few owned computers, is a significant achievement of media planners in higher education.

Media planners would benefit by basing their interventions based on the comparative standing of various educational media as understood through the viewing patterns presented with the help of the findings of the study.

It is suggested that measures be on to improve the viewership, listening frequency, the priority being on the latter, which is found to be the least frequently used educational media among the students in the area of study.

Since majority of the respondents have not used any of the media for educational purposes, the top priority is to be given to strengthen the educational usage of the powerful electronic media. Use of electronic media at educational institutions is found to be low. The usage needs to be enhanced in order to facilitate the increased usage of the media for educational purposes, as indicated by the previous suggestion. Creation of awareness among students about educational media should be taken up on a massive scale with a sense of urgency. Local inputs and interaction should be made a regular feature in the educational radio. Programs and contents in regional and locally understood languages should be featured for more duration and frequency than it is being done at present. In order to achieve localization of educational contents of the electronic media, well-equipped media centres carrying out research and producing need based programs should be created in each University. Campus based electronic media systems could be introduced to produce and present programs of specific educational needs.

9

Comparing the Internet and other Nontraditional Media with Traditional Media

Elections have witnessed the traditional media's monopoly on campaign communications threatened as candidates relied on a host of nontraditional media such as the Internet, radio and television talk shows, morning talk shows, MTV, and late night talks shows to present their message directly to the American people-much to the chagrin of the mainstream press.

Reporters from the mainstream media chastised candidates for relying on the nontraditional media of talk and interview shows in the 1992 and 1994 campaigns, charging that appearances on venues such as Larry King Live and the morning talk shows allowed candidates to sidestep the tough grilling they could expect from the traditional media in favour of "softball questions" designed to boost their image.

However, studies indicate that questions posed by the audience members in call-in programs often focused more on issues than those asked by journalists, who tended to focus on the strategy of the candidates. Others have suggested that the nontraditional media have improved the public's issue knowledge by providing more opportunities for citizens to see candidates and to hear them discuss issues.

In addition, the nontraditional media allow voters to speak directly to the candidates or host which might increase campaign interest among those previously indifferent about the political process. Venues such as talk shows may also humanize candidates and improve their image in the eyes of the public by allowing them to appear directly before the public unfiltered by the traditional news media.

Although the rise of the talk shows in 1992 represented a new strategy for employing existing broadcast media, the introduction of the Internet into the media mix in 1996 represented the birth of a new medium. While supporters argue that the Internet may eventually alter the dynamics of the election process much like television did when it overcame newspapers' campaign dominance, the emergence of the Internet only produced muted criticism from reporters.

Some press pundits charged that the Web provided another high-tech means for candidates to bypass the traditional press, and that while information on candidate Web sites appeared objective, it was the product of the candidates' spinmeisters. However, reporters did not heap as much criticism on the Internet as they did on talk shows four years earlier for at least two reasons.

First, journalists recognized that candidates' Web sites were rich, albeit slanted, sources of information about their issue positions as well as for up-to-date news on the campaign. Second, all the major news organizations rushed to put their own sites up with more indepth and up-to-date information than in their own publications. These sites paid dividends; media and other nonpartisan Web sites were swamped with people trying to log on to get the most recent election returns while network ratings plunged.

While several observers have commented on how the rise of the nontraditional media has influenced how candidates conduct their campaigns and how the traditional media cover them, less attention has been paid to the influence of the "new media" on the public's image of the candidates and their knowledge of the candidates' issue positions.

Studies that have examined the differences between the effects of traditional and nontraditional media on political attitudes and behaviours have produced conflicting results. Previous studies were also conducted before the Internet emerged as a means to reach voters as well as to attract campaign volunteers and funds.

This study will examine the extent to which heavy users of the Internet and other nontraditional media differ from heavy users of traditional media in their knowledge of the issue stances of Bill Clinton and Bob Dole after controlling for demographic and other political variables. This study will also examine whether nontraditional media users differ from those who use the mainstream media on images they hold of Clinton and Dole.

The Nontraditional Media in the 1992 Presidential Campaign Although politicians have relied on nontraditional media to present their views directly to the American people at least as far back as the 1930s when Franklin Roosevelt addressed the country through his "fireside chats," the candidates' use of such media was unprecedented during the 1992 campaign.

The three candidates made ninety-six appearances on Larry King Live, Donahue, and the three network morning shows alone in the year preceding the election in an effort to court voters. The candidates' appearances on nontraditional media produced some of the most vivid and lasting images of the campaign: H. Ross Perot coyly announcing on Larry King Live that he would run for president if he received a mandate from the American people; candidate Bill Clinton donning dark sunglasses and a flower tie to play the saxophone on the Arsenio Hall Show; and Clinton being queried whether he wears boxers or briefs on MTV's Choose or Lose.

Furthermore, the candidates' reliance on "new news" has been credited, at least in part, with boosting voter turnout to its highest level since 197210 and for spurring the traditional media to focus more attention on the issues. The Nontraditional Media in the 1996 Presidential Campaign

The 1996 election, however, should have allayed fears that reporters would become irrelevant to the campaign process because candidates' use of nontraditional media decreased sharply. Clinton relied on more traditional means of campaigning in order to appear more presidential. While Dole made some appearances on radio talk shows, he largely avoided the talk show circuit after he attacked Today Show co-host Katie Couric and the rest of the media for questions about his statement that tobacco was not addictive. The candidates allowed their surrogates to campaign on nontraditional venues.

For instance, Elizabeth Dole rode in on a Harley with Jay Leno to begin the Tonight Show, and the challenger's wife also offered a Top 10 list to David Letterman on his talk show. Neither candidate made extensive use of talk radio either, although Dole warmed up to the medium near the end of the campaign. However, Congressional candidates crowded the airwaves and during the Republican primaries, candidates such as Pat Buchanan relied extensively on talk radio to reach potential voters at little cost. This study, then, will also allow a comparison between the effects of the nontraditional media in an election like 1992 when they were used extensively to 1996 when they were not.

THE INTERNET IN THE 1996 PRESIDENTIAL CAMPAIGN

The Internet emerged as the dominant "new media" in the 1996 campaign, one that indeed represented the birth of a new medium rather than simply a different strategy for using an existing one. All the major candidates running for president in 1996 created their own home pages, cyber campaign offices that featured speeches, position papers, pitches for funds and volunteers, and, in some cases, audio and video clips.

While a political Web page presently receives less exposure than a single television commercial, it is hardly ignored. The Republican National Committee reported that more than 8,000 people signed the site's guest book in the first few months of operation. More important, the home page of their candidate, Bob Dole, received more than 3 million "hits" during the first six months it operated.

More than 10,000 joined the campaign e-mail list, and 1,700 registered to vote. Similarly, Bill Clinton and Al Gore bragged that their site receive 1 million hits in its first ten days. While the candidate sites might be onesided and sanitized, many news and nonpartisan organizations have created their own sites of political news and issue stances of the candidates. The Internet is also increasingly becoming an important part of political reporters' beats to find updated news and candidate issue positions as well as to "listen" in on discussion groups to get a sense of the public's attitudes toward issues and the candidates.20 Political observers predict that the Internet will transform the election process in the near future away from TV soundbites toward more substance as the sheer volume of news and issue information on the Web will allow voters to readily compare candidates' stances on issues and determine how issues will directly affect them.

21 Proponents also claim that the Internet will shift the locus of power away from corporations and special interest groups as individuals can lobby policymakers directly through e-mail and download information for themselves, bypassing the traditional media.

Also, grassroots organizers can become "hightech colonial pamphleteers" by creating home pages or electronic newsletters to distribute information to like-minded individuals or to spread their message through e-mail or discussion groups. Critics are far less sanguine, arguing that the Internet is likely to reinforce the existing political structure by providing a new, powerful tool for lobbyists and entrenched interests to influence government. Also, because the poor will have little access to the Information Superhighway, the Internet may actually increase the gulf between the "haves" and "have nots." Some experts predict that the Internet will be a primary way candidates campaign in the future-perhaps as early as the year 2000. The 1996 election served as the test-drive year for politics on the Internet as candidates struggled to learn how to use the new medium to best reach voters. Therefore, the Internet served as added exposure for candidates, rather than the main avenue for campaigning. As media critic Edwin Diamond noted, "It's a man with a belt wearing a pair of suspenders. It ain't the pants, and it ain't the belt."

NONTRADITIONAL MEDIA AND POLITICAL KNOWLEDGE

While few political observers would argue that the emergence of the nontraditional media altered the nature of campaigning, they differ on the effects of the "new media" on political attitudes and behaviours. Specifically, past studies are divided about whether the nontraditional media contribute or hinder the acquisition of political knowledge with results often depending on what medium is examined.

Recent studies have disputed the notion that talk radio listeners come from the lower socioeconomic strata and that talk radio has little impact beyond creating or reinforcing social isolation. Talk radio listeners are those who perceive they have the most at stake in the political system: the wealthy, white Republican male.

Consequently, talk radio listeners report greater interest in politics than nonlisteners, and they voted in greater numbers over the past four elections. Studies have consistently found that talk radio is linked to political knowledge and participation, even after controlling for other factors.

Frequent talk show listeners are not only more politically knowledgeable, but they also think they are better informed than other citizens. Listeners also say they attend to talk radio to keep up with news and to gain information they cannot find elsewhere.

Researchers are split on whether television talk show use contributes to political knowledge. On the one hand, research by Lemert and associates disputed the notion that the talk-show audience was composed of "helpless souls, unable to evaluate independently what they were seeing and hearing."

Heavy viewers were highly educated, had strong feelings of internal efficacy, and were generally interested in the campaign. More important, heavy viewers knew more about the views of the candidates than light viewers. Finally, while voters were more likely to view talk shows as a more helpful source of campaign information than all traditional forms of media except for debates, heavy talk show viewers were also heavier users of more traditional media such as television and newspapers. The talk shows supplemented, rather than replaced, more traditional forms of campaign information. However, several studies have found little relationship between talk show use and political knowledge.

For instance, Miller and associates found that viewing daytime talk shows such as Donahue and Oprah tended to be negatively related to political knowledge, suggesting that those who watched daytime talk shows showed little interest in political information and thus did not seek out more conventional sources of information.

Similarly, McLeod and associates found that talk shows were not significantly related to issue accuracy among a cross section of voters and negatively related to issue knowledge in their panel study. However, like the Lemert study, talk show viewing was linked to high political interest, internal efficacy, and use of more traditional media. Similarly, Waluszko, Weaver and Drew, Price and Zaller, and Hollander found that television talk shows were unrelated to gains in political knowledge. The discrepancies on the links between nontraditional media use and political knowledge may result, at least in part, because of different definitions of what constitutes nontraditional media. For instance, Waluszko restricted "new news" to radio and television talk shows while Hollander examined talk shows, late night talk shows, and MTV. Miller and associates expanded the definition of nontraditional media to include entertainment content such as daytime talk shows like Oprah, comedies like Saturday Night Live, and situation comedies such as Murphy Brown, while McLeod and associates considered debates, polls, and ads as nontraditional media. Indeed, Hollander and Chaffee and associates discovered that the influence of nontraditional media on political knowledge depended on which medium one examined. While watching talk shows was linked to increased campaign knowledge, MTV and late night talk show viewing was negatively related to campaign knowledge. While there seems to be no agreed-upon definition about what constitutes nontraditional media, scholars suggest that they entail presenting public affairs information in forums in which the message is unfiltered by a mediator and the public becomes a participant by being able to directly interact with the public official or with a host, or, in the case of the Internet, with other individuals.

For the purposes of this study, "nontraditional media" is defined as talk shows like Larry King Live, radio talk shows like Rush Limbaugh, MTV, and late night talk shows. While the political Web site on the Internet also qualifies as a nontraditional medium, it will be analysed separately because it represents the birth of a new medium rather than simply a new strategy for employing an existing one.

NONTRADITIONAL MEDIA AND CANDIDATE IMAGE

Studies suggest that the nontraditional media may have a greater influence on candidate image than on political knowledge-at least for certain candidates. Pfau and Eveland Jr. found that nontraditional media influenced perceptions of the candidate's competence and image.

Similarly, Elliott and Wickert found that nontraditional media use was positively related to images of both Clinton and Perot, although it had no influence on attitudes toward Bush. However, McLeod and associates only found that talk shows influenced images of, and feelings toward, the candidate who relied most on nontraditional media: Perot.

Results, then, suggest that the nontraditional media can have different effects on different candidates, with the effects being the most pronounced for those candidates who rely more on such media. Previous results suggest, then, that the influence of the nontraditional media depends on what political attitudes and behaviours one examines and which medium is examined.

The nontraditional media appear to have more influence on affective attitudes such as image than cognitive ones such as political knowledge. Also, "new media" that is heavier in information content, such as radio talk shows, will increase knowledge more than entertainment-oriented forums such as late night talk shows or MTV. This would suggest that the information-rich Internet could produce larger information gains than the talk shows that dominated the 1992 campaign.

INTERNET AND POLITICAL ATTITUDES/ BEHAVIOURS

Only recently have scholars examined the extent to which the Internet is linked to knowledge gain and other political attitudes and behaviours. Several recent studies have dispelled the notion that the Internet is "a haven for isolated geeks who are unaware of important events occurring outside their cavelike bedrooms." Internet users are more politically knowledgeable than the average citizen. In addition, Web users are politically interested and active, report high levels of political efficacy, are more likely to vote, and more likely to seek out information from the media than the general public. Furthermore, politically active Internet users score higher on these measures than general users. However, no studies could be found that examined the relationship between Internet use and images of candidates.

While evidence is just beginning to accumulate on whether Internet use does increase political knowledge, evidence suggests it should. If the ability of a medium to produce knowledge gain is increased by its information content, then those who regularly visit political Web sites should be high in political knowledge. Political observers tout the sheer volume of campaign information available on the Net through candidate Web sites, nonpartisan sites such as PoliticsNow, and online publications, contending that it could transform media coverage away from sound bites toward more substance and produce a generation of "cybergenic candidates" where issue stands will matter more than good looks and soundbites.

While the large volume of Internet information is only seen by a fraction of the voter-the Pew Research Centre found that about 12 percent of the voting age population used the Internet for political information in the 1996 election and about 3 percent listed the Internet as their primary source of informationS—those who do rely on the Internet may be highly motivated to seek out political information, and information found there may influence their voting decisions. Studies by the Freedom Forum suggest that people who have visited politically oriented Web sites are political junkies, watching CNN, Sunday public affairs programs and C-SPAN, and reading more newsmagazines than the average voter. They are also more than twice as likely to have read a political book in the last year.

Political Web site users are more likely than the average voter to have graduated from college and to earn a high income, two characteristics associated with high political knowledge as well as likelihood to vote. This study will examine the influence of nontraditional vs. traditional media on knowledge of issue stances and images of candidates through a survey of 320 Jackson County, Illinois, residents conducted by trained undergraduate and graduate students as part of a media and politics course in July 1996.

The sample was drawn from local exchanges using random digit dialing procedures. Independent Measures. "Nontraditional media" use was defined as relying on talk shows such as Larry King Live, late night talk shows, MTV, and radio talk shows like Rush Limbaugh for information on the 1996 presidential campaign. Using political Web sites on the Internet will be treated as a separate nontraditional media because it represents a new medium rather than simply a new use of an existing one. The traditional media examined were newspapers, television network news, radio news, news magazines, news programs like Meet the Press and more "elite" broadcast outlets such as CNN, C-SPAN, and National Public Radio. Respondents were asked two sets of questions examining use of both new and traditional media, one that explored frequency of use64 and one that examined attention to the media. Both questions were asked of each information source examined in this study. Demographic and political attitude and behaviour measures were also included as independent variables. The demographic variables employed were income, education, age, gender, and race.

The political attitude and behaviour measures were likelihood to voting, political interest, strength of party support, and amount of political discussion. To measure likelihood of voting, the survey asked respondents to indicate on a 0 to 10-point scale the chances they were going to vote this year. Similarly, they were asked on a 0 to 10 scale their interest in the national election.

Participants were first asked to indicate whether they were strong Republicans, lean toward Republicans, independents, lean toward Democrats, or strong Democrats in order to gauge strength of party support. Answers were recoded into a 3-point scale of independent, lean toward 1 of the 2 parties, and strongly support 1 of the 2 parties. Political discussion was measured by a 5-point question: "On a scale of 1 to 5 where 1 indicates nothing at all and 5 indicates a great deal, how much have you heard about the 1996 presidential campaign within the last month or so through discussions with other people?"

DEPENDENT MEASURES

The dependent variables are knowledge of Bill Clinton and Bob Dole's issue positions as well as images of the two candidates. Political knowledge was gauged by totaling the number of correct responses to questions examining President Clinton and Bob Dole's stances on six issues: a constitutional amendment banning abortion, affirmative action programs for minorities, a ban on assault weapons, providing welfare benefits for illegal immigrants, term limits for Congress, and the North American Free Trade Agreement.

Image of the candidates was measured by asking respondents to evaluate Clinton and Dole on a 1 to 10 scale on several characteristics: friendly, warm, likable, honest, trustworthy, and leadership. The variables were combined into indices measuring images of Clinton and of Dole. The Cronbach alpha test for internal reliability was.88 for images of Clinton and.91 for images of Dole. Data Analysis. The data were analysed in three stages. First, frequencies were run on the media use and attention variables to compare how much respondents relied on the "new media" versus the traditional ones. Second, Pearson Product Moment correlations were run between the independent variables and the knowledge and image measures." Finally, hierarchical regression was used to measure the predictive power of each of the media measures. The predictor variables were entered in five blocks: demographics; political attitudes and behaviours (campaign interest, likelihood of voting, strength of party support, likelihood of voting, amount of political discussions); use and attention paid to traditional media (newspapers;

television network news; news magazines; radio news; news programs; and elite broadcast media such as CNN, C-SPAN, and NPR); use and attention paid to political Web sites on the Internet; and use and attention paid to nontraditional media (television talk shows, late night talk shows, MTV, and radio talks shows). The "new media" measures were entered last to test their influence after other possible predictors, including traditional media, were statistically controlled for.

TRADITIONAL VS. NONTRADITIONAL MEDIA USE

Political observers suggested that the "new media" of talk and interview shows had partially supplanted traditional media as information sources in the 1992 election. However, results from the 1996 media demonstrate the continued dominance of traditional media.

Those surveyed said they paid more attention to each of the traditional media than to the "new news." Respondents were more than three times as likely to say they used television news as the most popular nontraditional medium, television talk shows. Those surveyed were even less likely to use late night talk shows and radio talk shows-15% and 10% respectively.

Scores were even lower for attention to these information sources. MTV and the Web sites on the Internet were all but ignored as sources of political information with only 5% and 2%, respectively, regularly getting political information from these media. The results also suggest the dominance of broadcast media as a source of information. People relied on network television news the most for political information, and elite broadcast news sources such as CNN, CSPAN, and NPR challenged newspapers for second. Scores for media use tended to mirror media attention, although respondents were more likely to say they used television news than to pay attention to it.

CORRELATIONAL ANALYSIS: POLITICAL KNOWLEDGE

Past research has been split on whether nontraditional media contribute to increased knowledge of candidate issue stands. This study found that while traditional media were correlated with knowledge of Clinton and Dole's issue positions, only 5 of 20 nontraditional media measures were linked with knowing candidate issue stands.

Both use and attention to television talk shows correlated with knowledge of Dole's position stands, while talk show attention was linked to Clinton issue knowledge. Late night talk show use also correlated with Dole issue knowledge while radio talk show attention was linked to knowledge of Clinton issue positions. On the other hand, use of all the traditional media-newspapers, television, radio, news magazines, news programs, and elite broadcast media-correlated with issue knowledge, with news programs and elite broadcast media such as CNN and C-SPAN posting the strongest correlations. Similarly, attention to all the traditional media except television news correlated with knowledge of the candidates' issue stands. Again, attention to news programs and elite broadcast media recorded the strongest correlations, although attention to radio news was also strongly linked to knowledge of Clinton's issue stands. Generally, attention correlations were stronger than use ones.

Correlational Analysis: Candidate Image. Earlier research suggested that the nontraditional media may be more strongly correlated to candidate image than knowledge. Indeed, "new media" variables were more strongly linked to candidate image than the traditional ones; 7 of the nontraditional media were correlated with candidate image compared to only 2 of the traditional media measures. Radio talk show use and attention were both strongly linked to images of Clinton and Dole, with heavier users viewing Dole favorably and holding negative images of Clinton. Television talk show use and attention also correlated with positive perceptions of Dole, although MTV use was negatively related to Dole's image. Clinton fared better with the traditional media as television news use and attention were both correlated with positive images of the president. No other traditional media were correlated with images of the two candidates, and the Internet variables also failed to post significant correlations.

Regression Analysis: Political Knowledge. The hierarchical regression analysis revealed nontraditional media use and attention did not predict increased issue knowledge-but traditional media did not fare much better. No nontraditional media variable significantly predicted knowledge of the candidates' issue stands, although attention to radio talk shows was negatively related to knowledge of Dole's issue stands. In 12 of 20 cases, including all 4 Internet measures, "new media" tended to be negatively related to candidate issue knowledge. Nontraditional media use contributed about 4% of the variance to knowledge of Clinton's issue stances and 5% to Dole knowledge gain. But traditional media did not prove a strong predictor of issue knowledge either. Only one measure proved significant: attention to news programs like Meet the Press predicted knowledge of Dole's issue positions.

In addition, radio attention predicted knowledge of Clinton's issue stands before the "new media" media variables were controlled. Like nontraditional media variables, the traditional media explained only about 5% of the variance in issue knowledge. Standard demographic and political measures, however, were strongly related to issue knowledge, explaining more than 25% of the variance for both Clinton and Dole. Being male and highly educated were linked to knowledge of issue stands as was political interest. Likelihood of voting predicted knowledge of Clinton's issue stands, but not Dole's.

Surprisingly, support for a certain candidate did not mean higher knowledge of his issue positions. In fact, the likelihood of voting for Clinton or Dole was negatively related to knowledge of their issue stands. Strength of party support and amount of political discussion with friends were also unrelated to knowledge of issue stances.

REGRESSION ANALYSIS: CANDIDATE IMAGE

While nontraditional media variables better predicted candidate image than knowledge, they only weakly influenced candidate images after controlling for other factors. Two nontraditional media measures, Internet use and attention to political Web sites, predicted images of Clinton, and talk show attention fell just short of significance.

However, Internet attention proved negatively related to Clinton images, and the block of "new media" variables did not significantly increase the variance in Clinton's image. Only radio talk show attention predicted images of Dole, and in 6 of 10 cases, nontraditional media use was negatively related to images of Dole. Internet and other nontraditional media explained about 3% of the variance for both Clinton and Dole images.

Traditional variables had even less impact on candidate image. Attention to television news and newspaper use predicted images of Clinton, although newspaper use was related to negative images of the president. Only newspaper use significantly predicted images of Bob Dole, and the relationship was negative. Demographic variables did not fare much better. High income was related to positive images of Clinton. Age was the only significant predictor of Dole's image, with older voters expressing the most positive images of Dole. Political variables explained almost the entire variance in images of both candidates.

Not surprisingly, intending to vote for a candidate influenced whether respondents had a positive image of him. Similarly, strength of party support was related to positive images of both candidates. However, likelihood of voting in general was negatively related to images of both candidates. On the other hand, the politically interested had positive images of both candidates.

Post-mortems of the 1992 election raised the specter of whether public officials would sidestep the traditional media and largely conduct their campaign through the nontraditional media of talk shows and entertainment programming. New York Times reporter Maureen Dowd pondered, perhaps only partly in jest, whether presidential press conferences would be replaced by presidential call-ins on Oprah, whether the State of the Union message would be delivered on the Arsenio Hall Show, and whether Clinton would sell his agenda for change with an MTV campaign called "Rock the Deficit."

The Arsenio Hall Show did not survive to see the 1996 campaign, and the role of the nontraditional media in general was greatly diminished. Candidates made few appearances on nontraditional media venues, leaving such campaigning for their surrogates.

Not surprisingly, then, relatively few individuals said they had read or heard much information about the campaign on nontraditional media sources. Respondents were more than three times as likely to say they had seen a great deal about the campaign on television news as on the most prevalent nontraditional media source, television talk shows. Political Web sites and

MTV were almost ignored as information sources. Past studies have been split on whether "new media" contributed to political knowledge. They suggested, however, that more information-rich sources were most likely to be linked to political knowledge. This study offers little evidence that nontraditional media influence political attitudes and behaviours.

Three measures, use and attention to television talk shows and late night talk show use, correlated with knowledge of Dole's issue positions. Attention to radio and attention to television talk shows were positively linked to Clinton issue knowledge. However, once the nontraditional media variables were entered into the regression equations, none significantly predicted knowledge of candidate issue stands except radio talk show attention, which was negatively related to Dole issue knowledge.

Twelve of the 20 relationships were negative, including all 4 Internet variables. The poor performance of the Internet in improving voter knowledge does not mean that its proponents' hopes that the Web could transform media coverage and campaigns away from soundbites to substance are wrong, but simply premature. Only 2% of respondents said they got a great deal of information from political Web sites, numbers that parallel other studies that suggest about 1% rely on the Web for political information. But the Internet is in its infancy as a political tool; the majority of people in this country have yet to go online, and politicians are just learning how to employ this technology to reach citizens. As Bimber notes, in terms of both number of users and its influence on the political process, the Internet of today is much like television of the early 1950s.

Television did not significantly influence the political process until the 1960s and 1970s, so it may take a decade or more for the Internet to achieve some of the lofty goals predicted of it. Researchers will need to wait until at least the year 2000 to assess the influence of the Internet on the political landscape. This study supported earlier ones that suggested that the nontraditional media had a greater influence on images of candidates rather than political knowledge. In fact, the influence was greater than for traditional variables. Correlational analysis found radio talk show use and attention were positively related to images of Dole, while radio talk show listeners harbored negative images of Bill Clinton.

Talk show use and attention were related to positive image of Dole. However once other variables were controlled for, only 3 of the 20 relationships were significant and 1 of the significant relationships was negative. Not surprisingly, while radio talk show use and attention were positively correlated to images of Dole, they were negatively related to Clinton's image.

Unlike other new media variables that cut across political ideology, studies indicate that radio talk show listeners are overwhelmingly Republican. For instance, a Media Studies Centre poll found that Republicans outnumbered Democrats among regular political talk radio listeners by a 4-1 margin. Internet use was positively related to images of Clinton, while attention to the Internet was negatively linked to Clinton's image. The negative relationship between Internet attention and Clinton images may reflect characteristics of the politically interested Web user. Experts suggest that "netizens" tend to be libertarian and to be disconnected from Washington unless the government is actively attacking the Internet. Dedicated Internet users perceive Clinton as an enemy of the Internet because of his positions on cryptography, pornography, and copyright on the Net. In addition, studies find that Internet users report high levels of political distrust.

Dole's ability to benefit more from nontraditional media than Clinton reinforces previous studies that suggest effects are greater for those candidates who rely more on nontraditional media. As noted earlier, Clinton largely campaigned through the traditional media to appear more presidential.

While Dole did not rely heavily on new media, he did warm up to radio talk shows late on the campaign and used surrogates such as his wife to campaign for him on talk shows like Jay Leno and David Letterman. Overall, then, results suggest that the nontraditional media had less influence in the 1996 election than 1992 in part because its use by the candidates has declined considerably from the last election.

Although the correlational analysis indicated nearly all the relationships between the traditional media and political knowledge were significant, the traditional media, surprisingly, had even less influence than the nontraditional media ones once other factors were controlled for. Only one variable, attention to news programs, was connected to any of knowledge gain measure and only attention to television news was positively linked to image of either candidate.

Several factors could account for the lack of impact of traditional media, many of which would also apply to the nontraditional media. Probably the main reason for the limited influence of traditional media was methodological. Media variables were entered into the regression equations after demographics and political ones. Demographics and political variables accounted for close to 30% of the variance in knowledge and more than 50% in images of Clinton as well as a significant variance in Dole measures. This conservative test of the research questions meant that the media variables had a limited opportunity to influence knowledge and image. Other studies of both the presidential campaigns employing hierarchical regression also found the media had limited influence after controlling for demographic and political factors.

Another methodological limitation was that not all of the variables were normally distributed, so they had a reduced ability to influence the political attitudes. But campaign-related factors might also explain the weak relationships for traditional media. First, this study was conducted during the lull between the primaries and the national convention when little was happening in the campaign. The candidates were not feverishly campaigning, and the media were not covering the campaign extensively. Consequently, fewer than half of those surveyed said they were paying attention to the campaign on television news; scores for other media were lower.

However, a study conducted later in the campaign using the same traditional media measures found both new and traditional media had even less influence on political knowledge than they did in July, suggesting the time when the survey was conducted was not a major factor.

Second, the political climate was much different in 1996 than in 1992. Despite motor voter and other innovations to stimulate turnout, voter turnout fell below 50 percent, the lowest level since 1924.

Several scholars and political observers lamented that the major issue in the campaign was not the economy or health care, but the "sheer crashing boredom among the electorate." Indeed, a Pew Charitable Trust poll revealed that 73 percent of the respondents said they were bored by the 1996 campaign, and only 24 percent of the public paid close attention to the 1996 campaign, down from 42 percent four years earlier.

Dissatisfaction with the major candidates ran high; almost two-thirds of respondents to a September 1995 poll said they supported the formation of a third party. Public confidence in elected officials continued to slide, and public optimism for the future of this country was even lower in 1996 than when Richard Nixon resigned in 1974. In this poisoned atmosphere of voter alienation and apathy, it is perhaps not surprising that the public would express little interest in the campaign and would pay little attention to it. The media's ability to influence candidate knowledge is greatly reduced in a campaign when relatively few people express interest in it.

The rise of the alienated and apathetic voter in campaign '96 might also explain why the likelihood of voting for a certain candidate would be negatively related to issue knowledge about that candidates" and why likelihood of voting in general was negatively related to images of the candidate. Results from this study, then, suggest that the nontraditional media, as well as the traditional press, had limited influence in a 1996 campaign which may be remembered less for the voters sending Bill Clinton on to a second term of office than an alienated electorate that stayed away from the voting booth in droves. This study was conducted during a lackluster campaign and at a time when the Internet was getting its "test drive" as a new campaign medium. Campaign interest is bound to increase in the 2000 election. The race will not feature an incumbent, making it likely the public will witness a more competitive race. Future studies should compare results from the 2000 and 1996 election to determine the degree to which campaign competitiveness influences the degree to which the media impact political attitudes and behaviours. Future studies should also perhaps focus on the Internet and its ability both to increase candidate knowledge as well as to reconnect voters to the political system.

10

A Demand-side View of Media Substitutability

Competition among media for audiences and advertisers is fierce and unrelenting. In both local and national markets, with weapons ranging from prepackaged contests and promotions to drastic overhauls of talent and management, media wage war with one another to attract audiences to sell to advertisers. Often underlying these intermedia battles is a simple, if unproven, assumption: that mass media are interchangeable, competing in the same market for the same advertising dollars.

In this chapter, we report results of a two-stage study conducted to explore the media interchangeability assumption as it relates to national advertising. The study specifically addressed the question: What are toplevel advertising managers' judgments about the degree to which cable TV, broadcast TV, radio, newspapers, magazines, billboards, and place-based media are substitutable for one another in national media schedules?

Advertiser opinions were collected in two stages. In the first stage, we mailed questionnaires to a sample of 402 chief advertising managers with the leading 100 national advertisers. In the second stage, we personally interviewed another sample of 34 national advertising managers to validate and extend the survey results. As detailed in the following paragraphs, both practical and empirical observations about media substitutability and national advertising guided our research approach.

According to Picard, media substitutability may be more evident in the market for advertising than any other media demand area. However, there are both practical and empirical reasons to suspect that media will not be seen as completely interchangeable by advertising managers. Based on these reasons, we predict that:

HI: For national advertising campaigns, advertising managers perceive little, if any, substitutability among traditional media options. Practical Considerations. As any advertiser well knows, different media provide different access to different kinds of audiences, which in advertising terms are defined as target markets.

Media for all advertising are typically selected based on a host of factors, including product consumption patterns, media usage patterns and habits, market size and location, vehicle cost efficiencies, specific media qualities (i.e., time and space availabilities, mechanical characteristics, delivery patterns, support services, etc.), and audience characteristics (i.e, demographics, lifestyles, psychographics).

Advertisers and their representatives, agencies, independent buying services, and in-house media planners, take these factors into consideration when planning advertising, seeking the media mix that best serves particular communication needs before specific media buys are negotiated and finalized. Therefore, for practical reasons, we predict that traditional media options will not be seen as completely interchangeable for national media schedules by advertising managers.

EMPIRICAL CONSIDERATIONS

A few researchers have empirically examined the question of advertising media substitutability. For the most part, these studies have been confined to local advertising and to the newspaper medium relative to local media options. One study found that print media are the most likely replacements for newspapers; others suggest that other media are also considered by local advertisers.

Sentman found that when a local newspaper goes out of business in a market where more than one newspaper is available, local advertisers are more likely to substitute the other newspaper in their media schedules than another medium.6 In two related studies, Smith found that the majority of local advertisers believe small dailies compete with other media, not just other newspapers, for local advertising dollars.

According to the Smith studies, more than three-fourths of the surveyed ROP advertisers said they would look to another medium if newspaper ad rates increased by 20 percent; about 40 percent said they would substitute another form of print media for newspapers, while more than one-third said they would use a broadcast medium as a replacement; and insert advertisers indicated that direct mail and a combination of other print would be appropriate substitutes for small dailies.

A study by Cameron, Nowak, and Krugman found that direct mail is seen by local advertisers as the primary substitute for advertiser dollars, although cable TV and yellow pages could be considered. Ferguson, in a study of newspaper advertising rates and competition for advertising dollars in a market, found that an increase in the number broadcast stations is associated with lower newspaper advertising rates, but that presence of a competing daily newspaper was not significantly related to newspaper advertising rates.

Work by Dimmick and Albarran adapted niche theory from the field of ecology to examine the displacement of existing media by newer media forms.

Neither study specifically asked advertising experts about substitutability among media options. Nevertheless, the work is relevant to our study because the results are suggestive of patterns of substitutability in advertising media planning.

Niche theory suggests that the more similar two media are perceived by advertisers and consumers, the more likely they are considered replacement options for one another. In one study, Albarran and Dimmick combined niche theory with a uses and gratifications approach to explore how niche breadth, overlap, and competitive superiority apply to the video entertainment industries. The study found a great deal of overlap among types of video media. In a later study, Dimmick suggests that the approach helps explain the "video revolution." According to Dimmick, advertisers are proficient observers of changes in consumer media and audience compositions. As new media emerge that meet the same needs as already existing media, the two media overlap or compete.

Advertisers react to media overlap by altering their ad placement patterns. The medium that is considered superior on the gratification dimension is the one that attracts more advertising dollars. The study most relevant to our investigation was conducted by Busterna. Although there are arguably methodological grounds to question the absolute validity of Busterna's findings, his conclusions are suggestive, if not conclusive, and predicative of our hypothesis. Spurred by definition disputes and conceptual inadequacies in the published research literature, Busterna used secondary industry data to determine which media are in the same market with newspapers for national advertising. Specifically, he tested the concept of cross-elasticity of demand, using price sensitivity to define market boundaries: "In simple terms the cross-elasticity of demand measures the relative change in quantity demanded of a given product or service in response to a change in price of another good or service.

If two products or services exist as reasonable substitutes, then an increase in the price of one will result in an increase in the quantity demanded of the other." Demand functions for five media were tested: television (network and spot), consumer magazines, newspaper supplements, radio (network and spot), and outdoor. Regression analyses revealed that "cross-elasticity of demand between newspapers and other media is consistently nil across all media," meaning that none of the tested media resides in the same market for national advertising dollars. From the results, Busterna drew two conclusions: First, it is clear that advertisers do not possess significant price sensitivity between newspapers and other media to consider newspapers a viable alternative for advertising that was intended to be placed in other media. Second, claims of significant competition between newspapers and other media often come from those who have a newspaper industry (seller) perspective rather than an advertiser (buyer) perspective.

FOCUS OF THE STUDY

Our study goes beyond Busterna's examination of newspapers as a substitute for other advertising media, as well as the previous studies of media substitutability in local advertising. As described more fully in the following methodology section, we asked two samples of top-level managers of national advertising programs to evaluate the interchangeability of seven media options against one another, not just newspapers against other media.

The study was designed and executed to accomplish three objectives: (1) to provide more evidence on the question of media substitutability in national advertising; (2) to re-examine Busterna's finding about the substitutability of newspapers in particular; and (3) to augment Busterna's price-sensitivity-based "buyer perspective" with perceptual data like that reported by Dimmick and Rothenbuhler and Lacy.

RESEARCH METHODS

Stage 1: Survey of Advertising Managers. To test the study's hypothesis, we first conducted a mail survey of top-level advertising managers, the individuals with large American companies who are responsible for spending national advertising dollars. Following Busterna's suggestion, we wanted to avoid the sampling error of studies conducted by Dimmick and Rothenbuhler and Lacy. In their studies, the researchers sampled executives with media organizations (i.e., supply-side representatives) on the assumption that media are active agents in deciding what advertising will be scheduled.

However, as pointed out by Busterna, the active agent in advertising media planning is the advertising executive, not the media executive. Therefore, we sought buyer judgment of media substitutability rather than seller judgment since it is the buyer of advertising, not the seller, that fuels intermedia competition. Sample and Mailing Procedure. Advertising Age's list of "100 Leading National Advertisers" and the Standard Director of Advertisers were used as the sampling frame. Four hundred-two individuals listed as the chief advertising officer (i.e., brand manager, advertising director, vice president of marketing, marketing communications, or advertising) for each of the 100 advertisers' corporate, division, and/or subsidiary organizations were selected as survey participants.

A notification postcard was sent to each of the 402 advertising officers one week prior to the mailing of questionnaires. The postcard informed the individuals of the nature of the study, requested their participation, and informed them that questionnaires would be arriving in seven to ten days. One week following the notification, the questionnaires were mailed.

Each questionnaire was accompanied by a cover letter and a postage-paid return envelope. Three weeks after the initial mailing, a second mailing was sent to nonrespondents. Four weeks later, a third mailing was executed. The third mailing was followed two weeks later by a reminder letter. A copy of the questionnaire was not included in the fourth mailing. Of the mailing of 402, a total of 91 completed, usable questionnaires were returned: 43 from the first mailing, 16 from the second mailing, 22 from the third mailing, and 10 from the reminder mailing. Eleven questionnaires were returned incomplete and/or unusable, 42 were "returned to sender," and 19 were returned with notes of refusal, for an adjusted individual response rate of 28%.

The 91 usable questionnaires were completed by individuals with 50 of the 100 national advertisers, for an advertiser response rate of 50%.

The individual response rate is consistent with other surveys of advertising managers. A sampling of studies published in the Journal of Advertising, journal of Current Issues and Research in Advertising, and Journal of Advertising Research between 1981 and 1996 found that reported response rates ranged from 21% to 33%io, with an average of 32%.

Questionnaire Construction and Pretest. An eight-page questionnaire was used to collect the survey data. The questionnaire was modified from one used in a past survey of agency media specialists. That questionnaire was stringently pretested with five advertising specialists located in New York, Chicago, Cincinnati, and Atlanta and produced a return rate of 54%.

The questionnaire contained seven sections, three of which are relevant to the focus of this study. The other four sections asked questions about media selection criteria and media-provided advertiser services.

National Advertising Definition. Included in the survey instructions was the following definition: "National ad accounts are accounts for brands/ services that are distributed or available in most or all of the U.S. The advertising for these accounts need not be national. Coverage may be regional." The definition was developed from interview information collected in the aforementioned advertising media survey and a search of basic advertising texts. The definition was provided to frame the construct for the respondents in an effort to reduce potential response variance.

Respondent Qualification. The first section asked one question: "Do you feel qualified to voice opinions about the appropriateness of media (i.e., TV and magazines) for national advertising campaigns?" The question had two closed-end options, yes and no, and was included to screen out respondents who felt unqualified to answer questions about national advertising and media substitutability.

MEDIA SUBSTITUTES

The fifth section contained seven traditional advertising media options, cable TV, broadcast TV, radio, newspapers, magazines, billboards, and place-based, formatted in a matrix with "media to be replaced" listed ina vertical column and "appropriate media substitutes" listed in corresponding horizontal rows.

The respondents were asked about media substitutability in the following manner: Sometimes because of factors beyond advertiser control, one media type must be substituted for another in national campaign planning. The list in the left-hand column below contains several media options.

For each medium in this list, please indicate those media that you believe are appropriate and reasonable replacements from the list of substitute media provided. Please indicate your belief by circling each medium you consider to be an appropriate substitute.

RESPONDENT BACKGROUND

The final section of the questionnaire contained six questions designed to collect background information from the respondents about their age, gender, education, present title/position, and years of advertising experience. Education information was collected on a categorical basis. Open-ended questions were used to gather the other background information.

QUESTIONNAIRE PRETEST

Although a version of the questionnaire had been pretested previously, we pretested the modified version because it contained three additional items: the respondent qualification question, the media substitutability measure, and several additional respondent background questions. Three advertising managers with Chicago- and Atlanta-based advertisers agreed to participate in the pretest. The pretest was conducted using both mail and personal interviewing techniques. First, agreement to participate was secured by telephone contact. Pretest questionnaires were then mailed and returned completions were followed up by phone calls to discuss any identified problem areas. No serious problems were uncovered. However, the format of the media substitutability measure was slightly modified to facilitate the response task (i.e., spacing was changed to enhance readability). Before final printing, the format change was cross-checked with the three pretest participants.

Stage 2: Personal Interviews with Advertising Managers. Using the same directory sources as the survey stage of the study, 50 additional advertising managers with large national advertisers were identified and contacted by telephone. Thirty-eight officers agreed to be interviewed; however, interviews could be arranged with only 34 of the 38.

Ten days prior to the scheduled interview, each participant was mailed a copy of the data analysis, with instructions asking them to consider and explain what the results indicate relative to their professional experiences. All interviews were conducted by the same procedure and protocol: the study's purpose was reiterated and the participant was asked to interpret patterns in the survey data and to explain what the patterns suggest about the question of media substitutability for national advertising accounts. Following are profiles of the two sets of respondents and the results of both the survey and interview stages of the study. Wherever appropriate, the survey and interview results are integrated.

RESPONDENT PROFILES

The majority of advertising managers who participated in the survey were male (73.6% male vs. 26.4% female) and under the age of 45 (57.3% under 45 vs. 42.7% over 45). Nearly all were college graduates (96.7%), with 56% having a graduate degree. Almost half had more than 15 years of professional advertising experience (48.4%io), either on the agency or client side of the advertising business. Just over one-fourth of the respondents had more than 20 years of professional advertising experience.

The profile of the 34 interviewed managers mirrored the characteristics of the survey respondents. Male managers outnumbered females (76.5% male vs. 23.5% female). The majority were under the age of 45 (55.9% under 45 vs. 44.1% over 45) and nearly all were college graduates (97.1%), with half having a master's degree. Fifty percent of the interviewees had more than 15 years in advertising, and almost one-quarter had more than 20 years of advertising experience.

QUESTION OF MEDIA SUBSTITUTABILITY

Not surprisingly, all 125 ad managers considered themselves competent to consider the issue of media substitutability and national advertising. The 91 respondents who returned useable questionnaires answered yes to the qualifying question about ability to judge media for national advertising campaigns. The 34 interviewees responded yes when asked about their abilities to consider the question during the opening phase of the interview session.

Each medium was perceived an acceptable substitute for another in national advertising planning. Analysis of the response frequencies and mean ratings revealed interesting patterns in the ad managers' judgments.

Consistent with the frequencies, substitutability among the six media is suggested by the means: every medium, on average, had at least one substitute mentioned and all but placebased were identified as a substitute for at least two other media. Cable TV had the highest mean number of mentions as a replacement (2.44) and placebased had the lowest (.83).

The mean number of mentions of cable TV as a substitute was significantly higher than those of the other five media, whereas the mean mentions of radio as a replacement was significantly higher than the means of three media: magazines, broadcast TV, and place-based media. The broadcast TV mean was significantly higher than the mean mentions of place-based media.

The interview results were consistent with the survey results. The consensus among the interviewed managers is that media are replaceable in national advertising schedules. All of the managers told us that they considered both media and audience characteristics when trying to determine national media schedules. They acknowledged that there are clearly times when one medium will do a better of job of communicating a message than another medium. However, in many cases, availabilities in geographic markets, timing considerations, media costs, and other conditions force managers and their representatives to consider substitutes.

As two managers put it: Though we prefer not to substitute, there are circumstances which dictate a change of direction in media planning. If you can't afford ABC, CBS, then you consider what we can do with a combination of magazines and USA, TBS, ESPN, or whatever other cable options are out there. The key is trying to deliver a message to a certain audience at a certain place and time, with effective exposure in a cost efficient manner.

Media are interchangeable, not in that they are all the same, but in the fact that it's audience delivery, message exposure, and cost which drive the typical national ad schedule. Yeah, there are options; there is an option for every medium because it's not media per se. It's what is being delivered by the medium that counts, and that what is the right audience.

Media is a negotiated process. The ideal often differs from what is planned for and what results. The issue of replacement comes down to a simple point-audience delivery. If you can't get it with a television schedule, then you back up and look at other combinations.

It's difficult to talk about it, but when you get down to it, media provide access to audiences-some deliver a specific audience better than others. From my experience, while not preferable, there are always acceptable substitutes in some combination. Sure national media are replaceable or substitutable for each other. Every competitor can't be in TV at the same time. You've got to look for other media to break through TV clutter, to out smart the competitor in another medium. Costs, audience, and message impact they are the factors that determine national media schedules, not media types.

One interesting factor mentioned by several of the ad managers was value-added opportunities, promotional incentives offered by media as inducements for media space and time sales. As suggested by two managers, these inducements sometimes persuade planners to took beyond time and cost when comparing media options.

We work with media to service our needs in ways beyond running our ads. Merchandising, joint-marketing efforts are important to us in stretching our promotional dollars. If a magazine comes to me and says I'll feature your product in a special section on house repair or gardening, and I'm considering buying TV spots, I'll try to do a cost analysis.

The extra offered by the magazine might offset a higher actual cost between different media. Like in any situation, cost is a relative thing. In today's planning environment, media extras are important. If a newspaper group comes to me and says they can get us premium space with a large retail chain in X number of cities, then I'm gonna listen. The same is true of media that offer to tiein our line with contests and special programs, for example, radio. Rates are important, yes. But, unless there's a tremendous difference in total schedule cost, sometimes the "extras" offset money differences. The whole process is more complex than comparing CPMs, and media incentives play a big part. Same is true with consumer incentive programs; advertisers are the consumers targeted by media sellers.

From the frequencies reported, it is apparent that not all substitutes are perceived alike; there are patterns in the responses which suggest that certain media fall into specific categories of substitutability. There is substantial agreement among the managers about the substitutability of both forms of television advertising. Cable and broadcast TV are considered highly appropriate substitutes for each other, with nearly 8 of 10 managers having judged one medium an appropriate and reasonable replacement for the other. Other combinations were identified as acceptable at the 40% to 50% range. Five of 10 managers judged newspapers and magazines acceptable substitutes of each other (52.8%/56.2%).

Radio was seen as a reasonable replacement for newspapers (53.9%), and cable TV an acceptable substitute for both radio (56.2%) and magazines (49.7%). Four of 10 thought billboards and place-based media were acceptable substitutes for each other (41.6%/39.3%). The same percent judged newspapers an acceptable substitute for radio (42.7".io), and radio a reasonable replacement for both cable TV (41.6%) and billboards (41.6%).

Thirty of the 34 interviewed managers agreed with the survey respondents-that is, media fall into specific replacement groupings. The most interesting and common explanation offered for categorization is the belief that creative decisions drive media decisions.

You have to understand once a creative approach is decided upon, then media are planned around that approach. Media are considered, but they are secondary in my view. Look at it in terms of give and take. Once creative is determined, there is no replacement. Sure media differ in how they deliver and impact messages, but they can be interchanged to some degree. Creative can't.

TV for TV, print for print. What's surprising about that? A point of fact is creative and media work hand-in-hand - they are like hand and glove. In my experience, creative drives the process, and when it comes to media If you can't get network broadcast spots, you're going to look at cable. Same is true in print, and in reminder type ads - billboards.

We often prefer to buy network TV spots because of coverage and message delivery impact allows us to demonstrate our brands at a pretty cost effective level. But if we have to we go with cable advertising in markets where we can't get the numbers with network Or because the spots aren't available We look to cable. Cable is relatively cheap, you can buy lots of spots at different times, on different networks. I certainly understand and agree that television is substitutable for TV. I see the same situation with print and out-of-home reminder media, like outdoor in store, or whatever.

A similar observation about magazines and newspapers was made by 9 managers. Said one manager: Look, when you are trying to run a print ad there's a reason— you want to deliver a specific type of message to a particular type of audience. Suppose you want those people to spend sometime with what you are saying to control exposure.

For whatever, if I can't get a magazine in a particular market-let's say a business mag-I'm not going to TV? A whole different ballgame there. No, instead, I'm going to look at newspaper options, particularly the business pages. Another example that comes to mind is a business magazine like Business Week or Fortune The ability of cable TV, newspapers, and radio to transcend media form was attributed to the fact these media are sometimes looked upon as secondary options in national advertising planning.

Radio is a great medium, especially for local advertisers. I think what you see is this radio is generally regarded as filling gaps in a national schedule building audience coverage, increasing total impressions when time can't be purchased in TV. It's a secondary medium for most national advertisers, a fall back option. Other managers explained it this way: We use radio and newspapers to fill in holes in our schedule. We like magazines because of their specialization and extras. If we buy radio or newspapers, we are supplementing. I suspect that the same is true of users of cable TV. Cable is used to supplement network schedules and spot buys Why is radio a reasonable replacement for cable TV and billboards?

Simple. Radio is not a primary option for most national advertisers. If you can't schedule enough TV or print to meet your market-by-market objectives, you fill in with radio if creative allows it. Radio is secondary in national ad planning, not primary. Contrary to our hypothesis, these results suggest that there is a degree of "perceived substitutability" among traditional media options for national advertising planning. The results also call into question the absoluteness of Busterna's finding that newspapers do not reside in the market for national advertising dollars with television, magazines, radio, and outdoor. It appears from our data that national advertising managers put traditional media in certain boxes, at least perceptually, when considering schedule substitutes. These findings are not particularly surprising if it is true advertising experts place media into national and retail boxes as well.

As for newspapers in particular, our findings suggest that newspapers compete directly with magazines and radio for national advertising expenditures. Though we would agree with Busterna that newspapers do not compete with every medium, the medium is not perceived by national advertisers in isolation, separate and distinct from other media options.

Considering the evidence provided in our depth interviews, we would argue that the issue of substitutability in national advertising comes down not to the issue of media type per se, but to other considerations such as audience delivery, communication effectiveness, and value-added opportunities. As suggested in the interviews, media are replaceable in national advertising because of similarities in form and function, that is, the physical and qualitative properties of each medium. Apparently in national advertising planning, when the first option is not available or too costly, then, the second option is considered on the same principle as the medium of choice-the ability to deliver the largest percentage of the targeted audience at the right time with the most frequency and the greatest communication impact.

In his economic analysis, Busterna focused on one factor of media selection-space and time costs. Our findings indicate that cost is not the only factor that plays a role in the decision to select a medium, including the decision to replace one medium with another.

For a variety of competitive and creative reasons, a medium may be used in a national media schedule even though it is more expensive on an overall cost basis. Actual media costs are important; however, unique communication qualities of a medium, delivery of a target audience (which would make a medium more cost efficient even though it is more expensive), value-added opportunities, as well as other factors certainly affect the relative cost of a medium as much as time and space cost.

In fact, surveys of how advertising specialists choose media for both national and retail campaigns convincingly demonstrate that, while media costs are essential to the media selection process, selection decisions are driven by a medium's ability to effectively reach a specific audience. Even cost-per-thousand data, a better measure than overall cost data adjusted for inflation (constant dollars) in determining the value of a medium because the measure considers the relationship between cost and audience delivered, overlook the effects of such factors as added-value opportunities, creative considerations, and audience characteristics. All things considered, we suggest that differences between the newspaper-specific findings of the two studies are attributable to the temporal nature of Busterna's media data. From his analysis, Busterna concluded that leaving the large rate differential between national and retail ad rates in newspapers makes sense from a managerial view because advertiser demand for newspaper space is somewhat inelastic.

Hence, he advised newspaper executives not to expect to get increased advertising business from advertisers in other media with national rate reductions. The problem with Busterna's recommendation is that during the time period of his data, 1971-1985, national newspaper advertising made up a small percentage of total U.S. advertising spending; it declined steadily from 4.96% to 3.53%. There was very little variability in the amount of national advertising in newspapers.

It is possible that the slope of the demand curve for newspapers would have been flatter (i.e., a sign of more inelastic demand), with more variation in 1971-1985 data, if national newspaper ad rates had been lowered significantly during the period. However, it is quite possible that trade-offs between media options already existed as the result of relative cost considerations; perhaps national advertisers were using newspapers less than magazines and radio on the basis of relative cost versus actual cost, for example. Those advertisers who were consistent users of newspapers during the 1971-1985 period might have found them an effective and efficient way to reach their target audience, despite the national/retail rate differential. If our findings accurately reflect advertising manager perceptions, we suggest that a reduction in the national/retail rate differential may have attracted national advertisers from magazines and radio to newspapers during 1971-85.

There is also reason to suspect the relative price variation between newspapers and magazines may have been more dramatic than reflected in Busterna's data as the result of differences in another non-cost factor, valueadded opportunities. During the period, magazines became much more specialized and the number of magazine options offering specialized audiences increased dramatically.

According to the MPA Handbook, the number of domestic consumer magazines which accepted national and broad regional advertising increased from 874 in 1970 to 1,492 in 1985. By 1995, the number of domestic consumer magazines increased to 2,454. As these magazines became more specialized, they also increased the number of value-added opportunities to national advertisers. Newspapers were much slower to jump on the value-added bandwagon. In addition to rate reductions, it is possible that newspapers may have attracted more national advertising dollars if the medium had countered magazines with its own value-added opportunities during the 1971-85 period.

PRACTICAL AND RESEARCH IMPLICATIONS

The implication of our findings for the practice of advertising is that media should be sold against other media, but not in the straightforward, one-for-one manner of selling one medium against every other medium. Rather it is suggested by these findings that sales representatives pitch their time and space directly against.media perceived as acceptable substitutes among national advertisers.

For example, national ad sales pitches for newspapers would be more productive by focusing on magazines and radio as the competition, not on television. Pitches for billboards would work best against other out-of-home options, not against print or electronic options.

Sales programs for radio would be more effective if positioned against newspapers, cable TV, and billboards, whereas sales efforts for cable TV would be more productive targeting broadcast TV, radio, and magazines. In each case, sales efforts should not concentrate exclusively on "absolute" cost differentials to sell media options.

National advertisers are interested in relative cost as much as absolute cost, and media must compete on non-cost competitive factors such as impact of message delivery, creative fit, and value-added opportunities.

For researchers, the implication of our results is that questions of substitutability and other comparative inquiries must be asked of buyers, not just sellers of media. As with any one-shot survey, our study needs to be replicated among another sample of media buyers. While the acheived response rate was in line with other relevant industry studies, the rate was less than desired. Replication would confirm and enhance interpretive validity

Other studies on agency buyers, media sellers, and perhaps marketby-market comparisons are needed to flesh out our findings. To extend our findings beyond the seven studied media options (e.g., syndicated TV, spot TV, network TV, internet), localized and specific market comparisons are needed to "tease" out differences and to expand the scope of the findings from general media options to specific market-based options.

Others studies are needed to examine, among other things, (1) the relationship between what national advertisers try to accomplish with their advertising and how media substitutability is affected by different creative approaches, and (2) the effects of over-time variation in factors such as actual media cost, valueadded opportunities, and new media introductions on patterns of media usage and substitution.

It would also be worth studying additional forms of advertising media, including new media options such as Internet advertising and direct mail advertising, and other categories of advertisers such as localized or retail advertising to compare and contrast opinions of media substitutability among national advertisers.

In the final analysis, these findings add to what is known about national advertiser opinions of substitutability among seven traditional media options. However, many other questions about advertising media substitutability need exploration, from many methodological viewpoints. Until those studies are conducted, we suggest that media, including newspapers, are substitutable to a certain degree and compete with each other in specific patterns for national advertising dollars.

11

Operationalizing and Analyzing Exposure

Measurement or manipulation of exposure is the foundation of research examining effects of mediated information such as news, music videos, Internet sites, and advertising. It is equally fundamental to studies of intentional influences on that environment such as behaviour change communication campaigns.

Our ability to test theory and to establish media or campaign effects is a function of our ability to successfully manipulate or measure exposure to mediated communication, and to analyse effects of that exposure. Exposure, in principle, is a straightforward concept.

McGuire's information processing model, for example, distinguishes exposure as the prerequisite for subsequent attention, comprehension, and retention. Accordingly, we may define exposure as the extent to which audience members have encountered specific messages or classes of messages/media content. However, operationalizing such a definition is a messy business. This definition says exposure refers to a person's merely encountering the messages, whether or not they are noticed enough to be remembered. After all, noticing the relevant messages in the communication environment is almost certainly confounded with variables that may predict attention to the content of that message, such as prior knowledge or involvement with the topic.

It is also quite possible that exposure may leave an affective if not a cognitive impression of some kind, even if the messages have not been attended to well enough to be remembered. However, if messages are not processed thoroughly enough to be recalled, how can exposure be self-reported? As a result, operations for exposure either take the conservative position of estimating exposure from the possibility of exposure, absorbing the error associated with not actually encountering the messages of interest, or use various techniques to obtain self-reports of exposure, and then use various strategies to control the effects of selective attention due to prior knowledge or involvement which would otherwise undermine causal claims.

Each available approach involves significant trade-offs and uncertainties. Some of these strategies have recently been evolved or incorporated into studies of exposure, making a critical review of methods used to study exposure effects timely.

USING SELF-REPORT MEASURES OF EXPOSURE

The most straightforward way to assess people's exposure to mediated communication is to ask them. Given the thousands of messages and other mediated content to which an individual is exposed in a month, the accuracy of such recall is often problematic. Since exposure to messages and media is, outside of the research lab, volitional and self-selected given prior knowledge, involvement, and other variables typically associated also with outcomes of interest. The direction of causality is also problematic. The task of the media effects researcher using self-report measures is to minimize these problems insofar as possible. The issues with respect to such operations are well-recognized and will therefore be only briefly reviewed here.

Global Self-report. One may simply ask respondents how often they watch the news, play "first-person shooter" video games, or listen to conservative talk-show radio programming. Perhaps the best-known, though widely criticized, example of such analysis is found in early cultivation research in which amount of television viewing was correlated with fears concerning crime and violence. Problems include the lack of specificity regarding the actual content of media exposure represented by global self-report,Which would result in underestimates of effect sizes and lack of control for third-variables and reverse causality.One strategy to address effect size problems is to increase specificity of exposure measures. Asking about frequency of watching specific crime dramas and reality cop shows is more precise than asking about overall TV viewing if one is interested in effects of violent TV content.Specificity of media exposure measures should include separate measurement of media types (such as television, radio, and newspapers) as well as of media content. Another approach to obtaining detailed information about specific media use is media diaries. Respondents are asked to record all of their use of specified media over some time frame. Problems include motivating respondents to provide complete and accurate record keeping, and the time-consuming task of coding and entering data from such diaries.

A primary weakness in the use of global self-report measures is the inevitable uncertainty concerning the exact nature of the relevant content of the media to which respondents report exposure. This uncertainty can largely be removed when content analyses of those media are conducted in conjunction with the survey of exposure self-reports.

Such content analyses permit quantification of specific elements of media content, such as valence of coverage, sources used, and ethnicity of people portrayed. This should facilitate more precise theoretical specifications of mechanisms as well as increasing predictive power. The claim that one has characterized the content of a medium is only convincing, however, insofar as one has successfully defined a corresponding population of messages and has randomly sampled or taken a census of those messages. Recall and Recognition. More precise than global exposure self-reports, but also more resource-intensive, are exposure self-reports that involve the recognition or recall of specific messages. In recognition measures, messages (or sometimes verbal descriptions of specific messages) are presented to the respondent. In recall measurement, the respondent is asked to describe content of messages that he or she has seen, which then must be analysed by coders to assess the accuracy and completeness of recall.

To use these methods, one must have a relatively small population of messages from which to sample test messages (for recognition measures) or against which to compare open-ended recall measures. Such approaches, then, are typically more appropriate for the evaluation of specific media-based campaigns than for studies of the existing media environment, unless one is interested in the impact of specific programs, articles, or other messages. In general, recognition measures appear to be preferred over recall for several reasons. Coding of free or cued recall is time-consuming, difficult, and error-prone. More important, people who process messages with relatively little attention are likely not to remember them in the context of a free recall task, but are more likely to recognize them.

Therefore, recognition measures are probably less confounded with variables related to attention such as prior interest in the topic than are recall measures, and therefore are closer to the conceptual definition of exposure. One of the principal problems of recognition measures, however, is the tendency of people to report recognizing messages that they in fact have never seen. The primary reason is probably respondent uncertainty: people are exposed to a great many messages on most topics, and it is easy to mistake a message presented in a recognition task with other rather similar messages that one may have seen. Other possible reasons include social desirability-the belief by a respondent that he or she "should" have seen the message-or simply response set when other messages in a test group are in fact recognizable. A simple strategy for handling this problem is through use of foils or ringers. These are messages that could plausibly have been of the type being tested, but were never shown and are different enough from messages actually shown that legitimate confusion is unlikely.

Recognition of foils can be used as a statistical control for response set and social desirable response bias; analysis of foils in a treatment/control design also suggests that simply using a "might have seen" response category, and coding it as "never seen," can reduce error due to false recognition.

Analysis of foils/ringers and "maybe" responses are useful for reducing the impact of false recognition, social desirability, and response set, but they do not address underlying problems concerning direction of causation, third variable explanations, and selective exposure.

THE DOSE-RESPONSE PROBLEM AND USE OF COVARIATES

As Hornik points out, the relationship of amount of exposure to media effects is a key applied question, on which the expenditure of many millions may depend. Establishing a "dose-response" relationship between exposure and outcomes also goes a long way towards validating the effect of a class of messages. Unfortunately, in field contexts amount of exposure is self-selected, not manipulated.

Exposure is typically a mediating, rather than a truly exogenous, variable: It may be substantially influenced by both baseline scores on an outcome variable and by many possible third variables (also known as endogeneity). Baseline scores can only be effectively controlled in longitudinal research.

Use of statistical controls or covariates can manage third variable problems-to the extent that they are well-measured, that all relevant third-variables are identified and incorporated into the model, and that no variables are mistakenly included as covariates when in fact they are mediators of effects. This ideal scenario can only be approximated, and there is always a substantial degree of uncertainty concerning the appropriateness of one's choices of control variables. Moreover, large numbers of covariates make for cumbersome models that use up degrees of freedom and statistical power (overparameterization), and can only accurately account for variables with a linear relationship to the outcome variable.

One statistical method recently applied to exposure studies in the evaluation of the National Youth Media Anti-Drug Campaign is the use of propensity scoring. This was done because this government-sponsored campaign was national in scope and begun before the evaluation began.

Absent control groups, control over exposure levels, or a baseline, evaluators were dependent on assessing dose-response effects while trying to control for all the many variables that might predict variation in exposure to campaign advertising. Propensity scoring involves building a statistical model predicting the likelihood of a given level of exposure from a variety of exogenous variables that are likely to be related to exposure. A single vector can be calculated from this model and applied to adjusting the outcome of interest for this propensity to be exposed.

This strategy has a number of desirable statistical qualities. Analyses are not encumbered with a long series of control variables-even if hundreds of covariates are incorporated in the model used to create the propensity score, only one propensity weighting must be used in adjusting a given analysis. Moreover, propensity scores do not assume a linear relation to the outcome as covariates do, and can be balanced over levels of the outcome variable.

Propensity scoring, then, addresses the degrees of freedom and linearity problems with covariate analyses, but remains as dependent as traditional covariate analyses on identifying all key third variables and measuring them with a minimum of error. Moreover, researchers using propensity scoring may be especially prone to inadvertently using mediators as covariates, because there is no price paid in statistical power or model complexity by adding in additional variables to the propensity score model.

A critical assumption when covariates are used is that they are all exogenous-that is, none of them in fact serve as mediators of exposure effects. For example, in political communication, one might want to use political discussion as a covariate, under the assumption that it might predict exposure to political coverage in the media as one seeks out information to use in such discussions. However, if effects of political coverage are mediated by political discussions (which might, for example, encourage incorporation of new information learned from the media into knowledge structures), then its use as a covariate or as part of propensity scoring might help eliminate media effects that in fact are present.

Managing Problems of Causality Using Longitudinal Analyses of Exposure. Causality and Endogeneity. The problem of reverse or reciprocal causality (or the endogeneity of exposure) is, as noted above, a fundamental challenge in most media effects questions. Research in selectivity suggests people are likely to seek out, process attentively, and remember information that interests or is relevant to them. These selectivity m echanisms, then, are likely to increase self-report of exposure to a given type or class of messages.

For example, consumer research shows that people who have an interest in a type of product are more likely to report having seen such advertising, more aggressive youth are more likely to seek out violent media content, and more politically involved people process mediated information with more attention. One cannot ascertain in cross-sectional data whether exposure items are measuring exposure, or salience of the type of information conveyed to people predisposed to seek out and recall such information. For example, in political communication, cross-sectional studies that link exposure to political knowledge may inflate the strength of such relationships. People who have an interest in and are knowledgeable about politics are probably more likely to seek out and recall mediated information, as well as having such mediated information increase their knowledge. Conversely, youth exposed to an anti-drug advertising campaign may be more likely to notice and recall such messages if they are experimenting with or using drugs, which would militate against finding favorable impacts of exposure in cross-sectional data.

In fact, one might state as a general principle that cross-sectional analyses that assume unidirectionality exaggerate the relationship between exposure and outcomes when the messages are consistent with the outcome, and underestimate it when the messages-as in many health prevention contexts-are intended to decrease a behavioural or attitudinal outcome of interest that may in turn be predictive of attention to the message.

The true relationships cannot be estimated with confidence. Structural equation models or instrumental variables may be used with cross-sectional data to estimate reciprocal paths. Causal models of cross-sectional data can provide useful initial evidence regarding the relative strength of reciprocal relationships, but can hardly be regarded as providing definitive evidence.

LONGITUDINAL ANALYSES, SELECTIVE EXPOSURE, AND CAUSALITY

One approach to reducing these problems is to use longitudinal data analysis. Studying longitudinal effects of exposure on change in political knowledge or marijuana use, controlling for prior levels of knowledge or use, is more convincing with respect to causal influence than are cross-sectional analyses, as one can control the time-ordering of effects and the influence of prior scores on the outcome measures; in other words, one is testing the effects of exposure on change in the outcome variable.

The simple use of lagged prediction, however, may not go far enough; the contribution of selective exposure may be to some extent controlled (insofar as it is captured by the influence of baseline scores on the outcome variable), but it is still not understood unless it is explicitly modeled. Use of longitudinal data permits comparisons, for example, of nested structural models positing selective exposure effects versus selective exposure plus media effects paths.

In such models, model fit for a stability model plus the lagged selective exposure effect can be assessed. Fit can then be reassessed with the lagged media effect path added, and a chi-square difference test computed to ascertain whether adding the media effect path or paths to the selective exposure paths resulted in a statistically significant improvement in model fit.

Cross-lagged panel regressions, however, have been criticized as being statistically inferior to growth curve models. Growth curve models focus on analyzing individual respondents' developmental trajectories in a longitudinal data set, and identify coefficients for averaged trajectories that can serve as variables in a regression or structural equation model.

Multi-level growth curve models can also separate out effects of "trait" and "state" components of predictor variables, which can be important in analyzing effects of media exposure. For example, the author and colleagues used multi-level growth curve models to test the "downward spiral" hypothesis that while aggressiveness in adolescents tends to increase use of violent media content (selective exposure), this exposure would reinforce that aggressiveness (media effects). Use of the multi-level model made it possible to look in particular at effects of variation in aggressiveness over time and not simply at aggressiveness as a trait, which is less likely to be subject to media influence. By modeling both selectivity and media effects, using either growth curve or more familiar cross-lagged models, one can move beyond simplistic discussions of competing causal directions and specify ways selectivity and effects of exposure to media content may reinforce each other or cancel effects out.26

INSTRUMENTAL VARIABLE APPROACHES

Still another approach to improving causal inference in pre-post and other longitudinal designs is to utilize instrumental variables, a technique widely used in econometric analyses. Instrumental variables in the present context are variables that are associated with exposure but not with the outcome of interest. A classic hypothetical example (described by Hornik) would be an international development effort in which some members of the population are blocked from receiving a radio broadcast because of a mountain blocking radio reception.

Area of residence-if not confounded with income, social status occupation, and so on in ways that might also be related to outcomes of interest-can then serve as an instrumental variable estimating relationships between exposure and outcome, and exposure-outcome relationships can be estimated using two-stage least squares methods, irrespective of possible reciprocal relationships between exposure and outcome. The problem is that it is often difficult or impossible to identify variables strongly predictive of exposure that are conceptually and empirically independent of the outcome of interest. As a result, exposure studies using instrumental variables to control endogeneity are at best a rarity.

THE PROBLEM OF LAGGED EXPOSURE EFFECTS

There are significant challenges to analyzing exposure using lagged longitudinal analyses, besides logistical issues such as cost, confidentiality, and respondent mortality. Effects of message exposure may be short-lived. If so, longitudinal lags (typically one-half year or more) may be too long to detect lagged effects of message exposure, especially for a message processed incidentally and with little attention, such as with advertising. A more sensitive way to capture the effects of message exposure, especially regarding short-lived effects as in the case of advertising, is to use time-series analyses. Such analyses, however, are most effective when exposure measures are not dependent on self-report, and therefore are discussed later.

EXPOSURE AND ATTENTION: CONCEPTUAL AND ANALYTIC ISSUES

McGuire's information-processing model of persuasion highlights exposure and attention as the two prerequisite conditions for message influence. Some media effects research treats these variables as additive, controlling for exposure before analyzing the effects of attention.

Other research argues that effects of exposure should be weighted by attention,The latter argument is attractive at first glance. Certainly, it is likely that the degree to which exposure affects an individual is a function of the amount of attention that individual pays to the message. However, this is also methodologically problematic.

Attention is inherently confounded with the prior knowledge, interest, and attitudes that give rise to attention. Such prior variables might independently be related to the outcome of interest independent of exposure. Weighting exposure by attention might produce effects that are primarily due to attention's antecedents, not exposure.

Moreover, there are serious statistical questions raised by using multiplicative terms without using the additive terms in the same model. If such an approach is to be explored, use of the main effect terms as well as the weighted term is to be recommended.

ESTIMATING EXPOSURE FROM THE POSSIBILITY OF EXPOSURE

An alternative to exposure self-report measurement is to identify or manipulate the possibility of exposure to a set of messages in a given population. The classic way to do this is through experimental manipulation in a laboratory setting or in the field. Experimental manipulation, however, is not the only way to study possible exposure.

One may use instead reach and frequency, using the traditional media planning terminology. Studies of advertising can take advantage of data concerning amount, type, and placement of advertising available (at non-trivial cost) from Nielsen and other market research firms. If one is working in cooperation with advertisers, as in the evaluation of a counter-advertising campaign, one can use media buy records to identify levels of possible exposure. Conceptual and methodological problems with respect to using each of these methods to operationalize exposure are discussed below.

EXPERIMENTAL MANIPULATIONS OF EXPOSURE

Of course, the only certain way to demonstrate causal relationships between exposure to media content and subsequent effects is through experimental designs. There are good reasons, though, that such studies do not fully dominate the media effects field. The following briefly reviews the problems and opportunities associated with experimental manipulations of exposure. Laboratory Experiment. Experimentation is well understood by social scientists, but it may be useful to note issues that have particular impact in research on effects of exposure to mediated messages.

For example, the complexities of selective exposure, information clutter and competition, the casualness with which much information is processed in real-world settings, the social contexts in which messages are received and discussed, and the cumulative effects of exposure to many hundreds or thousands of messages over a period of years cannot typically be reproduced in the laboratory. Experiments build theory and help elucidate processes, but these theories and models must be tested in the social environment as well.

The choice and presentation of message stimuli to which research participants are exposed in particular pose difficult problems.There has also been considerable debate over how possible it is to cleanly manipulate message variables, and the appropriate ways to analyse message differences in an experiment. Several researchers have argued that the key distinction is between true manipulation of a message (e.g., varying the source attribution) and operationalizing a message variable by presenting participants with various exemplars of different types of messages, such as humorous versus fear-inducing advertisements.

There is some consensus that in the latter case at least random effect models are appropriate, as the message variable has been operationalized through selection of examples rather than through a crossed experimental manipulation. Use of random sampling to create a pool of experimental stimuli to be used in an experiment more closely approximates the real media environment, and results in a more ecologically valid operationalization of exposure than would otherwise be the case.

Manipulation of exposure can be made a little less artificial by providing people messages outside of a laboratory environment. For example, some market research firms maintain panels of people who have agreed to serve as research respondents. Respondents can be sent experimental stimuli, thus providing a high degree of control over exposure outside of a lab setting. Similar me the Internet and then randomly assigned to experimental conditions.

FIELD EXPERIMENTS AND QUASI-EXPERIMENTS

The gold standard for any study of media or campaign effects is the group randomized trial, in which entire communities are randomly assigned to media treatment and control conditions. The strength of inference such studies make possible is impressive. Communication effects are studied in "real world" community settings, with all the complexities of audience selective exposure and attention, multi-step flow, and community process intact.Communities are in many respects a natural unit of analysis for exposure to mediated communication, as broadcast areas for radio and television, and circulation areas for newspapers, largely correspond with physical communities.

Media markets typically become the necessary unit of randomization in field experiments in which broadcast media or newspapers are involved. As noted earlier, this approach assumes that research participants have been adequately exposed to the message simply because they reside in a media treatment community. Such an assumption makes for a conservative test, given the degree to which exposure depends on access to specific forms of media and selective attention to the messages provided.The primary difficulty, though, is that the gold standard requires lots of gold. The expense of community intervention trials, such as those using media markets as the unit of randomization, has increased tremendously with the recent expectation that community trials be analysed using clustered or nested analyses in which the primary unit of analysis is the community. This represents a very serious challenge for researchers. Communication interventions typically have small effect sizes. Such effects are non-trivial given the ability of such campaigns to reach much or most of a population. However, an expectation that such studies should be analysed at the community level of analysis reduces power to detect effects considerably.

The costs of community-level media intervention studies precludes in most cases obtaining an adequate number of communities to assure reasonable power. For example, the author and colleagues are currently analyzing results from a field study of 16 communities to test the effects of using media in communities and schools to reduce teen substance use.

Effects on virtually all attitudinal and behavioural outcomes are significant or highly significant when analysed at the individual level (with an N over 3,000); some outcomes of interest, though, no longer remain significant analysed at the community level (N = 16), though fortunately major intention and behaviour treatment effects remain statistically significant even at the community level. Effect sizes even for outcomes that go to non-significant, though, are relatively robust relative to typical campaign interventions.Group randomized trials, then, have a substantial risk of resulting in Type II error that might mitigate against socially important findings.

Sophisticated journals will accept analyses of studies where treatments are applied at the community or institutional level (e.g., schools) that do not conduct a full hierarchical analysis of the data, but normally expect that these analyses are statistically adjusted for community-level or other clustering effects using procedures such as generalized estimating equations.

CROSS-OVER DESIGNS

Another model-the cross-over quasi-experimental design-has the potential to permit field experimentation in which media markets are used to manipulate exposure, but at a much lower cost than community-randomized designs. Cross-over designs, in which a control group is given the intervention treatment after post-test is completed on the original treatment group in the expectation that an effective treatment should replicate effects on the control group, are commonplace in biomedical research. Indeed, such designs are standard when withholding the treatment entirely raises ethical problems.

Such cross-over designs are, unfortunately, a rarity in media effects research. One example is a recent study of anti-marijuana advertising that compared two similar communities in Kentucky and Tennessee, one community exposed to the advertising, one the control. This would hardly have been considered a publishable design, but for the use of the cross-over procedure.

Successful replication of treatment effects in the control community eliminates many alternative explanations for treatment effects, such as uncontrolled variability between communities or history effects.

It is conceivable that history effects might have generated experimental effects first in the experimental community and then in the erstwhile control community, while simultaneously lowering effects subsequent to exposure in the original experimental community-but the probability of such a pattern seems small indeed. As noted below, the explanatory power of this cross-over design was also enhanced by the use of time-series data collection.

Cross-over designs using only a few communities exposed and unexposed to a media treatment do not rise to the same unambiguous evidentiary standard as the community-randomized designs described above.

However, they provide an attractive alternative to community-randomized designs to explore important research questions that would otherwise be impossible to study rigorously in the field given resource constraints, or when ethical or political considerations require that communities receive equivalent treatment exposure.

TRACKING STUDIES AND OTHER TIME-SERIES ANALYSES

Another technique in the cross-over study of anti-marijuana advertising was the use of rolling cross-sectional data collection and interrupted time-series data analysis to assess exposure effects. Rolling cross-sections involve collection of data at regular, closely spaced time points, such as every week or every month, typically over at least 30 or more points in time.

Interrupted time-series can be used to statistically test for the effect of an intervention in changing the slope of the outcome behaviour as plotted against time. Such analyses can also potentially be used to estimate the "half-life" of message effects and, if carried out long enough, can identify confounds such as seasonality effects that might otherwise lead to misinterpretation of longitudinal findings. Face validity of intervention findings are much enhanced when time-series analyses show that desired effects closely follow increasing distribution of and exposure to the messages of interest, and that these effects decay predictably when message exposure is withdrawn.

Rolling cross-sectional data collections and the resulting time-series data sets are known in the advertising industry as tracking studies. Tracking studies take advantage of a unique aspect of paid advertising campaigns: precise knowledge, on a week-to-week basis, of advertising placements and the consequent reach and frequency, or possible exposure, of the communication effort. Typically, tracking studies have modest objectives, testing for ad and brand recall and recognition to ascertain whether expenditures are achieving expected levels of awareness. However, such studies can also be used to assess impacts on self-reports of attitudes and behaviours. Causality in such analytic models is relatively unambiguous, as exposure can be measured exogenously, using Gross Rating Points (GRPs) or other measures of exposure inputs, and not through exposure self-report. It is also possible to use self-report measures of exposure in time-series analyses; however, assertions about causal direction are much weaker when self-report measures of exposure are used than when reach and frequency measures operationalize exposure.

The assumption that messages placed were actually seen is an uncertain one, but should lead to conservative estimates of effects free from selectivity and other confounds. Another approach to the use of time-series analyses to investigate exposure effects has been pioneered by David Fan. Fan and others using similar techniques assume exposure, and link rolling cross-sectional outcome data with rolling cross-sectional content analyses. The latter poses significant logistic challenges, which have been addressed through computerized content analytic strategies using key terms to identify stories on a topic and the valence of the story.

AP wire stories represent the media environment. Time-series analytic techniques are applied to test the association of fluctuations in amount and valence of media coverage with fluctuations in relevant public opinion polling that is carried out in an on-going way. Such an approach has limitations. The AP wire is an imperfect indicator of all U.S. media coverage. There is no measurement of individual-level exposure to such news as a mediator of coverage effects on attitudes or behaviour-again, this method focuses on possible versus actual or self-reported exposure.

It is possible that third variables may drive both coverage and behaviour (though this possibility can be tested through examination of evidence for a slight lag in exposure effects on outcomes). Many of these limitations, however, should increase conservativeness of findings. The more serious limitation is that these techniques can only be employed for exposure to media for which on-line sources over time are readily available, and for outcomes that are tracked regularly through on-going surveys.

When such studies are an option, however, they permit exceptionally robust inference concerning real-world effects of media exposure on national populations. The array of designs and analytic techniques available to study effects of media exposure permits convincing inferences when results triangulate across methods. This is illustrated in particularly concise and dramatic fashion in a recent meta-analysis of media violence studies, in which studies are separated by method, variation in effect size by method indicated, and the overall convergence of effects shown.

Media effects theories are theories of process, of cause and effect. Longitudinal designs that permit modeling of process over time or field experimental designs that permit unambiguous causal tests are where maturing theories must find their supportive evidence. Longitudinal designs also permit-indeed, they demand-explicit theorizing regarding the role both of selective exposure and media effect.

In the realm of media campaigns, rolling cross-sections and time-series analyses offer researchers the opportunity to evaluate campaign impact with a precision that has previously been unattainable, and cross-over designs may increase the viability of quasi-experimental studies.

Simple cross-sectional surveys and small-scale experiments provide excellent opportunities to ascertain if theoretical propositions and hypothesized mechanisms are viable and worthy of further exploration. They are insufficient to test whether these mechanisms operate as hypothesized in the larger social world. Expanded use of more sophisticated designs and methods is necessary if the media effects and campaigns research area is to continue to advance.

12

Phenomenological Medium Theory

For in the piece, besides addressing the problems concerned with Marxism in late, reflexive modern, neoliberal democracies, Derrida conjures a number of these specters, ghosts, spirits—hauntings—which he deals with through this logic of the ghost, hauntology. The word itself is, of course, a Derridean invention which plays at once on the subject of the spectral and the essence of Being. Medium theory, most often in the phrase "the medium is the message," has had a contentious history vis-a-vis media and cultural studies. This chapter argues that, along with that of Karl Marx, the spirits of Harold Innis, Marshall McLuhan, and Martin Heidegger haunt us on a regular basis in media and cultural studies.

If they already exist in ghostly form, perhaps by exorcising them through the logic of the specter, we can allow them to comingle with the living via historical materialism, Marxism, and phenomenology, along with a Heideggerian "questing for technics."

Daniel Czitrom once noted that "for the most radical and elaborate American media theory, one must look to the work of two Canadians, Harold Adams Innis and Marshall McLuhan."

Innis's central claim regarding media and power as having been ossified in the political economy canon is surely without question, cemented into thousands of bibliographies as firmly as anyone else in Canadian historiography. Beyond the field of political economy, however, there has clearly been some renewed interest in Innis's place within the media studies canon in recent years.

In his introduction to the 1994 rerelease of Understanding Media, Lewis Lapham wrote that Marshall McLuhan makes sense now more than ever, and, though he made this proclamation over a decade ago, little has changed. That was just following Wired magazine's 1993 launch, whereby they labeled McLuhan their "Patron Saint" on the masthead.

And beyond these examples, there is no denying the signs that abound, indicating the presence of McLuhan in contemporary discourse. For many, his pseudo-prophetic conjectures are now only beginning to show their clarity with regard to the "Internet Age." This is to say that Innis and McLuhan are a presence; they haunt us, to be sure. By placing medium theory in this historical context, it will be shown that its epochal history of communication demands to be dually understood in terms of Marxian materialism and phenomenology. The final section will discuss Martin Heidegger's "technological question" with relation to the Derridean deconstructive, hauntological apparatus, in order to juxtapose both the parallels and incongruities of these disparate philosophical tendencies.

EPOCHAL HISTORIES

To adapt Todd Gitlin's famous comment regarding the overzealous application of Gramscian hegemony theory, if medium theory explains everything, it explains nothing. And while this is a shortcoming of a field that is all too inclusive (cultural studies, I feel, suffers this same malady), the historical possibilities medium theory provides are still worth noting, for, as grand theories go, they don't get much grander.

Medium theory, specifically in the historical work of Innis, McLuhan, and Ong, has such an impressive scope that it draws upon the entire history of humanity, complete with its "social upheavals" and its "growth of languages, techniques, inventions, arts, and sciences". Each lays out an epochal history with nuanced classification.

For example, for Innis, all communication media were biased in terms of time and space, thus creating what he termed "monopolies of knowledge" for the dominant culture. Time-biased media are durable and difficult to transport, whereas spatially biased media are light and can be moved across space with relative ease, speed, and accuracy. Following Innis's lead, McLuhan divided human history into three distinct eras based on the dominant medium of communication that characterized the period.

Thus, mankind may be seen as having three epochs: the oral tradition, which stretches from the moment man first acquired speech to the beginning of literacy roughly five thousand years ago, the literate era, which extends from the invention of writing to the creation of the electric telegraph, and, lastly, the era of electric communication, beginning at the first telegraph usage in 1844 through today.

Walter 1. Ong, heavily influenced by McLuhan (who was Ong's teacher and master's thesis advisor), doesn't simply recapitulate the work of his forebear, however. Rather, he sees the history of man as divided into four stages of communication and culture—orality, chirography, typography, and electronic orality, or what he refers to later as "literate orality" and "secondary orality" to describe the complex and contradictory blend of old and "new" found within the media environment. From within this paradigm, we can begin to see that media are not conduits, rather, they are active agents of cultural and psychological change. And while I have only provided a perfunctory gloss of the historical and theoretical uses of medium theory, a simple perusal of this theory's grand theorists clearly emphasizes the breadth and scope that becomes incorporated.

It also becomes clear that this approach is historical materialist (not dialectical materialist) in nature. If we take the power that a particular medium might hold over its niche within the historical context, we might term its underlying biases as a kind of dominant ideology, though its "effects" might not be relationally understood without the benefit of hindsight.

The dominant ideologies at work in the biases of these communicative forms would thus incorporate subordinate technologies and their uses, rendering them politically quiescent and overshadowing alternative modalities via the concealment of reactionary social realities. Thus, the mechanics of dominant communicative forms are inherently powerful enough to bypass social contradiction and reify its position within the social, political, and personal consciousness. Underlying this technological manifestation is, of course, a specter in itself: the classic thesis from The German Ideology.

Historical materialism is the theory of social change, developed by Marx and Engels, in which history is divided into a series of epochs (or modes of production), each characterized by a distinct economy and class structure. Historical change in this view is fueled by the progressive expansion of the productive capacity of the economy, as well as the development of technology and the forces of production. This becomes manifest in class conflicts and revolutions. ne of the reasons the historical materialist approach works so well in both Marxism and medium theory is that it shows that ideas actually come from somewhere and gives an agency. Ideas and social change don't fall from the sky, and the appeal to this is clear in both schools of thought.

Dialectical materialism, in Marxist terms, encompasses those aspects of its philosophy beyond its theory of history (such as metaphysics, ontology, and epistemology). The term wasn't used by either Marx or Engels, but later became the dogmatic philosophy of the Soviet Union, building on works such as Engels's Dialectics of Nature. Dialectical materialism, for our purposes here, might be characterized by its materialism and rejection of skepticism. The material world, in this view, is held to have a primacy over the mental, so that the material is a precondition of one's consciousness (which would seemingly make sense for someone like Innis, McLuhan, or Edmund Carpenter). The material world is then knowable through the realm of empirical studies. Beyond focusing solely on its materialism, the philosophy itself is dialectical, in that it sees reality in its ever-changing state of development, arguing not simply that change exists in the world, but rather that the reality of that world is characterized by varying properties and their emergence.

THE "BIAS" OF INNIS

Innis's research can clearly be classified as both idealist and materialist, with an evident emphasis on the latter. As William Westfall notes, "Instead of recounting the gradual unfolding of an idea or series of ideas (such as political liberty, responsible government, or autonomy) it turned history toward the ongoing ramifications of a body of material factors in a geopolitical and economic setting." For obvious reasons, this parallels Marx's notion of the economic base, supporting a historically derived superstructure. Innis, however, avoided Marxian theory and "he certainly did not truck with socialism". In a 1948 essay, he makes clear the limits of Marxism and its approach and claims to be utilizing "the Marxian interpretation to interpret Marx".

While this would seem a worthy undertaking, Innis never really fulfills the promise in any of his published writings. It is worth pointing out, however, that he uses the term "Marxian," as opposed to "Marxist," which implies the source, rather than the tradition that sprang from it. Class-consciousness and any sort of concept of ideology, both of which are mainstays of Marxism, are glaringly absent in Innis's staple research (such as his work on fur or cod, etc.), which is why I am not linking him on that level. What is very present are the material conditions of production, and a sense of the cyclical nature of history (which Marx inherited from Hegel). Interestingly, Innis's later work, which valorized the oral tradition, is quite similar to Marx's notion of primitive communities.

The centrality of Innis's presence in critical communication and media studies is his focus on what he termed "bias." What began for Innis as a very specific problem (how does form influence power?) ended with what was almost an overarching theory of social and cultural analysis, the notions of spatial and temporal bias as the dominant way of understanding communication and, thus, power. For Innis, the world that one studies could not be positivistically regarded as a conglomeration of facts that one could objectively analyse according to the traditional methods of the social sciences. For Innis, these "facts" all reflect a series of values; a certain level of cultural factors that were ontologically subjective in nature thus biased all facts. Further, the social scientist was him- or herself biased by the cultural assumptions of the environment in which they were immersed.

One of the reasons for Innis's turn towards the study of "biases" inherent within particular communicative forms as an enabler of empires/networks of power is that, from a broader perspective, this problematic is but one of a larger philosophical and methodological issue—the shortcomings of rational empirical science, particularly in regard to the historiography of religious phenomena—that a number of disciplines were attempting to confront at the time of Innis. He, like so many others, had to deal with this on levels both abstract and personal. He sought to establish some kind of methodology which would allow the social sciences to explore the world objectively, and he tried to find a way for the social scientist to escape the gravity of the social environment so that he or she might gain some measure of freedom in order to deploy what Innis was trying to develop. For Innis, the problem of bias itself needed to become part of the solution, thus making necessity a virtue. He would accept the fact that both sides of the subject—object dialectic were shaped by the bias, but it would be the bias itself that would become the subject matter for his social scientific analysis.

For Innis, there were patterns that would become apparent, when looking historically, in the way that bias influences particular cultures (such as whether or not a medium is time-biased or space-biased). Thus, for Innis, by examining the patterns and elements of history via their continuity and predictability, one could essentially construct scientifically sound statements. Hence, to "rescue objectivity, one should study the shape of subjectivity: The only element in society that was not relative, Innis seemed to argue, was relativity itself". For Innis, the patterns of bias were themselves ecological reflections of the relationships that were tied to social processes, all of which could be studied empirically. We might, then, begin to understand Innis's representation of the social order as being a system of hierarchies with social reality on the surface and a system of bias on a level just below.

Beneath everything was what Innis often referred to as "primal cultural factors." The contemporary world, for example, is biased towards a certain attitude regarding time that is directly correlated to a system of communication (i.e., the world might be considered smaller now than ever before). And for Innis, in the last major project of his life, with the bias of communication as a starting point, one can begin to conceptualize the entire history of mankind.

Rereading McLuhan and Innis Through Marxism and Phenomenology

In the following section, I wish to render problematic the theory of medium of communication, as expressed in the work of Innis and McLuhan, in two ways. Beyond a traditional reading which might stem from structuralism and political economy, I wish to offer an alternative interpretation, which I believe to be truest to the epochal historiographies of Innis and McLuhan, and which might be called Marxist and phenomenological.

For both thinkers, central is the notion of space and time, and the conditions by which they are experienced (in the widest phenomenological sense) within a given social/historical condition, thus constituting a position within that history's hierarchy of production through the media of communication (in the Marxist sense). For Innis and McLuhan, media (or communication) are key in constituting the limits of what is humanly experience-able. But key to understanding these limits are the manners in which they are experienced, thus locating power in the realm of social formations (as laid out by Innis in his studies of empire). In other words, the medium institutes a system of social order, based on biases that are both spatial and temporal, that is constitutive of life itself.

While Innis is clearly concerned with the social influences of the materiality of communication (though his history is far more pluralistic than would be a Marxist revision), it is in McLuhan where we find the concept of the media environment pushed to its (il)logical conclusion by claiming that media (no matter what form they may take) have no intrinsic qualities whatsoever, but the characteristics they hold are distinctly dependent on their relationship with the media environment as a whole and the given translations of experience between media forms.

This, I would argue, is an implicitly Marxist and phenomenological stance, though McLuhan would probably have argued it as a purely rhetorical posture, whereby media maintain a social influence only through an originating matrix beyond the medium in question. This is why, for McLuhan, media have no intrinsic content as such. But while this might help us in establishing a line of phenomenological enquiry in the Innis-McLuhan genealogy (to incorporate Foucault's idiom), how can we begin to rethink media of communication in terms of historical materiality from a Marxian vantage point?

If we are to follow McLuhan's conjecture that media of communication should be understood as extensions of the corporeal system whose kinaestheses (or bodily motions/expressions) consist of representative modes of expression and interface with the unseen media environment, we are then pushing McLuhan into the realm of pure reification. I wish to locate this interpretation in its opposition with the tendency to theorize the materiality of communication media through a focus on the commodification ritual as seen by orthodox Marxist approaches to a medium. Rather, I would note that the key difference in this dichotomy has already been combed over by Marx himself in his infamous "Theses on Feuerbach" wherein he distinguished the reference of his historical materialism to "human sensuous activity, [or] practice" from the "materialist doctrine that men are products of circumstances and upbringing, and that, therefore, changed men are products of other circumstances and changed upbringing" as proposed by Feuerbach.

In this sense, media of communication (from language itself to literal channels of discourse and desire) can thus be experienced as active rather than simply descriptive and representative, or referential, of an already constituted object/experience. So while the message may have meaning, it is ultimately overshadowed by the medium as message itself.

It is in the critique of McLuhan by Raymond Williams (Television) where these worlds converge. Here we find an instructive confrontation between McLuhan's modernist sensibilities, his essentially postmodern theory of media, and Williams' Marxist theory that explicitly recognizes the constitutive power of media. In European thought, the critique of modernity in the twentieth century was primarily developed via the phenomenology of Husserl and Heidegger and the negative dialectics of the Frankfurt School, converging on questions of technology and the instrumentalization of reason within modernity. I call McLuhan's theory ultimately postmodern in that it does not situate the media environment within a larger totality, but uses the plurality of media itself as the impetus for any investigation of culture. Communication media are thus a manifestation of culture itself—not the other way around.

For Williams, on the other hand, media (or the material expression) of communication are purely a force of production. Williams felt that a failure of traditional Marxism was the relegation of issues concerning communication to the superstructure (removing it from the base and turning it into a second order process), thereby "missing the inherent role of means of communication in every form of production". Therefore, analyses of the role of media (and the medium of communication) must be understood within the larger totality of the capitalist mode of production.Hegel once said, "Every philosophy can be nothing but its own epoch comprehended in thought" (qtd. in Korsch). To unpack this in terms of McLuhan and Innis's medium theory, we are left with a crystallization of interest, which then becomes the way in which we understand our period in relation to history.

Through philosophy (and I would argue all of this is a philosophically discursive approach to the ontology of media) we can define the conflicts and the dominant interest of an era. This is what it means to conduct a philosophical analysis and this is why medium theory needs to be understood in reference to both its Marxist and phenomenological underpinnings. For if we are to begin to understand the materiality of our media environment, we must think outside of the discourse of "effects" and construct a new philosophical, critical theory of communicative constitution and representation. It is also worth noting some of the similarities between Innis and McLuhan for the purposes of relating them to a Marxian concept of history. Although the lineage and legacy of the McLuhan-Innis connection has been discussed ad infinitum, one thing remains controversial: Who was more important (as if this is a question worth asking)?

The problem that has risen from McLuhan's notoriety is that much of what Innis had to say in his major challenges to the future of communication studies has been overlooked (generally) in the process of separating his later work (such as Bias and Empire) from the ways in which they were discussed by McLuhan. For example, it is important to stress that McLuhan and Innis diverge sharply when Innis's critical quality and his social consciousness become the focal point.

Both shared a common "bias" about how to approach communication historiography; both manifest a keen interest in the classical tradition and its importance to both the humanities and the social sciences; both relate communication to culture as a value-laden term; both view the mode of communication as the formative process in the growth of structures of knowledge production, as well as structures of feeling within a culture; both would insist that there is an inherent aesthetic factor in the development of communication theory; both had a profound distrust of contemporary mechanization; and both wrote their histories with a sense of irony (Theall). I will now to turn Heidegger and technology to examine the place of deconstruction within communication.

HEIDEGGER/SPECTRALITY/PRESENCE/TECHNE

Derrida, in his turn to hauntology, examines the spectral (or ghostal) effects in any sensorial experience or interaction (communication, mediation) in order to illustrate that what appears present is always already contaminated, infected by what is absent (for Derrida this phenomenon is and must be associated with the general function of signs and their iterability).

With Spectres, he argues that the past can never be fully exorcised from the present. Today we live in a world haunted by multiple specters of Marx, for example, in terms of the political and philosophical landscapes.

From the specters of communism and totalitarianism to the articulation of class distinction and consciousness, from the millennial tensions of evangelicalism to those standing against the rising tide of neoliberalism, these ghosts haunt continually even as the contemporary moment superficially appears to be moving past Marx and towards what Fukuyama has termed the "end of history." What we must remember about these hauntings, however, is that they are examples of erasure in action. The Union of Soviet Socialist Republics no longer exists in a material sense, yet the politics of memory are such that its flame is perpetually rekindled. Like a corpse, the remains remain. In French hantologie sounds the same as ontologie because of the silent "h." This is part of Derrida's infamous play of differance, which I would argue has an extremely medium-centric attitude. Since the differance is an impossible possibility, it cannot exist outside of its communicative form. Differance can be read, thus privileging writing, and can only exist in speech as a possibility.

As McLuhan would say, the medium, is of course, the message. Hauntology is an offering to us, an offering of an alternative, not an opposition, to ontology. Its homonymic emphasis, then, is the nonpresent presence it presents the specter posing a fundamental challenge to ontology.

By focusing not on presence in a purely Heideggerian way, hauntology calls into question the very distinction between being and nonbeing. Like differance, hauntology exceeds (and precedes) the ontological. But it is Heidegger's spirit that allows us to consider the role of techng in our current context. Sterne writes, "It is true in conversation, in large-scale media systems, in human-animal interaction, and in the most subtle dimensions of encountering others. Communication is, above all else, a techne." Techne in contrast with those things that merely derive from nature (physis) or chance (tyche).

It is a word which has numerous connotations each of a somewhat ambiguous nature. Aristotle's stays the most famous designation, wherein it is both practical art and practical knowledge, meaning both the process by which things in the world are produced and the knowledge that accounts for said production. Referring to this Aristotelian model, Heidegger notes that techne, "reveals whatever does not bring itself forth and does not yet lie before us, whatever can look and turn out one way and now another".

Heidegger's "Question Concerning Technology" is arguably the single most important work in the field of the philosophy of technology. Essentially what is happening here is Heidegger attempting to uncover the essence of technology so that we can have what he calls a "free relationship" with it.

Once we understand the real essence of technology, we will learn how to experience it within its own bounds. Now according to Heidegger, what we have until now failed to understand is that the essence of technology isn't technological. It is not, in other words, something like a neutral tool or gadget. Technology is thus instrumental, a means to an end, a human activity that is geared toward the manipulating and controlling of things.

So, in this view, means produce ends, just like causes produce effects. Heidegger is not denying that this is accurate rather this definition represents only this causal, instrumental meaning of the means to the end. He reminds us of the ancient Greeks and their broader conception of causality; a cause is something that brings something about or that which is responsible for something. The four causes articulated by Aristotle that Heidegger points to are explanations, explanations of what something is made out of, what it is to be a something, what it produces, and what it is for. Together the four causes are responsible for bringing something into appearance (Heidegger uses the Greek here, poisis).

Poiesis is the Greek term for creation or production aimed to bring about an end, as opposed to doing or action such as praxis. These causes create presence, bringing it forth, "out of concealment into unconcealment." The essence of technology then for Heidegger is not a means but a way of revealing (or aletheia). In other words, it's a kind of truth. Yet the way that technology (or techne) reveals is problematic. It places an unnatural and unreasonable demand on nature: It forces the assumption that nature supply us endlessly and efficiently.

Humans then, the supposed masters of technology, are challenged in this way, becoming what Heidegger refers to as "standing reserve." Consider the phrase so ubiquitous today: "human resources." Heidegger calls this way of revealing the world Ge-stell or "enframing," a way of ordering people to see the world and each other—as more or less just a stockpile of reserves to he manipulated. Enframing happens both in us and in the world; for Heidegger it is the revelation of a certain kind of being (essence) (both in human beings and nature) as a standing reserve. Particular kinds of technology in the ordinary sense of gadgets and tools and machines only respond to this enframing—they are the consequence, not the cause, and, as such, help reveal things as standing reserve (for Heidegger this is true of modern science as well). The danger of technology here is twofold. First, Heidegger finds that we ourselves are this standing reserve. Second, in our role as human standing reserve, we tend to think that we are masters of everything. The truth of the matter, for Heidegger, is that we cannot see ourselves or understand the world clearly.

Enframing keeps that essence of things concealed; it obscures other ways of seeing things, particularly revealing as poiesis (bringing something into appearance). The danger here is the partial, incomplete enframing that is revealed. Poiesis is ultimately the essence of technology. What Heidegger is arguing is that we need to realise this essence and stop construing technology as mere instrumentality (as a mere means to an end), and overcome the illusion of our pretension that we have complete mastery and control over things. The "saving power" of technology, for Heidegger, is that the essence of technology is ambiguous. The very instrumentality (techne) that threatens us also saves us (as poiesis).

With the accelerated growth of technology in the modern era (consider Norbert Wiener's famous "change changed"), we find two millennia worth of metaphysics standing in the way of language, prioritizing information transmission and efficacy, threatening the prospects for aletheia, the truth of Being, our shared reservoir of preontological understanding of un-hiddenness or discovery. For this reason, Derrida's hauntological turn (and differance) offers a more vigorous means of approaching media and communication through considering than do either conventional metaphysics or traditional ontology. In this way, if truth exists as a "coming to presence," then the technological manifestations of communicative action, as laid out by the medium theory of Innis and McLuhan, disrupt presence by imposing themselves on the (pre)ontological limits of the very engagement. Therefore to speak of communication after Derrida after Heidegger is to speak of a kind of "artifactuality," whereby artificiality, actuality, artifice, and textuality become intrinsically linked in the materialist explanations of the communication environment.

For Derrida, artifactuality refers to the textual production of communication and information by means of the contemporary structural apparatus—teletechnology, or, simply, "the media". There is, thus, a responsibility in responding to and analyzing the media. "Hegel was right," Derrida observes, "to remind the philosopher of his time to read the papers daily. Today, the same responsibility obliges him to learn how the dailies, the weeklies, and the television news programs are made, and by whom".

Given an understanding that our mediated world is both "actively produced" and, considering the phenomenological medium theory of Innis and McLuhan, "performatively interpreted," mediation is not merely an abstract philosophical concept, but also a deconstructive artifact. The metaphysical presence of every object of being necessitates the projection of itself toward that end. It is this presence and projection that allows us to identify with forms of communication and to rationalize the mediatization process.

If each form renders a different ontological status, then there exists the possibility to disintegrate and distill these essences down to a primordial core, whereby the deconstruction of mediation is possible, and communication itself may be imagined as a possible impossible. Communication as (im)possible centre is often rendered problematic (and possible) through this sense of iterability. For example, for Soren Kierkegaard, mediation is explicitly linked to repetition, as he describes in his philosophical narrative on Constantin Constantius: "Mediation" [Mediation] is a foreign word; "repetition" [Gjentagelse] is a good Danish word, and I congratulate the Danish language on a philosophical term. There is no explanation in our age as to how mediation takes place, whether it results from the motion of the two factors and in what sense it is already contained in them, or whether it is something new that is added.

Almost two decades ago, Derrida faced a video camera in Toronto and discussed film and television, in Kierkegaardian form, as "a ghost dance" (la danse des fantomes), contemporary technologies like film, television, telephones live on or off of, ill some way, a ghostly structure. Film is an art of the ghost, which is to say, it is neither image nor perception The voice on the telephone also has a ghostly appearance.

It is something neither real nor unreal, something which returns, is reproduced—finally, it's the question of reproduction. From the moment when the first perception of an image is linked to a structure of reproduction, we are dealing with the ghostly. Sometime later, again on camera, this time at a conference, he rebuked a group of architects in Japan about the necessity to take what he now called "telefacture," or the facsimile, seriously, the need to attend to the new structure of spatio-temporal differance constructed by new techniques of telecommunication, by new powers of production as well as reproduction—information, images, discourse, and even the event in general.

The event itself, like the concept of experience and of the testimony that claims to refer to it, finds itself affected, in its inside, beyond the public-private opposition, by the possibility of the shot and of reproduction from practically anywhere to anywhere. Derrida is here now moving slightly beyond Heidegger and exorcising the ghost of Walter Benjamin, who once observed of media's iterability:

You can regard all these things as eternal (e.g. storytelling, narration), but one can also see them as temporal and problematic, even dubious. Eternal things in narration. But most likely entirely new forms, genres. Television, gramophone and so forth bring all this to an ominous bottom line. And within these early notes for the storyteller essay Benjamin goes on to articulate a fear that it is all repudiated: narration by television, the hero's words by the gramophone, the moral by the next statistics, the storyteller by what one knows about him Tant mieux. Don't cry. The absurdity of critical prognoses.

FILM INSTEAD OF NARRATION

This is Benjamin's antiessentialist response to the domination of traditional ways of thinking about new communication forms. Essentialism, one of the more enduring philosophical doctrines that responds to metaphysical inquiry into the nature of things, states, essentially, that a thing is a thing and is what it is, and not some other thing, because of inherent, immutable properties. Essentialist philosophical positions thus espouse truths that transcend specific times. The recent trend from essentialism toward more perspectivist (and multiperspectivist) approaches to deeply philosophical questions has resulted in the reification of structural binarisms within thought itself. For example, if we follow the lineage of contemporary critical theory and & construction, we find Hegel on one side, as a builder if you will, and someone like Heidegger on the other dismantling such buildings (Desilet 152).

Medium theory, in that it tends to neglect the spectral effects at work and forces us to remain prisoners of a metaphysics of presence, is closed by its own essentialist view of communication technology. Post-Heideggerian deconstruction can allow us to break with these limits and open the idea of mediation, for as we are often quick to forget, deconstruction was and is simultaneously structuralist and antistructuralist.

According to Heidegger, "metaphysics is Platonism," for "throughout the whole history of philosophy, Plato's philosophy remains decisive in changing forms." Medium theory, like structuralism then, is an ideal of form, an "ideal of metanarrative social cohesion, the idea; of language transparency".

Although the structural conditions make possible systemic changes (and indeed system formation), they also come to represent all that falls away and out of reach of what makes the very system possible.

Placing communication in conversation with phenomenology, deconstruction, and medium theory, encourages and engages (and hopefully will force) ruptures of thought, (ir)resolutions, promises to remain (re)opened, secrets hidden and exposed, sutures closed but oozing, reason and logic at their limits, aporia as understanding.

(Post)Structural Theories of Mediation (?)In this chapter I have provided a brief overview of some characteristics of medium theory and shown how they relate to the writings of Karl Marx and Heidegger's technological question via a series of "hauntings." Would Marx buy into medium theory? This is an ill-conceived question, for it carries an incorrect assumption—that Marx is concerned with ontological essences rather than with their historically determined and ever-changing function. For Marx, all issues must be dealt with historically. In this sense, we can see how, for him, the "mediums" might be somewhere in the superstructure, not the base.

Are Innis, McLuhan, and other medium theorists trying to move their object of inquiry from the superstructure (culture) to the base (history/economy)? For Innis, the answer might be a clear yes, but for McLuhan it might get a bit more complex. While Marx embraced new technology, he did so within the context of his time and place (not to be confused with being a technophile of the late twentieth century).

In that way, Marx was actually glorying in the city, with its consolidation of workers and its centralizing of scientific discourse. For Marx, this was the gods getting put in their place, not some kind of manifest technological utopianism in the form of a retribalized global village, replete with media, both hot and cool. Even though there are a number of similarities, as I have shown, in the spheres of Marxism and medium theory, one is still not the other (all medium theorists aren't Marxists, much like all Marxists obviously aren't medium theorists). McLuhan never critiqued anything from a Marxist/Marxian perspective.

For example, he never seemed concerned that radio and television were set up as purely commercial endeavors and never touched on the emancipatory possibilities or hindrances of any particular medium. For Marx, the goal was bringing about in the proletariat a class-consciousness to change their situation. For him, it was about holding up revolution before the masses.

This is why the phenomenological aspects of orthodox Marxism are theoretical, while still only using empiricism. This is similar to McLuhan's call to pay attention; he was never just some promoter of the latest gadget. McLuhan, like Marx, was trying to raise consciousness in the masses and hold the possibility of a better tomorrow before their eyes.

As with Marx, you must make up your own mind what you want from someone like McLuhan. In that sense, both sadly have become whatever the interpreter says they are. The bottom line is that they raise interesting questions, and that might he the most we can ask of theory at this point in our own (post)historical context. Derrida's theory of deconstruction, then, anticipates a poststructural turn in the changes in mediation, attempting to destabilize the rally of meaning in univocal logo-centrism by dismantling the logic it hides. It is an interpretive gesture similar to Mark Poster's commentaries on electronic writing, in that both attempt to "understand the volatility of written language, in its instability and uncertain authorship."

Thus, language is a destabilization of subjectivity and Derrida can apply these qualities to all forms of writing (differentiating only partially between media form). Deconstruction, then, might be interpreted as Derrida's interpretation of the metaphysical ramifications of the medium. Poster's concern, on the other hand, is much more in line with that of Innis and

McLuhan (though with a more explicit Marxist-Foucauldian slant), in that he distinguishes the differences of media form to assess the significance of these differences as enacted by the new communication technology.

And, unlike the materialism of Innis's time-space biases, Derrida (deconstruction) and Poster (poststructuralism) offer an interpretive approach that could intermingle with traditional medium theory in a way that would permit the exegesis of communication form in a manner that suits the glissandos of electronic media culture.

Derrida, who, for example, has long been an almost entirely unacknowledged theorist of the media, gives time for a detour in Specters of Marx to highlight the threat telecommunication poses to aletheia, noting that teletechnology obliges us more than ever to think the virtualization of space and time, the possibility of virtual events whose movement and speed prohibit us more than ever (more and otherwise than ever, for this is not absolutely and thoroughly new) from opposing presence to its representation, 'real time' to 'deferred time,' effectivity to its simulacrum, the living to the non-living, in short the living to the living-dead of its ghosts.

But if we begin to consider the problematic at work in a deconstruction of the mode of communication, we would undermine the entire logic of mediation (a la Derrida), whereby no medium is adequate to communicate because of the infinite play of differences. Since mediation itself, in poststructuralist terms becomes a play of difference, there isn't simply a reversal of hierarchy at work (such as the changing dominance of communicative form found in the epochal historiographies of Innis, McLuhan, and Ong). If there is a breakdown in this centre-margin dichotomy we are putting the active verb function of the mode of communication itself under erasure (sous rature), after Heidegger and Derrida, pointing to the inadequacies in the logic of communication form.

Since the medium is of central import (medium theory), yet it is unnoticed if communication is happening (the logic of successful communication), we find that mediation is then both there and not there, present and absent, alive and dead, material and spectral. Thus, if we are to actively disrupt the logic of the communication form, might it be more appropriate to say: The medium [begin strikethrough]is[end strikethrough] the message?

As communication scholars, we must phrase this intentionally with the impossible possibility intact. To place something under erasure, one must of course, write the differance into existence. To elaborate: Derrida, in taking up the practice of sous rature, shows that neither the word "speech" nor the word "writing" are adequate to describe the more abstract play of differences that exist. Both speech and writing function for Derrida as a play of difference. And what he's doing here is not simply reversing the hierarchy that makes up Western thinking about communication—making writing central while marginalizing speech (as in the infamous cover to La carte postale), he's putting both terms "under erasure." And he does this by infamously drawing an "X" through them, crossing them out, but leaving them present. And so, to put a binary opposition found in structuralism and communication under erasure, you could write the words [begin strikethrough]speech[end strikethrough] and [begin strikethrough]writing[end strikethrough] as such. This is a device Derrida borrowed from Heidegger and it simply means that both speech and writing are inadequate to describe the general differences common to both.

But the problem is, in discussing them, Derrida cannot simply do without them; they must be used. A clear, rhetorical criticism of putting something under erasure is that it allows us to essentially have our cake and eat it too, so to speak. By using this deconstructive strategy, we're able to use a word or a concept, while simultaneously indicating its inadequate or undecidable nature. Here are the origins of "arche-writing." It is an invention and an invitation, an expression that illustrates that binaries like speech and writing are really just the spoken and written forms of this play of difference.

Yet, because of the necessity to write this practice into existence, and by that I mean that this can't exist without the dichotomy of the speech-writing dialectic, we can see how Derrida is somewhat painted into a corner, relying essentially on what he's seeking to deconstruct. And here we return to the specter, the hauntological. The work of Harold Innis and Marshall McLuhan does breathe a ghostly life into the subjects of late modernity, technology, postmodernity, power, and possibilities of communication discourse, and each have much to offer cultural studies of communicative form and the material logic of power.

The work of Innis is complicated and laced with a certain darkness. His communication project remained unfinished (a fact that Paul Heyer, for one, thinks would have remained even if he had lived another ten years). The reason for this is because it is open-ended. Innis provided a wonderful map of what communications historiography could be. And for all its pseudoapocalyptic, speculative, quasitheological, proselytizing excess, McLuhan's probes regarding technology and culture remain some of the most sustained in the cultural theory of the twentieth century, at the crux between the modern and the postmodern, and have the opportunity (and do) to bridge the gap between Nietzsche, Mumford, and Heidegger and Baudrillard, Kittler, and Virilio. It is up to the rest of us to use these maps to discover and explore the worlds they describe, and, in doing so, resurrect the specters of Innis and McLuhan, allowing them to join Marx and Heidegger. and once we are in the presence of the specter incarnate, once we have accepted the material realities of what they have to offer cultural studies, this will mark the end of the spectral, and we will be haunted no more. But is this what we want, what we wish, what we desire—what we need? We need these specters, these ghosts. Is it really the goal to be haunted no more? We often consider an exorcism to be a removal, but how will this help us? This chapter has offered an understanding of communication in a manner that is at once historical (in the epochal sense), material, linked to spatial and temporal constraints and limitations, as well as both enabled and constrained by the techne and poiesis of the (post)modern lifeworld.

A phenomenological medium theory, coupled with an historical materialist understanding, offers a clarity with which we can glimpse this world. These ghosts of media and cultural studies don't haunt us, so much as we are simply standing on their shoulders. There can be no communication outside this discourse—one that links meaning with materiality and mediation with technology. Language itself is at the heart of this spectral turn, for, as Derrida reminds, there is no "before the machine" (technology), just as there can be no "before language" (communication) or "before capital" (materiality). "These machines," he writes, "have always been there, they are always there, even when they wrote by hand, even during so-called live conversation". The material nature of communication allows us to peer at the power of techne. And of all these modalities, all these glissandos, it is the spectral voice that will guide us into new worlds and new lives.

13

Electronic Media of the 21st Century

Since the beginning of the 20th century, government has enacted various pieces of legislation that regulate the communications industry. Limited space on the electromagnetic spectrum has been the justification, or rationale, for regulating the communications industry. The limited frequency space prevents anyone from actually owning any portion of the spectrum. Proliferation of media other than broadcast, such as cable systems and the Internet, had weakened the limited-space argument. Along with amendments and revisions to regulatory legislation, there have been complete rewrites since the first communication legislation was enacted in 1910. Rapid technological advancements provided the requirement for such modifications and rewrites.

This chapter has two objectives. It first examines the development and enactment of the Telecommunications Act of 1996, which is a complete overhaul of telecommunications regulation. Accordingly, it examines the political and social issues debated between the legislative and executive branches of government before the new legislation was signed into law.

Second, this chapter explores the new issues and implications created by the passage of the legislation and its effects on the telecommunications industry in the 21st century. This exploratory chapter highlights only portions of the telecommunications act that relate to broadcast or cable regulation. Other than acknowledging that telephone companies now can offer cable service, regulatory issues of the telephone industry in particular are not examined. Primarily, this chapter provides and examines highlights of regulatory changes relating to technology and programming issues in broadcasting and cable.

TELECOMMUNICATIONS ACT OF 1996

Despite the amendments and revisions that have been added throughout the years, Congress saw no choice but to completely replace the obsolete Communications Act of 1934. Because communication technology has grown by leaps and bounds over the last few years, the Communications Act of 1934 was considered an antiquated document. Edmund L. Andrews states that advances "in technology and rapid change in the marketplace have made [the

1934 act] increasingly outdated and, many experts believe, [the 1934 act] has been harmful to competition and consumers." For that reason, Congress decided to replace the 1934 act with a new, more modern piece of legislation that would adequately regulate the electronic media of the 21st century.

While attempting to change current telecommunications regulatory legislation, both the Senate and the House of Representatives passed bills. Both bills had basically the same objective: "to allow all telecommunications companies to compete head to head in one another's markets, with as little government regulation as possible."

The leading supporters of the Senate bill, S. 652, included former Commerce Committee Chairman Larry Pressler (R-South Dakota) and Ernest Hollings (D-South Carolina). The Senate version of the bill passed 81 to 18 on June 15, 1995. On August 4, 1995, the House of Representatives; passed its version of the telecommunications bill (H.R. 1555) with a vote of 305 to 117.

The leading supporters of that bill were House Commerce Committee Chairman Thomas Bliley Jr. (R-Virginia) and Telecommunications and Finance Subcommittee Chairman Jack Fields (R-Texas). A primary objective of both the Senate and House bills was to "promote competition in the telephone and cable markets while easing regulations on cable prices and broadcast-station ownership." The debate for such a bill was "propelled by the widespread sentiment in Congress and the telecommunications industry that legislation is needed to spur competition and investment in advanced telecommunications networks."

A House and Senate conference was established to reconcile the differences between the two bills. The conference consisted of eleven senators and thirty-four representatives. Some of the committee members only addressed certain parts of the legislation. For the bill to replace the 1934 act several issues needed to be resolved. There were specific issues that President Clinton stated he could not support in the House version of the bill. Furthermore, the Clinton administration stated that it was "committed to enactment of a telecommunications reform bill." Additionally, there was strong debate regarding the issue of what to do with the digital spectrum.

Television stations eventually will change from an analog channel to a digital channel, and former Senate Majority Leader Bob Dole (R-Kansas) wanted the remaining channels to be auctioned. There also is debate regarding the amount of spectrum the government plans to make available to broadcasters. Auctioning of the channels was expected to raise billions for the U.S. government.

After all of the negotiations, Congress passed the Telecommunications Bill on February 1, 1996. In the House the vote was 414 to 16, and in the Senate the vote was 91 to 5. After passage by Congress, the bill was sent to President Clinton, who signed it on February 8, 1996. In regard to the passage of the bill, Carney stated: "In the course of one afternoon.

The House and Senate swept away sixty-two years of telecommunications policy, paved the way for a more dynamic information superhighway, [and] suppressed decades of bickering between industries. This will be the biggest change in the government's role in communications since 1934."

TELECOMMUNICATIONS ACT HIGHLIGHTS

The Telecommunications Act of 1996 still requires broadcasters and cable companies to continue to observe the "public interest, convenience, and necessity" rule. As Krasnow, Longley, and Terry observe, the FCC' s powers to regulate are limited, at times, because of the fact that regulatory decisions must be based on the "public interest" standard.

The public interest standard is mentioned and maintained throughout the Telecommunications Act. As specific regulations are presented, there is some discussion regarding how well it was embraced by all parties involved in the process of creating the legislation.

BROADCAST OWNERSHIP

The primary issues that the House, Senate, and the president had trouble resolving included particulars relating to broadcast ownership. Both the Senate and the House wanted television national audience caps regarding broadcast ownership changed from 25% to 35%. Further, both the House and Senate wanted the ownership caps for radio to be eliminated completely.

After negotiations, it was determined that station ownership could not exceed 35% of the nation's TV homes. For radio, the national ownership limits were eliminated while the local ownership limits were relaxed.

The 1996 Act repealed the duopoly rule for radio station ownership, stipulating that in a market with forty-five or more stations an owner may operate eight stations, in a market with thirty to forty-four stations an owner may operate seven stations, in a market with fifteen to twenty-nine stations an owner may operate six stations, and in a market with fourteen or fewer stations an owner may operate five stations.

The Republicans pushed for even fewer regulations in this area, but eventually accepted the suggestions of the Democrats. This caused some anger among those in the Republican party because of the perception that the Republicans allowed the Democrats to gain the upper hand with this issue and several others.

OPEN VIDEO SYSTEMS

Before the Telecommunications Act, there existed a "cross-ownership" restriction that prevented telephone companies from offering cable service in the same areas where they were offering telephone service. The cross-ownership restriction provided cable companies protection from the large, established telephone companies. The 1996 Act lifted the cross-ownership restriction in an effort "to stimulate local competition in the multi-channel video market." The Act allows telephone companies to provide video services in one of four ways: (1) as an over-the-air provider; (2) as a common carrier; (3) as a cable television operator; or (4) as an open video service. The open video service is a newly created hybrid service(30) that allows telephone companies to offer video services and act as both a cable system and common carrier simultaneously.

The 1996 Act requires that if demand is greater than existing available space, the telephone company cannot control more than one third of its system's capacity. These open video systems are not franchised locally. Local authorities, however, are allowed a portion of the open video system's revenues, which is similar to franchise fees that cable operators are required to pay to municipalities. Also, traditional cable systems may opt to offer video services via an open video system and thereby avoid many regulations that normally apply to cable systems and to avoid all of the regulations that apply to common carriers. Open video systems are required to provide channels to local noncommercial and commercial broadcasters.

Healey states that open video system operators must abide by cable regulations that do the following: (1) require the operator to pay for any commercially broadcast programs that it carried voluntarily; (2) bar the duplication of certain network, sports, and syndicated programs; (3) regulate contracts to transmit programs known as carriage agreements; (4) bar the billing of programming that customers had not requested but had not canceled either; (5) bar program distribution arrangements that prevent competition; (6) protect customer's privacy; and (7) bar employment discrimination.

Unlike the regulatory issues discussed thus far, other issues required several months of negotiations. Before agreements were reached, the Senate and House of Representatives agreed upon several things rather early in the process:

- Broadcast licensing;
- Advanced television and spectrum flexibility;
- Direct broadcast satellite;
- Must-carry rules;
- V-chip and TV program ratings;
- Cable deregulation;
- Signal scrambling for indecent programming;
- Cable right of refusal of public and leased-access programming;
- Closed captioning; and
- FCC funding.

BROADCAST LICENSING

The agreement reached regarding broadcast licensing extended the license terms for television and radio to eight years. The previously amended 1934

Act allowed for television licenses to be renewed every five years and radio every seven years. The 1996 Act streamlines the license renewal process by automatically renewing broadcasters' licenses if: (1) the station has served the public interest standard; (2) if there have been no serious violations by the licensee of the rules and regulations of FCC; and (3) if there have been no other violations by the licensee that might constitute a pattern of abuse. Competing applications are reviewed only if a license is not renewed. The 1996 Act also requires broadcasters to maintain a "summary" in their public files of all complaints they receive from viewers pertaining to violent programming.

ADVANCED TELEVISION SERVICES AND SPECTRUM FLEXIBILITY

The Telecommunications Act of 1996 allows the FCC to assign licenses for advanced television services, and the licenses are limited to existing television stations. Advanced television service is defined as digital broadcasts. If the broadcaster receives a second channel, then one of the two eventually must be returned to the U.S. government. The public interest requirement continues to apply to the second channel if one is assigned to the broadcaster.

Critics suggest that broadcasters are getting a "sweet" deal by having the new digital frequencies automatically assigned to them rather than having to purchase the rights to use the new frequencies. Former senator Bob Dole believed the provision was a multibillion dollar give-away.

Andrews stated, "Government officials estimate the licenses would be worth anywhere from $11 billion to $70 billion, if the Government auctioned them in the way it is doing for licenses to operate new wireless phone services."

DIRECT BROADCAST SATELLITE (DBS)

Complete control of "direct-to-home satellite services" is granted to the FCC under the Telecommunications Act of 1996. This prevents local communities, including homeowners associations, from prohibiting direct broadcast satellite dishes. The must-carry rule was established in April 1965 and requires all cable companies to carry the signal of local stations within a sixty-mile radius of the system. The must-carry rule is maintained in the new telecommunications bill. The Telecommunications Act requires the FCC to act upon must-carry complaints within a 120 days of the filing date.

Additionally, the Act stipulates that markets are to be defined by commercial publications that delineate television markets based on viewing patterns (or Nielsen's Designated Market Area map) when considering the must-carry issue.

RESTRICTIONS ON OBSCENITY, INDECENCY, AND VIOLENCE

The 1996 Act established the fines for transmitting obscene, lewd, lascivious, filthy, or indecent material with intent to annoy, abuse, threaten, or harass another person at $250,000 for individuals and $500,000 for corporations. This includes broadcasting media, cable systems, and computer networks. Section 501 of the Telecommunications Act of 1996 is cited as the "Communications Decency Act of 1996."

Immediately after the Communications Decency Act was passed, there was a challenge as to whether it was constitutional. There were several lawsuits filed, and in mid-1996 at least two federal courts prevented its enforcement. In June of 1997, the Supreme Court, in a 7-to-2 decision, ruled that Internet communication indeed was protected by the First Amendment.

In Reno v. American Civil Liberties Union, the court stated that the Internet deserved the same protection as, media such as books, magazines, or newspapers. Thus, the Supreme Court essentially invalidated Title V of the Telecommunications Act. The Supreme Court dismissed the government's argument that if children were not prevented from accessing indecent material over the Internet then the Internet would not grow to be an important and pervasive media outlet. The government's rational was that the general public would not access the Internet because of the risk that children might be exposed to indecent material. The Supreme Court rejected this argument stating that it was unpersuasive.

V-CHIP AND TV PROGRAM RATINGS

The Telecommunications Act requires television sets to be sold with a V-chip, or violence chip, which allows for the "ability to block programming based on an electronically encoded rating." The entertainment industry was required to develop a ratings system for "violence, sex and other indecent materials and to agree voluntarily to broadcast signals containing such ratings." The bill requires the FCC to develop a ratings system if the industry fails to meet that requirement. The FCC was charged with the duty of overseeing the development of standards for blocking technologies.As a result of such findings, the Act states that there is a "compelling governmental interest" in providing parents the means to block such influences.

CABLE DEREGULATION

The 1996 Act deregulates cable rates for the expanded basic tier which usually includes such networks as MTV, Lifetime, ESPN, and Cable News Network. The cable companies are allowed to increase prices on the expanded basic tier within three years of the telecommunication bill's enactment (or on March 31, 1999).

The bill requires that equipment rates continue to be regulated. Further, the Act allows for the complete deregulation of small cable companies, defined as including 50,000 or fewer subscribers. The Act allows for cable systems to be free from rate regulation if "a telephone company offers cable service by any means that is comparable to the competing cable system."

SET-TOP BOXES

With the 1996 Telecommunications Act, consumers now are able to purchase their own set-top boxes in retail stores. Cable companies are allowed to continue providing set-top boxes, but they no longer may subsidize the boxes by subscription fees. Discussion over this issue caused the "first major impasse" on the telecommunications bill.

Cable companies opposed the sale of set-top boxes in retail stores, asserting that it would "freeze the current technology in place." The new rules regarding set-top boxes were designed to prevent theft of cable services. The rules expire in a market where: (1) there are competing multichannel video providers, (2) there are competing sources of set-top boxes, and (3) where the rules stifle competition and do not promote the public interest standard.

SIGNAL SCRAMBLING FOR INDECENT PROGRAMMING

The bill requires cable operators to scramble any audio or video of programming that subscribers deem "unsuitable" for children. This service must be provided at no extra cost to the subscriber.

CABLE RIGHT OF REFUSAL OF PUBLIC AND LEASED-ACCESS PROGRAMMING

Under the new bill, cable companies can refuse to broadcast programs that contain "obscenity, nudity, or indecency."

CLOSED CAPTIONING

The Federal Communications Commission was required to look into the possibility of making closed captioning a requirement for video programming. The Telecommunications Act of 1996 stipulated that the FCC can waive the requirement for certain classes of programs if closed captioning is economically burdensome.

FCC FUNDING

Finally, the bill authorizes appropriations needed by the FCC to carry out the provisions of the 1996 Act. Quello' s comment could not have been more foreshadowing. Others held similar opinions regarding the future of telecommunications regulation.

Approximately a year after Quello's remark, both the Senate and the House of Representatives introduced different versions of a bill that essentially would do exactly what Quello suggested, that is, modernize the regulatory framework under which the entire telecommunications sector operates.

Simply put, modernization was needed because when the Communications Act of 1934 was enacted, telephone, telegraph, and radio defined the field. Today, "television, cable, cellular, and satellite only scratch the surface of modern digital telecommunications." Hence, a new piece of legislation was needed to accommodate technological advances. The Telecommunications Act of 1996 serves as that modernized regulatory framework for the telecommunications industry that Quello suggested is needed to help in the proliferation of new media. The 1996 legislation essentially creates "one marketplace for telecommunications services " Technological developments will transform the multimedia world as we know it today.

The Telecommunications Act of 1996 attempts to regulate media as a whole rather than as individual entities. Chong suggested this approach was needed for there to be a healthy and prosperous development of multimedia technology in the United States. To illustrate how just one aspect of the telecommunications bill attempts to converge the electronic media, examine the overlapping markets of the telephone and cable companies.

The cable companies will be allowed to offer telephone services and the telephone companies will be allowed to offer cable services. Fundamentally, the 1996 Act takes a deregulatory approach and relies on the marketplace as a control over electronic media policies and procedures. The telecommunication legislation diminishes barriers that have prevented widespread competition and work toward the convergence of all media. Because of the belief that competition is good, the Act allows for competition between and among different telecommunication outlets. As one could expect, new competition is not welcomed by the entire electronic media industry.

For example, the industry opposed the cable-telco cross-ownership rules. Only time will allow observers of the telecommunications industry to determine the new legislation's effectiveness. The Telecommunications Act has created an ironic juxtaposition. Technology and programming were specific areas that the new legislation attempts to deregulate, or regulate in certain circumstances (e.g., violent programming). The foundation of the legislation is built upon deregulatory theory. Head, et al. Suggest that there are many motives fueling efforts to deregulate, such as a need to discard outdated rules, simplify complex rules, ensure that rules actually can achieve their intended objective, and lighten administrative roles.

Additionally, they suggest that deregulation also originates from ideological motives stemming from the belief that the government should play a limited role in the everyday lives of Americans. This approach relies on the marketplace to regulate industries.

Yet the marketplace approach of regulating industries does not always work effectively. On one hand, the Telecommunications Act of 1996 essentially promotes the convergence of technology by disassembling the cross-ownership restriction and by establishing specific regulations regarding the promotion of direct broadcast satellite, set-top boxes, closed captioning, and cable deregulation. On the other hand, it attempts to regulate programming through must-carry rules, v-chip technology, signal scrambling for indecent programming, and cable right of refusal of public and leased-access programming. Meyerson suggests that if "these new combinations do not compete with one another, then the Act may have only permitted the creation of large, deregulated monopolists (or oligopolists)." Monopolies were just what the Clinton administration wanted to prevent.

Finally, another juxtaposition includes the requirement that program ratings be implemented. The industry was required to create a ratings system that would be content-based and would alert parents about programming they might want to prevent their children from viewing by way of the new v-chip. Initially, the industry created ratings that were age-based. Critics argued that the age-based system would not provide enough information to make a decision. The industry argued that content-based ratings would be confusing and that advertisers might not want advertise during programming that had a perceived negative rating. Eventually, the industry adopted a content-based ratings system. Overall, it will require time to determine the effectiveness of the Telecommunications Act of 1996.

14

Audience Valuation and Minority Media

All advertiser-supported media Organizations operate in what is best described as a dual product marketplace. That is, media organizations produce one product—media content—that is either given away or sold in an effort to attract the second product—audiences. The attention of these audiences is then sold to advertisers seeking consumer exposure to commercial messages. The audience and content markets are tightly inter-related. Success or failure in the "content market" is dependent upon success or failure in the "audience market" and vice versa.

For this reason, policymaking involving the preservation and enhancement of competition and diversity of sources and content within the media industries has been—and continues to be—guided by research on how various market and institutional factors affect what media organizations are able to charge for their audiences.

One recent manifestation of this general concern with source and content diversity involves the viability of minority-owned media outlets. Per the directive of Congress (Telecommunications Act of 1996), the Federal Communications Commission (1996) initiated an investigation into the barriers affecting minority-owned media outlets and the associated availability of minority-targeted programming.

One of the barriers that may face minority-owned and -targeted media outlets is the possibility that minority audiences are valued at a much lower level by advertisers than majority audiences. If this is the case, then minority-targeted media outlets face a substantial hurdle to remaining viable, as their ability to monetize their audience is compromised by lower advertiser valuations of their target audience. Lower audience values lead to lower revenues, lower levels of investment in programming, and an overall diminished ability for such outlets to compete and remain viable.

In this way, the nature of the content market (in terms of the diversity of available sources and content offerings) is affected by the dynamics of the audience market. This study investigates the possibility of lower valuations of minority audiences through a quantitative analysis of the determinants of the value of commercial radio station audiences.

MINORITY MEDIA AND DIVERSITY POLICY

The general policy imperative that drives concerns about the viability of minority-targeted media outlets stems from policymakers' long-standing commitment to diversity in the sources of information and the content that these sources provide.

The diversity principle extends, in part, from the traditional democratic theory notion of a well-functioning "marketplace of ideas," in which citizens' abilities to participate effectively in the democratic process are contingent upon their abilities to consider a wide array of ideas and viewpoints from a wide array of sources. Diversity concerns have economic motivations, as well, since policymakers have sought to maximize the choices available to media consumers, thereby increasing their overall satisfaction.

The availability of content targeting minority interests has long been perceived as an important means of providing such content diversity. As the FCC (1948) noted as far back as 1948, "It has long been an established policy of the Commission that the American system of broadcasting must serve significant minorities among our population". Research has demonstrated that minority audiences focus much of their media consumption on minority-targeted programming and outlets—and even increase their media consumption—when such services are available. This suggests that such content is highly valued by its target audience. It is important to emphasize that such diversity is seen as benefiting not only those who are targeted by minority-appeal content, but those whose tastes are "majoritarian" as well.

For the "marketplace of ideas" to enhance citizen knowledge and the consideration of diverse viewpoints, citizens must be exposed to diverse points of view. It has been argued that this exposure diversity is particularly vital within the context of minority media so that greater cultural understanding and social cohesion can be achieved. In an effort to identify the potential barriers facing minority-targeted media content, the FCC commissioned a study of the value of minority audiences to advertisers. The results of this study raised the possibility that advertisers may place significantly lower values on minority audiences and that these lower valuations may arise, in part, from advertiser misconceptions about minority spending patterns and product purchasing decisions.

A recent NTIA survey raised similar concerns about the challenges associated with selling minority audiences to advertisers (National Telecommunications and Information Administration, 2000). The NTIA survey found that minority broadcast station owners cited obtaining advertising as their most common difficulty. Lower advertiser valuations of minority audiences have significant implications for the viability of minority-targeted media outlets since the provision of minority-targeted content potentially involve financial challenges not faced if more mainstream content options are pursued.

In such a situation, the diversity of content long valued by policymakers can be undermined by the valuations placed upon different segments of the media audience by advertisers.

AUDIENCE VALUATION

Those minority audiences may be valued at a lower level than majority audiences may be a reflection of the basic economics of the audience marketplace. Advertisers typically value various audience segments differently, based upon their demographic characteristics. These demographic characteristics are presumed to correlate with purchasing power and purchasing behaviour. Thus, for instance, younger audience members generally are valued more highly than older audience members (i.e., 50+) due to factors such as their presumed greater inclination to switch brands, their higher levels of disposable income, and their lower levels of availability in the media audience. Income is another important factor that guides advertiser valuations of media audiences.

Some products and services are likely only to be purchased by consumers of certain income levels. For this reason, advertisers frequently will use income as a variable by which to screen out certain media outlets. There are a number of possible reasons why ethnicity may factor into audience valuations as well. To a certain degree, ethnicity correlates with income. The median family income for Whites is almost $46,000, compared with approximately $30,000 for African Americans and $33,000 for Hispanics. Thus, advertisers seeking higher-income consumers may avoid minority-targeted media outlets. It is also the case that African Americans and Hispanics consume significantly more television and radio on a weekly basis than Whites.

The associated greater ease with which minorities can be reached by advertising messages may reduce their value to advertisers. Finally, some within the minority media community argue that advertisers form their valuations of minority audiences on the basis of severe misconceptions about minority product preferences and purchasing habits, which leads to a devaluing of minority audiences. Regardless of the reason, there is a growing body of evidence that such "minority discounts" do exist. Ofori's analysis of commercial radio stations found that stations with formats that targeted minority audiences earned less for their audiences than stations with general interest formats.

However, because this analysis focused only on formats, and not on audience composition, no strong conclusions regarding the relationship between audience composition and audience valuation could be drawn. An earlier analysis by Webster and Phalen found that greater proportions of non-Whites in a market had a significant negative relationship with the average cost of reaching 1,000 television viewers within a market.

This analysis controlled for income variations across markets, suggesting that ethnicity was not simply a proxy for income. The Webster and Phalen study focused on advertiser expenditures at the market level, leaving open the question of the existence of such effects at the outlet level.

No research has, at this point, directly examined the relationship between actual demographic composition of media outlets' audiences and advertiser valuations of these audiences to see if there is a significant relationship between audience ethnicity and audience value. The study presented here attempts to fill this gap through an analysis of a sample of commercial radio stations. It is important to emphasize that lower valuations of minority audiences may make economic sense from an advertiser's perspective. Regardless, such lower valuations may undermine the viability of minority-targeted media content. Such impediments to the economic viability of minority-targeted media could undermine the principles of source and content diversity that long have been objectives of electronic media regulation in the United States.

Given the nature of the policy issue, this analysis utilizes a dependent variable—the power ratio—that provides an indication of the extent to which an individual station is capable of monetizing its audience. Power ratios are computed by dividing a radio station's share of the total radio advertising expenditures in its market by its share of the total radio listening audience in that market. Thus, a power ratio greater than 1 suggests that a station is able to capture a share of advertising dollars that exceeds its share of the total audience. Such a station is "overselling" its audience. A station with a power ratio of less than 1 is capturing a share of advertising dollars that is lower than its share of the listening audience. Such a station is "underselling" its audience. Because the power ratio controls for audience share, it provides a measure that is uniquely well suited to assessing the impact of audience composition on audience value.

Power ratio data were obtained from the 1999 Media Access Pro commercial database produced by BIA Research. For the regression analysis, the natural log of the power ratio was used as the dependent variable. This transformation was conducted in accordance with the conclusions of Bates' research into the various methods and models employed in the analysis of the value of broadcast audiences, which found models employing such a transformation to be both theoretically appropriate and to provide a better fit to the data than models without such a transformation.

An emphasis on audience composition has been maintained for the independent variables, as well. Station power ratios for 1999 are regressed against Fall 1999 Arbitron data on the demographic composition of individual stations' audiences. Thus, instead of incorporating each station's ratings or share points, or raw number of listeners for the different demographic groups listening to each station, this analysis employs percent composition data.

Arbitron provides data on the percentage of each station's audience that is comprised of various demographic groups (according to age, gender, and ethnicity). Thus, for example, Station A's audience may be 40% African American, while Station B's audience may be 80% African American. Clearly, such figures provide no indication of which station has the larger number of African-American listeners. Station A may reach more African Americans than Station B if Station A's total audience is much larger.

The use of pure composition figures was deemed most appropriate given the nature of the dependent variable. Using raw numbers or rating/share points would not as effectively address the issue of the viability of minority-targeted media outlets, given that minority-targeted media outlets are not defined in terms of audience size, but in terms of the extent to which the composition of the outlets' audiences consists of minorities.

Arbitron breaks down each station's audience into men and women for seven age Categories. Arbitron provides data on the average quarter-hour percentage of each station's 6:00 a.m.-to-midnight audience that is comprised of each of these demographic categories. For the purposes of this analysis, these demographic categories were collapsed to produce two independent variables: (a) the percentage of a station's audience comprised of men within the ages of 18 to 54, and (b) the percentage of a station's audience comprised of women within the ages of 18 to 54. These two demographic categories roughly represent the audience groups with the highest demonstrated value to advertisers.

Thus, it is presumed that there will be a positive relationship between MEN1854 and WOM1854 and station power ratios. Broadcast band was included as a dummy variable (AMFM; 0 = AM; 1 = FM) to account for the likelihood that FM stations are able to charge more for their audiences than AM stations because of the better sound quality of FM signals.

The station's average quarter-hour share (6:00 a.m. to midnight) of the listening audience (SHARE) also was included as an independent variable to account for the possibility of advertisers paying a premium for larger audiences, independent of the composition of those audiences. Although this analysis focuses on the issue of audience composition, research has suggested that advertisers will pay more on a per audience member basis for larger audiences. Such patterns may be due to the efficiencies derived from engaging in fewer transactions in order to reach the desired number of consumers. Or, this premium may be derived from the value advertisers associate with the likely greater reach of a single ad placement relative to two ad placements that achieve the same level of audience exposure.

In the latter case, there is the possibility that some consumers appeared in both audiences (unless the advertisements are run simultaneously on different channels), thus the overall reach in the latter case is lower. To capture the ethnic composition of each station's audience, the two composition-based ethnicity variables provided by Arbitron were employed. The first of these is the percentage of a station's average quarter-hour audience that is African

American (AQBLACK). The second is the percentage of a station's average quarter-hour audience that is Hispanic (AQHISP). It is important to note that Arbitron does not report ethnic composition for stations in all of the markets that it measures, but only in those markets where there is a significant minority population; nor does the company provide data on ethnic groups other than African Americans and Hispanics in any of its markets.

A number of market-level variables were included as control variables to account for the possibility that station power ratios vary in accordance with market size and demographic fluctuations. Two ethnicity variables (percent Hispanic in the station's market [HISPANIC]; percent African American in the station's market [BLACK]) were included, as was per capita income in the station's market (PERCAP).

Market size was controlled using total radio advertising revenues in the market (MARKETREV). This variable was very highly correlated with other potential measures of market size, such as total population and number of radio stations in the market. The use of a market-size variable that most directly reflected market value was deemed most appropriate, given the nature of the issues being addressed.

The inclusion of these market-level independent variables addresses the possibility that variations in market size and demographics affect audience share and revenue share (the two components of the power ratio) disproportionately, independent of a station's audience composition. Perhaps a more likely relationship involves possible interaction effects between audience ethnicity and market conditions. Thus, for instance, the extent to which African-American/Hispanic audience composition affects audience value may be different in markets with higher African-American/ Hispanic compositions than in markets with lower African-American/Hispanic compositions, given the different supply and demand dynamics for African-American/ Hispanic audiences in markets that are heavily African American/ Hispanic versus those that are not.

Similarly, in larger or wealthier markets, advertiser demand for African-American/Hispanic audiences may be different than in smaller or less wealthy markets. For these reasons, six interaction terms were created.

Two inter action terms were created for interactions between audience ethnic composition and market ethnic composition to address the possibility that the effect of audience ethnicity on audience value varies in accordance with market ethnic composition, Two interaction terms also were created for interactions between audience ethnic composition and market size to account for the possibility that the effect of audience ethnic composition on audience value varies in accordance with market size.

Finally, two interaction terms were created for interactions between audience ethnic composition and market per capita income to account for the possibility that the effect of audience ethnic composition on audience value varies in accordance with per capita income in a station's market. Utilizing interaction terms typically raises problems of multicollinearity between the main effect independent variables and their associated interaction terms. The recommended procedure for reducing such multicollinearity problems is to "centre" each main effect independent variable used in the computation of the interaction terms.

Centreing involves subtracting the independent variable mean from the independent variable value for each case. These centreed independent variables were then used as the main effect variables in the multivariate analysis and to compute the interaction term used in the multivariate analysis.

Although it would have been desirable to also incorporate data on the average income levels of the audience members for each station studied, such data were not available via the data sources obtained for this analysis. As was noted above, station-level audience income delta are not part of Arbitron's syndicated reports (the reports obtained for this study) and are only available to Arbitron clients for an additional fee.

This limited availability of audience income data even to advertisers likely limits the extent to which such data are employed in radio buying decisions. Regardless, such data would have made it possible to separate the effects of income from the effects of ethnicity. Given, as was noted above, that ethnicity is correlated with income, it is possible that advertisers are using ethnicity solely as a proxy for income. Although previous research has provided evidence that contradicts this assumption, the analysis presented here cannot address this issue directly. However, as was noted above, even if lower valuations of minority audiences are largely a function of lower income levels, such lower valuations still could undermine the source and content diversity that policymakers traditionally have sought as well as the provision of content serving minority interests and concerns.

Finally, it is important to address a number of limitations in the scope of the database. First, Arbitron does not measure all radio stations in the United States. Of the roughly 13,000 radio stations in the United States, only about 6,000 are in Arbitron-defined and measured radio markets. Moreover, as was noted above, Arbitron does not provide data on the ethnic composition of station audiences for all of the radio markets it measures. Generally, Arbitron only provides such data in markets where there is a significant minority population. These factors limit the number of stations eligible for analysis and weight the stations included in this analysis toward those in markets with large African-American and Hispanic populations.

The number of eligible stations was limited further by the fact that not all commercial radio stations report their revenues to BIA Research (BIA's reported response rate is roughly 80%). In cases where station revenues are not reported, it is impossible to compute the power ratio that serves as the dependent variable for this analysis.

Due to these limitations, within this data set there is a total of 810 stations with Hispanic audience composition (and revenue) data, 1430 with African-American composition (and revenue) data, and a total of 461 commercial radio stations with reported revenues and with both African-American and Hispanic audience composition data available.

It is this latter set of stations that is the focus of this analysis as these stations represent the only context in which it is possible to investigate simultaneously the effects of both of the minority-audience characteristics at issue on audience value. In sum, while previous research has explored the relationship between audience ethnicity and audience value via market-level demographic data, market-level CPMs, and differences in power ratios across program formats, the approach outlined here moves beyond these approaches by directly examining the relationship between the audience composition of individual media outlets and their ability to successfully compete for available advertising dollars.

The mean power ratio of stations that target minority audiences was first compared to the mean power ratio of stations that do not target minority audiences. For the purposes of this analysis, minority-targeted stations were defined as those stations for which the majority of the station's average quarter-hour audience (i.e., greater than 50%) is comprised of African-American and/or Hispanic listeners. In this means comparison, stations with a minority audience of greater than 50% (n = 121) have an average power ratio of.82, compared with an average power ratio of 1.06 for other stations (n = 340). This difference is statistically significant at the.01 level. As these results suggest, minority-targeted stations tend to undersell their audiences, meaning that their share of the total radio audience is greater than their share of the total radio advertising revenues in their markets.

Of particular importance is the fact that correlations between the main effect variables and their associated interaction terms generally are modest. Before these variables were centreed, some of the correlations between main effect and interaction terms were as high as.90, a level indicative of a potentially serious multicollinearity problem.

There remain, however, a few strong correlations between some of the interaction terms. There is a similarly strong correlation between the Hispanic versions of these interaction terms. However, tolerance statistics for all four of these independent variables are reasonably high (ranging from.39 to.52), alleviating concerns about multicollinearity in the multivariate analysis.

Hierarchical regression was employed due to the inclusion of interaction terms. When working with interaction terms, hierarchical regression is necessary in order to determine whether the interaction terms provide significant explanatory power beyond that provided by the main effect variables. Using hierarchical regression in this context also makes it possible to better examine the relative contribution of market-level versus station-level independent variables. (Given the nature of the dependent variable, it was presumed that station-level independent variables would provide greater explanatory power than market-level independent variables).

The first set of independent variables entered into the model was the market-level control variables. These variables alone explain none of the variance in station power ratios. There is a negative relationship between modulation type and power ratios, with AM status having a negative effect on power ratios.

Both the MEN1854 and WOM1854 demographic composition variables are positively related to power ratios, indicating that the greater the extent to which a station's audience is composed of men and women 18 to 54, the greater the station's power ratio. A station's overall audience share (SHARE) also is positively related to a station's power ratio, providing evidence that sellers of audiences are able to charge a premium on a per audience member basis for larger audiences. Finally, in terms of ethnicity, both the AQHISP and AQBLACK variables are negatively related to power ratios, suggesting that ethnic composition exerts a downward pressure on a radio station's ability to monetize its audience. The magnitude of the beta coefficients indicates that the age/gender independent variables are the most important in terms of explanatory power, followed by the ethnicity variables. The AQBLACK and AQHISP coefficients are similar in size, though African-American audience composition seems to exert a slightly stronger downward pressure on audience value than Hispanic audience composition.

The six interaction terms were added to the equation. The addition of interaction terms explains only an additional 5% of the variance in the dependent variable (the adjusted R2 increases from.32 to.37); however, this improvement in explanatory power is significant at the.01 level.

Only one of the six interaction terms is statistically significant. The significant negative coefficient for the AQHISP*MARKREV interaction term indicates that the magnitude of the negative relationship between Hispanic audience composition and station power ratios decreases slightly as market size increases. The analyses presented here represent the next step forward in determining the extent to which advertiser valuations of minority audiences affect the viability of minority-owned and minority-targeted media outlets. The results conform to those of previous studies, which found that minority audiences are more difficult to monetize than non-minority audiences.

This study also has extended previous research by examining the value of minority audiences at the level of individual media outlets and by employing detailed data on the demographic composition of the audiences for those outlets. Future research should seek to better separate possible income effects from ethnicity effects.

From a media policy standpoint, however, whether lower valuations of minority audiences are purely a function of income or also are a function of other factors such as advertiser perceptions of minority spending and product usage patterns, the implications for diversity in the electronic media are the same—the viability of minority-targeted media content suffers.

It is important that these findings be placed within the broader context of the economics of minority media. Minority-targeted media content suffers from not only the potentially lower valuations of minority audiences but also the fact that, by definition, it appeals to a small audience. Smaller audiences mean smaller revenues, particularly when the audience is not highly valued by advertisers (if the small audience segment being targeted is highly valued by advertisers, then, of course, revenue potential increases).

Recall that this analysis also found that stations with larger audiences are able to charge more on a Per audience member basis than stations with smaller audiences, a finding that further illustrates the compounding negative consequences of being a niche programmer. These economic handicaps result in lower incentives to produce such programming and, consequently, lower levels of availability of such programming. Moreover, lower levels of audience size and value both exert downward pressures on the production budgets of minority content, which further undermine the ability of such content to compete and remain viable. The smaller and less valuable the potential audience for a media product is, the smaller the likely investment in programming. At the same time, research shows that audiences are drawn to content with higher production budgets over content with smaller production budgets.

Together, these processes create a situation in which minority content loses some of its appeal—even to minority audiences—relative to majority content. The differential in production budgets may be enough for some minority audience members to find the majority content more appealing than the content targeted at their particular interests and concerns.

Such defections further undermine the viability of minority-targeted content and contribute to the availability of minority audiences in non-minority content that further discourages advertisers from advertising on minority-targeted media outlets. In the end, the lower valuations that advertisers place on minority audiences feed into an economic process that works against minority-targeted content being able to compete and remain viable in both the audience and content markets.

The end result is lower levels of availability of minority-targeted content. This Perspective suggests that policymakers seeking—at the general level—to preserve and promote diversity of sources and content in the electronic media, and seeking—at the specific level—to promote minority ownership of media outlets and the production of minority-targeted content, need to investigate new strategies and tactics.

Previous policy initiatives, such as minority preferences in the license allocation process and minority tax certificates, have focused on increasing the likelihood of minorities becoming owners of media outlets. The results presented here suggest that if policymakers want to preserve and promote minority-targeted media outlets, their efforts may need to address the barriers not only to establishing such media outlets but also to maintaining the financial viability of such outlets once they are established.

Possible mechanisms might include subsidies for minority-targeted media outlets or education campaigns designed to counter any advertiser misconceptions about minority media audiences that may be driving down their value. Of course, such recommendations are premised upon the notion that existing levels of minority-targeted media content are not sufficient.

Whether—and to what extent—this is the case is a question that is beyond the scope of this analysis. The analyses presented here suggest that the economic handicaps associated with targeting minority audiences may lead to a disconnect between the availability of minority audiences and the availability of minority-targeted media content. Future research should explore this issue in greater detail. However, in order to effectively address this issue, and the necessity of a policy response, policymakers need to work toward establishing more concrete objectives in terms of the desired levels of both ownership and content diversity in the electronic media marketplace.

15

Preparing the Next Generation of Journalists

The news industry has been undergoing a fundamental paradigm shift since the end of last century. An increasing number of media companies around the United States, such as the Washington Post in Washington, DC, Media General in Virginia, the Tribune Company in Chicago, and New England Cable News, have taken solid steps to merge different media such as newspapers, television stations, radio stations, and online journalism companies to disseminate news content on multiple media platforms.

As a result, in a metropolitan area, one company would own print, TV, and online venues. Media call this industrial trend "media convergence," though the concept means much more than media mergers. Media convergence muddies the lines among broadcast journalism, print journalism, and online journalism, leaving college journalism educators to wonder whether traditional journalism programs have become dinosaurs.

After surveying 200 newspaper publishers worldwide, the World Association of Newspapers (WAN) found, "Despite a somewhat gloomy outlook for wholesale convergence in media companies worldwide in the near term, convergence is already being implemented with varying degrees of enthusiasm and speed among the world's media companies".

The Innovation International Media Consulting Group estimates that at least 100 of the world's multiple media companies are planning and implementing integration strategies. South and Nicholson drew a sketch of a converged media company:

Daily journalists need to embrace the 24-hour news cycle, with continuous deadlines. And the story needs to be reported and produced for a multi-platform audience. That may mean delivering content first to the Web and cell phones, a streaming video broadcast later in the day, a TV talk-back interview still later, and a "second day" interpretive story for the next morning's newspaper.

Dominic Gates (2002) pointed out, "Convergence with broadcast and online media is the shape of things to come for newspapers." The trend remains controversial. Critics complain that such cross-ownership of both a television station and a newspaper in the same market is a threat to democracy because it limits the number of voices1. Delegates of the Communication Workers of America, a 60,000-member guild, passed a resolution in June of 2002 at the group's annual convention in Las Vegas, pledging to increase public awareness about the risks of ongoing media convergence. The delegates complained that shrinking media markets are a threat to editorial diversity and job security.

In 1975, the Federal Communications Commission (FCC) ruled that no new broadcast licenses would be granted to companies that own a major daily newspaper and a local television station in the same city. Fairness & Accuracy In Reporting (FAIR) calls on the FCC to roll back limits on media consolidation. The Newspaper Association of America (NAA), on the other hand, has asked the FCC to appeal the rule. On June 2, 2003, the FCC voted 3 to 2 to relax or eliminate some ownership restrictions, such as a rule barring media companies from owning television stations in markets where they publish daily newspapers. Although some lawmakers and advocacy groups are still fighting in the courts and on Capitol Hill to overturn the FCC's new media ownership rules, these rules will be likely to encourage cross-media ownership in the years to come.

The mergers have raised questions about whether they are good for the craft of journalism itself. Critics complain that by requiring journalists to be jacks of both trades, print and broadcast, the journalists will be masters of none. Robert J. Haiman, president emeritus of The Poynter Institute, compared the media convergence trend to an Amphicar, a cross between a boat and a car. The Amphicar, hawked in Florida during the 1950s, flopped. "It flopped because people quickly discovered that while it really was an ingenious combination of a car and a boat, it was a lousy car (because it also had to be a boat), and it was a lousy boat (because it also had to be a car)".

Willingly or unwillingly, many news practitioners' functions are gradually changing or are expected to change as media convergence rolls on. For a reporter in a converged media environment, knowing how to write is probably no longer enough. S/he could be expected to write the same story for different media in a timely manner.

Ideally, s/he can readily talk in front of a video camera. As a photographer, knowing how to tell a story both in video and in still images is more and more in demand. A designer should know how to prepare still graphics for print, moving graphics for television and dynamic graphics for the Web. At the online version of the Chicago Tribune, for instance, staffers are supposed to cover stories, take pictures, operate video cameras, and create digital pages. The editors, too, need a wider variety of skills than the traditional paper editors. Along with infrastructure changes and the attempt to create synergy among the various media outlets, a new breed of journalists-digital or multimedia journalists-is expected. As media jobs become more demanding, some news practitioners are beginning to team up to complete projects. At the same time, fear, confusion, and frustration from news practitioners are creeping into newsrooms. Carr wrote: "Convergence frightens many people who wonder whether their current skill sets have prepared them for-or will even be needed in-that great undiscovered country, the future.

This is probably the primary reason why I still find such great hostility to convergence among certain journalists." Killebrew (2001), a mass communications professor from the University of South Florida, suggested that "journalists must be prepared to either crosstrain themselves or seek training from other sources while management must be prepared to give them the opportunities and time to do so."

The 1999-2000 president of the Association for Schools of Journalism and Mass Communication (ASJMC), Shirley Staples Carter, questioned whether, in the midst of the "Internet revolution," programs are prepared to educate journalists of the future. When specifically talking about writing, Keith Hartenberger, manager of news and programming for Tribune Regional Programming, said that journalism schools should make their students aware of the many ways to present the news. "It's a multimedia world out there," he said. "If you're just being prepared to write newspaper stories, you won't be prepared". "At some point, this [cross-media training] is something we're going to expect from everyone".

Media convergence, as a trend that is gradually shaping the landscape of the media industry in the new century, has called into question the conventional journalism school practice of having separate tracks-print, broadcast, etc. Journalism educators around the country also are trying to figure out what they should do, if anything, to better prepare students for the converged media. For instance, should journalism educators consider merging different sequences such as magazine, newspaper, broadcast, and photojournalism, or still teach all such courses as if they were unrelated media? "Traditionally defined segments of the communications industry are less and less distinguishable for technological and market convergence," observed Moon. Are college journalism educators themselves both theoretically equipped and technologically prepared to teach their students for converged media? What do media companies expect from future news practitioners? What do current news practitioners in converged media feel is lacking? For both news practitioners and professors, the two most urgent questions cry for answers: Should journalism schools train specialists or fit for-all generalists? And how should college journalism education balance the teaching of critical thinking and technical skills?

Apart from all these education-related questions, we are also interested in finding out what are the driving forces behind the media mergers, who are regarded as the beneficiaries of this trend, and how people's political beliefs are related to their attitude toward teaching media convergence in colleges? These questions pertain closely to college journalism education, which has been the subject of debate and criticism for two decades. A national survey was conducted among colleges, daily newspapers, and commercial television stations to explore the issue of how journalism schools should prepare students for the trend of media convergence from the perspectives of news editors, news professionals, and journalism professors. The study measured the level of general support for convergence education and determined if a new model of journalism education was called for.

If so, it examined whether consensus existed among the three groups on the direction educators should take when revisiting program designs. Where consensus was not apparent, divisions among the sample of educators, editors, and reporters were defined. The goal of the study is to provide evidence that will help journalism educators make informed decisions about how to respond to media convergence in their curricula and courses and lay an empirical foundation for further discussions and conversations about media convergence. The search results show that media convergence is a comparatively new topic in media research, though articles about it have inundated the Internet, magazines, and newspapers. Most research writings appeared no earlier than 1998. Many writings have addressed one of the toughest questions: What is media convergence? How to define "media convergence" had a direct bearing on how we conducted this study. Out of these writings, we identified four categories of media convergence that directly affect how journalism will be taught in colleges.

CONTENT CONVERGENCE

As Tremayne noted, decades ago, the term media convergence referred to the content convergence between competing newspapers and even among newspapers, magazines, and television. Today, pure content convergence continues on the Internet. For instance, the St. Petersburg Times has incorporated local Channel 10's TV news into its online newspaper though they are independent business entities. In other words, media convergence may not necessarily be tied to media merger. Form convergence (or technological convergence). Around the mid-1990s, as Tremayne and Wurtz noted, computer technology and Internet technology made possible the convergence of all forms of mediated communications including video, audio, data, text, still photo, and graphic art for "on-demand" audiences. Using these different forms to tell news stories on the World Wide Web has been widely regarded as the future of mass communication regardless of the fact that most online news sites have had a hard time making ends meet, let alone making a profit. Form convergence, often called technological convergence, has been a fundamental force to guide and lead convergence in the market, industry, and regulation.

CORPORATE CONVERGENCE

Since the late 1990s, media convergence has been escalated to the level of media mergers. The News Centre located in Tampa, Florida, owned by Media General, and the Tribune Interactive, owned by the Tribune Company, for instance, are the products of media mergers.

In The News Centre, WFLA-TV, The Tampa Tribune, and Tampa Bay Online operate out of the same building. They share daily tips and information, spot news, photography, enterprise reporting, franchises, events, and public service. Each of the three entities in The News Centre has its own independent newsroom, but they issued a joint statement of coverage principles, titled "News Centre Pledge".

The Tribune Interactive has brought together the interactive functions of the company's four newspapers and more than a score of television stations including WGN-TV and CLTV. The individual media outlets have their own newsgathering staff, but their coverage is enhanced by their multimedia desks in the Chicago Tribune newsroom and the Tribune Media Centre in Washington. "A synergy-team of print editors and TV news veterans at the Chicago Tribune work together to manage resource sharing and the relationship". Media merger has made both content convergence and form convergence handy. Corporate convergence via vertical and horizontal integration, mergers, alliances, and acquisitions will make traditionally defined segments of the communications industry less and less distinguishable.

Role convergence. Russial identified several examples of role convergence in newsrooms. For instance, the roles of reporter and librarian, the roles of copyeditor and compositor, the roles of graphic artist and Web designer, and the roles of photo editor, darkroom technician, and photographer are all converging in different media. In more recent years, content convergence, form convergence, and especially corporate convergence have sparked more in-depth role convergence among news practitioners.

For instance, Victoria Lim from The News Centre in Tampa revealed at a February 2002 conference on media convergence at the University of Florida that she primarily works as a television reporter for WFLA-TV, but she also has to write for the company's newspaper, The Tampa Tribune, as a senior consumer investigative reporter and for the Web company TBO.com on a daily basis; at the time of the conference, she was working on 31 stories.

A newspaper reporter may also produce a newspaper in QuarkXPress or serve as a TV news anchor, while a newspaper photographer may shoot video stories or produce interactive online stories in Flash. Role convergence requires that both reporters and editors re-equip themselves both journalistically and technologically. Of the four types of convergence, role convergence has the most direct effect on future journalism education. Within the media industry, there are serious doubts about whether training cross-media journalists is possible or desirable. When asked whether reporters of the future must be equally skilled in print, TV, and online, Forrest Carr, news director of WFLA-TV at The News Centre in Tampa, said no. He said he believed that there would always be areas of specialization and students may still choose specialties, but said that it no longer makes any sense to pretend print journalists and electronic journalists are in different professions. On the other hand, he said that journalists who have skills in TV, print, and online media certainly will be more valuable to their employers; and he emphasized that prospective employees must be willing to work in an environment where reporters cooperate across platforms.

In most cases currently, he said, cooperating across platforms simply comes down to the sharing of tips and information. Charles Kravetz, the vice president for news and station manager of New England Cable News (NECN), the largest regional news network in America, concurs with Forrest Carr.

When asked "Do you see a time when all journalists will have to be able to file stories on all platforms (print, TV, radio, online)?" Kravetz said: "I am not sure that is the way it is going to work out. This notion we had that one-journalist-fits-all-media is perhaps not that realistic. There are very few people we will talk about in the future that are TV/newspaper/internet reporters".

Gates agreed, "The 'backpack journalist'-a superhack master of multimedia who can do it all and who routinely packs a laptop and a video camera along with the tape recorder and steno notebook-may be the subject of avant-garde j-school courses, but it's not likely to become the norm."

Some other media executives have tried to define the extent to which role convergence is expected. Gil Thelen, executive editor and senior vice president of The Tampa Tribune, for instance, gave suggestions to journalism educators based on his two years of experience in The News Centre.

"The fully formed, all-purpose, multiplatform, gadget-laden journalism grad is NOT what we're looking to hire. Journalism schools must continue to produce graduates who are competent in one craft area: reporting, design, producing, directing, editing." However, Thelen encouraged journalism schools to train writers to write for print, online, and broadcast and train print photographers to learn how to shoot and produce TV packages. Thelen said that cultural resistance is the biggest hurdle for converging newsrooms, and that employees or current journalism students need to learn to cooperate and collaborate across newsrooms. What is unclear is whether these media administrators' predictions are limited by the status quo of the current generation of news practitioners who might not be very well prepared for convergence or who might even resist the notion of media convergence.

At Brigham Young University, students with multiple skills are more valued and feel more comfortable in the converged media environment. In addition, sharing tips and information does not entail convergence. Reporters have been doing this for decades. It seems that keeping convergence only on the level of sharing tips and information can hardly justify the high cost of rebuilding infrastructures like The News Centre.

We are interested in finding out what expectations media companies have for future journalists. From news professionals' self-evaluations of their preparedness for media convergence, we should also be able to infer what is most desirable in the media industry nowadays.

In the face of increasing demand for technically skilled journalists-conversant with QuarkXPress, Photoshop, Avid, and Dreamweaver and able to crunch statistics using spreadsheets and other statistical methods in order to uncover the hidden story-should longstanding staples such as ethics, law, and theory remain at the heart of journalism curricula?

Or should such materials, commonly grouped together as "critical thinking", share equal hilling with technology or "skills" training? In other words, how should journalism schools balance the teaching of professional skills and that of critical thinking in an era when technology penetrates every facet of news gathering, preparation, editing, production, and delivery?

Convergence further complicates this age-old battle in journalism education. Abraham noticed that the goal of most restructuring in journalism institutions is to provide an integrated skills environment where students would get the chance to practice the skills of multimedia production. Abraham argued: "The role of journalism academy should be very different from that of the industry. Its role should not simply be to inculcate skills that will help students to flag down jobs. They should aim to provide a scholarly background for a deeper intellectual understanding of our lives, media forms and of communication in general".

The dean of the University of Nevada at Reno thinks the ability to use multiple media skills is essential. Brigham Young University, which has built a working converged newsroom into its curriculum, expects students to graduate with multiple skills. University News Director, Dean Paynter, said, "We expect our students to more than anchor, more than report, and more than produce. The best ones can do it all, including write for the newspaper". Mitchell Stephens (2000), professor of journalism and mass communications at New York University, holds up the other end. "In a world where corporate pressures on 'content providers' seem to be increasing and civic affairs decreasing, the argument for emphasizing the basics does have much to recommend it."

Thomas Kunkel (2002), dean of the Philip Merrill College of Journalism at the University of Maryland, sums it up: "Today's journalists, first and foremost, must be strong critical thinkers who know enough about geography, history and the human condition to understand why events play out as they do. They must be intellectually curious. They should speak a second language. They should read something other than Jim Romenesko's MediaNews site. They ought to have a world view." A controversy in late 2002 at Columbia University demonstrates how volatile the argument is currently. The debate arose when the graduate school of journalism at Columbia University halted its search for a dean. The new university president, Lee Bollinger, wanted to re-evaluate the school's mix of craft versus theory (Babcock), and the move created a flurry of opinion about the journalism school's existing curriculum.

This critical curriculum question is often reflected in the questions of whether and how new technology classes should be included in the existing curriculum and how they should be taught. Some journalism schools are preparing to embrace the wave of media convergence in their new curricula by converging print and electronic media sequences to adapt to the industrial trends and the new technological environment.

Blanchard and Christ warn that universities with limited resources will no longer tolerate duplicating specializations with separate courses such as writing for television, writing for newspapers, writing for public relations, and writing for advertising. Blanchard and Christ add that the communications revolution (the media's convergence and related trends) is making journalism and mass communication's traditional sequences obsolete.

Actually, Blanchard and Christ's opinion is not something new. Early in 1972, the University of Iowa School of Journalism already eliminated its sequences but at the expense of being denied reaccreditation by ACEJMC. About thirty years later, their decision seemed to be finding more sympathy.

Many schools are still exploring where to go. In October 2001, seventeen professors and leaders of new media from thirteen journalism programs across the country gathered in Berkeley, California, and had a discussion about new media in journalism education. The University of Nevada, Reno, offered several different elective courses in new media, but it did not have a special sequence. It was struggling with how to incorporate them in other classes. The University of Florida had a concentration in online media, which was equivalent to other concentrations such as reporting and editing and photojournalism. Students who were not in that concentration couldn't always squeeze in the online media courses because they did not have any leftover électives they could take in the school. American University had three divisions, journalism, public communication, and visual media, but they did not work together very well most of the time.

The University of South Carolina was restructuring its graduate masters program in newspaper leadership and was focusing it on convergence. The University of Maryland had an online curriculum, but it was not formally structured as such. Northwestern University had an introductory New Media course at the undergraduate and graduate level, which was offered as an elective. It was packed with everything from new skills training to wrestling with the business issues of new media to actual production. After three admission cycles, enrollment declined. The University of Minnesota established the Institute for New Media Studies, which merged broadcast journalism and print journalism programs to make them a concentration with the idea that future journalists would work in a multi-channel environment and should know how to operate within all those channels. Although editors and academics sometimes agree on the qualifications a journalism student needs, an ideal curriculum doesn't always include convergence preparedness courses. In a 2000 poll, editors and educators agreed "on the same five of 14 types of knowledge considered most necessary for journalism graduates and listed them in the same order of importance".

Technical skills were not mentioned in the top five, surpassed instead by "understanding of a journalist's responsibility to the public, understanding of the ethics of journalism, knowledge of current events, broad general knowledge, and knowledge of government". With so much variance across universities, we are interested in finding out how many journalism schools have revamped their curricula to prepare students for the trend of media convergence, what professors' attitudes are toward teaching critical thinking vs. teaching technical skills and training generalists vs. training specialists, and what editors' and news professionals' attitudes are toward the same issues. In this regard, several scholars and news practitioners have tried to give advice to journalism professors and students in the context of media convergence.

In 2002, David Bulla from the University of Florida presented his "Media convergence: Industry practices and implications for education" to the AEJMC annual conference in Miami. This is the first research writing of its kind. The theme of the paper is the closest to that of this study. Bulla's study looked at the changing nature of contemporary mass communications practices, focusing on multimedia or converged journalism. It described what scholastic journalism scholars are doing to prepare their students for these changes and provided recommendations to educators about how to update curricula to account for convergence. The research questions for that study were: (1) what are journalism educators currently doing to incorporate convergence into their curricula; and (2) what abilities, skills, and attitudes do professional journalists expect from their newest employees? Media convergence in Bulla's study was defined as multimedia journalism, which means reporting, writing, and disseminating content in two or more media platforms.

Because of the controversy about media mergers, Bulla tried to find answers to some hot issues concerning democracy including: Does corporate media merging reduce public discourse and hinder democracy? Will it ultimately mean the need for fewer and fewer reporters, as the development of other technology has meant a decline in the number of employees in other areas of the production process? All these questions pertain to our study.

Bulla obtained a sample of 114 news practitioners working at newspapers, television stations, wire services, magazines, radio stations, and online publications in the United States. The sample was randomly selected from Editor & Publisher and Yahoo lists of media companies in the U.S. Media Web sites. With a response rate of 36 percent, Bulla interviewed 41 news practitioners. Bulla also interviewed college educators, but he did not state how he sampled them. What is unclear is the extent to which the Yahoo list and Editor & Publisher list overlap each other and if a sample from two potentially overlapping lists is any longer a random sample. In addition, since Bulla's questions were almost all unstructured, that is, he conducted interviews,10 he did not really need a random sample.

Researchers strive for depth rather than breadth and don't mean to claim external validity in the statistical sense by conducting interviews. Finally, if he did need a random sample, a sample of 114 people with a 36 percent response rate could be statistically defective because of big statistical errors. Bulla needed a better research design to make his study valid and reliable.

Some scholars doubt whether journalism school professors are theoretically and especially technologically prepared to teach media convergence. In an article written for Journalism Education magazine, John Irby, a professor from Washington State University and a veteran newspaper editor and publisher, for instance, was concerned about the disconnection between the newsroom and the classroom.

Irby (2000) asked: Are universities and educators effectively preparing students for the work force? Do educators understand what newspapers are looking for in future reporters and editors? Does the newspaper industry have a responsibility in the division between educators and professionals? Are journalism educators "discounted" by professionals who believe those who teach couldn't succeed in newspapers? Irby said older generations of newspaper reporters also appeared on radio and television periodically though they had no training; they never even felt like it was part of their job and thus did not take it very seriously. But now, he continued, print journalists do need to take it seriously; journalism educators need to re-evaluate, and probably modify, the separatetrack approach in training print and broadcast journalists.

Irby believed that there is still a need for specialization, but he told students to take both broadcast and print courses and told them that computer literacy is as crucial as the old-fashioned kind. A study about the impact of media convergence on journalism education without consulting Robert J. Haiman's article "Can convergence float?" (2001) should be considered incomplete. Haiman's fervent talk against media convergence raised some challenging questions that educators must face. Haiman, president emeritus of The Poynter Institute, argued that the converged media world is one from which good journalism, and good journalists, are going to be in great need of defence. He stuck to his notion of the mission of good journalism he stated 40 years ago: "To inform the public about the public's business, creating a society that is equipped with the knowledge it needs to make the right civic decisions more often than it makes the wrong civic decisions, and thus helping to perpetuate self-government and democracy."

Expressing his deep concern for journalism, Haiman said: "I think that convergence may end up being good, maybe even very good, for media companies. I fear, however, that it is going to be bad, and maybe even very bad, for journalism." He continued to explain:

I think it is going to be bad for journalism because, even if it goes as well as it possibly can, I believe that it is going to distract journalists, journalism teachers, and journalism students away from that single most important imperative of the craft - to create an informed society capable of intelligently governing itself. And if it does not go well, I fear it is going to subject journalists to time, resource, craft, and ethical pressures, all of which will be bad for journalists, bad for journalism, and bad for the country.

In his talk, Haiman mentioned a top education reporter who had done a "superb job" for more than 18 years. Now, he had to do short reports for the TV station with which that newspaper was converged.

However, "he's not exactly ready for prime time." After this reporter retires, Haiman is afraid that that he will be replaced by "someone who may not report like a buzz saw and write like a dream, but who probably will report and write education okay and who will also look good and sound good on television." "When that happens," he continued, "the journalism quality of all of the education reporting coming out of that converged news operation is going to go down." We believe that few people would disagree with Haiman's point that quality content is the king, to use his own words, but Haiman's above comment could be limited, again, by the performance of the current generation of reporters who are not prepared for media convergence.

Haiman was suggesting that a future reporter who has been trained to work for different media platforms and who has learned more about reporting would produce reporting of less quality. In our study, we would like to find out to what extent Haiman's concern is shared by editors, news professionals, and professors. While convergence is still in its infancy, Haiman suggested that journalists, journalism students, and journalism teachers do three "terribly important things":

- For journalists who want to keep good journalism alive in the converged world to take a blood oath to fight, scrap, kick and scream whenever any attempt is made to dilute good journalism values.
- For journalism schools and journalism teachers to offer students the right curriculum to function best in that converged world, and this does not mean offering new courses in convergence.
- For journalism students to emphasize the right areas of study and take the right courses so they will be able to defend themselves against the evils of convergence, prosper in that new world, and contribute to the effort to sustain informed self-government.

Haiman said, "If we decide to teach anything about convergence at Poynter, that is the lesson I hope we'll teach."

To students, Haiman said that the journalists who will be the most successful in the converged world are the same ones who are the most successful today, and they are the ones who are best trained in six areas: reporting, writing, editing, ethics, and media law, research techniques and specialized knowledge such as business, finance, law, science, health, aging, and the environment.

Since the top reporter in education Haiman mentioned can hardly survive the converged media world, our question is whether gaining knowledge in these six areas is sufficient and what else, if any, students need to learn. Do students need to learn any new skills? What new skills do news practitioners need? Also, we would like to see how the attitudes of the respondents from these three groups toward media merger affect their views of how to train future journalists. As South and Nicholson (2002) commented, "If the industry doesn't agree on what new skills journalists need, it will be hard for journalism schools to know what to teach."

LARGER CONTEXT OF THE STUDY

The questions concerning teaching skills vs. critical thinking and training specialists vs. generalists are not new. They have been contextualized in ongoing conversations across disciplines over decades on many campuses in the United States. But such conversations take on new meanings in journalism schools when many reporting jobs today are becoming high-tech-oriented and many news companies are demanding high-tech skills from new hires upon their graduation. The impact of such industrial demands on universities brings us back to the core issue-the role of the university in the shaping of the young souls in its charge.

In other words, how should a university achieve the desired product-a truly educated human being for newsrooms. The question of teaching skills vs. critical thinking winds down to a perennial competition between acquiescing pervasive vocationalism with its emphasis on skills training in an attempt to enable college students to survive outside academic institutions and establishing the relevance of the broad spectrum of knowledge to the career goals and lives of individuals. E. D. Hirsch argues: "Narrow vocational education, adjusted to the needs of the moment, is made ever more obsolete by changing technology What is required is education for change, not for static job competencies". Probably no one has better expressed than Joanne G. Kurfiss the importance of imparting critical thinking as skills of analyzing and constructing arguments, as construction of meaning, and as the manifestation of a contextual theory of knowledge.

"Critical thinking can result in a new way of approaching significant issues in one's life or a deeper understanding of the basis for one's actions. Or it might result in political activity". Along the similar line as Kurfiss's critical thinking theory and unlike Allan Bloom, who condemns the introduction of non-Western materials into the university curricula so as to protect the curriculum from the contamination of ideological conflict, Jerry Herron also highly promotes the teaching of critical thinking by calling on faculty to bring their conflicting ideologies into open engagement so that students can discover what is at stake in different ideas and can see their representational meaning.

The questions are whether universities should totally give up the teaching of skills today and how the needs of the job market and the goal of college education can be in harmony. In other words, can the teaching of common traditional content and the teaching of higher order skills join forces? Patracia Graham, ex-dean of the Harvard Graduate School of Education, argues that we need both commonality and flexibility in American education and there is no reason we cannot have both at once.

The question of training specialists vs. generalists is an extension of a larger conversation about reforming the fragmented curricula in higher education. Often classified as "cultural right," Ernest Boyer, Allan Bloom, and E. D. Hirsch share similar views about the problems in higher education. They point out that the university now is anarchistic.

There is no vision of what an educated human being is. The curriculum is disjointed and disciplines are fragmented into smaller pieces. Undergraduates find it hard to see patterns in their courses and relate what they learn to life. Careerism conflicts with the liberal arts.

And finally, schools have failed to thoroughly carry out the educational goal of promoting mature literacy for all our citizens. They all agree that an educational reform is needed to teach more common traditional content apart from the higher-order skills that are commonly emphasized.

Boyer calls for a balance between individual interests and shared concerns while the actual priority is given to the latter. To promote a liberal education, Boyer advocates the "integrated core" or "enriched major"-a program of general education that introduces students not only to essential knowledge, but also to connections across the disciplines, and, in the end, to the application of knowledge to life beyond the campus.

Boyer points out, knowledge becomes important only when we use it and apply it to humane ends; therefore, the undergraduate experience should not only generate new knowledge, but channel that knowledge to the service of the society. It is a matter of invigorating "the claims of community while protecting with full vigour the dignity and origins of each individual," to use Boyer and Kaplan's words. In a similar vein, Bloom calls on teachers to look toward the goal of human completeness and to provide students a liberal education, in which learning is both synoptic and precise.

To Bloom, liberal education feeds the student's love of truth and passion to live a good life. It also requires that a student's whole life be radically changed by it. Bloom offers an ivory tower vision of the university-"the good old Great Book approach"-undergraduate students spend four years reading certain generally recognized classic texts for answers to philosophical questions of personal and human identity and aspirations. Bloom thinks that man may live more truly and fully in reading Plato and Shakespeare than at any other time because then they are participating in essential being and are forgetting their accidental lives.

In accordance with Boyer's and Bloom's points of view, Hirsch argues that "the greatest human individuality is developed in response to a tradition, not in response to disorderly, uncertain, and fragmented education" and "only by accumulating shared symbols, and the shared information the symbols represent can we learn to communicate effectively with one another in our national community". However, Hirsch places emphasis more on the content of education, ensuring that students acquire all the "right" elements of knowledge that will enable them to get along in the Real World. He believes that neither the content-neutral curriculum of Rousseau and Dewey nor the narrowly specified curriculum of Plato is adequate to the needs of a modern nation.

Hirsch calls for a curriculum, including extensive curriculum and intensive curriculum with an emphasis on the former, which is traditional in content and provides students with a common core of cultural information. "The conception of a two-part curriculum avoids the idea that all children should study identical materials" Hirsch says. Based on our literature review, media convergence in our study is defined as the assimilation of media content for multiple media platforms. Media convergence may involve any combination of the convergences of media contents, media forms, media companies, and roles of news practitioners.

Our general research question is how college professors should prepare students to cope with media convergence. To be specific, should college professors prepare generalists who can competently work in multiple media platforms or prepare specialists who know inside out how to work for one particular medium platform? And how should journalism schools balance the teaching of critical thinking and technical skills? Corresponding to these two questions, we also would like to find out if college journalism educators themselves are both theoretically equipped and technologically prepared to teach their students about media convergence. The study serves both as an attitude finder and a fact finder.

We believe that professors, editors, and news professionals are the best candidates to answer these questions. Editors represent the media companies to hire news staffers with news reporting abilities desired by the company. News professionals work in the forefront of news reporting and know best about what news reporting abilities they need. The attitudes of the editors and the current generation of news professionals toward media convergence will have a great implication on future journalism education. Professors run journalism schools, and they have the final say about where their schools are going. Their attitudes toward journalism education in terms of media convergence will have the most direct influence on the kind of education journalism students will receive and how the students will perform in tomorrow's media.

Editors include daily newspaper editors in charge of newsroom operations or online news operations and news directors in charge of newsroom operations in a commercial TV station with news content, both in the United States. News professionals refer to non-management news staff, such as reporters, anchors, photographers, designers, producers, Web staff, etc., working in American media companies. Journalism professors are defined as full-time instructors with any academic rankings who teach journalism courses in a U.S. journalism school, department, program, or division, which could be administratively affiliated with an institution with a name like College of Communications or Department of Communications Studies.

To obtain opinions about media convergence, we could have targeted our survey only at those editors and news professionals in a converged media environment. The opinions obtained from those editors and news professionals, however, could be biased. Those media companies that have not gone through convergence must have a reason for not doing so. We also wanted to find out what they are doing about convergence. Balanced views both from the converged and un-converged media companies will better assist colleges in their strategic planning.

We conducted a national survey among editors, news professionals, and journalism professors with three different versions of online survey questionnaires posted on a school Web site. Respondents were asked to fill out the questionnaire online and submit answers online as well. The answers went through a commercial form handler and reached the primary investigator's email address.

By doing so, the primary investigator had no way to detect who answered the questionnaire unless the respondent voluntarily revealed his/her email address to request the findings from the study. There were twenty-two questions in each of these three questionnaires. Almost all questions were close-ended. About half of the questions used a 5-point Likert Scale from "Strongly Agree" to "Strongly Disagree." Some questions across the three questionnaires shared similarity, so that comparisons could be made when analyzing data.

A text field was created for respondents to provide feedback to the survey freely. The textual answers in the text field will be reported along with the statistics to illustrate and explain the quantitative findings. All questionnaires went through pilot tests. The unit of analysis was each participant. In order to conduct a systematic random sampling of editors and news professionals, we needed a list of newspaper editors and TV news directors in the United

States and a list of newspaper and TV news staffers. We found that such lists did not exist, though lists of newspapers and lists of TV stations did exist in multiple places online like Editor & Publisher Yearbook and Broadcasting Sr Cable Yearbook. Therefore, we decided to construct our own.

To do so, we went through two steps. First, we constructed a combined list of daily newspapers and TV stations so that we could sample these news institutions. Second, we visited the Web sites of all sampled news institutions to find the email of the editor/news director and the email of one news professional randomly chosen. Then, we visited each of those Web sites to find the email address of the managing editor, chief editor, online editor, or equivalent in each of those dailies and sent out a survey invitation email to him/her.

In total, we extracted 674 TV stations with a valid URL. Since this population is smaller than that of the newspapers, we over-sampled it. Instead of sampling every other four, we sampled every other station. Then, we visited each of those Web sites to find the email address of the news director or equivalent in each of those TV stations and sent out a survey invitation email to him/her. We also sampled one news professional out of each of the sampled U.S. dailies and TV stations for the survey. Since there was always more than one professional in a company, we simply randomly clicked on one name and picked him/her and made sure that s/he was on the news staff.

Then, we sent him/her a survey invitation email. If an individual email address was not available, we replaced it with a generic email address and specified whom the email was for. S/he was asked to fill out a questionnaire that was worded in a slightly different manner. In total, we successfully sent out invitation emails to 398 news professionals. We also needed to conduct a systematic random sampling of college journalism professors, but we were disappointed that all lists we found had many J-schools, even major ones, missing. In total, the new list contains 205 alphabetically ordered U.S. J-schools that contain 2,194 journalism professors. We sampled one out of every four professors from the virtually running list of all journalism professors across the schools. For instance, if a school had six journalism professors, we picked the fourth one; then, the second journalism professor from next school was picked. We sent an invitation email to every professor in the sample. In total, we successfully sent out 500 emails. The three samples of editors, news professionals, and professors included 1,421 cases. We understood that nonresponse had been a serious problem with online surveys in recent years.

In order to counter possible low response rates in our survey, we created three samples for editors, news professionals, and professors containing roughly 500 people for each group, which were much larger than the sample sizes for populations recommended by Mildred Patten (2000) in her book Understanding Research Methods: An Overview of the Essentials so that, if low response rates occurred, we could base our confidence limits on the actual number of responses themselves. We also sent out one reminder email to the samples, which drastically boosted the response rates, especially for professors and news professionals.

FINDINGS AND DISCUSSION

After two weeks of online data collecting in November 2002, we received 223 responses from professors (a 44% response rate), 151 responses from editors (a 29% response rate), and 142 responses from news professionals (a 35% response rate). The overall response rate is 36%. As Singletary (1994) notes, returns of 30% to 40% are common in mail surveys.

The response rates of this online survey seem typical. However, the response rates are still comparatively low. A response bias is potentially present. Many respondents (41%) left textual answers to explain and illustrate their answers to the close-ended questions and/or made comments on the topic. By the end of 2002, 19% of the newspapers and commercial television stations with news content in the United States had gone through media mergers. Being merged or not has to do with the size of a company. Larger companies tend to have been merged while smaller ones have not. Roughly half of the news professionals surveyed (48%) reported that they produced news content for multiple media platforms on a routine basis; that was true both in merged media (50%) and non-merged media (48%).

In other words, media merger is not the precondition for practicing news for multiple media platforms. The pressure on news professionals to learn to produce multimedia content is also felt in many non-merged media companies. This finding confirms that media convergence is not necessarily related to media merger. A typical editor or news director was a man (71%) between 36-45 years old (42%) with a bachelor's degree (76%) who had worked for at least two media (57%) for more than 20 years (53%). A typical news professional was either a man (52%) or woman (48%) between 26-35 years old (43%) with a bachelor's degree (84%) who had worked for at least two media (60%) less than ten years (62%).

Editors had generally worked for more years than news professionals, but they did not have more multiplatform experience than news professionals. As more news companies are practicing cross-media reporting with or without their companies being merged, it is important that editors with multiplatforrn experiences are chosen to direct newsroom businesses. Many editors need cross-media training more urgently than news professionals do if the news company they work for produces news contents for multiple media platforms on a daily basis.

Should J-schools Train Specialists or Generalists?

Gil Thelen (2002) said that writers should learn how to write for multimedia and still photographers should learn how to shoot videos, but he was not interested in hiring people with multiple sets of skills. We designed four questions to test how popular Thelen's opinion was. The majority of the respondents (84%) agreed or strongly agreed with Thelen that journalism students should learn how to write for multiple media platforms. One-way ANOVA shows significant difference among the means for professors (4.35), professionals (4.05), and editors (3.99). Tukey HSD post hoc tests show that professors were more positive on this statement than editors and professionals, while no significant difference existed between editors and professionals.

A similar number of respondents (85%) agreed or strongly agreed with Thelen that journalism students with a visual emphasis should learn how to produce and edit photos, videos, and online interactive images. One-way ANOVA shows significant difference among the means for professors (4.55), professionals (4.22), and editors (3.91). Tukey HSD post hoc tests show that professors were more positive on this statement than professionals, while professionals were more positive than editors. Most respondents (78%) agreed or strongly agreed that all journalism majors should learn multiple sets of skills, such as writing, editing, TV production, digital photography, newspaper design, and Web publishing.

Oneway ANOVA shows significant differences among the means for professionals (4.28), editors (3.99), and professors (3.86). Tukey HSD post hoc tests show that news professionals who worked in the forefront of news production felt this need more deeply than other respondents. Editors also had such an expectation for them.

There is no significant difference between editors and professors. These findings support the growing evidence that news professionals are being asked to wear multiple hats. The findings also indicate that Thelen's view has its market at this moment when news professionals with multiple sets of skills are highly desirable but not easy to find. Such a view may change as more journalism graduates equipped with multiple sets of skills enter the job market. The professors' textual answers show that some of the difficulties J-schools have come across include the lack of a friendly curriculum, lack of credit hours to include the components of convergence content, lack of willing cooperation among faculty from different sequences, and lack of expertise, interest, or even time for some professors to develop new courses on convergence.

When asked whether journalism students should still have a specialization, such as writing, photojournalism, broadcasting, and new media, over half (63%) of the respondents agreed or strongly agreed. Over a quarter of the respondents (28%) were negative and 9% were not sure. One-way ANOVA mean comparisons show no significant difference of attitude among professionals (3.42), editors (3.51), and professors (3.72).

Comparing the support rate for this question to those for the first three questions, it is fair to argue that editors, news professionals, and professors emphasized the importance of cross-media training more than that of specialization, though they believed that specialization should not be neglected either. Currently, students in many J-schools specialize in one area by subscribing to a sequence such as news-editorial, magazine, photojournalism, and broadcast. When asked whether sequences should be reorganized considering the trend of media-platforms merging in the industry, 56% of the professors agreed or strongly agreed, 22% were not sure, and another 22% disagreed or strongly disagreed.

The concept of sequences is being shaken among professors though it is still being accepted as a legitimate means of training students in various specialization areas in some J-schools. Speaking on behalf of herself and her colleagues, Professor offered some special insight on this issue:

We can't teach for the "now." We have to prepare students for when they graduatewhich in most instances is now five years out. And, we feel a commitment to expose them to all types of writing in all platforms so they can be flexible about their career choice at the front end of their academics. Then, they can apply the skills to a specialty area where they are totally proficient. "Flexible" is a key term repeatedly seen in editors' and news professionals' textual answers as a suggestion for future journalists. Editor 's statement is typical: Our job descriptions are open ended and new hires understand that they are being hired for their skills. They may be hired today to cover the city beat. In six months or in two weeks, if necessary, a person with Quark skills may be asked to fill in or shift duties to include pagination of a particular section. It is important that hires stay flexible.

The new hires, wrote Editor, "need to understand that the information they gather and process can have many different uses, audiences and shelf lives. They need to understand the complexities of the audience mix and be able to respond." "Those unwilling to be flexible may find themselves in a difficult scenario later in their careers".

From a different perspective, Professional concurred: "Students must be flexible, have a vigorous skill set and be prepared to get laid off and move around in the changing media arena." In short, "young journalists must be prepared to fill a variety of roles if they hope to succeed". "The most successful journalists are those that take on assignments willingly, can learn and want to learn". Specialization in journalistic jobs is still honored, but is losing its favour to cross-media capability in converged media. Today, professionals with different specializations team together to work on multiple media projects. Tomorrow, it is likely that one-man bands will be more and more desired in newsrooms.

Most respondents (93%), especially professors, agreed or strongly agreed that journalism students should both learn technical skills, such as online information search and Web design, while learning critical thinking skills in media law, ethics, etc. One-way ANOVA shows significant difference among the means for professionals, editors, and professors. Tukey HSD post hoc tests show that professors were more positive on this point than editors and professionals, while no significant difference existed between editors and professionals. But, should journalism students spend more time on learning critical thinking skills than on technical skills? Opinions were divided. More than half of the respondents (62%) believed that should be the case, but 19% of the respondents were not sure and another 19% of them did not agree. Oneway ANOVA shows significant difference among the means for professors (3.21), professionals, and editors. Tukey HSD post hoc tests show that editors were more positive on this point than professionals, and professionals were more positive than professors.

Throughout all the answers from the three groups of respondents, critical thinking was highly regarded as being more important than technical skills. Editors, news professionals, and professors all liked to see good stories, and good stories come from good thinking ability. An editor said: "Journalism graduates need to have a broad, well-rounded education; be critical thinkers; have the ability to write clearly; have a serious work ethic; and know computer basics - in that order". "You can teach a monkey to type," echoes a writer. Therefore, he strongly suggested that J-schools "get more critical thinking skills pounded into the skulls of the students". While highly emphasizing the importance of critical thinking ability, editors did not mean to neglect the importance of teaching technical skills in schools. We will develop this point when we discuss the next question.

Comparing the professors' highest mean for the first question and their lowest mean for the second question, it is clear that professors saw critical thinking as highly important, but preferred a comparatively balanced approach for the teaching of the two sets of knowledge. One professor's comment illustrated this observation: Knowing technical skill alone will not make you a "good" journalist. Critical thinking is vital not just to a career but to life itself. Without developing your ability to discern and evaluate, you will become "the prey" of society. Next, a technical skill is critical to a career in journalism today. Even print Journalism is very high tech these days and all electronic media require extensive computer knowledge as well as other technical skills. I would place critical thinking skills first on your list of things to do because a developed mind will make it that much easier to develop a creative and technically sound understanding of the technical side of the business.

From a holistic view, there was no substantial disagreement between classrooms and newsrooms when we examine the issue of teaching critical thinking vs. teaching technical skills. Compared to Terry's 2000 poll, this study shows that professors gave a higher status to technical skills in journalism curricula in 2002 than they did in 2000. This is a period during which media convergence garnered its momentum. In short, all respondents generally agreed that J-schools should place emphasis on teaching critical thinking, but at the same time, should not neglect teaching technical skills. News professionals were asked, "If you wish to possess the technical skills you don't have now, do you prefer to learn them at work or wish you had learned in school?" Editors were given the same question with a slightly different wording. Chi-Square test shows that the difference between editors and news professionals is significant. This finding well supplements the findings from the preceding questions. It suggests that editors not only looked at future journalists' critical thinking ability, but also hoped that future journalists would already possess the skills needed in a converged newsroom when they are hired.

On the other hand, most professionals preferred that they spend most of their school time on gaining critical thinking ability and learn skills largely at work. The professionals' general preference, to some extent, also reflected their need for technological update at their current positions, so that they can better qualify for multimedia productions.

Many editors and reporters said that school is the best place for journalism students to explore every facet of the media and acquire basic technical skills, though some advanced skills can only be learned on the job. Learning skills while in school, they said, can build confidence and an expansive and broad understanding of the entire field and help with damage control and communication in newsrooms. "If editing and the technical skills were more prevalent in college courses," wrote a multi-tasking editor, "I think I could stave off a lot of headaches when the students become professionals." An internship was the news professionals' and editors' most recommended venue for enhancing and learning more technical skills and gaining other practical experience. Reporter said: "While I value my college education, my internship and first job provided me with the most valuable skills today."

Another reporter said: "While education is great, students who work in media while in school fare much better in the real world." Some editors had complaints about graduates with a 3.5 GPA but no practical experience and no published news work. An anchor/reporter said that it is important even "for a freshman or sophomore in college to visit a newsroom and shadow someone. So many students wait until they are juniors and seniors to do this and then they realise they made a mistake in selecting their major. You will learn more by watching and doing". One reporter said, "To remain competitive, education must continue throughout a career".

The implication of the discrepancy from this finding suggests that Jschools should place emphasis on teaching critical thinking, expose students to new technology, and design a comprehensive internship program for students to gain real-world knowledge and further develop their crossmedia technical skills. Both editors and news professionals were given this unstructured question with slightly different wordings. We read through all the answers, and categorized them into the following nine facets in random order:

Multimedia production: producing and editing news stories on video, for the Web, and for print; re-purposing the same story for different media. New technology: knowledge of software for producing video, Web sites, graphics, newspapers, and magazines; knowledge of how to operate a computer and use the Internet. Good writing: knowing how to write to make people remember and/or take action, write about the beats with an expert's view. Good editing is also expected. Critical thinking: having good news judgment, understanding what is legal and ethical, knowing how to report with insight, knowing how to crunch statistics.

Computer-assisted reporting: expert's knowledge of conducting online information search, database knowledge. On-camera exposure: how to report like a TV news anchor before a camera for a newspaper reporter. Visual production: A newspaper writer must know how to take photos, or a TV reporter must know how to shoot video.

SECOND LANGUAGE: KNOWING HOW TO FLUENTLY SPEAK AND READ A FOREIGN LANGUAGE

Time management: well organizing time to work for multiple media platforms; the ability and willingness to work as a team to produce multimedia news stories. Then we ranked these facets according to the percentage scores each facet got separately from the editors and the news professionals:

This ranking shows more agreement than disagreement between editors and news professionals. No matter how technology changes and whether media are converged, editors and news professionals believed that learning how to write good stories is still the top priority and writing is the very basic skill all news professionals should learn.

One editor pushed the importance of good writing to the extreme: "I've worked in markets 170 to 20, and having training in multiple media will not help you get a job, but being a good writer will". Most editors and news professionals, however, did believe that learning multimedia production, new technology, and computer-assisted reporting are also among the top priorities. "I would strongly urge students to prepare themselves to the best of their ability to be able to report/edit the news in a variety of platforms and to learn how to truly engage readers/listeners/viewers in what they are writing about," said Editor. Editors and news professionals both believed that it is not very important for a newspaper reporter to learn how to talk like an anchor in front of a video camera. This skill was even regarded as being less important than knowing how to speak a second language. Some editors and news professionals also mentioned learning how to manage time for producing multimedia news stories.

Editor hoped that journalists in a converged environment would learn to avoid "extra" work by working "smarter" and with greater awareness of the requirements of the different publishing media.

This finding, again, shows that editors valued critical thinking ability more than news professionals did. Editors wanted news professionals to be good thinkers first, and the latter wanted most to learn how to express their thinking in different media. Since some authors such as Haiman expressed the concern about the possible decline of work quality if news professionals have to "re-purpose" stories for multiple media platforms, we tried to find out to what extent this concern was shared by editors and news professionals. Opinions split. Thirty-eight percent of the editors and professionals agreed or strongly agreed that the quality would deteriorate, 40% disagreed or strongly disagreed, and the other 22% were not sure.

Editors and professionals showed no significant difference on this attitude T-test. Such a concern was not prevalent in the news industry.

In response to such concerns, the news director from a converged media company wrote: "When reporters do cross platforms we give them the time to finish the project for all three platforms. Quality does not suffer. If we were to try to force reporters to cross platforms while operating under daily deadlines then quality could suffer depending on the nature of the story and the extra time consumed". Another editor summed up this issue: "Some employees can capably handle multiple media and tell stories effectively. Others cannot. Certainly strong technical skills and training can help, but it's not just dependent on that; it depends more on the attitude and aptitude of the journalist".

Quality multimedia work also involves a solid understanding of different cultures in different media. Editors both for and against media convergence noted the difficulty of merging different media with different cultures, and editors in those merged media called for flexibility in aptitude and willingness to cooperate across platforms. For instance, Editor wrote: Clarity of what convergence means to the news organization is vital and often lacking. This causes unneeded anxiety. Managers have to realise that each medium has its own culture, language, skill set and timetable and is naturally skeptical of anything unfamiliar. It is also true that these same journalists' stock in trade is learning a new culture, language, skill set and timetable-on a daily basis.

Therein lies the hope for an efficient news operation running on all cylinders and an effective -maybe even happy-staff. If most editors and news professionals are not concerned about the quality of the work prepared for multiple media platforms and if news professionals are given enough time to complete their cross-media work, there is little reason to worry that future journalists, if well trained both theoretically and technologically for multiple media platforms, will produce work of poorer quality.

Training students to practice news in multiple media platforms will help bridge newsroom cultures from different media and eventually erase such differences. We have noticed that no significant statistical differences existed between the editors and news professionals from the converged media companies and their counterparts from the not-yet-converged media companies when they answered the questions reported above.

How are J-schools Coping with Media Convergence?

From 1998 to 2002, about 60% of the J-schools in the United States redesigned their curricula or developed new courses to prepare students for practicing news in multiple media platforms. A typical journalism professor was a man (71%) between 46-55 years old (42%) with a doctoral degree (63%) who worked in news media for one to ten years (48%), may still be practicing news (45%) in one way or another, and conducted academic research (66%).

More professors claimed that they were theoretically equipped (81%) than technologically prepared (53%) to teach students how to report news in multiple media platforms. More than half of the professors (57%) had not taught any journalism courses in the last five years where skill sets were beyond their own expertise; 25% of the professors taught one such course and 11% taught two. Nevertheless, the majority of the professors (84%) added content about media convergence either to their existing courses or to new courses or participated in cross-media team-teaching in the last five years.

Worries, concerns, and, sometimes, misconceptions about media convergence appeared in professors' textual answers. For instance, a professor from Montana said: "convergence is not happening". A professor who no longer practiced news said, "In my judgment, the writing portion of preparing news for print and for the Web is exactly the same". Another professor maintained that it was not necessary to teach cross-media news practicing because "few 'want ads' for newspaper reporter and editor positions specifically listed multimedia platform skills as required or preferred experience for new hires".

Many professors worried that media mergers would restrict the number of voices in a community. They regarded media mergers as a grand experiment in the profession and waited for the FCC's ruling on the cross-ownership of different media in the same market. Wait-and-see-that was the strategy some universities took for teaching media convergence. One professor said that he needed to see the substantive contribution media convergence could make before he would be more serious about this phenomenon.

He said that J-schools should be cautious about embracing convergence. Some other universities didn't have the time and resources to teach convergence courses or make major curriculum changes. Most professors, however, did believe that media convergence was a reality; and "anybody serious about practicing media needs at minimal an acquaintance with various media and at best multiple competencies," as Professor said.

Many professors (and editors and news professionals as well) had a clear opinion as to which comes first, teaching critical thinking or teaching technical skills. While acknowledging the need for incorporating media convergence content in curricula, especially the technological components, professors cautioned against sacrificing conceptual and theoretical courses such as law, ethics, history, cultural studies, critical perspectives, etc.

Professor analogized critical thinking as meat and potatoes and technical skills as dessert and side dishes and argued that "the meat and potatoes need to come before one begins to worry about the dessert and side dishes (or side shows)." This viewpoint was popular. Professor wrote: It's the message, not the medium, that is of paramount importance. If students cannot understand and appreciate the underlying concepts, principles and ethics of journalism, then they cannot produce the type of content that will be of value to a free society. A thorough grounding in journalism must come before any training in tools. The tools are means to an end, not the end in and of themselves.

Incidentally, a reporter had similar thoughts: The medium isn't the message, the message is the message. In short, the fundamental analytic and synthetic skills of the news writer are paramount to the message. The medium does not alter the reporter's craft of interpreting news events in the context of the society in a way that will make sense for the receiver of the information.

Additional skills may be desirable, but for the most part they can be learned on the job. Obviously, the more skills one can offer, the better the employment opportunity. Those ancillary skills should not come at the expense of thorough proficiency as a news writer. We fully understand why these respondents emphasize the teaching of critical thinking and the fundamentals of good reporting over the teaching of technical skills, and we strongly agree with their opinions.

But, we also see the danger of over-stretching the point by treating the two sets of knowledge as two opposing poles. Those arguments are based on the presumptions that message and medium can be easily separated, content and form can be detached, and readers for different media are from the same population. But, is that right? It is true that content is the king. It is true that "the medium does not alter the reporter's craft of interpreting news events." News practice, however, is not only about news-gathering and writing. It also includes production, editing, and delivery. Without a solid grasp of grammar and style, how can a writer effectively express his/her good analytical thinking?

Without knowing the available features and limitations of online news delivery, how can messages be constructed to their fullest potential? Without understanding the technical difference between video news and print news, how can messages be constructed appropriately? In the digital era when almost all steps of news transmission involves technology, if professors don't teach students technical skills, will the computer majors, who know little about news practices, be expected to produce newspapers, TV news, and online news? Writers, for instance, do not necessarily have to be conversant in constructing news reporting with Flash for online presentation or know how to operate a video camera to shoot video stories. But knowing the principles and rules of news video-taping and what Flash or other software can offer will surely help writers more effectively convey their messages and better cooperate with visual reporters. Creativity distinguishes artists and artisans.

Critical thinking ability distinguishes master journalists and technical writers. But artists must first know what artisans know and a master journalist must possess all that a technical writer knows for a living. Skills are intrinsic instead of extrinsic to ideas. Teaching critical thinking and teaching technical skills are not mutually exclusive. Teaching journalism students how to express their critical thinking with conversant technical skills in different media seems to be a big challenge for J-school professors in the years to come. From the professors' textual answers, we have observed different philosophical approaches to teaching convergence.

Unlike some professors who took the wait-and-see approach, a professor from the University of Texas at Austin claimed that "convergence is already happening, and journalism schools should be leading the parade and not following it". A popular viewpoint was that "skills across platforms must be taught, but more importantly storytelling, ethics, and critical thinking skills should be even more important in the journalism school curriculum". One professor from Texas Christian University said that it maintained the existing sequences but required broadcast students to take print courses and vice versa.

Team-teaching was an often-used approach in some J-schools such as Indiana University for courses involving multiple sets of skills while professors learned from each other. Another professor, from the University of Colorado at Boulder, said convergence meant that "students work together to produce multimedia content for the Web-not that each individual should attempt to become proficient in all media". To overcome the hurdle of the ratio limited by the ACEJMC accreditation standards between journalism courses and liberal arts courses, a professor from Bowling Green State University suggested that journalism undergraduate students stay for five years and devote the fifth year entirely to practice.

Some professors said that journalism students only need to know a little about the practices in media other than their own while some other professors firmly maintained that students should "be the master of many arts and the explorer of all". All respondents were asked, "Do you think that merging media companies such as television station, newspaper, radio station, and online news from a local area will benefit any of the parties listed on the left?

Check all entries that apply." The entries included "The general public," "News professionals," "Media companies," "Nobody," and "Not sure." We designed this question about the legitimacy of media merger as a barometer for testing the respondents' political view on media convergence. We presumed that a respondent's answer to this question could be related to his/her way of answering other questions regarding teaching media convergence or requirement for new hires. Most respondents (66%) from all three groups pointed to media companies as the beneficiary of media mergers. In comparison, only 37% of the respondents said that media mergers also benefit the general public, and even fewer (27%) said that media mergers benefit the news professionals.

By reading the percentage numbers horizontally, we can find that consistently fewer respondents believed that media mergers benefit the general public or news professionals; also consistently more respondents believed that media mergers benefit media companies. It is also noticeable that 47% of editors believed that media mergers benefit the general public while the other 53% didn't. Editors' opinions on this point were roughly equally split. This finding indicates that media merger is a grand experiment in the media industry. Its benefits to the general public, which can better legitimize media mergers, are to be explored in the years to come.

By reading the percentage numbers both vertically and horizontally, we also find that editors were the most positive about the benefits media mergers could bring to all three parties while professors were least sure of such benefits. It is logical to reason that management personnel, such as editors and news directors and the companies they represent, are the primary forces behind today's media merger movement. The question is that, since most professors, editors, and even news professionals believed that media mergers do not benefit news professionals and hardly benefit the general public, why do most news professionals still want to be trained to be cross-media practitioners and why are so many Jschool professors enthusiastic about training such graduates? Considering the editors' most positive attitude toward media convergence, we wonder if news professionals are under the pressure to do so, and J-school professors are under the pressure to follow the industrial trend. Our surmise is partially corroborated by some textual answers.

A news anchor from a merged media company agreed that new hires should have received cross-media training in writing and visuals and should possess multiple sets of skills. She showed her understanding for media mergers: The merging of media companies is almost a daily occurrence. The pool of entities providing news services is shrinking. I think there is a danger that the public will lose in this race for media giants to accumulate wealth. At the same time, with the amount of competition in the industry from cable networks, the Internet, DVD's etc., I see the financial need for companies to merge to survive. A newspaper reporter also from a merged media company expressed a similar feeling: "I am not all for the media convergence At the same time I find it quite beneficial to be savvy in all branches of the industry. It helps the journalist become more knowledgeable about her or his job". News professionals were not alone in having such feelings. Here are two excerpts from two professors who have expressed similar feelings: It's a harsh reality that I checked the box saying that news companies are the ones that are sure to benefit from media convergence. It may not be great for the public or even for news professionals who are going to be asked to bring more and more skills to the table and to have more and more responsibility on the job. Even so, convergence in one way or another is gonna happen and we need to prepare our students.

Finally, my answer on merging media companies reflects my disdain for the corporatization and concentration of control in the media. I think we ought to train mass communicators for a converged world, but as professors we ought to fight like hell against media mergers. Very few respondents (19%) believed that media mergers benefit all three parties, the general public, news professionals, and media companies, but about one third of the respondents (35%) believed that media companies are the only beneficiaries to such a practice. These 35% respondents, who were almost equally proportionally found in editors, news professionals, and professors groups, could be regarded as the most critical toward media mergers. We compared these 35% respondents with the rest of the sample and found no significant difference in their answers concerning the necessity of teaching journalism students cross-media writing and visuals and teaching multiple sets of skills.

Always, more respondents believed that professors should teach all those things. In short, the respondents' political view was not directly tied to their views of teaching students cross-media practices. As an experimental industrial trend, media convergence in the sense of media mergers is still in its formative stage. Whether it will sustain its momentum to reach popularity in the nation and how its advantages balance against disadvantages are yet to be seen. While there seems to be a good deal of support for cross-media education, on some questions, professors are more gung-ho than editors and news professionals about the trend. The legitimacy of media mergers needs repeated tests before such mergers can be truly accepted as a healthy development and a full-force education of media convergence can be seen in many in J-schools. Media convergence, however, is not tied to media mergers. Media convergence, initiated and made possible by digital technology, is more than media mergers propelled largely by financial considerations. More pervasive is the media convergence in the senses of content convergence, technological convergence, and especially role convergence, which have occurred not only in merged media companies but also more in non-merged ones.

No matter whether media mergers will continue, the other three forms of media convergence, which are not subject to the FCC regulations, are likely to continue to develop. Most editors and news professionals in this survey are not from merged media companies.

Many editors, news professionals, and professors do not yet see media mergers as beneficial to the general public and news professionals. But, their backgrounds and political views do not prevent them from sharing with other respondents with different backgrounds and political views many opinions regarding where future college journalism should go. Such common understanding is shaping a force to push forward the education of media convergence in campuses nationwide. To better direct newsroom businesses in a converged media environment, many editors need cross-media training. Many opportunities are out there for news companies and universities to work together to explore the issue of media convergence and provide mid-career professionals and editors cross-media technological training.

It seems sensible that opportunities for learning multimedia skills should be made available both on campus and through off-site continuing education programs that are geared for midcareer news professionals as technological developments continue to evolve. Multi-dimensional news reporting in multiple media platforms will be tomorrow's way news is presented. Therefore, dealing with media convergence in college journalism education is an urgent necessity. The wait-and-see strategy will place a Jschool in a disadvantaged position over the long run.

These findings tell us that J-schools do need to provide cross-media knowledge and experience to their students, so that the latter can better qualify for cross-media jobs in the future. Media convergence poses both challenge and opportunity to J-schools for them to reconsider their current curriculum design, sequence setting, faculty composition, teaching methods, and internship approaches. Many professors, editors, and news professionals have expressed concern that media mergers will eliminate voices in a community, thus potentially eroding democracy. However, media mergers did not start only these days. As a TV reporter wrote in the textual answer, when she first went to Philadelphia years ago, there were five daily papers.

Now, there are two; and they are both published by the same company. Philadelphia is not alone in such media reduction. The question is whether the general public feels that it is less well-informed than it was thirty or forty years ago and that democracy has been eroded by such media reduction prior to media convergence. This is a topic for another study. Nevertheless, students should be exposed to such a legitimate concern and learn to take a critical look at the phenomenon of media mergers. J-schools should continue to teach critical thinking courses and meld critical thinking components into the teaching of all courses. Critical thinking is the cornerstone of journalism education. However, technology courses or course components should also be given the status they deserve.

In other words, there should be a balanced curriculum to include both kinds of courses, and many cross-media related courses should contain both components. An ideal curriculum should balance the load of technical skill-based courses and critical thinking courses, weighting toward the latter. Critical thinking and technical skills can go hand in hand rather than being competitors for class time. A balanced curriculum can help students better gather, produce, edit, and deliver quality news; more creatively and professionally materialize their ideas; and make them better fit into the market, especially in an economic downturn.

University of Florida professor Melinda McAdams, one of the Washington Post's first online editors, told colleagues that if colleges don't teach journalists the technical skills they will need, no one else is likely to take on the responsibility." The reality they'll face in the world is they'll have to teach themselves". The classroom should be the first stop for students to at least get exposed to and get familiar with the technology for cross-media practices, though they can become more proficient with such technology through internship and their future jobs.

With all that said, technology courses should not dominate journalism students' education, and technology should not be taught for the sake of technology. Technology must serve the purposes of doing good journalism. Apart from teaching students multimedia productions, new technology, and computer-assisted reporting, J-schools still need to place good writing-the very basics of being a journalist-as the top priority for all journalism students regardless of sequences or specializations.

Many respondents point out that the teaching of technology should not be at the expense of the teaching of critical thinking. Many J-schools have no more elective hours for students to learn cross-media technology within the existing parameter of curriculum. For such schools, curriculum redesign is a necessity. Though some J-schools such as Indiana University School of Journalism have eliminated sequences to provide a comprehensive education to all journalism students, we expect that sequences will continue to exist for some time in some other J-schools. However, it has become increasingly important to encourage students from all sequences to learn technology and reporting skills from other platforms.

Sequences in many J-schools are regarded as dinosaurs because it no longer makes sense to teach broadcast and newspaper, for instance, as two unrelated bodies of knowledge in the era of media convergence and students can opt for a specialization without sequences but with professors' advice. Most respondents expect that future journalists will be competent in producing news in multiple media platforms while being particularly strong in one area. It appears that students will be prudent to opt to specialize in either print or television and take several electives in a secondary platform, either radio or online journalism. Versatility and specialization should be equally important.

The majority of the editors do expect that future writers will be able to and willing to write for multiple media platforms, and photographers and designers will create multimedia visuals, though such expectations will not be converted into requirements in job ads for a while because "too many newsroom dinosaurs have to die off first," as Editor put it. But chances are they will, as Nelson (2002) predicted. Most editors even expect that new hires will possess multiple sets of skills to become "superhack masters of multimedia," to use Gates's term. The needs are out there, but whether the training of such superhack masters will become the norm, as Gates questioned, largely depends on whether J-schools are willing and able to develop those "avant-garde" courses. Apart from the technological aspect, students also need to learn to cooperate and collaborate across newsrooms so as to bridge different newsroom-cultures.

Students need to be both theoretically and technically prepared for media convergence. The findings from this study show that more than half of the J-schools in the United States have redesigned their curricula or developed new courses to cope with media convergence, but professors need to be better prepared technologically. Team-teaching is one approach to solve the problem, but will the teaching of media convergence be more effective if a professor at least knows as much as a student in a convergence class will learn? Does the Gestalt psychological principle "the whole is more than the sum of its parts" also apply in such a context? Professors normally learned little or no technical skills while studying in a J-school doctoral program.

Their technical knowledge inherited from their previous media experience is easily dated. More than half of the professors (54%) no longer practiced news after they began to teach, as we found out in this study. In some cases, professors know less technical knowledge than their students do. Therefore, in the middle of heavy teaching and research, updating and learning more technical knowledge for teaching convergence is a big challenge for many professors. Learning from each other during team-teaching is, of course, a good way of learning, but professors also need to find time to do self-teaching to gain more in-depth knowledge. J-schools should provide financial support for professors to attend new technology workshops.

Being exposed to or involved in community news reporting in a multiple-media-platform environment, if possible, is an even better way of learning new technology for professors. Attitude and aptitude, together with time management ability, will be the key to producing quality work in newsrooms.

Since editors and news professionals are not prevalently concerned about the quality of work currently re-purposed for multiple media platforms, there is no reason for them or professors to be concerned that students being trained on multiple media platforms will be jacks of all trades but masters of none. Students need to learn how to re-purpose their work in a timely manner and control the quality of their work in a professional manner.

One editor said it best: "To sum things up, journalists need to be prepared to hit the workplace running. With limited resources and cutbacks across the country, the new hire will be the person who is the most skilled, coupled with energy and willing to be flexible as needed." Media convergence is a comprehensive topic. Many sub-topics related to this study are yet to be explored. For instance, how can the general public benefit from media convergence? Does the general public in markets where media are converged think that they are less well-informed and that democracy has suffered in their areas? How can news professionals benefit from media convergence?

What are the typical differences between the career lives of the news professionals in converged media and the career lives the same news professionals led before the media were converged? We call on mass communication scholars to continue to study media convergence to shed more light on this phenomenon that will affect every one of us.

Index

G

H

I

J

L

M

N

O

P

Q

R

S